THE MINNESOTA ETHNIC FOOD BOOK

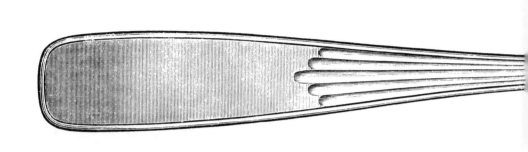

The

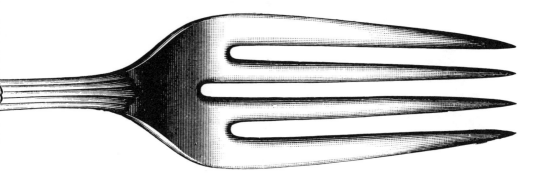

Minnesota
Ethnic
Food Book

Anne R. Kaplan
Marjorie A. Hoover
Willard B. Moore

Minnesota Historical Society Press, St. Paul, 1986

Line drawings by Chris Wold Dyrud

Minnesota Historical Society Press
St. Paul 55101

Manufactured in the United States of America
10 9 8 7 6 5 4 3 2

International Standard Book Number:
  0-87351-197-2-Cloth
  0-87351-198-0 Paper

Library of Congress Cataloging-in-Publication
Data

Kaplan, Anne R., 1951–
  The Minnesota ethnic food book.

  Includes indexes.
  1. Cookery, American. 2. Cookery,
International. I. Hoover, Marjorie A., 1928–
II. Moore, Willard B. (Willard Burgess),
1931– . III. Title.
TX715.K186 1986   641.5   86-8519

To the ethnic cooks of Minnesota

CONTENTS

ACKNOWLEDGMENTS

The success of this project depended, to a large degree, on the good will and interest of the people of Minnesota. Through our research we met literally hundreds of people who patiently explained their traditions, stood by while we poked around in their kitchens, invited us to their religious services and club meetings, posed for photographs, and offered the names of others who might help. All of these persons deserve our sincere thanks. Among them, however, very special thanks are due to: Jeanne Blake for many hours spent translating from Hmong to English and back again in homes in the Twin Cities and Rochester; Vu Yang and his family, Minneapolis, for preparing and serving a Hmong feast under the eyes of researchers so that the proper questions could be asked; Diana Rankin and Marlin Heise for leads and introductions in the Hmong community; Pauline Mueller, Trudy Mahady, Helga Parnell, and Mary Ann Hauser for a very special introduction to German cuisine; Robert Dueñes, Owatonna, for sharing his thorough knowledge of the area's Mexican-American community; Rosa Coronado de Collyard, St. Paul, for her insights into Mexican and Mexican-American foodways; and Geraldine Kangas, Aurora, for her help with fieldwork and photo research among the Finnish Americans of Palo and Aurora.

Members of many ethnic institutions went out of their way to be of help. Without the special assistance of the following people, this book would lack some of its flavor: Arden Haug, assistant pastor of the Norwegian Lutheran Memorial Church, Minneapolis, Liv Dahl, Sons of Norway, the Wedding Circle at the Bethlehem Lutheran Church, Minneapolis, the Kontakt Club of the Twin Cities, Randi Johansen, Jim and Anna Bateman, and Shirley Morton; the Volksfest Association of St. Paul; Karen Muller and the Danish American Fellowship and Center, Minneapolis; the American Swedish Institute, Minneapolis; members of the Pilgrim Baptist Church, St. Paul, especially Estelle Dorsey and its pastor, Dr. Earl Miller; the staff and congregation of Our Lady of Guadalupe Roman Catholic Church, St. Paul; Rabbi Bernard S. Raskas, Lois Brand, and Phyllis Brody of Temple of Aaron, St. Paul; and the staff at Ingebretsen's Scandinavian Foods, Minneapolis.

A C K N O W L E D G M E N T S

Sincere thanks are also due the scholars who helped through all phases of the research, especially Professor Marion J. Nelson, University of Minnesota, Minneapolis, and Dr. Greta Swenson, who shared insights into Scandinavian culture in Minnesota; Ruth A. Myers and Joyce M. Kramer, both at the University of Minnesota, Duluth, for their help with the Ojibway chapter; and Professor Timothy Dunnigan, University of Minnesota, Minneapolis, for his with the Hmong chapter.

Finally, this book would not have been possible without the sharp eyes and astute questions of Sally Rubinstein and the careful checking of Deborah Swanson, both of the MHS Press, or the nimble fingers of June Sonju, who typed and corrected numerous copies of chapters and recipes, many of them right before lunch. And last but not least, thanks to Roy Hoover and Jim Moss who valiantly tasted their way through this book, from "first draft" cooking attempts to the final recipes.

FOREWORD

Minnesota is home to many more than the number of ethnic groups included in this book, and each is a significant part of the state's folklife. Given limitations on time, space, and cost, the authors chose to present a sampler of ethnic foodways, to describe a range of cultures in the state, including some that have high visibility as well as some that do not. Rather than attempt a superficial statewide survey, fieldwork for each chapter was conducted in selected ethnic communities. Broadbased library and archival research yielded additional material. The result shows a general pattern of ethnic foodways for each group, a pattern that nevertheless accommodates embellishment and variation.

Deciding on groups to include in this book was a difficult task. Regional similarities shared by the various European, Indochinese, and Middle Eastern cultures helped guide the selection process. Middle and Near Eastern influences were represented, for example, in the Greek, South Slav, and Jewish chapters; hence, the Lebanese and Syrians, two communities that maintain some very distinctive, traditional foodways, were omitted. Norwegian-, Danish-, and Swedish-American foodways were grouped in a Scandinavian chapter with an introduction that explores points of similarity and difference. Chapters on the South Slavs and the British offer a similar approach. Czechs, Slovaks, Poles, Irish, Luxembourgers, Chinese, Japanese — the list of possibilities for future research could go on and on. This study only begins to chronicle Minnesota's ethnic foodways; perhaps others will take up where this book ends.

Readers familiar with any of the foreign-language terms that appear in this volume may be surprised at some of the spellings employed. In many cases names for foods exist in dialect form — and not all members of any ethnic group speak the same dialect. In some cases, no one interviewed could spell a given word with any sense of confidence; in others, researchers amassed variant spellings for the same term. And languages that contain sounds lacking in English pose additional difficulties to translators and transliterators. In an attempt to reconcile different spellings and to provide clear, recognizable terms, the editors have consulted modern dictionaries and, where they exist, reputable cookbooks. Words not included in those references are reproduced here as they are used in the ethnic communities.

Much of the information presented in this book was gathered in interviews and conversations and is preserved either on cassette tapes, some of which have been transcribed, or in handwritten field notes. All research materials are on file in the collections of the Minnesota Historical Society.

The recipes included at the back of this book were chosen to help illustrate some of the points made in the essays. Whether ceremonial foods or mundane, these dishes were among the ones most often named as important or common parts of a group's traditional foodways. All of the recipes were carefully tested, a process that involved preparing versions of the same recipe collected from different people, checking the results against products made by ethnic cooks, referring to published recipes (if they existed) for guidance, sometimes combining elements from several versions, and clarifying wordings and measurements that might stump cooks unfamiliar with a particular dish or method of preparation. The final recipes, then, are composites that have received close attention; they will produce an authentic product without forcing the novice to puzzle out the likes of "Stir. Pour in pan and cook until done."

INTRODUCTION:
ON ETHNIC FOODWAYS

Tell me what you eat, and I will tell you what you are." This oft-quoted maxim of the nineteenth-century philosopher and gastronome, Jean Anthelme Brillat-Savarin, posits a direct correlation between foodways and identity. Since his delightful volume, *The Physiology of Taste*, first appeared in 1825, Brillat-Savarin's saying has passed from truism to cliche. Nutritionists, historians, sociologists, anthropologists, and folklorists, in exploring the relationship of what one eats and what one is, have quoted, paraphrased, and rearranged his saying. If nothing else, the dictum has provided food for thought; superficial and catchy though it may be, it captures and expresses some underlying truth, almost universally perceived, that the things we eat can say a great deal about us — who we are, where we came from, our current social, cultural, economic, and religious circumstances, and what our aspirations might be.

The term "foodways" nicely captures all of these nuances. Folklorists first began using the word in the 1970s in an effort to discuss traditional behavior that was more than merely preparing a particular recipe at a particular time, behavior that reaches into many aspects of daily life. At a simple church supper, for example, food is the focus of an event that brings people together for social and spiritual interchange. Potluck suppers did not originate for religious purposes, but their symbolic message nicely fits Christian belief: everyone gives a little so that many may eat. The details of the meal are more concrete: what kinds of foods are appropriate, who will bring what dishes, what program will be presented, who will perform all the necessary tasks. Members of a church community know the answers to these questions, which have evolved from the traditions of past suppers. In Aitkin, for example, being allowed to bring food to the supper rather than washing dishes afterward is a sign that a girl has come of age. In sum, there is much more to a humble church supper than Jell-O salads and hamburger casseroles. The meal encodes religious and social beliefs as well as hierarchies of age, skill, and status. Foodways are "a whole interrelated system of food conceptualization and evaluation, procurement, distribution, preservation, preparation, consumption, and nutrition shared by all members of a particular society."[1] Ethnic foodways, however, pose a slight problem for this definition.

Contemporary ethnic groups are, in general, much more loosely structured than "a particular society," and membership in them is far from absolute. They are "reference group[s] invoked by people who share a common historical style . . . based on overt features and values, and who, through the process of interaction with others, identify themselves as sharing that style."[2] Ethnicity, then, is basically a function of different culture groups operating within common social contexts, and such interactions are increasingly frequent in American society. We live in a multicultural setting. It is not uncommon to have two sets of grandparents of two different nationalities or even parents of two different ethnic backgrounds. The daughter of a Norwegian-American father and a British-American mother, for example, may identify with either or both of her ethnic traditions. After her marriage to an Italian American, she may learn to cook foods from his family traditions as well. And, in addition, she may also indulge her love of Mexican and Oriental foods. She is of mixed ethnic background, and she is also an American living in Minnesota. All of these factors influence her as she shapes her foodways, choosing items and practices from the traditions and resources available.[3] To put it another way: Ethnic foodways in Minnesota, as elsewhere, operate on two levels. They are a unified system of beliefs, symbols, and actions as described in the definition of foodways above, but they are also part of the larger contexts of American, as well as international, cuisine. No ethnic foods exist in a vacuum, nor are they preserved in a pristine state, uninfluenced by their surroundings.

In fact, it is the multicultural setting that makes ethnic food ethnic. Immigrants sooner or later learn that "Americans" (or members of other ethnic groups in America) do not eat the same things in the same ways as they themselves do. Thus the common food that first-generation settlers considered everyday sustenance gradually takes on a new luster (or stigma, depending on the people and the situation): it is special, it is different, it sets them apart from other groups. In contrast to what surrounding peoples are eating, it has become "traditional" or "ethnic" food. Stories are common about school children and laborers — whose parents or even grandparents had emigrated — discovering to their surprise that their bag lunches differentiated them from their peers. Sandwiches on crusty Italian bread were sometimes enough to mark their bearers as ethnic.[4]

Ethnic foodways are rarely identical to those in the homeland. In the first place, specific ingredients may be unavailable in the new land; substitutions are inevitable. More important, however, are the influences of a new setting, for as food is an integral part of life, so are foodways intrinsic to social and cultural life. As life styles change — both work habits and leisure-time activities — so do foodways. Recipes are modified to accommodate changing time commitments, technology, and ingredients. Occasions for eating traditional foods change; religious or calendar holidays become prime times for eating ethnic food.[5] New foods are incorporated into the everyday diet. Common foods of the immigrant generation are reserved as ethnic treats for special occasions. After decades in America sharp intraethnic demarcations soften. As village or regional loyalties begin to be replaced with national ones, some blending of food traditions occurs.[6] Neapolitan women, for instance, learned to make Calabrian specialties and began to consider themselves — and their foods — Italian. Changes also occur in the Old Country and may be introduced into the ethnic communities by returned visitors. Black families seeking their roots in the Caribbean, for example, bring home recipes for curried goat; Norwegian Americans discover that few people in their ancestral homeland still eat lutefisk. Recent immigrants infuse a knowledge of modern German or Finnish gourmet cookery into the ethnic communities. As a result, ethnic foodways maintain not a direct correspondence but a dynamic relationship with the immigrants' Old World cuisine.

This last point is an important one to remember. Too often we are overwhelmed by the sentimental fallacy that change is an enemy of tradition. This view is basically ahistorical; it focuses on a particular recipe (with or without its social context), removes it from the stream of time, and holds it up as "authentic." Any deviation from this one version is not read as a change, but as a loss of tradition. In reality, however, people — even during previous centuries in the Old World — constantly alter traditions to fit their lives; a static tradition is, most likely, a dead one. Ethnic foodways are far more than surviving relics of Old Country cuisines. A South Slav potica cake, for example — the quick-bread version of a traditional yeasted delicacy — shows how foodways evolve and change with new contexts. By altering the form and preserving the flavor, South Slav women demonstrate their commitment to tradition in the midst of their new status as women who work outside of the home. Precisely because such traditions can be altered to fit circumstances, they are a valuable index of human creativity as well as of the ways people balance cultural continuity with change.

Of all of the ethnic groups included in this volume, nowhere is this delicate balancing act more apparent than among the Hmong. Having lived in Minnesota for barely a decade, at the longest, these people retain much of their traditional culture, including foodways. Eating Hmong food is the norm, rather than a festive highlight of a holiday or other special gathering. In addition, their everyday life is rich in other kinds of customary behavior that relates to food: cooks use homemade knives, cutting boards, and other implements, people speak proverbs or narrate legends to account for certain practices such as eating hot peppers, avoiding certain substances, or offering food to visitors, and families maintain traditional etiquette for serving and eating food. Yet the Hmong daily confront new ways of doing things, and, like the many immigrants before them, they are eager to accept some changes while trying to maintain their cultural integrity.

Watching Hmong ethnicity evolve may give observers a sense of the general process of adaptation in a new setting; whether or not we can deduce from their experience the way it was for the nineteenth- and early twentieth-century immigrants is another matter. For while the other groups included in this book were faced with the notion of America as a melting pot and were encouraged (or forced) to abandon their traditional cultures, the Hmong emigrated in an era when the prevailing ideology encompassed cultural pluralism and ethnic pride. How successful these people will be in directing their own acculturation remains to be seen. At present, however, the Hmong, keeping their traditional culture firmly in mind, stand at a very different point on the continuum of continuity and change from the other ethnic groups discussed in this book.

What are ethnic foodways, and, more specifically, what are ethnic foodways in Minnesota? The creation of food from raw ingredients is a cultural process that varies from individual to individual, group (be it religious, regional, racial, ethnic, or national) to group, and location to location. Various peoples, for example, observe taboos against eating particular items that are considered prime foodstuffs by others; observant Moslems and Jews do not eat pork or any other by-products from pigs. Likewise, ethnic groups follow sometimes strict rules governing the proper ways to process or combine ingredients, thereby transforming them into acceptable food. Again, the Jewish proscription against mixing meat and dairy products — each acceptable when eaten alone — in a single dish or meal can be cited. Another instance is the elaborate techniques of chopping, marinating, or spicing essentially raw meats, such as steak tartare (called "cannibal" by some Minnesotans), sushi, or the Hmong nqaij liab, in order to bring these substances into the realm of what is considered edible by humans. Finally, different religious rites set aside specific fasting times during which participants abstain from certain kinds of food or all foodstuffs for a set period. The point is that such rules and taboos are dictated by cultural beliefs, not biological necessity. And this system of cultural rules and beliefs is the invisible structure upon which is built the distinctive food-ways of each ethnic group.[7]

Styles of presentation also characterize certain ethnic traditions, most specifically setting them apart from eating patterns in the United States. Whether they be second- or third-generation descendants of immigrants who generally consider themselves American or recently arrived Hmong refugees, many people contrast their traditional serving styles to a generic "American" one of placing all foods, save dessert, on the table at the same time. When Italian or German Americans enjoy a traditional meal, it is in courses, each presented with new tableware. Russian Jews (and Russians) believe that a dinner is not dinner unless it begins with a soup course — salads are American. Hmong people are adamant about serving rice and vegetable-meat dishes in separate bowls and keeping the foods discrete on individuals' plates.

Taste or flavor is a more tangible factor that distinguishes one ethnic cuisine from another, and this factor, too, is based on cultural (as well as individual) predilection. Researchers have yet to answer the question of why certain villages, nations, or even regions of a continent prefer certain flavors and eschew others. To some degree, geography and climate limit foodstuffs locally available. But exploration, conquests, travel, and trade, sometimes going back to ancient times, have made many nonindigenous ingredients locally available. While scholars study the phenomenon, the popular imagination cherishes stereotypes about ethnic cookery: all Scandinavian food is bland, all Mexican dishes are fiery, Italian food depends on generous amounts of garlic and tomato sauce, and so forth. As the chapters in this book will show, these generalizations, although they may contain a kernel of truth, do not hold true across the board.

Along with favorite ingredients, most groups also have preferred techniques for preparing foods. Southern blacks, for example, traditionally simmer greens and meats for hours, the Hmong often chop and stir-fry their protein-vegetable combinations, while Italians commonly layer crusts or noodles, filling, and sauces. Nevertheless, there are but a finite number of structural possibilities and cooking techniques for "constructing" food; consequently, dishes from various ethnic cultures are bound to resemble each other somewhat. Italian manicotti, Jewish blintzes, Hmong spring rolls, and Mexican enchiladas, like the Anglo-American sandwich, all involve wrapping a starchy jacket around a form of protein. As a novice Jewish cook was advised when trying to visualize how her kreplach should look, "Think of it as a won ton!"[8]

The limited number of forms and cooking processes, combined with common historical, environmental, and cultural experiences, helps account for the similarities in cuisine shared by diverse groups. Despite the historical enmity of the Greeks and Turks, for example, their foodways bear some resemblance, and the same is true of cultures in the Near and Middle East, within Indochina, and throughout the regions of Europe. In very broad terms, the cookery of the world can be divided into regional cuisines similar in general characteristics but distinctive in detail.

The topic of ethnic foodways in Minnesota raises some perplexing issues. Can a state, a political entity carved out of a geographic region, affect ethnic foodways? Have ethnic Minnesotans and their foods made any impact on the state? While it would be difficult to prove that political boundaries materially influenced foodways, the state's climate and geography, in some cases, caused the immigrants and their descendants to modify or change some practices. Some people emigrated to Minnesota from a completely different geographic zone. South Slavs substituted berries for apricots and other warmth-loving fruits that they were accustomed to growing. Greeks grew grapevines for the leaves, which they stuff to make dolmades, but, like the Italians, bought California grapes for winemaking because the growing season in northern Minnesota was too short for the vines to produce fruit. Hmong people find alternatives to the banana leaves they traditionally used to wrap food, and so forth. Not all changes, however, resulted from necessity rather than choice. Many European immigrants, for example, were delighted by the availability of refined white flour, an upper-class commodity in Europe, and happily replaced darker flours and whole-grain breads with a less healthful, more prestigious alternative.

Ultimately more important to the shape of ethnic foodways than climate and geography were the socioeconomic conditions people faced in Minnesota. The Ojibway present the most radical example: white settlement caused profound changes in their traditional pattern of life and livelihood as farms, cities, and industry replaced prairies and woodlands. Laws regulated their traditional food-gathering practices such as hunting, ricing, and fishing; the government attempted to turn them into farmers; federal food allotments introduced them to foods like salt pork, beans, and bacon; and Indian agents and other government or church workers taught them to can fruits and wax vegetables. These vast changes are especially ironic, since from the perspective of classic immigration theory, the Ojibway take the role of a "host society" rather than an immigrant group.[9]

In less traumatic ways, members of other ethnic groups shaped their foodways to fit the Minnesota environment. In many instances they showed a good deal of ingenuity in maintaining traditional practices; for example, people as diverse as Greeks, Italians, and Hmong have found places to gather wild greens in urban environments. Members of numerous immigrant groups over the years have planted gardens with seeds carried from their homelands, traded across ethnic lines for particular ingredients, started their own businesses to manufacture, import, or simply merchandise hard-to-find food items. Income seems to have had less effect on traditional foodways than peer pressure, the efforts of social workers and dietitians who sought to "Americanize" immigrants, and prevailing concepts of what foods were prestigious. The Great Depression and subsequent economic crises caused many Americans to adjust their foodways; members of some of Minnesota's ethnic groups claim that hard times brought them back to the simple foods of their ethnic heritages.[10]

Settlement patterns certainly affected the overall shape of ethnic foodways, as many of the people who became neighbors in Minnesota shared their recipes and customs. Residents of the state's iron ranges exemplified this kind of exchange which occurs, to a greater or lesser degree, whenever different nationalities interact. Food columnist Eleanor Ostman summarized the process of sharing that was mentioned by many people interviewed for this book: "It wouldn't be a wedding on the Iron Range without Potica, the [South Slav] walnut-rolled sweet bread, or Sarmas, the [South Slav] meat-stuffed cabbage rolls. Pasties [Cornish and Finnish], Porketta [Italian], Pulla [Finnish] — we all grew up with them no matter our ethnic heritage, because if our families didn't make them, our friends did."[11] Intermarriage often promotes this kind of mingling, when spouses share traditions or when the primary cook learns to prepare items from the spouse's heritage. But so does regular social interaction. Hmong people in the Twin Cities have adopted elements of Lao and Thai cuisine because the ingredients are readily available in Oriental groceries. Germans who live in predominantly Norwegian towns in the Red River Valley have learned to make Norse delicacies.

There is no question, then, that some changes have occurred as a result of Minnesota's multicultural environment. Whether or not the state provides a particularly fruitful setting for ethnic interaction, however, is difficult to gauge. Those familiar with traditional cultures on Michigan's Upper Peninsula report similar conditions,[12] and it is reasonable to assume that these are widespread. Yet, according to one source, in neighboring Wisconsin, "The border each [ethnic] group established around itself was almost as formidable as an Old World frontier. Commonality of the immigrant experience was usually shared just with landsmen. . . . Gastronomically, such divisions were every bit as rigid. As happens today, new foods were approached with caution."[13] Clearly, the reciprocal relationship of ethnic groups, their eating patterns, and a particular environment such as a state is a topic well worth further investigation.

One thing for certain, however, is the impact that ethnic cooks have had on Minnesota's local markets. Even large chain stores respond to the cooking needs of their patrons in particular neighborhoods, stocking specialty items like fresh mustard, collard, and turnip greens, fish sauce and a variety of Oriental noodles, packaged kosher ingredients and mixes, frozen phyllo leaves, Swedish meatballs and sausages, and so forth. And the state also supports a fair number and variety of ethnic groceries and meat markets which serve patrons from diverse ethnic groups. These stores are rich resources for the scholar as well as the cook; their contents can tell much about neighborhood settlement patterns in addition to ethnic and interethnic shopping habits. The owner of a Mexican grocery in St. Paul, for example, noted that many "Anglo" people, currently enthralled with Mexican food, shop in her store. She also has many Hmong customers whose cuisine does not resemble the Mexican one but who use some of the same ingredients. Similarly, Sicilian Americans shop in Oriental food stores for frozen squid, Finns may go to Jewish delicatessans for smoked salmon, and several specialty groceries on St. Paul's West Side stock Mexican and Lebanese items under one roof.[14]

Most of the institutions that support ethnic life in Minnesota — churches, synagogues, fraternal organizations, and clubs — have at one time or another published cookbooks. These volumes are ostensibly produced as fund raisers or to satisfy those who enjoy a particular ethnic dish but do not know how to prepare it. In a sense cookbooks serve as a public relations device, but more precisely they are a statement about ethnic identity, one of the barometers of the times. The ladies' aid society of a Minneapolis Norwegian church, for example, published a cookbook in 1942. The first eighty pages were devoted to American recipes, many of them typical of depression-era foods: tuna-noodle and hamburger casseroles and Jell-O "surprises." At the back of the book, a mere eleven pages described "Scandinavian Delicacies." Nine years later the tide toward ethnic cooking had begun to rise, and the same group published another edition with the same cover illustration, but the 128 pages carried almost entirely Norwegian recipes.[15]

Ethnic cookbooks help preserve and disseminate recipes, and they present another research source for the student of ethnic foodways. Yet they should be approached with caution. Who uses them? When? Why? How? Many cooks, for example, frequently amend published recipes, their improve-

ments reflecting changing tastes or trends, as well as individual predilection. Ethnic cookbooks and newspaper descriptions of particular holiday
foods followed by a recipe convey little of the cultural and even less of
the behavioral context of ethnicity or foodways. Cookbooks offer few clues
to the significance of a particular dish or its place in traditional life.[16] Furthermore, many cookbooks, because of insufficient space, must ignore
regional distinctions or stylistic differences. One lefse recipe, for example, seems to stand for all lefse when, in fact, the bread exists in dozens
of variations. And traditional dishes are sometimes adapted with the help
of American commercial enterprise. Potato flakes, for instance, may replace freshly peeled potatoes in the lefse recipe, especially if it was developed for a public function, such as a Christmas bazaar, where quantities
of bread are needed. In short, published recipes are not always reliable versions of home-cooked ethnic foods, even though they may accurately reflect
the shortcuts some cooks take if pressed for time.[17]

Similarly, eating in ethnic restaurants or frequenting events staged for
the public gives but a glimpse of true ethnic foodways. In fact, such public meals may alter or blur the proper presentation and meaning of popular foods. Dishes that have a formal, distinct, and functional place within
the context of a traditional meal or social occasion are often randomly listed
on restaurant menus or laid out informally as part of a mix of delectables
on a bazaar table at a county historical society or a country church. Eating
in such a setting is a little like visiting a museum full of beautiful tools
with no explanatory labels: one appreciates the artifacts but must guess
at their meaning or function.

As dietitians and social workers charged with changing immigrant eating habits were quick to discover, familiar foods are preferred for more
than their nutritional value.[18] Traditional foodways prove to be intrinsic
to the way a particular group views itself and its relation to others, to the
natural world, and, often, to a deity. Aside from providing sustenance,
foods (with attendant ritual) are also at the core of traditional medical practices, whether for something as serious as removing the evil eye (see Mexican chapter) or ensuring good health for mother and unborn child throughout pregnancy and the early postnatal period (Hmong, Scandinavian
chapters) or as minor as treating the symptoms of a cold (British, South
Slav chapters).

But perhaps the most consistently important end to which ethnic foodways are put is a symbolic one. Serving food — any food — is a sign of hospitality and sociability; we can learn a great deal by paying close attention
to the kinds of foods offered, the occasion for socializing, and the place

where eating occurs. Foodways tell the canny observer about social intimacy and distance, background, and aspirations — in short, the kind of impression one hopes to make, the image one wants to project, and the relationship binding those who gather to eat.[19] When Americans choose to serve their traditional ethnic foods at any occasion, they communicate a message about identity, focusing attention on their membership in a group with a particular background and set of values.

Ethnic foods may be offered at casual or formal gatherings, in public or private settings, to members of the same ethnic group or to "outsiders." And even at a casual, private affair like a family supper, the choice to serve ethnic foods is of symbolic significance; using foodways to project or to teach about one's identity is not confined to feeding a curious public. On an everyday basis, for example, when parents prepare and serve traditional food in the ritually or socially proper manner, they are teaching their children about their heritage at the same time that they are celebrating their own ethnicity and reassuring the larger community of a continuity of tradition. The process of communication and reinforcement is the same, whether the participants are an Ojibway family sharing venison stew, a third-generation Finnish couple eating rutabaga casserole and fish soup, or a recently resettled Hmong family eating pork with hot pepper sauce.

Likewise, at annual religious and secular holidays and on special occasions such as weddings, birth celebrations, and funerals, members of a group reaffirm their identity through the foods they serve and eat. And it is not only individual identity that is celebrated, but each person's membership in a unique group, the members of which share certain cultural traits such as traditional foodways and the knowledge of their appropriate uses and contexts. Thus the foods and foodways of any group help establish a cultural boundary which serves both inclusive and exclusive purposes, uniting those within its bounds and distinguishing that particular group from all others.[20]

The power of foodways to symbolize one's status was not lost on many immigrants or their heirs. While constraints of time and money caused some temporarily to reject traditional foodways, the fear of being marked a "greenhorn" (foreigner) prompted others to try to eat American food, especially in public. Consuming large pieces of meat, such as beef steaks or pork chops, and conspicuously displaying processed, or "store-bought," foods in place of homemade items were signs of success, American style. The soul food movement (see Black chapter) and the subsequent celebration of American cultural pluralism in the 1970s turned this trend around to some extent, publicly proclaiming pride in heritage as symbolized by foods both distinctive and humble in origin.

Currently, Americans perceive theirs as a pluralistic society, and open expression of ethnicity is appreciated. Even so, not all ethnic foods are deemed appropriate for public notice. Most cultures have certain well-liked foods, such as menudo (tripe soup) among Mexican Americans, greens among blacks, or pasta fagioli (noodles and beans) among Italian Americans, which members think project a derogatory image of themselves, symbolizing poverty, peasant origins, or the willingness to consume foods of doubtful origin. These dishes are reserved for private consumption. After all, many cultures have suffered name-calling and discrimination based upon the foods they allegedly prefer: French "frogs," black "coons," German "krauts," and so forth. These slurs operate on the principle that people who eat food we consider inedible, for whatever subjective reasons peculiar to our culture, are somehow less human than we.[21]

Consequently, members of ethnic communities often make predictably safe choices when occasions call them to present their foodways (and thus themselves) to the public. The foods that are offered as badges of ethnicity, whether at a festival, a religious observance to which outsiders are invited, or an ethnic New Year's celebration, for example, usually maintain a delicate balance: They are "exotic" or distinctive enough to convey an ethnic image, yet they are "tame" enough to appeal to the uninitiated. And, to spare embarrassment at events meant to generate good will, they are often easily handled "finger foods" such as tacos or miniature Greek pitas (pies) — actually appetizers or snack food, and not celebrative fare. Traditional foodways for public consumption convey ethnicity, in reality a complex web of interactions and allegiances, in simplified, favorable, and easily perceived images.

But if ethnic foodways are used to draw boundaries, to separate "us" from "them" (in either a hostile or a supportive manner), they may also be used to bridge the gap between nationalities. Selectively sharing food, as noted, is a basic form of hospitality. Sharing ethnic food is a rudimentary way of giving strangers and friends a glimpse of one's culture while projecting a positive image of one's self and one's group.

NOTES

[1] Jay A. Anderson, "Scholarship on Contemporary American Folk Foodways," *Ethnologia Europaea* 5 (1971): 57. On church dinners in Aitkin, see interview of staff of KKIN/KKEZ Radio, Aitkin, November 13, 1984.

[2] Anya P. Royce, *Ethnic Identity: Strategies of Diversity* (Bloomington, Ind.: Indiana University Press, 1982), 18; Abner Cohen, "The Lesson of Ethnicity," in Abner Cohen, ed., *Urban Ethnicity* (London: Tavistock, 1974), xi.

[3] On the ways in which family members may "negotiate" a menu, see Judith Goode, Janet Theophano, and Karen Curtis, "A Framework for the Analysis of Continuity and Change in Shared Sociocultural Rules for Food Use: The Italian-American Pattern," in Linda Keller Brown and Kay Mussell, eds., *Ethnic and Regional Foodways in the United States: The Performance of Group Identity* (Knoxville: University of Tennessee Press, 1984), 79–84.

[4] See, for example, interviews of Theresa Inzerillo, Minneapolis, June 7, 1982; Michelina Dreyling, St. Paul, May 10, 1982.

[5] In fact, foodways associated with holidays (especially religious observances) or rites of passage are most likely to be maintained in their traditional forms and contexts. Among everyday dishes, traditional baked goods and desserts seem most likely to be preserved.

[6] Food often becomes symbolic of regional differences or strife. In an opinion column in *Asian Business and Community News* (St. Paul), November 1985, p. 15, Dac Tuong Tuan, a Vietnamese immigrant wrote: "Time only perhaps can erase the discrimination between Northerners and Southerners who belong to the same Vietnamese nation. . . . Southerners gradually learned to eat the bind weed (a kind of vegetable) fried with garlic and Northerners realized that raw bean sprouts are also delicious."

[7] The anthropological literature is replete with references from many viewpoints on food taboos, avoidances, and preferences. See, for example, Marvin Harris, *Cows, Pigs, Wars, and Witches: The Riddles of Culture* (New York: Random House, 1974); Mary Douglas, *Purity and Danger: An Analysis of the Concepts of Pollution and Taboo* (London: Routledge and Kegan Paul, 1966) and *Food in the Social Order: Studies of Food and Festivities in Three American Communities* (New York: The Russell Sage Foundation, 1984); Roger Abrahams, "Equal Opportunity Eating: A Structural Excursus on Things of the Mouth," in *Ethnic and Regional Foodways*, ed. Brown and Mussell, 19–36; Frederick J. Simoons, *Eat Not This Flesh: Food Avoidance in the Old World* (Madison: University of Wisconsin Press, 1963). On the nature-culture distinction, see Claude Levi-Strauss, "The Culinary Triangle," *Partisan Review* 33 (1966): 586–95 and *The Raw and the Cooked: Introduction to the Science of Mythology*, vol. 1 (New York: Harper & Row, 1969).

[8] Interview of Lisa Schlesinger, St. Paul, November 10, 1981. For a lighthearted treatment, see *Minneapolis Tribune*, April 11, 1982, p. 1K, tellingly titled "It's the same the whole world over (and it's a pancake)."

[9] For a description of these changes from an Indian perspective, see Ignatia Broker, *Night Flying Woman: An Ojibway Narrative* (St. Paul: Minnesota Historical Society Press, 1983).

[10] For an analysis of a broad range of regional food customs during the Great Depression, see John Charles Camp, " 'America Eats': Toward a Social Definition of American Foods" (Ph.D. diss., University of Pennsylvania, 1978).

[11] *St. Paul Pioneer Press*, September 20, 1981, Accent sec., 12.

[12] See, for example, interviews of Natalie Gallagher, St. Paul, January 25, 1983, Helen and William Sysimaki, Duluth, August 24, 1983.

[13] Harva Hachten, *The Flavor of Wisconsin: An Informal History of Food and Eating In the Badger State, Together with 400 Favorite Recipes* (Madison: State Historical Society of Wisconsin, 1981), 27.

[14] Interviews of Maria Silva, St. Paul, May 15, 1984, Eila Eilers, Duluth, August 24, 1983, T. Inzerillo, Minneapolis, June 7, 1982.

[15] Ladies' Aid Society of Norwegian Lutheran Memorial Church, *Cookbook of Tested Recipes* (Minneapolis: The Church, 1941, 1950).

[16] See Lynn Ireland, "The Compiled Cookbook as Foodways Autobiography," *Western Folklore* 40 (1981): 107–14; Edith Horandner, "The Recipe Book as a Cultural and Socio-Historical Document," in Alexander Fenton and Trefor M. Owen, eds., *Food in Perspective: Proceedings of the Third International Conference on Ethnological Food Research* (Edinburgh, Scotland: John Donald Publishers Ltd., 1977), 119–44.

[17] The incorporation of premixed, instant, or convenience foods into traditional ethnic cooking is in step with the use of these foods in American life. Leaving aside judgments of aesthetics or quality, this trend supports the argument that traditional foodways should be regarded as an integral part of everyday life, rather than as a sacrosanct preserve untouched by modernity.

[18] See, for example, Bertha M. Wood, *Foods of the Foreign-Born in Relation to Health* (Boston: M. Barrows and Co., 1929).

[19] See, for example, two works by Mary Douglas, "Deciphering a Meal," in Clifford Geertz, ed., *Myth, Symbol, and Ritual* (New York: Norton and Co., 1971), 61–82, and "Food as a System of Communication," in Mary Douglas, ed., *In the Active Voice* (London: Routledge and Kegan Paul, 1982), 82–124.

[20] A good introduction to this topic is the book edited by Brown and Mussell, *Ethnic and Regional Foodways in the United States*. For a caution against simplistic interpretations of ethnic foodways, see Janet Theophano, "It's Really Tomato Sauce But We Call It Gravy: A Study of Food and Women's Work among Italian-American Families" (Ph.D. diss., University of Pennsylvania, 1982).

[21] For more on the phenomenon of labeling a group with reference to a notorious food, see William W. Weaver, *Sauerkraut Yankees: Pennsylvania-German Foods and Foodways* (Philadelphia: University of Pennsylvania Press, 1983).

Maddy Moose pouring hot maple syrup into tins, where it will cool and harden into cakes, Long Lake, 1984

THE OJIBWAY

Hunting and gathering have always been part of the Ojibway life cycle, and the processes of procuring sustenance from the land are well documented as far back as the seventeenth-century observations of missionaries and fur traders. Traditionally, the Ojibway migrated in the spring to obtain sugar sap from the maples, in the summer to find berries, wild greens, and herbs, in the fall to harvest wild rice, and in winter to kill game and spear fish. Consequently the lunar phases of the yearly cycle were identified by food availability. For example, September was Moon of Ricing, and April was Moon of Sugar Making — names that modern Ojibway remember although they may no longer seek that food from the land.[1]

Today, as in former times, important occasions in Indian life are associated with food — naming a child, marriages, deaths, the change of seasons, and religious events. Many aspects of food and diet are sacred to the Ojibway; they are intertwined with religion and provide a guide to the treatment of the land and its products. Plants, trees, animals, and grasses all have a purpose and are a gift that the Ojibway hold in reverence. Because this bounty was placed on earth to be used as food or medicine, it must be managed carefully to ensure its presence for generations to come. Wild rice, maple sugar, and various wild game are integral parts of religious feasts and private powwows. This sacred use of food is a personal matter that most Ojibway prefer not to discuss.[2]

By the late twentieth century the Ojibway depended less upon the land, but there was hardly a family that in some way, or to some degree, was not fed by the world of nature. Areas that were once woodlands have been urbanized, thereby reducing the potential sources of food supply. Wild greens and berries that grow along roadsides and railroad tracks are sprayed with herbicides, which renders the growth unfit for human consumption. Land formerly given to Indian peoples has been alienated and settled on by non-Indians. Even so, Indians residing on the Grand Portage and Fond du Lac reservations try to follow traditional food-gathering practices, and Ojibway living in Duluth and other Minnesota cities return to the land whenever possible. Short of this they rely on the generosity of friends and relatives who share the natural bounty.[3]

Long before the Ojibway arrived in Minnesota, the land was inhabited by Dakota (Sioux) bands. As encroaching settlers and rival Indian tribes forced the Ojibway to emigrate from their homeland on the eastern seaboard, they moved first to the Sault Ste. Marie area of Michigan. Later some of them traveled over the north shore of Lake Superior until they reached the present site of Grand Portage. A second and larger group left Sault Ste. Marie to follow the south shore of Lake Superior to Madeline Island, one of the Apostle Islands in Wisconsin. A third migration took the Ojibway into the heart of Dakota territory, and, after a series of wars with their traditional enemies, they occupied the land as far south as Mille Lacs Lake.[4]

Tribal life changed drastically, however, as white settlers moved westward, and in the 1850s treaties began to remove many Ojibway to reservations. By 1867 there were seven Ojibway reservations in Minnesota: Grand Portage, Fond du Lac, White Earth, Mille Lacs, Nett Lake, Leech Lake, and Red Lake. The Red Lake Reservation has a formal tribal council and its own medical clinics, schools, police force, and businesses — fisheries, a lumberyard, and commercial rice harvesters and processors. Red Lake is the only reservation that refused to accept the allotment of lands to individuals but instead retained common tribal ownership. The other six reservations have incorporated as the Minnesota Chippewa Tribe, yet each maintains an individual governing body called the Reservation Business Committee (RBC). At Grand Portage, for example, the RBC owns a large hotel (Grand Portage Lodge), and at Fond du Lac the RBC conducts a bingo operation and manages a furnace factory.[5]

Before the mid-twentieth century the roles of men, women, and children were clearly defined. In most instances the men hunted and fished and butchered the meat. Women cooked, gathered berries, herbs, and wild greens, raised meager crops, processed the animal hides, and preserved the meat. Children helped in all of these activities, observing the procedures and practices and learning by doing for their own later use as adults. The family as a whole was involved in ricing and maple-sugar making.[6]

Until the early reservation years, Indians in general used two thousand different foods derived from plants alone, not to mention the available wildlife. Nuts, berries, greens, onions, turtle eggs, camas bulbs, leeks, Jerusalem artichokes, and numerous other foodstuffs formed part of the Ojibway diet.[7]

Because of the nomadic life the Ojibway led, they frequently prepared one-pot meals over an open fire. Whenever weather permitted, this fire would be outdoors, but on rainy days or in the depths of winter it was moved to the center of the large wigwams, which housed one or more families. Foods were cooked in a birch-bark container suspended from a tripod over a low fire that provided continuous heat. The cooks dropped hot rocks, taken from the coals, into the water-filled bark containers, which would not burn as long as there was water in the vessel. The rocks brought the water to a low boil sufficient to cook all the ingredients of the one-pot meal. Later the manomin (wild rice) or napodin (dumplings) might be added.[8]

Cast-iron kettles replaced birch-bark containers as the Ojibway began an exchange of goods with the white people, especially the fur traders. Some kettles were made with a heavy, hoop-shaped handle so they could be suspended over the fire, while others were supported by three legs and could be placed directly over coals or low flames. Later, as part of the treaty arrangements, the United States government gave some Ojibway bands copper kettles of similar style. The iron and copper pots proved to be superior replacements for the birch-bark containers as they were more durable and allowed a higher heat for cooking. Many families still possess these early kettles and use them in the woods during ricing time or maple-sugar season.

American Indians were introduced to salt by fur traders, and it later became part of their allotments of food and supplies from the federal government in accordance with the treaties of 1845 and later. Prior to this time foods were seasoned only with maple syrup or maple sugar; salt, however, was quickly incorporated into Ojibway cooking. It was also used in food preservation, especially after the Scandinavians who came to fish Lake Superior's north shore waters showed the Ojibway how to salt down fish for winter storage.[9]

Most government-issue foods were nonperishable staples and were originally part of the Indian allotments. Surplus commodities were substituted for allotments in the late 1950s, discontinued in subsequent years, and resumed in 1980. Older people at Fond du Lac remember trips to Esko in a horse-drawn cart or wagon to pick up macaroni, raisins, flour, salt pork, oatmeal, canned goods such as tomatoes, and other allotment foods, many of which remain in the diet of Ojibway to the present.[10]

Salt pork, one item consistently on the allotment list, was customarily served with hominy or was used to season wild game. Although salt pork is used less often today because of its high fat content, small amounts are sometimes added to boiled dishes for flavor or laid in strips over baking venison, moose, duck, coot, or fish. In some families salt pork is boiled to remove some of the salt, then sliced, fried crisp, and served with oatmeal.

Oatmeal and macaroni were used to such an extent that today many joke that they are "traditional Indian foods." Oatmeal as a breakfast cereal is cooked very firm and served with bacon fat over the top. Leftover oatmeal is sliced and fried, often in bacon fat, and accompanied by fried onions, perhaps topped with catsup.

Plain macaroni is sometimes served as a hot dish, seasoned with butter or margarine, but more often it is mixed with canned tomatoes. Many women today make more elaborate tomato-macaroni casseroles by adding canned meat and cheese. In addition, some older Ojibway still enjoy a dessert of macaroni mixed with milk and maple syrup or canned tomatoes with sugar on them. Macaroni, plain, simple, or mixed with other ingredients is called "macs" by many people, or, for reasons no longer remembered, "skeds" or "skeddies" by others.

Lamb — a meat the Indians never learned to enjoy — was included in the early allotments. The Ojibway soon stopped trying to use it and instead traded it to nearby non-Indians for potatoes and other garden produce.

Indigenous foodways have succumbed to a variety of other forces. In the 1920s and 1930s youngsters were sent to government boarding schools where the training was meant to change Indian habits, including foodways. Soon they were eating white bread, pies, cakes, beef and pork roasts, and chicken. Girls in food preparation classes or who worked in the homes of school staff members learned how to prepare many new dishes — some of which are used today. Later, as some of these Ojibway women married Swedes, Poles, French Canadians, and Scots, they cooked only the foods their husbands enjoyed.[11]

Many Ojibway remember very poor times during the depression years and into the early 1940s. Women made soups and stews that stretched wild meat and fowl and added dumplings and wild rice to extend them further. One woman said, "I remember relatives who had Campbell's bean and bacon soup . . . as being very wealthy."

In more recent years, with the increased incidence of diabetes, high blood pressure, heart disease, and gallstone problems in the Ojibway population, the movement to curb sweets, salt, cholesterol, and fat has changed diets even further. Many in public health nursing and educational programs on the reservations hope that the contemporary Ojibway diet will reintegrate traditional foods that were relatively free of salt, fat, and sugar and were high in fiber. The meals provided for the elderly on the reservation are carefully planned, and fruit is usually the only dessert served. At the Fond du Lac Reservation menus include wild-rice dishes and donated wild game so that some of the traditional foods can be prepared for those who remember them best. The school lunch program at Fond du Lac introduces children to nontraditional but nutrient-rich foods. Fat and salt are kept at a minimum in preparation of such favorites as chili, sloppy joes, Spanish rice, grilled cheese sandwiches, or a hamburger patty fixed with gravy and served over rice, and fruits are always available for dessert. [12]

Ojibway foodways were modified by exposure to diverse white cultures and their attendant pressures to change the Indian way of life. When the Fond du Lac Reservation near Cloquet was formed, the government hoped that the Indians would become farmers. Some of the Ojibway sold their allotted lands to non-Indians, most of whom were Scandinavians and Finns who raised pigs, cows, and chickens and planted gardens and crops. Not only were the Indians introduced to fresh pork, but they also learned from their new neighbors the technique of making headcheese, a practice retained today. Milk, previously absent from the Ojibway diet, was adopted as a beverage and then rejected because it created digestive problems unless it was cooked in foods or used as a processed, canned product. Few Ojibway raised dairy cattle because of this condition. [13]

Peddlers of Rawleigh and Watkins products also left their mark on the Ojibway diet. These men traveled from house to house in rural areas, selling spices, herbs, extracts, mixes, and miscellaneous other household items. Several women remember that it was an important day when one of these salesmen called with an array of new and interesting products.

Going to the sugar bush, the forested area where the sugar maples grow, has been part of Ojibway family life for generations, each family retaining its own particular location over many years. Permanent shelters, called "sugar-bush cabins," or wigwams once housed the families, but later tents became more popular. [14]

Today, middle-aged Ojibway relate many childhood memories of sugar-bush times when the elders of the family were always in charge of sugar making. First, the trees had to be tapped in a precise operation. An ax slash marked the spot for the insertion of the spigot, and a birch-bark container (later a bucket) was attached to collect the sap. Children usually had the task of making trips back and forth between the trees and the open fires carrying the containers of sap. Next the sap was boiled in as many as a dozen kettles, which in some cases were the heavy cast-iron or copper pots obtained in fur trade or allotment days. As much as ten hours of labor on the part of many workers was required to boil down enough sap to produce one pound of sugar, and four to five hundred trees were often tapped to obtain enough sugar for the needs of one extended family. [15]

As the sap boiled down, it turned first into a thick maple syrup, some of which was cooled and stored in jars and bottles. The remaining liquid was boiled further until it was reduced by half. This thick syrup was then poured into small molds, pans, or even cone-shaped, birch-bark containers where it was left to harden into sugar cakes, which were used for treats or special gifts or as part of religious ceremonies. The rest of the boiled syrup was poured into a wooden trough especially constructed for making bulk maple sugar. Using a heavy wooden utensil similar to an old-fashioned potato masher, the workers "mashed" this thick liquid — nearly solid as it cooled — much in the same motions one might use with potatoes. When cooled it resembled granulated sugar and was used in cooking or sprinkled on oatmeal or other foods or dissolved in cold water for a refreshing summer drink. Some sap, however, was used just as it came from the trees to make a bracing hot tea.

Many Ojibway continue these traditional practices in the sugar bush but use new ways to tap the trees and gather the sap, in part because current laws make it difficult to continue the old processes. On the Fond du Lac Reservation no wood may be cut in the area of the maple trees, so the Ojibway must haul in all wood necessary to keep the fires going. Some families are experimenting by carrying the sap to their homes in large containers with plastic lids. Sap, however, spoils quickly, and this home processing does not always turn out well. Another law, which prohibits anyone under sixteen years of age from working in the sugar bush, reduces the number in a family who can help with the project.[16]

Maple sugar has always been enjoyed as a sweet, and the syrup is still used by older Indians on vegetables, cereals, fish, and wild rice. In addition, for some it has medicinal qualities, for others an element of sacredness, and for all, it is a symbol of good relations among people and harmony between them and their religious world. Those Ojibway who continue the maple-sugar process today "feel the presence of our ancestors." According to tribal custom, after all the activity is completed the forest is to be left as the sugar-makers found it. The Ojibway believe that "Nature gives to us, and we have great respect for it."

Gathering wild rice (actually the kernel from an aquatic wild grass called *Zizania aquatica* by botanists and manomin by the Ojibway) is an important food ritual involving all members of the family. The elders guide the young, and every family assigns tasks, drawing upon the strengths and experiences of each person. Lakes with large rice beds were frequently divided among families, just as the sugar-bush locations were. Groups went out long before the rice was ripe and tied bright ribbon or twine around the stalks, marking only enough rice to supply them for the year ahead.[17]

The actual method of harvesting has remained unchanged since it was described in the early writings of missionaries. Two people in a canoe glide slowly through the rice. One person poles and guides the canoe while the other, using a pair of cedar sticks about two feet long, called "knockers" by the Ojibway, harvests the rice. One "knocker" is used to bend the grass over the canoe and then the other beats the rice heads gently, shaking the kernels loose into the bottom of the boat. When the grass is released and returns to an upright position a few kernels fall into the water, becoming the seeds of next year's rice. Since all the rice on the stalk does not completely ripen at one time, the ricing team makes several trips through the area to harvest the crop.

Ricing is still an integral part of autumn for many Ojibway, and families continue to journey to the same lake or lakes as did generations before them although they no longer mark the stands of rice. Because there are only a few lakes in the Grand Portage area, the Ojibway there have either riced elsewhere in Minnesota or in Canada or traded fish for rice with other

Porky White testing the consistency of maple sugar, Long Lake, 1984

Mrs. Peter Fields parching wild rice, Nett Lake Reservation, April 1946

bands. Urban Indians receive it as gifts, buy it from others, or return to the reservation for ricing.

Parching wild rice begins as soon as it is unloaded from the canoe. Before the Ojibway received metal utensils as part of their allotments, they spread the rice to dry on birch-bark sheets or flat rocks. The availability of washtubs changed these techniques. Currently a pit is dug in the ground for a fire, and posts are driven in around it to support the tub above the flames, thereby facilitating the continual addition of firewood. About nine quarts of rice at a time are poured into the tub and stirred with an old canoe paddle or a hand-carved wooden implement. The rice is carefully watched and stirred only until it is a greenish-brown color — much lighter than the dark brown associated with commercially processed wild rice. By Indian standards dark rice has been parched far too long and indicates that metal drums heated by gas flames have been used.

When the hand-parched rice turns the right color, it is removed from the heat, and small amounts are placed in winnowing — or finishing — baskets made of birch bark. Many Ojibway still own and treasure the baskets and equipment that their parents used. In winnowing, the rice is tossed into the air and the loose hulls blow away in the breeze. Another pit is then dug, and either a wooden, canvas, or metal container is put in the bottom. The kernels that still have hulls on them are placed in small amounts in the pit. An Ojibway dons moccasins or clean rubber boots and dances in a shuffling motion on top of the rice, loosening any remaining hulls. This dancing continues until most of the rice is clean, but some hand cleaning at the end may be necessary. When the process is completed the wild rice is stored in a cloth sack or pillowcase that permits air to circulate. Hand-parched wild rice is never stored in a closed container because its high moisture content will cause mildew.

Some men have put together handmade parching machines, usually a small drum attached to a motor. In this way they can still exercise a careful watch over the color and conclude the parching when the rice is just right. Still others have made finishing machines that separate hulls from kernels. Wild-rice hulls, when first harvested, have small, single, wiry hairs on them that adhere to skin, mouth, and eyes and cause an itch. In the past these hairs were a constant irritation, but ricers learned to use chewing gum to remove them from their skin.[18]

Wild rice is still an important staple food for the Ojibway in northern Minnesota. Preparing rice is simple — simmer it in boiling water until the kernels burst open, drain, mix with butter or bacon fat, and serve. Hand-parched rice, because of its moisture content, cooks in only twelve to fifteen minutes. The flavor of this rice is full-bodied and needs no seasonings or sauces to heighten it. Many Ojibway use the rice in pancakes, muffins, stuffings, casseroles, and soups. Hand-parched rice can also be popped. Every cook has a different method for popping the kernels, but basically most add a tablespoon of rice to hot fat for a few seconds until the rice pops, doubling in size. The process is repeated until a bowlful is ready to eat, either lightly salted or mixed with maple sugar.

Fish, once crucial to the survival of the Ojibway during Minnesota winters, is still a mainstay in the diet of many Indians. Traditionally fishing was accomplished with nets and hooks in the open water and with spears and various hook and line arrangements through the ice. In January when the suckers come to cracks or openings in the ice for more oxygen, Indians can easily spear them. Ojibway at Grand Portage fish year round for trout and whitefish in Lake Superior while Indians at Fond du Lac catch northerns, walleye, sunfish, suckers, and bullheads in the inland lakes.[19]

Before the introduction of salt, fish were most often preserved by cleaning and freezing or by smoking. The winter cold provided a natural freezer enabling fishermen at Grand Portage, for example, to scale and gut their catch and hang the cleaned fish by their tails in a woodshed until needed

Henry Fields with his fish nets, Nett Lake Reservation, September 1947

for a meal. Another way was to layer the cleaned fish in snow. The bottom layer rested on a clean cloth and was covered with snow, and the entire catch was buried, layer by layer, in this fashion. Later the fish were chipped out and cooked. The old way of smoking fish was to build a rack out of young saplings about three feet above a good bed of coals. The fish were placed on the rack for many hours and periodically turned until they were flavorfully smoked and ready for storage. More recently the Ojibway have preserved fish in their home freezers or used various types of manufactured smokers.

Fish is served either boiled, baked, pickled, or made into cakes. Larger fish are boiled in salted water for ten to fifteen minutes and, traditionally, are accompanied by boiled potatoes and onions. Baked fish is covered with strips of bacon or salt pork. Fish cakes are a well-liked entree, and every family has its recipe for mixing flaked fish with crumbs, eggs, canned milk, and seasonings. Some women grind up sunfish, bones and all, add other ingredients, form the mixture into cakes, and fry them. Recipes for pickled fish use trout, whitefish, and bullheads.

Among those Indians living at Grand Portage, a popular food was whitefish livers, easily prepared by dipping in flour and frying in hot fat — a dish still enjoyed today. Both inland Indians and those living on Lake Superior are fond of roe or fish eggs. Spread on bread or crackers or fried quickly in a little fat, they are an unsurpassed delicacy.

In the bay by the community of Grand Portage is Grand Portage Island, but since the turn of the century it has been known as Pete's Island. Pete Gagnon ran a boardinghouse for lumberjacks who worked at Camp Nine on the Pigeon River and operated a store and trading post. The *America*, a ship that regularly traveled the north shore of Lake Superior, stopped there to take on barrels of salted fish from the local fishermen and discharge supplies for Pete's store and allotments for the Ojibway. Pete employed Indian women who, in the course of their work, learned a great deal about cooking for lumberjacks. Many of the women at Grand Portage today believe that it was here that their grandmothers learned about ham, lemon pie, white bread, and other lumber camp staples.[20]

Some Ojibway women periodically canoed to the island to obtain fish heads and throats (called "little stockings") that Pete saved for them. The cheeks were cut out of fish heads and used with potatoes and onions, boiled until tender, and the mixture thickened with corn meal to make a delicious stew. "Little stockings" were turned inside out and cleaned thoroughly before going into a soup or stew, frequently being served with the ever-present salt pork.

A wide assortment of wild game found its way to the cooking pots of the Ojibway: deer, moose, bear, rabbit, muskrat, beaver, raccoon, porcupine, partridge, duck, and coot were the most common. Due to the diminishing wooded area in Minnesota, these game animals are not found in the quantity they once were. Persistent hunters, however, can usually bag something for the family dinner. Ojibway today who live in the Grand Portage area continue to have more moose in their diet than those living elsewhere in Minnesota. Deer and moose cannot be hunted when the females are carrying or nursing their young, but enrollees (tribal members of the Grand Portage Reservation) may hunt during any of the other months. Deer and moose are favorite meats, often butchered into steaks and roasts or processed for ground meat and sausage. Bear is the least desirable and is hunted only if there is a need for meat even though the skins usually bring a good price. When a hunter kills a porcupine or beaver, it is generally frozen and kept for a special occasion, such as a dinner honoring the elders of the tribe.[21]

The freezer serves to store the winter's supply of game along with the catch of fish and marks a sharp contrast to the ancestral ways of preserving meats. Meat was often dried. It was then stored in cheesecloth bags or was placed on a canvas and beaten with a clublike utensil until it was reduced to powder thus providing a savory ingredient to mix with a kettle of wild rice. Some Indians also made a mixture of pounded meat, fat, and berries, often called pemmican. This high-protein blend made an excellent food to take on hunting trips, or it could be formed into patties and fried. Both the pounded meat powder and the meat patties were placed in covered birch-bark baskets and buried below the frostline until needed.

Women on both the Grand Portage and Fond du Lac reservations remember that their families in earlier days ate a great deal of rabbit. Children did the snaring; after school it was the job of twelve- and thirteen-year-olds to go into the woods and gather the rabbits caught in the previous day's sets and reset the snares. Elders taught them the precise technique — an arrangement using a filament of picture-frame wire with a slip-knot loop in its end and attached to a stick. The stick was secured in a bush by a rabbit run — where tracks were visible — and the wire positioned so that the rabbit ran headlong into the loop and was choked to death. After being skinned and cleaned, the rabbits were usually cooked in a pot with water until tender, although sometimes they were baked. Skins were cut into strips and woven in an intricate way to make warm reversible blankets, and rabbit feet decorated clothing.[22]

In addition to wild game and fish, water fowl formed part of the diet. Coots, slate-colored ducklike birds, were plentiful on the Fond du Lac Reservation and formerly were used often for one-pot meals. Today they are relished at special occasions. Seagull eggs were gathered in great abundance on the many islands in the bay at Grand Portage during the early part of the 1900s. One of these large spotted brown eggs was enough for a cake. Although one woman noted that they had a slightly fishy taste, "you got used to them." In order to ensure a supply of fresh eggs, some Ojibway regularly destroyed the existing ones in the nests, knowing that the gulls would lay new eggs overnight — these to be gathered the next day.[23]

Turtles as well as turtle eggs were once plentiful and occasionally eaten on all reservations. The eggs were boiled, shelled, and eaten out-of-hand with a little salt. Some remember that pigeons and snowbirds also were caught, cooked, and eaten. The snowbirds were attracted by corn meal scattered under a propped-up box. A long stick was used to knock away the prop and trap the bird. When the food supply was short, some Indians resorted to hunting loons despite their fishy taste and boiled them until tender.

The land provided other foods. Hazelnuts, available in the Fond du Lac area, were gathered, placed in gunny sacks, and allowed to dry until around midwinter. After the family shucked off the prickly hulls — a task hard on the hands — there was a tasty treat. Mushrooms supplemented the diet. Morels were the most plentiful, and these were fried for immediate consumption or dried for winter use.[24]

Adult Ojibway today recall gathering wintergreen or labrador leaves for tea. Pigweed, which grew in abundance around Big Lake in Carlton County, often furnished a meal and was usually cooked with salt pork. The juices and pan drippings were thickened with flour to make a gravy. Wild leek and onion were still part of the diet in the 1930s and 1940s as were various herbs. Milkweed stems were collected when they first appeared in the spring. Fiddlehead ferns, watercress, and dandelion were other wild greens Ojibway remember eating as children.

The summers were filled with berry picking beginning with strawberries and followed by June berries, raspberries, pin cherries, and blueberries. Whole families went picking, and everyone worked hard because each knew that the fruit would be canned, dried, or made into jelly or jam for the winter. An unusual type of canning was practiced in the Grand Portage area before jars were introduced. One woman relates that her mother took a dozen or so crocks (similar to butter crocks) out to the berry camp. After the many quarts of berries were picked, she washed them, put them in a large kettle with a little water, and brought them to a boil over an open fire. Twice she skimmed the scum off the top of the kettle and then filled the clean crocks with the cooked berries and juice. After cutting brown wrapping paper to fit the tops of the crocks, the woman made a flour and water paste. She applied the paste to the top of the crock and pressed down the brown paper to form a seal. When dry it was sufficient to keep the berries from spoiling until winter. After the crocks were opened, the berries were placed in a pan with sugar added, brought to a boil, and served. Sometimes they were mixed into breads or pancakes. Fruit supplied almost the only dessert eaten by the Ojibway.

The Ojibway in Minnesota practiced very little agriculture because the areas where they lived were too far north, too heavily wooded, and too poor in soil nutrients. The crop most often raised was corn, a non-native grain brought from Mexico in pre-Columbian times. The Ojibway on the Red Lake and White Earth reservations, where the land is more open, have been able to raise surplus corn, some of which they then trade for fish, moose, or whatever other bands had to barter. Although freshly picked corn is cooked and eaten for midsummer meals, most of it is dried for use later in the year. Indians frequently sell corn at powwows and some grocery stores stock dried corn.[25]

A few urban Indians have tried to grow corn on small plots; however, the process of growing and drying corn in a city environment is difficult. Harvested, roasted, and cut from the cob, it is best dried in the open air, but returning it to the house each night is a demanding and tiresome process. Some Ojibway spread it out on cloths on a garage floor while others dry it in small batches on a baking sheet in the oven rather than leave it unprotected in the open air. Corn chowder is a well-liked dish prepared from the dried kernels, and some Indians still make hominy, using the complicated process developed by their ancestors.

Ojibway bread was a staple part of the meal. Bannock, a heavy biscuit-like dough baked in a variety of ways, was one of the most widely consumed varieties. Some cooks made it in a cast-iron skillet propped up on its side by an open fire, using a good bed of coals. Some baked it in strips wrapped around the end of a two- or three-foot-long stick from which the bark was removed. The stick was first pushed into the ground to suspend the dough over hot coals and then was turned until the bread was cooked and browned. People today make bannock using this method when they are out in the woods. Bannock prepared at home is baked in pans of various sizes. A similar bread is "lug" or "lugaled" that includes the same ingredients: flour, baking powder, water, salt, and either lard or bacon fat. (It is not clear why the two names evolved for what is essentially the same bread.) Fruit is added to either of these breads in whatever proportion the family likes.[26]

"Fry" or "fried" bread has been part of Ojibway foods as long as people can remember. Although it has been described in food books and histories as part of the diet of Southwest Indians, no one seems to know whether they introduced it to Minnesota or whether it has always been an Ojibway staple. Some scholars believe that Indians throughout the United States invented fry bread to use the flour that was included in their government allotment. Fry bread is made from a stiff dough using flour, salt, baking powder or yeast, water or milk, and little or no shortening. Some women roll out the dough and cut it into triangles or squares, while others pinch off pieces of dough and pull the pieces into ovals, squares, or rounds with their hands. The thickness of the dough varies from very thin to three-quarters of an inch, depending on the preferences of the family. Whatever the shape, a hole is next poked into the center and the dough dropped into hot fat, sometimes using the old cast-iron or copper kettles. The bread cooks in seconds, and the crisp fried morsel is eaten plain or with sugar, jam, or syrup.

A typical one-pot meal often began with the preparation of fry bread. Then the frying fat was emptied out and water added to cook the venison, porcupine, beaver, or whatever was available. Fry bread is made for every Indian gathering and for powwows and community events in which the Ojibway participate.[27]

Ojibway on the Grand Portage Reservation have, since 1974, taken part in an annual celebration called Rendezvous Days held at the Grand Portage National Monument in early August. The Ojibway sell fry bread served with butter, jam, or sugar or split and filled with a hamburger patty. Wild-rice soup, moose-meat soup, venison or moose burgers, and "blanket dogs" — biscuit dough wrapped around a hot dog and deep-fat fried — are prepared for the hungry visitor. Similar food is available during Indian Awareness Days at the Fond du Lac Reservation.[28]

Another annual celebration, held during one weekend in August since 1984, is called Ni-Mi-Win, which means "everyone come and dance." This event, billed as a family reunion of the Ojibway nation, attracts hundreds of Ojibway as well as white people to Spirit Mountain, a recreational area near Duluth. In addition to many hours of dancing by several hundred Ojibway of all ages, the festival features an Indian art show, crafts demonstrations and sales, and a series of lectures on Ojibway culture and current issues. Popular contemporary and traditional foods are sold to the hundreds who attend — fry bread, wild-rice soup, buffalo and venison burgers, and blanket dogs in abundance. Special meals of venison, corn, and other traditional foods are sometimes also featured.[29]

Increased public awareness of Indian traditions and the desire for more understanding has led to the inauguration of several school programs that include some exposure to Indian culture and foodways. Public schools in Grand Marais, Grand Portage, Carlton, Cloquet, and the Twin Cities plan field trips to the woods during the sugar-bush season. Thus Ojibway students whose families no longer carry on this tradition can observe part of their cultural heritage, and non-Indians in the school can watch and appreciate this activity. Other programs are designed to teach about such subjects as winter trapping and fall ricing in the world outside of the classroom during different times of the year. In the Duluth public schools Indian social studies curriculum, the various foods obtained from the land are discussed, methods of harvesting explained, and some cooking demon-

*Porky White showing Maggie
Sengoge, a student at Heart of
the Earth Survival School,
Minneapolis, how to tap a
sugar maple, Long Lake, 1984*

strated in the classroom. One of the most popular units is the section on making fry bread.[30]

The Ojibway school on the Fond du Lac Reservation has special dinners for graduation, Easter, Christmas, Thanksgiving, New Year's Eve, and All Saints' Day, each sponsored by the Reservation Business Committee. Featured foods are baked or boiled fish, roasted venison, duck or coot in a stew or soup with wild rice, fry bread dipped in maple syrup, and apple pies sweetened with maple sugar.[31]

Living on the reservation is directly related to the retention of traditional foodways. At Grand Portage, Indians continue to gather and prepare fish, game, and maple sugar. Ricing remains a strong tradition on the Fond du Lac Reservation as does hunting and some fishing on the inland lakes. Schools in both areas, on and off the reservation, are committed to teaching Ojibway customs and traditions, hoping to preserve them. Although individuals' roles have changed through the years, the family as a close cooperating unit has remained constant. Reverence for the elders and joy toward the young continue to draw families together for special celebrations, and food — wild-rice dishes, fry bread, soups or stews made from game, and boiled fish or fish cakes — is always part of these occasions.[32]

Several centuries of outside influences have altered indigenous Indian foodways practices and contributed to health problems. Allotments and surplus commodities have supplied processed, canned, and packaged foods high in fat, sugar, and salt. To compound the problem, peer pressure among the young and, until recently, the general nationwide food trends have popularized nutrient-poor foods. Many Ojibway, on their part, no longer care to spend a large amount of time on the old labor-intensive foodways.

Despite these changes, Ojibway tribal attitudes toward life — not the least of which involve food — have persisted and still offer the non-Indian many principles. Whether it is during the maple-sugar season or while gathering other foods, the Indian has always viewed the world as an integrated place in which people, nature, and animals exist together in perfect harmony. Frugal use of the bounty of the land, an awareness of the balance that exists in nature, and a caring for the environment so that it is preserved for generations to come — all are standards the nation as a whole could well adopt.

NOTES

[1] Timothy G. Roufs, *The Anishinabe of the Minnesota Chippewa Tribe* (Phoenix, Ariz.: Indian Tribal Series, 1975), 39–45. The names of the months are listed in Edmund Jefferson Danziger, Jr., *The Chippewas of Lake Superior* (Norman: University of Oklahoma Press, 1978), 11–13; Betty Gurno, "Months," in David Martinson, ed., *A Long Time Ago Is Just Like Today* (Duluth: Duluth Indian Education Advisory Committee, 1977), 54–55; interview of Sandy Shabiash, Carlton, November 10, 1983.

[2] Interviews of Larry Aitkin, Office of Indian Education, University of Minnesota-Duluth, May 2, 1983, Billy Blackwell, Grand Portage, October 26, 1983, Amelia LeGarde, Duluth, July 2, 1984; Shabiash interview.

[3] Shabiash and Blackwell interviews.

[4] Here and below, see Mitchell E. Rubinstein and Alan R. Woolworth, "The Dakota and Ojibway," in *They Chose Minnesota: A Survey of the State's Ethnic Groups*, ed. June Drenning Holmquist (St. Paul: Minnesota Historical Society Press, 1981), 17–26; Roufs, *Anishinabe*, 45–58.

[5] For other reservation business enterprises, see *Duluth News Herald-Tribune*, March 2, 1986, p. 21.

[6] Interview of Vernon Zacher, Duluth, July 10, 1984; LeGarde interview.

[7] Waverley Lewis Root and Richard de Rochemont, *Eating in America: A History* (New York: William Morrow, 1976), 15–24; James Trager, *The Enriched, Fortified, . . . International, Unexpurgated Foodbook* (New York: Grossman Publishers, 1970), 90.

[8] Here and below, see interviews of Alvina Tiessen, Sawyer, January 24, 1984, Mary W. Deschampes, Grand Portage, November 22, 1983; Shabiash interview; Frances Densmore, *Chippewa Customs* (Washington, D.C.: Smithsonian Institution, 1929; St. Paul: Minnesota Historical Society Press, 1979), 39–44.

[9] Interview of Liza Thibault, Grand Portage, October 26, 1983; Root, *Eating*, 244–45.

[10] Here and four paragraphs below, see interviews of Peggy Couture, Sawyer, November 17, 1983, Margaret DuFault, Sawyer, November 17, 1983; Mary Deschampes and LeGarde interviews.

[11] DuFault, Couture, and Mary Deschampes interviews.

[12] Interviews of Rosemary Blanchard, Sawyer, October 21, 1983, Nora Hakala, Duluth, July 10, 1984, Joyce M. Kramer, Duluth, April 12, 1985; DuFault and Couture interviews. For another study of diet and health, see Sandra K. Joos, "Economic, Social, and Cultural Factors in the Analysis of Disease: Dietary Change and Diabetes Mellitus among the Florida Seminole Indians," in *Ethnic and Regional Foodways*, ed. Brown and Mussell, 217–37.

[13] Here and below, see interviews of Les Northrup, Duluth, July 11, 1984, Vi Foldesi, Duluth, July 11, 1984; Tiessen interview.

[14] Roufs, *Anishinabe*, 16–18; LeGarde interview.

[15] Here and below, see Thibault and Shabiash interviews; interview of Paul Buffalo (Chief Buffalo) by Joseph Drezenovich in files of Iron Range Research Library, Chisholm; Betty Gurno, "Maple Sugaring," in *A Long Time Ago*, ed. Martinson, 39–43.

[16] Here and below, see Shabiash interview.

[17] Here and four paragraphs below, see interviews of Walter Caribou, Grand Portage, October 26, 1983, Florence Greensky, Sawyer, November 7, 1983; Shabiash and Zacher interviews; Danziger, *Chippewas*, 12–13.

[18] Here and below, see Broker, *Night Flying Woman*, 117–19; Foldesi, Northrup, LeGarde, and Zacher interviews.

[19] Here and three paragraphs below, see Caribou, Thibault, Mary Deschampes, and Buffalo interviews.

[20] Here and below, see interview of Florence Deschampes, Grand Portage, November 22, 1983; Tiessen and Caribou interviews.

[21] Here and below, see Buffalo, Caribou, and Blackwell interviews.

[22] Densmore, *Chippewa Customs*, 161; Foldesi and Hakala interviews.

[23] Here and below, see Tiessen and Blackwell interviews.

[24] Here and two paragraphs below, see interview of Beulah Sayers, Duluth, July 3, 1984; Foldesi, Thibault, and Tiessen interviews.

[25] Here and below, see Danziger, *Chippewas*, 6–12; Broker, *Night Flying Woman*, 47–48; Sayers interview.

[26] Here and below, see LeGarde, Sayers, Foldesi, and Hakala interviews. Densmore, in *Chippewa Customs*, 41, notes "bread called 'Legolet bread' was made from flour and salt, mixed with water, and kneaded very hard into round, flat loaves. If the woman had a frying pan, she baked the bread in this pan, placed upright in front of the fire. If she had no pan she fastened the bread on sticks, which she stuck in the ground before the fire."

[27] Shabiash interview.

[28] Interview of Jayne Gagnon, Grand Portage, October 26, 1983; Shabiash interview.

[29] *News-Tribune and Herald* (Duluth), August 17, 1984, supplement; Kramer interview.

[30] LeGarde and Blackwell interviews.

[31] Florence Deschampes and DuFault interviews.

[32] Zacher and LeGarde interviews.

Evelyn Fairbanks with a bowl of potato salad, Minneapolis, 1985

THE BLACKS

Black Americans express two general attitudes about their culture in Minnesota. As in other regions, the descendants of early settlers have created a synthesis of old and new ways. Established black families claim theirs is a rich and supportive culture, textured by music, oral traditions, patterns of social and political import, and economic enterprise. Newcomers from the South since World War II, rooted in the older ways, decry what they view as a fragmented social network and a paucity of authentic folkways. Yet both groups retain a substantial and distinct culture, the core of which includes traditional foodways.

The food heritage of black Minnesotans is largely southern but heavily influenced by each family's subsequent experiences, whether in Pennsylvania or Nebraska, Baton Rouge or Chicago. And black life and concomitant foodways in the South varied, too, not only from state to state, or from urban to rural residence, but depending on whether people were servants in white houses or field hands. When talk turns to "roots" it refers, almost always, to the South. Unlike other groups of ethnic Americans who can make frequent visits to ancestral villages, Minnesota blacks, with rare exception, have not visited any part of Africa. Home and heritage are associated, more likely, with a farm in Oklahoma or a suburb near Atlanta. Most of the state's blacks are but distantly aware of the origins and uses of African foods such as okra, rice, and certain squashes. Yet references to Africa are heard, and the term "Afro-American" is used, especially when blacks consider their origins, cultural commitments, and political imperatives.[1]

The influence of Caribbean foodways upon Minnesota diets is more noticeable. Blacks are more and more frequently visiting the islands, particularly Jamaica. "It's as close to our roots as we'll ever come," said one woman, explaining her fascination with that place. While some go for the sun or the music, others penetrate more deeply, exploring the ideologies and the cuisine. "The food there was simpler and probably closer to slave food. Their dumplings were solid and hard. Just flour and water and they would sink into the pot you boiled them in. They ate them with stewed green peas and rice, mixed with kidney beans, salt beef, or pig tail, for flavor."[2]

There seems to be no part of the southern black foodways tradition which is not touched by the "peculiar institution" of slavery and by the subsequent system of segregation that continues in the United States, though in more and more subtle forms. The Slave Narrative Collection, part of the Works Progress Administration (WPA) Federal Writers' Project carried out in the 1930s, tells us a little of the earlier times. Segregation has been different from slavery. Few families can discuss foodways without recalling numbing experiences of having to go without food because "colored" were not served in most places. In the 1950s, for example, before shopping in a nearby town black families in the Deep South always had a substantial snack since they could not buy hamburgers and soft drinks at drug-store counters. Only in large urban centers could they hope to find nourishment at modest places like Woolworth's. Sometimes there were vendors, such as an old lady from the countryside, selling peanuts. And sometimes children were treated to two-for-a-penny candy, but no real food. Before the late 1960s, if the family planned a trip of more than a few hours duration, they packed a cooler or a basket with food, usually cold fried chicken, corn bread, Kool-Aid, and tea.[3]

Segregation also molded blacks' careers outside the South. Those who sought work away from agriculture often found jobs as cooks or waiters on railroad Pullman cars, in urban hotels, and at country resorts along the eastern seaboard. Those who served in the armed forces, before integration, were admitted only as stewards or were organized into black companies. Many, and especially women, learned to cook for white families — a direct extension of their roles in slavery days. Whites who could afford "colored help" preferred black cooks for their culinary skills and willingness to work long hours for low wages. This pattern emerged also on Minneapolis' north side in the era before World War II.[4]

Thus, even during an era of social segregation, white society's food preferences and resources were influenced, although subtly, by black tastes. And black cooks or other hired help, in turn, took home previously untried or unavailable dishes, thereby expanding their own horizons. This kind of exchange is but one example that shows how culture is not static but dynamic and subject to changes. Today many blacks continue to serve their communities and churches or to earn livings by catering large dinners, but seldom with a menu that is southern. Changes in cultural consciousness, costs, and time commitments are largely responsible for this shift.

From early times a certain self-consciousness existed among blacks who hoped one day to be accepted or successful in white society. Even to peers one might remark, "For dinner today we had a green vegetable," reluctant to admit to eating "greens."[5] According to those interviewed, traditional black foodways were sometimes consciously avoided or put aside following moves away from the South in hopes that children would not learn them and would thus grow more acceptable to the mainstream of American life. Such behavior paralleled the practice of praising children with light skin or hair of "good quality" (that is, less kinky).[6] This self-conscious and self-destructive attitude is still sometimes found despite black pride programs and an increased awareness of black cultures and their importance outside this country.[7]

Families were frequently poor and large, with as many as six to ten children. Black southern techniques of preparing meals which stretched available foods cheaply, yet deliciously, eased the task of cooking for a large family. Filling and nourishing, if possible, meals of things such as head-cheese, bread pudding, sweet-potato pie, beans and rice, or greens cooked for hours with ham hocks, made use of every scrap of food. Today, people recall this diet as one that families maintained and through which they held themselves together.[8]

Time passed. Mainstream America remained unavailable. From diverse black political and economic movements that became particularly visible in the United States in the late 1960s there emerged a movement to cele-

Estelle Dorsey baking sweet-potato pie, St. Paul, 1983

brate and emphasize the cultural importance of "soul food" both among blacks and to a non-black society ignorant of the food's historic and symbolic significance. "It was like coming out of the closet," commented one black Minnesotan. Another said, "To me, soul food is what got my grandparents and my parents through the depression. Things like chicken feet, boiled and the skin pulled off and cleaned and soaked in salt water. We fried all of it, even the neck. It kept families together, that food."[9]

Others, looking back, laugh at the term, believing it was an attempt to seem eloquent about something they knew as common and to some extent unavoidable. As one explained, "It seemed sort of funny, you know. I never used the term 'soul food' to describe what I ate, but it raised my consciousness about it. Whites didn't know what blacks ate. They just laughed at us."[10] Still another black Minnesotan, born in South Carolina, observed, "For some, the soul food thing was the right thing to do. It did some good. But my son-in-law hates chitterlings, hates them, but he has to have it sometimes. But they're expensive. Two ten-pound pails of chitterlings gets you about eight pounds for the table!"[11]

By the late 1960s soul food restaurants sprang up in many inner cities wherever blacks lived. These places also became popular with white liberals, the most receptive segment of the non-black population. And it became politically important among some blacks to serve some southern soul food at community gatherings and social events.[12] By the mid 1970s, however, blacks had gained limited entry to the mainstream of the work force and some appeared at managerial levels. African costume and radical hair styling became passé, but soul food did not disappear. It merely assumed its former name: "home cooking."

Field interviews revealed no such history of soul food enterprise in the Twin Cities, although today there are two soul food establishments, the Willa Grant Battle Restaurant in Minneapolis and Southern Belle in St. Paul. In addition, both cities have a variety of take-out spots selling ribs and barbecue. By contrast, a native black Minnesotan owns and operates a Minneapolis restaurant that offers some southern-style cooking — ribs, chicken and rice, Louisiana gumbo, and shrimp — as well as standard restaurant fare. To some extent, the restaurant's menu reflects the day-to-day eating habits of Minnesota's black population: a mix of standard American dishes, some selections of popular ethnic foods (Mexican, Ukrainian), but also a special and sometimes highly symbolic use of southern cooking — traditional foodways. Commenting on the black food tradition, the restaurant owner observed, "Soul food is available everywhere — at homes. In restaurants you have to offer something extraordinary but, at the same time, consistently excellent."[13]

According to local black Minnesotans, the core of their traditional home cuisine includes rice, eaten with a variety of beans and flavored with smoked chicken necks; black-eyed peas, crowder peas, or field peas of some variety (and there are many); stew made from home-grown vegetables and any meat available; green cabbage, collard and mustard greens, cooked at some length or "smothered" and flavored with ham hocks; sweet potatoes in pies, baked, candied, boiled, or mashed; chicken in many forms such as pot pies with bones and all left in, but usually fried crisp; pork products of all kinds from hams to hocks, depending on the purse, but also, traditionally, pig's feet, tails, stomach, or chitterlings, and "skins" — fried pork rind; "smothered" meats (usually cheaper, tougher cuts); certain wild game such as rabbit, raccoon, and possibly possum;[14] fried fish of every variety, usually served with bread to sop up the juices; corn grits, corn bread or hoe cake, and "light bread," meaning inexpensive store-bought white bread which is also used in bread puddings; cole slaw and potato salad, the latter considered somewhat more old fashioned; fruit,

Food as a focus for socializing at this unidentified family outing in St. Paul

canned and used in cobblers; and a wide variety of cakes, especially fruit cakes and jelly cakes, which are made in abundance at Christmastime.

Minnesota blacks adjust their core of traditional foods to suit individual tastes and regional origins. Many former southerners who married native-born Minnesotans claim that their northern spouses knew little or nothing of greens, grits, chitterlings, or field peas before marriage. On the other hand, those who have moved to Minnesota since the 1950s have discovered pizza, stuffed cabbage rolls Ukrainian style, a vast array of creamed vegetables, and potatoes mashed, baked, au gratin, and fried.

Distinctions also exist within the foodways of a particular region. Southern black cooking, for example, contains certain traditional substyles. Louisiana dishes such as jambalaya, filé gumbo, and similar spicy foods reflect a love of hot seasoning. In many families and in most ribs restaurants, vinegar and Gold Dollar Louisiana sauce or Gray's Jamaican hot sauce is kept readily at hand. Many families order by mail such condiments as crab boil, okra powder, and filé powder from the Gulf region. Some see this as a natural part of the southern tradition while others label it "ulcer food."[15]

The common term "boiled dinner" means different things to blacks from different regions. A south-Georgia-born Minnesotan claims it means cabbage cooked with salt pork. After a while, the pork is removed and the cabbage joined by potatoes or rice, carrots, chunks of browned beef roast, and tomatoes. The inclusion of "English" peas, turnips, and green beans is optional. The whole affair is served with corn bread. But for a woman from Oklahoma who grew up in North Minneapolis, "boiled dinner" consists of mustard greens cooked with ham hocks or smoked turkey and pinto beans.[16]

Corn bread, too, differs subtly from family to family. Basically, there are two kinds. One, for a festive event or a relaxed dinner, is made from corn meal, flour, and eggs and is baked in the oven. Corn bread usually accompanies any meal that includes stewed meat. When pressed for time, however, black cooks make the other variety, called "skillet bread," "hot water bread," or, by the older name, "hoe cake," on the stove top, sometimes in an iron skillet. Hoe cake — simply hot water and lard mixed with corn meal and fried — is stiffer than the other versions. Many blacks like to crumble it into a bowl of buttermilk as a snack or use it as turkey stuffing.

Corn-bread stuffing, called "dressing" if cooked separately in a pan, is also a point of taste difference. Many cookbooks and experienced black cooks insist on using green peppers in the dish; others, especially those with roots in the Upper Midwest, omit the vegetable, though they consider it a possibility within their repertoire.

Some families like to make homemade soups and others do not. Favorites are okra, mixed vegetable, chicken with vegetables, and turtle. As a rule, people use up leftovers in soup, although fresh ingredients, especially vegetables, are also added. One family looks forward to spring when huge snapping turtles lay eggs along the inland waterways of the upper Mississippi valley. At that time they hunt and capture the turtles and go through the laborious and time-consuming chore of trimming, skinning, and cooking the meat. Another family maintains its traditional Oklahoma recipe for ox-tail soup, learned from grandparents.[17]

Summarizing variations in traditions is difficult. While one person believes that a household's diet pretty much depends upon what the mother's mother used to cook, others respond that husbands, more than anyone, determine what will be served. A third party insists that her generation cooks very differently from her parents', and that parents often cooked for children according to that child's favorite dishes — chicken cacciatore, beef stroganoff, or fried chicken — all birthday requests at one time or another.[18]

Recently, blacks have adopted spaghetti with meat sauce as a mainstay for group dinners. A church event in late 1983, for example, included spaghetti, black-eyed peas, and corn bread. A snack served to a political gathering consisted of chitterlings, spaghetti, and cold beer. Pasta in other forms, too, is achieving a favored place in festive meals. Potluck dinners and even Christmas meals may include macaroni and cheese or a similar baked dish.[19] Mexican-style foods are also favorites for two contrasting reasons: they present dishes close to standard black fare — corn, beans, rice, and spices that include peppers — but in a different form. They also lead to new taste experiences like guacamole and papaya.

As in most groups with a strong traditional cooking style, many families borrow and intermix the old and the new. As a rule, the more traditional the menu, the longer it has to cook and the more old techniques are employed. Greens are simmered for hours, and this technique also yields the traditional by-product, "pot liquor." Chicken gravy, cooked with necks and backs included for flavor, is ready only when "it is smooth and glistens on top."

The tradition of cooking on top of a wood-burning stove is a historic and poetic image, which may coexist with microwave ovens, pressure cookers, and roomy freezers. Many blacks say they are attracted to the stir-fry style associated with Oriental cooking but which, in fact, closely resembles the reliable and simple one-pot meal found among many ethnic groups. Blacks today, unless deterred by deeply embedded preferences shaped by time or religion, are as time-conscious as all members of the society. They also seek out more nutritious dishes, avoiding fatty, deep-

Homecoming dinner at Pilgrim Baptist Church, St. Paul, October 1983, including (front to back) meatloaf, fried chicken, turkey, and baked macaroni and cheese

fried, and overcooked foods. Often, traditional southern cooking is modified to suit these modern tastes. Smoked turkey may replace ham hocks or other pork products in dishes of greens or beans and rice. Leaner foods — center-cut pork chops, steak, fish fillets, and others with lower cholesterol — are served more frequently. Minnesota blacks, however, can remain within their traditions and still select such nutritious foods as rabbit, which is sold in many stores and also is vended privately. To supply a household with this breadth of selections, blacks shop at larger chain stores but also seek out small and reliable shops for such traditional delicacies as headcheese. They also take time to visit farmers' markets on Saturday mornings for the freshest greens and fruits.

The modern and traditional foodways patterns intersect most obviously at holiday time and on special social occasions. Traditional menus ascend when blacks celebrate Emancipation Day in January or attend family reunions, a traditional southern event set for July 4. Christmas, the most festive time, requires preparations that begin in early November with cake baking. Fruit and pecan cakes are highly favored, but caramel, coconut, pineapple upside-down, lemon, and plain jelly cakes, too, are both popular and traditional. The Christmas cookie tradition, so visible among European ethnic groups, is barely acknowledged in black homes.

Christmas dinner will vary from one household to another. Many urban families set aside this day for visiting and entertaining guests. In their homes, a buffet is prepared which might include turkey or baked chicken, ham, corn bread, greens, headcheese with a vinegar dressing, sweet-potato pie, and several cakes. In another home, a two-generation Minnesota black family might enjoy a relaxed sit-down dinner of turkey with oyster and sausage dressing, sweet-potato pie and candied yams, snap beans, cranberry sauce, jelly cake, and apple cobbler. A third family with roots in Pennsylvania and the eastern shore of Maryland prefers baked ham, sweet-potato pie, black-eyed peas and rice, turnip or mustard greens, a custard pie, and a compote of oranges, shredded coconut, and pineapple called ambrosia.

If Christmas Day's menu allows some latitude, the New Year's Eve meal does not. Black-eyed peas and corn bread are served right after midnight to ensure good luck in the coming year. Explanations usually suggest that this meal must be humble and simply prepared — something easily attainable throughout the rest of the year — as if stating an unpretentious attitude toward the future at the outset. Some blacks of poor and rural origins realized in retrospect that they practiced this tradition, but it was hardly discernable to them as children, since they ate that meal frequently throughout the year.

For one family that grew up in Minneapolis but has roots throughout the Midwest, goat and lamb are springtime favorites, especially at Easter. One Jamaican recipe — curried goat — is popular among their friends, or the cook may marinate and roast the meat. Some people, in addition, use all the parts, making a soup from the head seasoned with allspice, thyme, and leeks and thickened with beans. In any event, lamb, goat, and possibly mutton are the only meat dishes in which black Minesotans would use garlic, a seasoning otherwise generally ignored.

Volunteers usually bring dishes of all kinds to supplement community and church food events that are organized and prepared by a committee. For a church homecoming dinner in October 1983, for example, a committee prepared sweet-potato pies, meatloaf, corn-bread dressing with green peppers, canned green beans cooked with pork, collard greens, black-eyed peas, and corn bread. But congregation members brought in a rich array of additions, including baked green cabbage with ham, fried chicken, peach and apple cobblers, corn-meal muffins, dinner rolls, zucchini with tomato sauce, baked chicken garnished with zucchini and green pepper, macaroni and cheese, baked squash, and Jell-O. Children and adults drank Kool-Aid served from a huge punch bowl. Pies and an enormous cake were served from a second table.[20]

THE BLACKS

The foods contributed for this and similar dinners demonstrate a food-use pattern that most black cooks acknowledge. Private black foods, things that seem intimate and even risky, are balanced by the public dishes that are easily shared within the culture. In the latter group are the easily recognized favorites: fried chicken, greens, sweet-potato pie, red beans and rice, catfish, sometimes buffalo fish, and ribs. Very private because they require expert cleaning and preparation or because they are part of the tradition which has become marginal are such items as tripe, pig tail, chitterlings, possum, and brains with scrambled eggs. Other dishes might be considered inappropriate in public because they are expensive, ostentatious, or excessively spicy. Private preferences, no matter how widely enjoyed, such as crumbled hoe cake in buttermilk, would not be served in public. And public food events also attended by non-blacks might have a neutral menu such as hamburgers, potato salad, and cold pop.[21]

Teen-agers and young couples tend to maintain some, but not all, of their parents' foodways. The old-fashioned "Georgia breakfast" of skins with hot sauce and a cola has become an afternoon snack in nutrition-conscious homes where oatmeal or eggs are served each morning. But the

Maceo Littlejohn carving turkey, St. Paul, 1983

father in that home may prefer leftover chicken and gravy served over freshly cooked grits, a hold-over from his farming childhood. All generations may avoid milk, owing to a well-documented, genetic intolerance. Buttermilk, though, remains a favorite among older people, and custards are popular. Many modern blacks have turned to yoghurt and even tofu as milk substitutes within their nontraditional diets.

With increased black mobility, interracial marriage is somewhat more common than previously. Children of these unions enjoy some balance of traditions. One woman, for example, whose father is black and mother is Japanese, has black relatives living in her neighborhood. The scale is balanced, however, by the occasional visit of her maternal grandmother from Hawaii. On Christmas, New Year's, and Thanksgiving holidays traditional southern foods are served. But when guests drop in or even when the father's relatives visit, Japanese foods are often prepared. The family

For Homecoming at the Pilgrim Baptist Church, 1983, Carol Richardson prepares a table of sweets; the homemade decorated cake is surrounded by peach and apple cobblers, slices of sweet-potato pie, and pound cake.

spice shelf holds ginger, garlic, and soy sauce next to the peanut oil and okra powder. This family is also attracted to Bahamian foods and sometimes enjoys a traditional Caribbean dish of rice, peas, and fish fillets.[22]

The generation of black Minnesotans born in the 1950s and later have tended to use traditional cooking or "soul food" more as a symbolic gesture than as a source of nourishment. Some symbolic behavior has been scorned by black intellectuals and political leaders as a condescension toward the less fortunate. In 1968, Eldridge Cleaver wrote, "Eating chitterlings is like going slumming to them [the black bourgeoisie]. Now that they have the price of a steak, here they come prattling about Soul Food. The people in the ghetto want steaks. *Beef Steaks.* I wish I had the power to see to it that the bourgeoisie really *did* have to make it on Soul Food."[23]

Indeed, "making it," as in the common form of greeting, "How you makin' it, man?" means surviving with dignity, a central goal in black culture. Scholarship has demonstrated, however, that class conflict and dignity are but two parts of a larger, more complex whole. More than class differentiation and blacks' participation in today's world, certain sources of black culture moved American blacks from slavery to ethnicity. Poverty alone does not explain any part of black culture or food; rather, they derive, in part, from slavery and racism and the fact of escaping from one but not the other.[24] Black foodways are no more a mere matter of economics than is the rest of black culture. With racism as the major source, black culture has become an ethnic culture, distinct from white cultures in America in both form and structure. Whatever happens to black foodways in the future must be considered by both blacks and whites in those terms.[25]

NOTES

[1] For a broader discussion of these issues, see Norman E. Whitten, Jr., and John F. Szwed, eds., *Afro-American Anthropology: Contemporary Perspectives* (New York: Free Press, 1970). The African roots of black foodways are demonstrated in a family-owned restaurant offering authentic Ethiopian cuisine in the University-Dale area of St. Paul.

[2] Both quotes from interview of Juan Turner, Minneapolis, January 1984.

[3] Kenneth M. Stampp, *The Peculiar Institution: Slavery in the Ante-bellum South* (New York: Alfred A. Knopf, 1956); Charles W. Joyner, "Soul Food and the Sambo Stereotype: Foodlore from the Slave Narrative Collection," *Keystone Folklore Quarterly* 16 (Winter 1971): 171–78; interview of Grace Rogers, Minneapolis, January 1984. For a somewhat different point of view of segregation and foodways, see William Faulkner, *Intruder in the Dust* (New York: Random House, 1948), and Zora Neale Hurston, *Dust Tracks on a Road: An Autobiography* (Philadelphia: J. B. Lippincott Co., 1942).

[4] Interview of J. D. Rivers, Minneapolis, January 1984, who recalls that Jewish residents on the near north side of Minneapolis frequently employed blacks as cooks. See also David Vassar Taylor, "The Blacks," in *They Chose Minnesota*, ed. Holmquist, 78. On Pullman porters, see Jack Santino, "Miles of Smiles, Years of Struggle: The Negotiation of Black Occupational Identity Through Personal Experience Narrative," *Journal of American Folklore* 96 (October–December 1983): 393–412.

[5] Interview of Becky Scott, Minneapolis, January 1984.

[6] Rogers interview.

[7] For a detailed study, see Thomas J. Price, "Ethnohistory and Self-Image in Three New World Negro Societies," in *Afro-American Anthropology*, ed. Whitten and Szwed, 63–73.

[8] Scott interview; interview of Aletha Halcomb, Minneapolis, February 1984.

[9] Interview of Pat Stroudes, Richfield, February 1984; Rogers interview. Among the black political and economic groups were the Black Power movement, the Black Panthers, Student Non-Violent Coordinating Committee, Urban League, National Association for the Advancement of Colored People, and the Black Muslims.

[10] Scott interview.

[11] Rivers interview.

[12] This phenomenon is thoroughly discussed in Robert Blauner, "Black Culture: Myth or Reality?" in *Afro-American Anthropology*, ed. Whitten and Szwed, 347–66.

[13] Interview of Rick Davis, January 1984. A large portion of his following comes from the Jewish population of St. Louis Park.

[14] Some informants related that possum, raccoon, and rabbit are all available through private contacts in North Minneapolis. A small sign is posted in a residence window with the word, "Rabbit," and "from that you know you can get it there"; Turner interview.

[15] Turner, Stroudes, Scott, and Halcomb interviews; interview of Ludie Thomas, Fridley, October 1983.

[16] Rogers and Turner interviews.

[17] Turner interview.

[18] Scott interview.

[19] Rivers interview; interview of Richard Parker, Minneapolis, February 1984.

[20] This event was held at Pilgrim Baptist Church, St. Paul. For background on this historic church, see Taylor, "The Blacks," in *They Chose Minnesota*, ed. Holmquist, 75–76.

[21] Rivers interview.

[22] Interview of Kim White, St. Paul, December 1983.

[23] Eldridge Cleaver, *Soul on Ice* (New York: McGraw-Hill Book Co., 1968), 29.

[24] Blauner, "Black Culture," in *Afro-American Anthropology*, ed. Whitten and Szwed, 357–64.

[25] Consider that early black residents of St. Paul referred to two neighborhoods with metaphors from their own foodways: "Oatmeal Hill" for a well-to-do section and "Corn-meal Valley" for the less prestigious one; Taylor, "The Blacks," in *They Chose Minnesota*, ed. Holmquist, 81. Also, consider the identity-switching of a twelve-year-old boy who refuses to eat chitterlings when visiting his grandparents at Christmas but insists that they are "good eating" when confronting his white friends at a potluck dinner; interview of Jackie Randelman, Minneapolis, January 1984, and Rogers interview.

Herlinda Velasquez and Cipriano Velasquez assembling tacos at Our Lady of Guadalupe Church, St. Paul, for the Mexican Independence Day celebration, 1985

THE MEXICANS

A young couple from Bloomington goes to a Minneapolis Mexican restaurant and orders enchiladas with sour cream. Four office workers in St. Paul go shopping and stop for a quick lunch of tacos and a tossed salad. A businessman closes a deal and escorts his clients to a stylish bar and orders margaritas and nachos while scanning menu entries of chimichangas and burritos. But a knowledgeable and experienced purveyor of Mexican foods in St. Paul insists, "If I were in Mexico today and asked for a 'burrito,' I'd be kicked by a real one! To us, a tortilla filled and rolled up is a taco, and that means a 'snack.' In Spanish, we don't even have the word 'chimichanga'!"[1]

Obviously, among those who prepare, sell, and consume what Minnesotans call "Mexican" food there is a wide variety of opinion and taste. Much of this conflict has to do with the region of origin of certain dishes. Putting aside consideration of what is served in the restaurants of Mexico, one may discern certain basic food patterns similar to those of other working-class people who have migrated to Minnesota and brought with them a cherished heritage of nourishing, tasty, and highly stylized cuisine. In its main form, Mexican fare is soupy, something to be eaten at a family table. It is not necessarily overly spicy although special sauces and fresh flavorings, such as chile peppers and limes, may be offered to suit individual tastes. Dishes include sopa (fine noodles or rice cooked in a broth) and caldo (a tangy beef and vegetable stew) with flour tortillas. Or, dinner might be a pot roast served with cooked pinto beans, a side dish of fideo (noodles), and tortillas. A migrant worker in Owatonna, who swears by his substantial dinner of caldo made with goat meat, fried rice served in a broth, and corn tortillas, laments the tastes of his children who prefer American processed or "junk" foods. "You cannot work on this food," he argues. "You have to work and this food has no strength in it!"[2]

The story of Mexican foods in Minnesota has much to do with the role of migrant laborers in the state's economic growth. Largely a twentieth-century phenomenon, migration from Mexico was spurred by unsettling political and economic conditions during the Mexican Revolution of 1911–17 and the dire need for farm labor during America's participation in World

War I. Sugar beet producers recruited Mexican nationals, and the 1924 government quota law restricting the immigration of Russian and German workers, among others, further enhanced the position of Mexican laborers in Minnesota's fields. Although the migration was generally seasonal, many brought their families and eventually "settled out" of the migrant stream, making Minnesota their permanent home. By 1930 a substantial Mexican population lived in the Red River Valley; the St. Paul-Ramsey County area, however, held the densest settlements. The depression years wreaked havoc with the migrants' lives when the sugar beet industry declined, but conditions improved when the United States entered World War II. Again, field and factory labor was in demand, and the high quality of Mexican migrant work was recognized and put to good use. By the late 1940s, Mexican Americans were well settled in the southern Minnesota counties, where they were employed in canning factories in Le Sueur and Owatonna by 1959. Grand Forks, North Dakota, and Rochester also had substantial numbers who chose to settle out.[3]

The 1960s saw a period of stability and strength as Mexican Americans demonstrated a large measure of ethnic pride in their cultural heritage, supported in some measure by state government agencies. The St. Paul settlement in the West Side Flats experienced some trauma in the 1960s when a flood-control project was initiated, and the mixed ethnic population of that area was forced to seek new locations. By the end of the 1960s, Mexican Americans in St. Paul had crowded into the West Side neighborhood near Roosevelt High School, most working in small businesses. At the same time, their rural counterparts had become well established in southern and western farming communities as dependable field hands on a permanent basis or as seasonal factory employees.

Not all of Minnesota's Mexican residents are descendants of migrant families. The Coronado family opened its first restaurant in St. Paul in 1945, the product of diligent work and culinary skill of people whose property holdings in Mexico and, later, Texas had been substantial.[4] Others had worked on small farms in Oklahoma or Texas and sought a more tolerant social environment for their families. Once settled and stabilized economically, Mexican Americans in Minnesota strove toward good education for their children, modern health care, and, in turn, strong and very visible support for their own cultural institutions — Our Lady of Guadalupe Roman Catholic Church (St. Paul), language programs, and neighborhood houses. In large measure, these institutions and the Mexican-American population continue to support and serve one another, and foodways programs are one of the most viable means of continuing this cultural pride.

Rosa Coronado de Collyard making corn chips and tortillas on the gas-fired machine that has been in her family for more than thirty-five years, St. Paul, 1986

Although many social groups and regions of Mexico and the Southwest are represented in Minnesota's population, the majority of people have migrated from northern Mexico and the border towns in Texas.[5] Their respective opinions, therefore, of what one calls "Mexican-American food in Minnesota" are mixed. Some claim that they prepare Tex-Mex cuisine, a hotter version of Mexican food which is almost always rolled up in a tortilla. Others feel that their tables are laden with true Mexican dishes. All concede that they frequently like to include "American" recipes in their family diet, and this balance may range from once a week to every other day, on the average. Typically, Minnesota's Mexican Americans reject the so-called Mexican restaurant fare, especially the fast-food products offered by franchises. People suggest that Twin Cities restaurants, for example, are too enthralled with flowery "tropical" drinks, and that although their menus offer a variety of dishes, the sauces and ingredients all taste the same, as if they were from a common pot.

When one engages Mexican Americans in conversation about their traditional foodways, certain ingredients, dishes, and preparations inevitably arise, no matter what their region of origin. Chile peppers are the subject of much discussion, as Mexican Americans believe that the place of the pepper in their cuisine is misunderstood. They stress that chiles, the basic ingredient in hot sauce, are traditionally a relish, served "on the side" for consumption at the diner's discretion. One woman, respected in the St. Paul community as a traditional cook, summarized popular opinion: "[Chile] pepper to us is optional, like salt is to you. . . . The true Mexican food is saucy food, like the French."[6] Mild, medium, or hot peppers are ingredients in many Mexican-American dishes, but their flavor is meant only to contribute to, not overpower, the overall taste. A side dish of hot sauce is then available for those who wish to spice up the meal. This style of cuisine allows a cook to produce a single dish acceptable to children with a taste for bland foods as well as those who crave spicier victuals.[7]

Through the 1950s jalapeño peppers were the most available variety in Minnesota. People grew their own in backyard plots, according to a St. Paul grocer. Currently, a wide array of chiles — in fresh, dried pod, and powdered form — are available in Minnesota's markets. Some people use the whole green jalapeño or serrano peppers. Many name the chile ancho ("ancho" means wide) as a favorite among the dried pods; in addition, cooks utilize the guajillo, pasillo, mulato, arbol, cascabel, Anaheim, red japonaise, and chipotle (smoked jalapeño). A number of women combine several varieties of pepper to achieve a balanced taste in a traditional dish such as mole (see below).

While powdered chile is available in Mexican specialty stores as well as American supermarkets, traditional cooks shun it as an inferior product. Although the pods, for example, must be cleaned and soaked, fried or toasted, and then chopped, pounded, or blended, most cooks agree that this processing yields a truer, purer flavor than that of the commercial powders.

Tomatillos are another cornerstone of Mexican-American foodways, a basis for sauces and relishes. Early Mexican settlers in Minnesota were unable to obtain these wild green tomatoes that grow covered with a papery husk. Subsequent immigrants apparently brought seeds with them, and those who were able to get some plants established soon had an overabundance of tomatillos. Successful gardeners canned their surplus for the winter months; some supplied local markets. In the 1980s Mexican specialty stores carry tomatillos throughout the year; they are imported from Mexico when the Minnesota growing season is past. One St. Paul grocer sells 160 to 180 pounds a month of this staple for which, many claim, no other flavor will substitute.[8]

When one asks about festive meals, one word always comes to the fore:

mole. Adventurous Anglos, who have been curious enough to ask, remember that this dish is usually chicken prepared with a sauce that includes unsweetened chocolate. There are, however, many kinds of mole — one is a light broth, another is dark, and there is the rich pipian mole that relies on ground sesame and squash seeds. Weddings, birthdays, anniversaries, and any special celebrative event in the Mexican-American community can be marked by mole, usually served over chicken, although turkey and even pork can be used. The actual process of preparation is complex and requires a fair amount of skill. First, mole can be prepared properly only with real Mexican chocolate. Much less sweet than American chocolate, it has a distinctive, almost granular, texture. A sauce blended from this chocolate, chile ancho, ground sesame seeds, and sometimes peanut butter is cooked with a little water, salt, and garlic. When ready, it is served over a steamed chicken and accompanied by Mexican-style rice which has been browned and then cooked in the chicken juices. Anglo guests at a dinner where mole is served are often repelled by its unusual appearance and more often by a simplistic explanation of the ingredients. To this extent, mole might be categorized as a private or "in-group" dish, appreciated most by those who know it best.

Even more restricted or private is the consumption of menudo, a traditional tripe soup which enjoys considerable popularity among Mexican Americans. It is commonly served as a weekend treat, partly because it takes a great deal of time to prepare and partly because, according to folk belief, it is an excellent cure for a hangover. A meal in itself, menudo is made from cooked tripe (experienced householders suggest preparing the tripe in a basement kitchen, away from the rest of the house), cut-up pig's feet, hominy, tomatoes, onions, cilantro, and other spices. It is served with slices of lime, finely diced onions on the side, and tortillas. For best results, one should begin the menudo on Friday and let it cook through Saturday. Or, if home preparation is not possible, several Mexican food stores and delicatessens carry the soup for their customers.

Equally rare in public or mixed company is the grandest of all Mexican delicacies — the pit barbecue or barbacoa. Once popular throughout the Southwest and at reunions and picnics in Minnesota, this feast is less frequently enjoyed now by Minnesota's Mexican Americans since it takes a great deal of time and requires a place to dig a large hole in the ground — something difficult to accomplish for urban dwellers living by the typical American time schedule. But memories are still sharp about barbacoa, for which one purchases an entire beef head and prepares a pit approximately six feet deep and four feet in diameter. A fifty-five-gallon drum is lowered into the pit, and a long, slow-burning fire is built in the bottom of the drum, which has been layered with large rocks. When the fire has burned long enough to heat the rocks and the drum thoroughly, the ashes are removed, and the beef head, wrapped in aluminum foil and wet burlap sacks and seasoned with lemon and other spices, is suspended by chicken wire in the drum. The top is sealed and covered with the hot ashes, and the whole affair is left to cook for five to seven hours. Removed, the head is served with tongue, brains, cheeks, and eyes intact. Skinned, the beef falls from the skull and is served with more lemon squeezed over individual portions, beans, rice, and tortillas. Sometimes the brains are removed and mixed with peppers and onions to serve as a special sauce for the beef.[9]

These dishes are specialties and can be enjoyed only rarely. The day-to-day diet of Mexican Americans in Minnesota in the 1980s is generally a mixture of dishes — some American, some Mexican, depending on what time, energy, and individual tastes will allow. When one is self-employed, it is typical to begin the day with coffee and rolls or sometimes hot chocolate instead of coffee, a Mexican tradition. Breakfast is enjoyed at about ten in the morning and may consist of huevos rancheros (eggs scrambled with onion, pepper, and cilantro) and sometimes chorizo, a Mexican sausage containing hot peppers, garlic, and other spices. In Minnesota, the potato has become an integral part of Mexican cooking, too, especially for breakfast. Cooks prefer to fry the potatoes and, when nearly done, add a cut-up hot dog, some scrambled eggs, and salsa verde (green sauce). Scooped up in pieces of flour tortilla, the dish is delicious and filling. Or, one prepares fried eggs, sprinkled liberally with finely chopped jalapeño peppers and served with bacon and tortillas. Children, as a rule, eat milder versions, and many prefer toast instead of tortillas.

Currently, this hearty breakfast is more likely to be postponed until the weekend, as most Mexican Americans follow the same work schedules as other Minnesotans. Their normal pattern is familiar: children breakfast on packaged cereals, and adults go off to work with coffee and little else. The children's tastes for institutional and commercial foods is further reinforced during the school lunch, and it is not until the evening meal that any hint of Mexican-style cooking is brought to the table. Then, even a jumble of American ingredients can become "Mexican." For example, picadillos is a favorite quick meal that calls for browned hamburger, cooked carrots and onions, garlic, cumin, and tomatoes, all simmered together and served with portions of sopa on the side.[10] Chicken and pork can be prepared in dozens of ways that are quick, simple, and similar to methods used by other ethnic groups, and children seem to prefer, for example, fish sticks, hot dogs, or tuna fish. Most Mexican-American mothers, nevertheless, find ways to maintain the Mexican style through flavoring, no matter what food item is requested.

The tortilla — corn or wheat flour — is a staple in the Mexican diet and is often so closely associated with some dishes that even the least traditional family member will insist upon having them. Corn tortillas, which are hand-formed from meal which is ground originally in a metate (stone trough), are more difficult to make than the flour version. They are the preferred form by far in central Mexico. Opinions vary about the origins of flour tortillas, but it seems that the border area between Mexico and Texas or Arizona might be their point of origin. Today, in Minnesota, many families still make their own flour tortillas, a simple process of mixing flour, salt, baking powder, and water, rolling out the dough with a rolling pin, and cooking them briefly on a stove top. Corn tortillas are readily available in a number of Twin Cities markets and are carried, along with flour tortillas, in the frozen-foods section of most supermarkets. Corn tortillas are most popularly used for tacos, enchiladas, and the snack, nachos with cheese toppings. They are also frequently put into soups instead of noodles or dumplings. Whether made from flour or corn, tortillas serve the all-purpose use that bread does in the Anglo diet. Leftover beans, fish, or rice, luncheon meats, tuna fish, even peanut butter can be used as a filling. They serve as a fork with traditional soupy Mexican dishes and are eaten as a filler: for example, a fieldworker in Owatonna uses tortillas to supplement his daily thermos bottle of sopa.

Even dry, leftover tortillas do not go to waste. Cut up and fried, they are the traditional snack item that inspired the current wave of mass-market, commercial corn chips. They are also the basis for chilaquiles, a dish that may be eaten at any time but is usually either breakfast or a light lunch. As with other traditional foods, chilaquiles can be made in a variety of ways; all, however, use tortillas that are no longer suitable for consumption in their original form. These are first cut and fried until crispy; next, tomato sauce — spicy or bland, depending on the individual's taste — is added to soften them slightly. At this point, recipes diverge. Some people add cheese and finely chopped raw onions, simmering the chilaquiles until the cheese melts. For people of little means, this dish was breakfast; those with more money might add eggs, cooked separately, to their meal. Other Mexican Americans scrambled eggs right into the tortilla mixture. Some added thin strips of beef to make a light lunch. In all cases, however, the initial object was to avoid wasting tortillas.[11]

In peasant families, the corn tortilla has served as part of the main protein source for centuries; the complement is the bean. In Mexico, regionalism and subculture determine what beans are preferred among the many varieties. In Minnesota the principal legume is the pinto bean. Currently, food preparers wash the beans thoroughly and cook them slowly, either in a crock pot or in a baking dish in the oven. Usually some pork or bacon is added for flavoring, and a whole onion is put in but removed when the beans are tender. Leftovers can be used as refritos — refried beans. The cold pintos are simply placed in a frying pan with lard, less if one prefers them dry and more if the preference is for a softer texture.

The other popular and traditional complement to beans in Mexican foodways is arroz (rice). Unlike Oriental or American preparations, the Mexican approach is to cover the bottom of a frying pan with lard, put in washed rice, and stir it over a low flame until brown. Then one adds a seasoning of onion and garlic and tomato sauce until the kernels are flaky and separate. Commonly referred to by Anglos as "Spanish rice," this is a favorite side dish for meat, fish, and poultry. Fideo or vermicelli is prepared in essentially the same manner — browned, seasoned, and combined with a sauce to attain a soupy consistency.

If the term "taco" covers a multitude of tortilla-and-filling combinations, the enchilada and the tamale are distinctive and specific dishes. Each family has a slight variation of method for making and seasoning enchiladas,

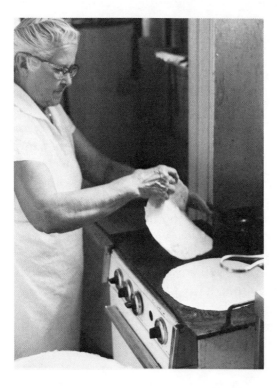

Bessie Peña making flour tortillas in her daughter's Owatonna restaurant, 1985

but one that appears to be standard is as follows: One dips a corn tortilla into a sauce based on chile ancho, salt, and garlic and immediately fries it in lard. As soon as the tortilla is soft, it is removed to a plate, cheese and chopped onions are added, and the enchilada is folded. Most Mexican Americans build a stack of small enchiladas on a platter before serving them hot. One may also use ground beef, or shredded beef from a roast, and goat cheese, popular among more traditional families, may be added. Left-over enchiladas can be reheated in a microwave oven, but this method is too close to restaurant techniques for most to approve.

The tamale is a major dish in Mexican-American culture. Whether pre-pared and served in the home or the church, it symbolizes devoted effort and commitment to tradition during a celebration. Tamales require much work and a great deal of practice; today, families depend upon the older generation of women to prepare them. Visiting the home of one of these women gives one a glimpse of the past — the early years of Mexican set-tlement in Minnesota's urban environments. The kitchen is a storehouse of herbs, powders, and condiments, but the basement is even more won-drous. There, the tamale maker keeps sacks of dried field corn, a grinder (possibly a metate or a hand-turned machine), tubs, and a stove or hot plate. It is here that most of the work for tamales is accomplished.[12]

When they first settled in Minnesota, Mexicans bought the corn des-tined for tamales from local farmers. Today, they might go to the Gray Milling Company in St. Paul and purchase corn that has been husked and shelled. Back in the basement, the cook shakes the corn to remove dust and any foreign particles and then boils it in a large pan with carefully measured portions of hydrated lime to loosen and remove the hulls from the kernels. As soon as the hulls float to the top, they are skimmed off, and then the corn is put through a hand grinder, the first stage of making a corn paste. After grinding, perhaps twice for a smooth consistency, the cook then further refines the paste by kneading it in the metate with a stone scraper made from volcanic rock. Some of this paste may be set aside to be made into corn tortillas, but most of it goes into cornhusks, the next step in the tamale-making process.

Mexican-American women aged in their fifties can remember sitting on the back porch and enduring the chore of removing husks from the ears of corn for tamales. Today, husks can be purchased in markets, thereby reducing the time and effort involved in preparation. In any event, husks must be thoroughly washed and dried. Meanwhile, the meat is prepared.

A pork roast is preferred. First, all fat is removed, and then the meat is boiled in a little water and, afterwards, shredded. A sauce is prepared of chile, garlic, and salt, to which small bits of fried pork may be added.

Some of this sauce may be used as a dip with corn tortillas, but the goal is to use it in the tamale.

Finally, all ingredients come together. The dried cornhusks are spread out and smeared with the corn paste. The meat and the sauce are used as filling on top of the paste, and the husks are folded into a pouchlike form. Each pouch, elevated so as not to become soggy, is carefully steamed in a pan with a little water, covered with a wet towel. This process occupies the greater part of a day. It is little wonder that the tamale is used only for special occasions and that family members with few commitments are called upon to perform this task.

The social context of Mexican-American foodways in Minnesota provides the clearest idea of what these foods mean and how they communicate symbolically with community members as well as outsiders. As would be expected in communities where the most intricate dish is set forth at the holidays, the Mexican-American family looks forward to tamales with their Christmas turkey, although tamales are sometimes served after Christmas Eve mass as well. In place of the traditional American mashed potatoes, the family enjoys arroz and tortillas.

Foodways enter into a traditional ritual also as the Mexican-American families observe Posada, the journey of St. Joseph and the Blessed Lady in search of an inn near Bethlehem. This event is planned for the nine days preceding Christmas and usually involves a minimum of nine families, each of whom takes a turn playing the innkeepers as well as the traveling couple. The Posada generally includes good friends whose social and spiritual involvement are compatible; often it is an extended family — cousins, in-laws, and siblings. The scenario is simple: Joseph and Mary approach the home and ask for shelter. A prayer is said and certain traditional songs are sung. Then the couple is invited in to join the other celebrants, and the food is brought forth. There may also be music and entertainment, such as the household can offer. Traditionally, the hosts serve coffee and Christmas cookies and other sweets, such as buñuelos (a crispy cookie made much like a flour tortilla, but without baking powder, and topped with sugar and cinnamon) or galletas which resemble hoya leaves and are colored red and green. There are also tamales and atole de maiz, a healthful drink concocted of finely ground corn meal, water, milk, cinnamon, and sugar. [13]

The community also observes the Lenten season through its foodways, preparing a wide variety of dishes without meat. Minnesotans of northern Mexican heritage have fewer seafood dishes than do coastal people, and Minnesota's fish cuisine does not play a major role in their Lenten diet. Nevertheless, the period is a time when certain tasty meals can be expected, notably meatless tostadas, sopa, and especially torte de camaron (shrimp

The Posada procession winds into Our Lady of Guadalupe Church for its concluding feast, December 1971; buñuelos and other Mexican pastries share the table with American-style sandwich cookies.

patties). Dried or powdered shrimp is purchased in cans or bags. It is crumbled, mixed with beaten eggs, formed into patties, coated with egg batter, and fried. These are served with a traditional tomato sauce flavored with onions and nopales (a type of cactus pickled in spices, which can be bought in the local markets). At this time, too, certain desserts are made, somewhat more than at other times of the year: cookies in special forms, sweet rice puddings, and the favorite, capirotada (bread pudding). The easiest way to make this delight is identical to the American recipe: a batter of egg and milk poured over dried bread and sweetened with sugar and raisins. An older recipe calls for deep frying all the pieces of bread whole, then adding chopped almonds, peanuts, and other nuts in the frying pan. Then raisins are added, and the whole affair is covered with a brown-sugar-and-cinnamon sauce and cooked on top of the stove, covered. Some prefer to put cheese on top to melt and mix with the other ingredients.[14]

An event less widely celebrated but still recognized within the Mexican-American community is the Quinceanera, the coming-out party for a fifteen-year-old girl. This rite of passage has a religious aspect since the girl, her family, and companions attend a special mass at church. But there is a secular portion, perhaps the dominant one, and specific dishes are expected. Mole de pollo (chicken mole) is always served with rice. If the family is less traditional or wishes to cater to non-Mexican guests, a baked ham or roast beef may also be served, together with the usual Anglo accompaniments. A multi-tiered cake is also presented, reminiscent of a wedding cake, complete with the figure of the young woman in a white gown at the top. Quinceanera is a special event in a young woman's life, for it marks her passage from childhood to womanhood. She moves from a position of observing the social scene to participating in it. She may begin to dance with male partners, go out on dates, and possibly even imbibe alcohol moderately. Wine is served for the adults, and if the party's principal figure tastes it, one looks the other way. Obviously, such parties are available only to those who have the means to afford them, and they are more generally found in the Twin Cities than in farming communities. In fact, many farmworkers know of Quinceanera but have never attended one. It is symbolically significant that a wedding party provides almost the identical foods.[15]

Mexican families who settled in Minnesota in the early years enjoyed many of the aforementioned special dishes, but it was difficult to obtain the necessary ingredients and spices in a state that was unfamiliar with the needs and tastes of Mexican cuisine. As might be expected, seasonal migrants brought ample supplies with them from their native villages in the Southwest. They, in turn, supplied those who had settled out. Even in the late 1940s, no cilantro, cumin, chile ancho, powdered shrimp, or Mexican chocolate was to be found in local markets. Consequently, owners of the earliest Mexican restaurants, all tiny places in which the family served as staff, had to send to Texas for bulk supplies, an expensive investment for a small-scale business. Twenty years later supplies were available in the Twin Cities, but a restaurant that opened in 1969 in Owatonna, for example, had to rely upon deliveries of condiments from St. Paul even though meat and corn were available locally.[16]

The introduction of Mexican restaurant cuisine to a cautious and conservative public was also a problem. One enterprising restaurateur in St. Paul strove to develop a clientele by taking her recipes to the public-school children and presenting a positive view of Mexican culture as a whole, thereby encouraging Anglos to try her wares. The experiment was highly successful, and many of those former grade-school children became her best customers. Another ambitious proprietor of a Mexican restaurant in the southern part of the state actually gave food away in order to encourage patronage. "They were afraid they might get sick, you know. They didn't want to take a chance. So, I just said, 'Here. Try it!' I just gave it away. Later, they came back little by little and tried other things." Women and children, she remembers, were the first to try something new. Men were more dubious about so much seasoning and strange shapes and textures. Today she is a popular caterer in the community and has had to move into larger space in order to accommodate her trade.

Traditionally, women are the preparers of food in Mexican and Mexican-American families. This role is very evident today as well. But male members of the family, particularly husband and eldest son, are also significant in determining what is eaten and when. In many families, even in full-time migrant homes, men will, on occasion, step in and prepare food if the wife is working outside the home. If both spouses are at home, the wife will prepare food, although the husband might be willing to help with minor tasks. In no case is there evidence of males preparing major dishes such as tamales, mole, or desserts, but they easily accommodate to the preparation of snacks and are the sole preparers of barbacoa and chicherrone — fried pork rind. (These cracklings are direct products of butchering and use animal parts in an unprocessed form.) The male role is most clearly presented in the words of numerous interview participants who recalled, for example, "Husbands ask their wives to cook what their mothers cooked." Or, "I would come home from _____ and she would always have that fixed for me because she knew I liked it." And, "Wives as a rule always have to get to know how their mothers-in-law cooked so that they can please their husbands."[17]

Meals in any home are the result of subtle negotiations. More than ethnic heritage and the income determine what is on the table. Changing time commitments in all parts of the household, social images and goals, and traditional sexual privileges may alter traditional foodways. The food preparer in Mexican-American homes may choose which dishes to serve; her decision, however, is influenced by those who demand, perhaps subtly and perhaps not, specific levels of seasoning, quantity, and intricacy in their cuisine. This balance may be illustrated, moreover, in marriages between Mexican men and Anglo women, some of whom have earned the reputation of striving harder to produce traditional foods for their families than many third-generation women of Mexican heritage. [18]

Within this matrix there are still other forces to observe. The recognition of, or the striving toward, some tangible middle-class status through acquired sophistication on American terms also affects foodways. Such dishes as turkey necks and hominy, calavasa (zucchini) simmered in onion, cumin, garlic, tomatoes, and chile peppers, or bombones (okra) cooked with cilantro and tomatillos might be considered gourmet ethnic food by outsiders but are often targeted as old fashioned or even unhealthy by the younger generations or upwardly mobile individuals. Guacamole, on the other hand, once one of the most difficult dishes to introduce to conservative palates in Minnesota, is now commonly eaten among middle-class urban people, whatever their ethnic background. It is especially popular in some chic health-food restaurants as a sandwich filling.

Finally, the form in which food appears is yet another variable in foodways today. As in some other groups, Mexican-American foods are slowly evolving from the one-pot, soupy preparations to platter foods or even finger foods. As a direct result of daily schedules and commitments, more and more mainstream Anglo dishes with Mexican seasoning and style are enjoyed in the family while the traditional dishes are relegated to holiday fare. The sopa and the tamale require patience for the cook and time seated around a table for the family. It is more efficient to cook items that are easily handled and can be consumed at varying times, as family members may eat at different hours of the day.

Another part of the Mexican-American foodways tradition is now nearly invisible, yet still viable. Traditional herbal teas, made from leaves once gathered in the fields and canyons of northern Mexico and now sold in packages there, in Texas and California, as well as in Minnesota's Mexican markets, are widely used in the ethnic communities to cure headache, relieve stress and constipation, reduce gas in the stomach, and to lower fevers. There are also long-term remedies for high blood pressure, infertility, and arthritis, but the most dramatic cure, one that has been witnessed by many of those in the community today, is the dispelling of fever and other dangers as a result of the mal de ojo (evil eye) — the curse of envy, brought on by admiring a child. The power to discern and dispel the ojo is restricted to certain sensitive individuals, often older women. Its causes and mechanics and the ensuing fever and torment are well documented elsewhere,[19] but central to the cure are the gift of the healer, the use of a raw egg, and prayers. Essentially, a stricken child runs a high fever and, if the healer determines that the cause is mal de ojo, candles are immediately lit around the child's bed, a raw egg is broken into a saucer and placed under the bed, and certain prayers are uttered over the patient. Eventually, according to observers, the child becomes calm and sleeps peacefully, and the fever subsides. After a little while, the attending adults will observe that the raw egg is thoroughly cooked and, moreover, a black spot is visible in the center of the yolk. "Young people are always skeptical at first. I was myself," commented a schoolteacher in St. Paul. "But then I saw it with my own eyes what was done. The fever was gone, the egg was cooked hard, and that spot was there. She said that the spot was where the evil was drawn out."[20]

Many of the basic foods preferred in the Mexican-American community have always been available in Minnesota: beef, beans, corn, poultry, pork and pork products, carrots, tomatoes, garlic, eggs, and dairy products. Inevitably, substitutions for hard-to-obtain ingredients were made. String beans are occasionally used in place of cactus in egg-and-shrimp patties. Other kinds of change are also apparent. Tortillas accommodate delicatessen luncheon meats. The potato has been added as a commonly used staple. And the flour tortilla has eclipsed the use of corn ones. At the same time, the mainstream of Minnesota cuisine also influenced the Mexican-American diet. Vegetable and chicken soups became a staple in households where meat was scarce. In the early settlement in St. Paul's West Side, Mexicans borrowed from their multi-ethnic neighbors and tried Italian, Slavic, and kosher foods. One woman remembers that her father, who used to go fishing, always delivered his catch of sunfish to a local kosher butcher shop and returned with a parcel of corned beef and rye bread.[21]

Mixed marriages also affected the traditional Mexican diet as it had come to be in Minnesota. A migrant's daughter, married to a Norwegian American, frequently prepares "Spanish rice," buñuelos, and tacos of hamburger and beans flavored with cumin and a little vinegar, but depends upon her mother for tamales at Christmas and is doubtful about planning a Quinceanera for her daughter.

Another couple combines the wife's Mexican heritage and the husband's

Mexican Independence Day queen enjoying a taco at the celebration in St. Paul, 1975

Swedish background. They do not mix foodways in a single meal but alternate styles throughout their weekly menu. On Christmas Eve, they enjoy the traditional korv (Swedish sausage), lutefisk with cream sauce, and lefse. On Christmas Day, the wife prepares tamales, chicken mole, and tortillas.[22] Throughout the year, most families in which one spouse is not of Mexican origin tend to prepare more sweet American-style desserts, but they also experiment more broadly with fresh vegetables such as broccoli, salads, and root vegetables. Urban and better-educated Mexican families, too, are in a transitional stage, beginning to eat fewer things cooked in lard and striving for a lighter diet that is lower in cholesterol.

As Mexican Americans move into public office and play more important roles in community affairs, their foodways tend to accommodate this broader perspective. For example, if a local district representative of Mexican heritage holds a political dinner at Our Lady of Guadalupe Church, the menu invariably is not spicy, possibly offering but a single dish that can be called Mexican — usually tacos. The theme is diplomacy, not intimacy; conversion, not affection.

Yet the church is also an arena in which families can seek collective support for the continuity of cultural traditions. For example, May 5 is the annual observance of Cinco de Maio, Mexican Independence Day. At this event a queen is chosen from among the many candidates in the community. To support their daughter's candidacy, extended families prepare and sell tamales, enchiladas, and other favorites after mass. Both the food and the money perpetuate the image of a heritage that is renewed for all generations who wish to participate.

But nowhere does self-image show more clearly than in language, especially in the spontaneous metaphors of conversation. In response to questions about such language images in the Mexican-American community, one St. Paul schoolteacher recalled: "A bunch of us were leaving the Guadalupe church after a meeting, six of us. And this one guy had a compact car and we had to squeeze in there. So he got out his key and laughed and said that we'd have to just fit in there like chilaquiles! Now, what does that mean? That's not an everyday dish like an enchilada at that church. It's something that is cut up in sections, and hot, and the ingredients are all crowded together. Not only crowded, but we're all part of the same scrumptious dish! Our personalities are different and we look a little different, just like those spices. But we fit together."[23]

NOTES

[1] Interview of Rosa Coronado de Collyard and Elmira Gomez Coronado, South St. Paul, January 24, 1984.

[2] Interview of Vincente de la Rosa-Valdez, Owatonna, August 9, 1984.

[3] Here and below, see Susan M. Diebold, "The Mexicans," in *They Chose Minnesota*, ed. Holmquist, 92–107.

[4] De Collyard and Coronado interview.

[5] An alternative term for this cultural group is Tejano (Texan), which implies their migratory and bicultural status.

[6] De Collyard and Coronado interview.

[7] Here and two paragraphs below, see interviews of Juanita Moran, St. Paul, June 20, 1983, Frank Rangel, St. Paul, March 30, 1983, Maria Silva, St. Paul, May 14, 1984; de Collyard and Coronado interview.

[8] Interview of Mary Morgan, St. Paul, May 21, 1984; Silva interview.

[9] Interview of Robert Dueñes, Owatonna, August 9, 1984. Spiced brains are also a favorite as a filling for tacos.

[10] Interviews of Margarita Romo, St. Paul, July 6, 1983, January 30, 1985.

[11] Interview of Laura Nystrom, St. Paul, July 14, 1983; Rangel and de Collyard and Coronado interviews.

[12] The author was privileged to visit such a home in Albert Lea where Guadalupe Dueñes demonstrated some of the techniques necessary for making tamales. For information on how groups of women share the task of preparing tamales, see M. H. de la Peña Brown, "Una Tamalada: The Special Event," *Western Folklore* 40 (January 1981): 65–71.

[13] According to Gloria Coronado Frias and Carmen Coronado Rodriguez, St. Paul, June 6, 1984, some families prepare a traditional sweet bread for these guests; embedded in the loaf are miniatures of Joseph and Mary. Whoever gets this portion of the loaf is designated host for the following night. Generally those playing the roles of Mary and Joseph actually remain as the overnight guests of their hosts. For more on Posada, see Stanley Brandes, "The *Posadas* in Tzintzuntzan: Structure and Sentiment in a Mexican Christmas Festival," *Journal of American Folklore* 96 (July–September 1983): 259–80.

[14] Silva, Moran, Frias, and Rodriguez interviews.

[15] *St. Paul Pioneer Press*, May 17, 1985, p. D1.

[16] Here and below, see interviews of Graciela Peña McGuire, Owatonna, August 9, 10, 1984; de Collyard and Coronado interview.

[17] Interview of Ramedo Saucedo, St. Paul, August 13, 1984; Dueñes interview.

[18] See Brett Williams, "Why Migrant Women Feed Their Husbands Tamales: Foodways as a Basis for a Revisionist View of Tejano Family Life," in *Ethnic and Regional Foodways*, ed. Brown and Mussell, 113–26. Similar negotiations are discussed at length for Italian-American households in Judith Goode, Janet Theophano, and Karen Curtis, "A Framework for the Analysis of Continuity and Change in Shared Sociocultural Rules for Food Use: The Italian-American Pattern," in *Ethnic and Regional Foodways*, ed. Brown and Mussell, 66–88.

[19] Many of the world's cultures fear the evil eye; see, for example, Louis C. Jones, "The Evil Eye among European-Americans," *Western Folklore* 10 (January 1951): 11–25. On Mexican beliefs, see Octavio Ignacio Romano V., "Charismatic Medicine, Folk-Healing, and Folk-Sainthood," *American Anthropologist* 67 (October 1965): 1151–73; Joe S. Graham, "Folk Medicine and Intercultural Diversity Among West Texas Mexican Americans," *Western Folklore* 44 (July 1985): 172, 188, 189.

[20] Saucedo interview. Stories about traditional cures are legion within the various ethnic communities, and the use of eggs is particularly prominent; see Hmong chapter, below. Other Mexican folk remedies using foods include sipping boiled tomatoes for a sore throat, soaking potato slices in vinegar and using them as a poultice on the forehead for fever, rubbing a mixture of lard and baking soda on the stomach for gastric pains, and eating a daily dosage of raw garlic to prevent colds.

[21] The shop was owned by the Goldberg family; Frias and Rodriguez interviews.

[22] Interview of Gary and Lee Smith, Owatonna, August 10, 1984; Nystrom interview.

[23] Saucedo interview. Our Lady of Guadalupe Church is named for the migrants' most beloved folk saint. See Williams, "Migrant Women," in *Ethnic and Regional Foodways*, ed. Brown and Mussell, 126. For an entertaining discussion on Guadalupe and Hispanic foods, see Gwyneth Cravens, "The M & J Sanitary Tortilla Factory," *New Yorker*, August 6, 1984, p. 59, 62, 64, 66.

THE BRITISH

British foodways have been part of the Minnesota scene since territorial days when the English, Scots, Welsh, and Canadians settled both in the Twin Cities and on small farms in the Minnesota River Valley. Still others arrived during succeeding years, settling in every county of the state. In the period of peak migration to Minnesota, 1890–1920, the greatest number of British—from Scotland, Canada (including the Maritimes), Wales, and England (including Cornwall), and the East Coast of the United States — arrived in 1890. There was employment in the cities, land to farm, and mining work on the Vermilion Iron Range with more to begin on the Mesabi. British immigration slacked off after World War I until dozens of war brides from the British Isles emigrated to join their husbands after World War II.[1]

It is difficult to discern characteristic ethnic foods for most British, whose roots in America and Minnesota are perhaps a century old. Favorite foods, long a part of family menus, have lost their ethnic identity, but pioneer cookbooks and reminiscences reveal that the early British settlers used recipes from the homeland. In Minnesota River Valley towns as early as 1850, for example, bakeries advertised fruitcakes, pound cakes, and traditional steamed puddings. Popular also were steamed brown breads, salt-pork cake, dried codfish dishes, bread puddings, boiled dinners, and molasses cookies and cakes. Although many of these are also considered New England dishes, their origins are in the British Isles.[2]

More recently, however, several events have promoted an awareness of ethnic foodways. Foremost was the American Bicentennial celebration in 1976 which prompted the organization of ethnic committees in many Minnesota cities. Not only did these groups help publicize traditional food, music, and culture but also many are still involved with local folk festivals, church celebrations, and events at cultural institutions such as the St. Louis County Heritage and Arts Center (The Depot) in Duluth, the Iron Range Interpretative Center in Chisholm, and colleges and universities. As a result, the public is more aware of the British influence on American foodways. To their surprise, many Minnesotans have discovered that some of these foodways are commonplace in their own homes.[3]

Many factors have affected British foodways. Through the centuries the Celtic, Germanic, and Norman cultures contributed to the development of English cuisine. And, after the New World settlement, the resulting commerce brought potatoes, sugars, chocolate, coffee, and new fruits to the homeland. Later, many of the British who were sent to India as employees of the East India Company or as part of the army acquired a taste for the spicy, highly seasoned food of the land. Then, in 1869 the publication of Isabella Beeton's book on all phases of cooking and household living, *Mrs. Beetons Book of Household Management*, made a great and lasting impact on British foodways. Many cooks heeded Mrs. Beeton's advice, and she became their helper and friend. Copies of the book crossed the ocean in the great wave of British immigration to the United States and Minnesota.[4]

All British, irrespective of their origins, share a love of certain foods. Breads, soups, scones, shortbread, tea and teatime foods, fish and chips and other fish recipes, meat pies, steamed puddings, and pasties are universally popular. Each is prepared somewhat differently depending upon the region of British provenance, and the names are unique to specific locales in Britain. Rolls, for example, are Chelsea buns in London, baps in Scotland, or Bath buns in Somerset. A biscuitlike quick bread goes by the name of scones in Scotland, singing hinnies in Northumberland, and Sussex heavies in Sussex. The list is virtually endless.[5]

British cooks make soup with beef, lamb, and chicken or with vegetables such as lentils, peas, or other garden favorites. Traditionally, vegetables and a chunk of meat or a whole chicken simmer in water until tender. Then the broth and vegetables are served as a soup, and the meat or chicken is removed, cut up or sliced, and eaten as the next course. Among the favorite soups are cock-a-leekie (leeks and chicken), Scotch broth (lamb shanks or beef and vegetables), and split pea flavored with ham or bacon. Substantial and flavorful barley was an ingredient used by many British cooks. Today substitutions are common, and stew meat, beef or lamb bones, or chicken necks and backs may be the basis of the broth.[6]

Many British Minnesotans remember washday from their childhood in the 1920s as the usual soup day. The soup kettle would be simmering on one side of the big kitchen stove, along with a steamed pudding, while on the other side a copper kettle contained the boiling clothes. Dishes were kept at a minimum on this busy day, and one bowl was used for the whole meal. The bowl first held the broth and then was wiped clean with a piece of bread. Next the sliced meat and vegetables were placed in the bowl, and after they were consumed it was wiped out with bread. Steamed pud-

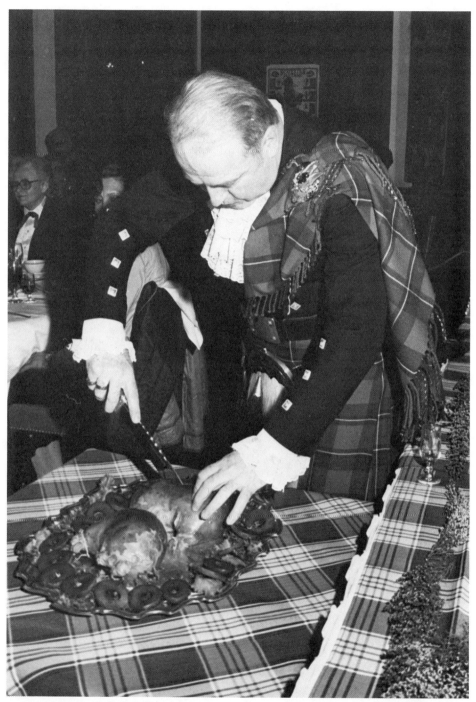

Judge David Bouschor performs the ritual carving of the haggis at the Robert Burns dinner, Duluth, 1984

ding, with a sauce, was the last course, and again the bowl received a final wipe so that dishwashing was virtually eliminated.[7]

The British like puddings. Although rice and bread puddings are popular, steamed or boiled ones — usually a combination of flour, ground suet or salt pork, fruits and nuts, and perhaps other ingredients — are the favorites. Where once puddings were wrapped in cloth and boiled in water, today's cooks usually mix the pudding, place it in a basin (bowl), cover it with a cloth tied in place, and steam it until done. A lemon sauce, soft custard, or hard sauce flavored with vanilla or brandy is always spooned over the pudding. These desserts go by many names — spotted Dick or spotted dog uses a suet dough with raisins and roly poly requires a sweet suet dough rolled around various sweet fillings and is also called bolster pudding or jam roly poly. Certain other desserts with currants and raisins are named cloutie dumpling in Scotland, plum duff in Sussex, and Helston pudding in Cornwall.[8]

At Christmastime, fruitcakes and "Christmas cakes" are stirred up, using currants, raisins, sultanas, various fruit peels, and numerous other ingredients. These cakes are baked at least eight weeks before the holiday and allowed to age until serving time. Plum puddings (which many food historians claim never contained plums, only currants, as "plum" meant "fruit" in early English recipes) use many of the same ingredients as the cakes but are steamed and then aged. Some people saturate each of these seasonal treats periodically with brandy or whisky for added flavor and moistness. It is considered good luck if all family members participate in mixing and stirring the batter, and some families also feel good luck will prevail if from year to year a Christmas pudding or cake is hung in a cloth at the back of a closet. Coins, a silver thimble, a ring, or other trinkets are usually hidden in the dough before it is baked, and family members look for these treasures in their servings. The cakes are frequently frosted first with an almond paste and then a fluffy white topping called royal icing. They may be decorated elaborately with Christmas scenes or simply with a sprig of holly. Sometimes warm liquor is poured over the cakes or puddings or liquor-saturated sugar cubes are placed on top, the liquor then being ignited and the flaming dessert brought to the table.

In Minnesota today there is a great variety of ways to conduct teatime, just as there was in the British Isles. For a while, immigrants were faithful to the customs of their home regions so the time of day for tea in Minnesota thus varied according to area of origin. Often the hour tea was served depended on family schedules and was delayed until children came home from school or the father returned from his work. Children drank a spe-

The Walton family, Minneapolis, at afternoon tea, about 1920

cial concoction, occasionally called French tea, made from one teaspoon of brewed tea in a cup of warm milk. As they grew older, the proportion of tea was increased and sugar added. Tarts, either slices or individual servings, small sandwiches, sliced cake, shortbread, scones, or sometimes small, filled crepes accompanied the beverage. If teatime were in late afternoon, then the family ate supper just before the children went to bed. In this case, supper was a light meal, possibly porridge and bread. In other homes the evening meal was called "high tea," a term denoting more elaborate food such as seafoods, savouries (cheese dishes), breads (including scones or oatcakes), sausage rolls, Scotch eggs (a sausage-wrapped hard-boiled egg), and shortbread or steamed pudding. These different teatime traditions are seldom practiced in Minnesota homes today, although some dishes or recipes remain family preferences. But one custom does remain. Whenever it is served, the mother always pours the tea, adding cream, sugar, milk, lemon, or additional hot water as desired. If "mother" is not there, then someone asks, "Shall I be Mum today?" or "Who's going to be Mother today?"[9]

Today tea drinking is a daily ritual for some, a weekend event for others, and a holiday or special occasion for still others. Many British who have substituted coffee as a daily beverage maintain that when a family problem or crisis arises the teakettle goes on the stove, as a good strong cup of tea helps one face situations more comfortably. They enjoy China teas or the stronger and darker India teas, which are available in specialty stores throughout the state. Whenever Minnesota Britishers take a trip to Canada they purchase their favorite varieties in quantity, and visitors from the British Isles know gifts of tea are always appreciated. Bags are used, although most prefer to brew the leaves in a tea ball. Traditionalists are very particular about the proper method of preparing tea: "You always take the teapot to the kettle so the water is hottest when it reaches the tea leaves."[10]

Minnesota British, whose love of fish is well known, aver that the state's lakes do not produce any species comparable to the catch available in seaside or river towns of Britain. Trips back home always include many visits to fish and chip shops for paper-wrapped servings, well doused with malt vinegar.

Childhood memories include dishes made from flounder, mackerel, rock salmon, cod, haddock, and skate. Scots remember Arbroath smokies (smoked herring), named after a fishing port, and salted mackerel — a breakfast favorite. Today, thanks to the availability of frozen fish, Britishers can include their deep-sea favorites in daily menus.[11]

British Minnesotans continue to combine vegetables in a variety of traditional dishes, many of which retain their regional names from the British Isles. For example, bubble and squeak, a combination of cabbage and mashed potatoes, is named for the sounds produced as the mixture sautes. Cooks from other areas give this same name to a hash, usually served on Mondays, which uses up the meat and vegetables from the large Sunday meal. But others call the vegetable dish colcannon. The mixture of turnips and mashed potatoes is also called by many names, including neeps and tatties, clapshot, or rumbledethumps. These dishes are said to "tone down the turnip and give life to the potatoes." To many British, rutabagas (sometimes called baggies) and turnips are interchangeable in name and use. In Minnesota, their names for vegetables caused some confusion. Many tell of going to the grocery store for the first time and asking for Swedes, another nickname for rutabagas. The confused grocers often replied, "We don't sell people here," or asked them to point out what they wanted.

Although the British tend to patronize bakeries more than Americans do, they generally make certain breads at home. Chief among the homemade goods are scones, a type of baking-powder biscuit. Often called an excuse for using butter, jams, and marmalades, they come in many forms: sweet scones, plain scones, scones with currants or other fruits. There are large ones, small ones, even pie-sized scones split and filled with fruit and whipped cream. Recipes vary; teatime scones are sweet while breakfast ones are plain. Milk, cream, or buttermilk as ingredients yield slightly different flavors. In the days when kitchens contained only open fireplaces, scones were made on a griddle (called girdle in Scotland) hung by a handle from a hook over the hearth. Some cooks today still use griddles to bake the bread on top of the stove, while others use an oven. After baking, the scones are quickly placed in a dish or basket and covered with a cloth so that none of the warmth is lost on the way to the table.[12]

Many British like tart Seville orange or grapefruit marmalade with a scone, while others prefer Lyle's Golden Syrup, a British product found in some supermarkets or speciality shops in the United States and in most grocery stores in Canada. The flavor is a blend of corn syrup, treacle (molasses), and honey. Originally sold in a tin, it now comes in glass jars. Its trademark, a lion with a hive of bees in its mouth, is based upon the biblical story that Samson told to illustrate "out of the strong came forth sweetness."

Many kinds of breads rely on saffron, the pungent, dried stigmas of one variety of crocus flower, for flavor. British cooks have for centuries used saffron. Francis Bacon, English essayist, philosopher, and statesman, once wrote that "What made the English people sprightly was the liberal use of saffron."[13] Perhaps that is true, but, more likely, it is the lovely pale yellow color and distinctive flavor that endear the seasoning to the British. Saffron bread — buns, loaves, and braids — is enhanced with currants, dark or golden raisins, candied fruit, or lemon peel. The Cornish in Ely made their saffron bread round with a knob on top and added saffron to a rich cake for Christmas and other holidays. Saffron usage has survived the years and continues today despite the high price for the small amount needed in an average recipe.[14]

Shortbread, once made exclusively in Scotland, became known throughout Great Britain once the internal mobility of the British increased. Actually a cookie, it contains only butter, flour, and sugar. Although in earlier years the dough was always mixed with the hands in a "gentle and loving fashion" — as older cooks still do — today most bakers make it in a food mixer or processor. They admit, however, that the best dough is still produced by hand, thus keeping the butter from becoming too warm and preserving the delicate texture. Originally, cooks rolled or patted the unbaked shortbread into an eight- or nine-inch circle on a baking sheet and then crimped the edges and scored the round lightly into pie-shaped wedges to facilitate cutting or breaking it after baking. The rounds were next carefully pricked all over, usually in a pattern, and baked in a slow oven to a lovely golden color. In Scotland the unbaked rounds were often pressed

Janet Petersen, Duluth, made shortbread for the Christmas season, 1985; these cookies are adaptations of the more traditional shortbread shape.

into a shortbread mold — a piece of birdseye maple having a design, usually a thistle, carved in it — unmolded and baked. Cooks also pressed the dough into rectangular pans and scored it in squares, which were also pricked with a fork.[15]

Early British Minnesotans saw their neighbors making cookies in a variety of shapes and decorating them with sugars, candies, and other toppings. Some then adopted cookie cutters to make squares, rectangles, and scalloped edges for their shortbread. Other Scots began to sprinkle their shortbread with colored sugar in patterns resembling the family tartan. Reacting also to these outside influences, some women even added oatmeal, raisins, currants, or vanilla to their shortbread.

Just as shortbread is identified with Scotland, the pasty is linked to Cornwall. Many regions claim the origin of this meat turnover that has become a staple food throughout the British Isles, but research indicates that the Cornish created them to make a good solid meal for the miners. The shape, the size, the ingredients, and the way the edges are crimped all vary by geographic area, a diversity that has carried over in Minnesota. For some Britishers pasties are everyday food while in other families they are prepared only for get-togethers on New Year's Eve or birthdays.[16]

Pasties are made from five-, eight-, or ten-inch rounds of flat dough, filled with meat and vegetables, folded over, and sealed. Customarily, pork pasties are made smaller than the beef. (Today the traditional round steak is often replaced with hamburger.) Some cooks slice the vegetables — potatoes, onions, and rutabagas — and place them in layers alternately with the thinly sliced meat on a round of dough. Other cooks are sure that dicing the vegetables before layering them with the meat produces a better product, while still others simply combine the diced vegetables and meat and spoon the mixture onto the pastry. Some add a pat of butter to each pasty before closing it up; others add suet. Usually three vent slashes cut on top of the pasty means made with rutabagas, and two slashes, without. Some families use this slash method to denote presence or absence of onion. A real pasty is juicy and flavorful and is not eaten with gravy or cat-

Phyllis Cook crimping the edges of a pasty, made as part of a regular fundraising effort at the Ely United Methodist Church, February 1977

sup; however, some members of the younger generation, used to eating foods with sauces, add catsup, mustard, or gravy. In any case, all agree that pasties are made properly "when the juice runs off your elbow as you eat them."

Pasty making outside of the home is the basis for many successful church fund raisers. The Methodist church women in Ely prepare pasties once a month and sell them for $2.50 apiece, regularly taking orders for eight hundred or more. In Hibbing the women at Wesley Methodist Church start with a circle the size of a dinner plate and use a pastry dough that is firm enough so that their pasties can be eaten out of the hand without crumbling.

Meat encased in pastry also appears as meat pies for which the British Isles have always been renowned. Pies were usually purchased in bakeries, but in the small villages where homes often had open fireplaces, women would prepare the pies and take them to the local baker to finish. Britishers brought their appetite for meat pies to Minnesota and still fix the various kinds at special times. Although they made pork, onion, and potato pies, ham and veal pies, and steak and kidney pies, the latter kind — containing round steak, lamb kidneys, gravy, salt, and pepper — seems to be the most popular today. Some women use a special basin (meat-pie dish), which is flat bottomed but deeper than the usual pie plate. Many British women brought theirs along when they emigrated; however, specialty stores today sell these dishes.

The flaky lard pastry on top of the pie (there is no bottom crust) is decorated with cutout shapes and brushed with an egg wash. At the center of the crust is a large open steam vent; a hollow china blackbird or other shape fills the hole, and the steam is directed out its mouth or top. Even though the authentic steak and kidney pie should be plain, some "muck it up with other things" such as mushrooms, herbs, and vegetables.[17]

Some foods, such as desserts and salads, and food uses, as in home remedies, are pervasive throughout Britain. Trifle, the dessert invented to use leftover cake, is one such dish. Scots claim it as their own, but with the mobility in the British Isles, it is no wonder that its popularity spread. Britishers brought trifle to Minnesota as a cherished family tradition. Made in layers in a deep, glass bowl (often a family heirloom of etched or cut glass), trifle is based today upon sponge or pound cake, lady fingers, macaroons, or a combination of these. After pouring liquor — sherry, brandy, or whisky — over it, the cake is allowed to stand overnight; those who do not have liquor in the house use orange juice. The next day, first a layer of fresh, canned, or thawed frozen fruit is added and then one of soft custard. The top is decorated with whipped cream and garnished with fresh fruit. Occasionally, fruit gelatin replaces expensive or unavailable fruits. Some British are loyal to Bird's custard powder, a boxed mix that is used extensively in the British Isles to make a custardlike vanilla sauce. Today as trifle rides the crest of national popularity, women's magazines feature exotic recipes using unusual fruit such as the kiwi, and specialty shops sell all sizes and shapes of deep glass dishes.[18]

Traditional British salads and sauces are quite simple. A typical salad consists of cucumber and pickled beet slices, wedges of tomato and lettuce, hard-boiled eggs, canned salmon or cold slices of meat, and olives all arrayed on a platter. It was the custom to help oneself to each salad item, arrange it on the dinner plate, and then apply salad dressing. This salad is served infrequently today, since many cooks make the Jell-O and tossed salads listed in popular cookbooks.[19]

British foods incorporate few sauces, although Worcestershire sauce has become a well-recognized export. Another favorite condiment is mint sauce, which is made from fresh leaves, vinegar, water, and seasonings and served with meat, especially lamb. For those without a garden, this piquant sauce is also available in grocery stores.

British mothers prescribed food remedies for common ailments suffered by family members. Toast with warm milk over it proved nourishing and settling to stomachs that were a little upset. When given to colicky babies, this dish was called "sap." Mumps were treated with a glass of Bermuda-onion juice. For a sore throat or cold, one cup of boiling water poured over one tablespoon of black currant jelly or jam was considered helpful, as was sweetened lemon juice in a little hot water. Cooked goose grease was always saved to be used as a salve for sores or burns or combined with mustard as a poultice for a sore throat. In many of the Presbyterian homes, people used no liquor except for cold remedies. Hot toddy, made with liquor (usually whisky), sugar, water, and a little lemon juice, was a common remedy. Even children might be given a small toddy when afflicted with a winter cold.[20]

The Scots, perhaps more than any other British group, have kept their food traditions alive in Minnesota. Clustered in many towns on the iron ranges, in Duluth, and in the St. Paul-Minneapolis area, they are also scattered all over Minnesota. Those in Duluth emigrated primarily from Ontario, Nova Scotia, and the Isle of Lewis, especially from its chief town, Stornoway. Immigrants from Nova Scotia and Stornoway picked Duluth primarily because of the building boom of the late 1890s and early 1900s.

Being carpenters of all kinds, they went into construction and ship building. Others from the Isle of Lewis were the city's early merchants and bankers.[21]

Before long there were enough Scots in Duluth to form the fraternal organization, Clan Stewart of the Order of Scottish Clans, with ritual and social events for all members and families. Women organized auxiliaries that scheduled luncheons and other meetings where traditional foods were served. Older Scottish residents say that they, or their mothers, would never have adjusted to their new homes had it not been for these organizations. Without these pioneer women, the ethnic foods and celebrations might have been lost through the years.

One celebration renowned in the early twentieth century in Duluth was the yearly picnic held at Fond du Lac, a site up the St. Louis River from the city. The day began when pipers led a parade from downtown Duluth to the dock, where the riverboat, *Montauk*, took revelers to the picnic site. Ham, oatcakes, and round currant cakes were always served because they traveled well. The day was spent doing country dances to bagpipe music and engaging in the Scottish games of "putting the stone" and "tossing the caber."[22]

The annual Scottish Country Fair currently held on the first weekend in May at Macalester College in St. Paul resembles this bygone event. The fair includes music, dancing, games, and food booths that sell sausage rolls, scones, cherry and sultana cakes, meat pies, and shortbread. It is one of many affairs that have continued since the Bicentennial activities began a revival of ethnicity. For example, Minnesota families, like those in other parts of the United States, regularly gather for Scottish dancing competitions. Duluth, Burnsville, and Mounds View are the sites for these meets, which create much local interest in all things Scottish. Ethnic foods — meat pies, shortbread, sausage rolls, tarts, and the like — are always a part of the day's experience.[23]

In early days of Minnesota settlement, Scots gathered to celebrate the January 25 birthday of revered Scottish poet Robert Burns with music, dancing, toasts, and food. With the passing of the immigrant generation in the 1930s, these occasions were abandoned but were revived in Duluth and the Twin Cities during the Bicentennial. In these places contemporary Scots and their guests enjoy a grand evening of food and poetry recitations. In the Minneapolis-St. Paul area both the St. Andrew's Society of Minnesota, Inc., and the Twin Cities Scottish Club have a Burns dinner, and although the menu varies for each group, haggis is always featured. In Duluth the event is held at the Kitchi Gammi Club; Burns is honored throughout the evening, as is the haggis, the food creation venerated in his poem, "Ode To A Haggis." Although few Scots today remember having this concoction at home, they thoroughly enjoy it at this celebration. The original dish consisted of the pluck (heart, liver, and lungs) of a lamb mixed with oatmeal, onions, and other seasonings and stuffed in a cleaned lamb's stomach to be steamed for several hours. A legend has persisted that haggis was first made in the early fourteenth century when Scotland was ravaged by English invaders, who left the natives only the worst parts of the animals. The hungry Scots made something edible from what they had — haggis. Those who make it at home today spoon the mixture into a casserole dish and bake it in the oven or simmer it gently in a boilable plastic bag.[24]

At Burns celebrations the chef carries the haggis out into the dining hall on a silver tray held high, preceded by pipers playing traditional music. The master of ceremonies toasts the haggis, and all raise their glasses in salute. Some in attendance may prefer to save their toasting whisky or Drambuie to pour over their portion of haggis. Whether this enhances or masks the flavor is not clear.

St. Andrew's Day celebrations also contribute to the maintenance of Scottish traditional foods. In Duluth at least two hundred people annually attend this event, held on St. Andrew's Day, November 30, or a Sunday evening close to that date at an Episcopal church, where a service celebrating the accomplishments of the patron saint of Scotland and the Kirkin O' the Tartan (blessing of the various clan tartans) is followed by high tea. This Scottish fare consists of roast beef and buns, horseradish, shortbread and other cookies, oatcakes, fruit, and trifle. In the Twin Cities area the St. Andrew's Society sponsors a similar event.[25]

Other Scottish and multiethnic celebrations help both to perpetuate and to publicize traditional foods. At the Iron Range Interpretative Center, one of the Ethnic Days, held each August since 1978, celebrates the British Commonwealth heritage with song, dance, and food. Scots at the annual Duluth Folk Festival sell scones, oatcakes, and shortbread. And the Scottish Heritage Sunday at the Hope Community Church in Virginia is crowded with smartly kilted men and women and their guests in plaid skirts, shawls, or ties. A social hour following the church service features tea and shortbread. In the Twin Cities, the Scottish Club, formed to promote Scottish culture, meets at least once a month for a social evening — a family event for members and guests. Traditional main dishes such as steak or steak and kidney pie, tattie soup, or fish and chips are featured.

When queried about early food habits Scots are quick to relate that their mothers and oftentimes they themselves learned to cook on an open hearth, sometimes with a side oven. A huge cast-iron pot for stews, soups, and other dishes hung from a hook; a griddle could also be hung there for browning oatcakes, scones, and other breads. Old Country food was simple, being made with fresh ingredients from their own gardens or the surrounding countryside. Breads of barley, rye, or oatmeal flours were baked in the side ovens. One reminiscent woman told how her her grandmother, who enjoyed baking bread, "balanced her large mixing bowl on one hip, held it with one arm and stirred with the other, and quoted the poetry of Robert Burns."[26]

Oatmeal, an early favorite because oats grew well in Scotland, was used in cakes and cookies but most regularly as porridge. It was similar to the long-cooking variety available today, simmered slowly the night before and reheated the next morning in a double boiler or over a pan of water. Adults who ate oatmeal as children now fall into two groups: those who will "never touch it again," or those who "must start the day with it." In the heavily Scottish area in Duluth nicknamed Oatmeal Hill (Hunter's Park), so the story goes, mothers always insisted their children start the day with that porridge. Friends who stayed overnight were also expected to partake. When asked where they had visited, the guests replied "Oatmeal Hill." In addition to the breakfast cereal, oatcakes (a cookie-cracker) were a staple in Scottish homes although they are not often made today. The dough, which includes bacon fat, is rolled thin and cut into squares or rectangles; once baked these are crisp and make a good accompaniment to cheese and fruit. Most importantly, some Scots claim, "oatmeal will make your hair curly."

While the Scots celebrated most holidays with ordinary food and simple gifts, they gave the New Year's Day, or Hogmanay as it is called in Scotland, special emphasis. This tradition they continue in Minnesota. Families from the Isle of Lewis always gathered in Duluth to celebrate Hogmanay, usually in the home of a fellow Lewisman. There was singing in Gaelic until the 1920s, bagpipe music, and much reminiscing. As was their custom, no liquor was served at these gatherings, but there were foods in abundance, including oatcakes and cheeses, shortbread, scones and accompaniments, and the ever-enjoyed tea.

The Cornish who left their homeland in search of work migrated to Minnesota's Vermilion Iron Range as early as 1882 and to the Mesabi in the 1890s. They had worked in the tin mines of Cornwall and had gained more experience in Pennsylvania, Michigan, and Wisconsin. A particularly large group from Quinnesec, Michigan, arrived in Tower in 1884; others from Ishpeming, Michigan, settled in Tower and neighboring Soudan at about the same time. So many were related, according to the old timers, that they were soon nicknamed "Cousin Jacks." They brought to Minnesota their traditional foods — saffron breads, doughnuts, stews, and the pasty, a food still found in bakeries and restaurants throughout northeastern Minnesota.[27]

Early Welsh immigrants settled in the Minnesota River valley in 1853; Blue Earth, Nicollet, and Le Sueur counties were the nucleus of a rural community that reached west into Brown County. While some of the men had been miners in Wales, most seem to have left central and northern Wales looking for land of their own. Families quickly founded enduring farming settlements and, despite movement of children to Mankato and the Twin Cities metropolitan area, a Welsh presence remains in the river valley to this day.[28]

Welsh people traditionally follow the kind of diet described in this chapter as British, but certain foods and occasions for consuming them, remain distinct. A profile of the Welsh community in the 1980s seems typical of many American ethnic groups: women of the "older generation," aged in their sixties and seventies, maintain what there is of traditional foodways; those one or two decades younger are rarely involved in ethnic cooking; but the "younger generation" shows revived interest in its heritage. These women have reclaimed old recipes from Welsh cookbooks or brought them back from trips to Wales. Thus, Welsh folk occasionally eat Welsh cakes, bara brith (raisin bread), leek soup, and lamb on St. David's Day (March 1) in honor of the patron saint of Wales. According to one community member, the ease of making most of the traditional recipes has prevented much modification — except in leek soup. Leeks are not always available, instant potatoes are a handy short cut, and food processors make quick work of the whole process.[29]

After the large influx of Britishers in the 1890s and 1900s, few immigrated to Minnesota until the years following World War II. Then, between 1947 and 1950, British war brides who were married to American servicemen formerly stationed in Great Britain rejoined their husbands. In wartime Britain with all of its shortages and rationing these women had learned to cook with few ingredients. They were pleased with Minnesota's plentiful food supplies, but they also enjoyed the packages of Bird's Dessert Mix, Lyle's Golden Syrup, flavored gelatin in flat sheets, and biscuits (cookies) sent from home. Many of the men they married were from strong

Irene Maio, Duluth, removing cooled and decorated Bakewell tarts from the pans, 1986

ethnic backgrounds, and the women lived at first with in-laws who were, for example, Finnish, Slavic, or Italian. They soon were cooking and learning new recipes from their mothers-in-law. Later, in their own homes, their menus often combined the newly learned Finnish soups and flat breads, Italian pasta or meat dishes, or Slavic potica and strudel desserts with dishes from their homeland.[30]

Another influence on these women was the Young Women's Christian Association's International Institute, which sponsored clubs for the new immigrants. In Duluth these groups included not only a social club, but also classes to teach the war brides "to cook American." In them the women learned to make Jell-O salads, ham with raisin sauce, and tuna-fish dishes. This group stayed together years after the classes were over, calling themselves the Rainbow Club, a name that they altered to the British Social Club at the time of the Bicentennial. These women often have a food booth at the Duluth Folk Festival, and they also serve their specialties, such as sausage rolls, shortbread, mince tarts, and Bakewell tarts, named after the town in Britain where they originated. The latter tart shell is made from a short-crust pastry, and it is filled with custard and ground almonds. Butterfly cake, a cupcake named for the pointed pieces of cake on top and containing a sweet filling, is also featured. When large convention groups are in Duluth, these same foods are sold at the St. Louis County Heritage and Arts Center along with the foods of other ethnic groups. At home, British Minnesotans continue to make traditional dishes such as meat pies, toad-in-the-hole (a sausage dish), lamb recipes, bread-and-butter pudding, and tarts with lemon curd, jam, or fruit.

British cuisine consists of more than the familiar roast beef and Yorkshire pudding, Christmas goose, and flaming puddings popularly perceived as British by readers of English novels. The cooking from these islands depends upon fresh ingredients prepared simply and served with few embellishments, allowing the natural flavors of individual foods to remain. Over the years in Minnesota, this national cuisine has blended with other foodways, resulting in few distinctively recognized British dishes. The influx of British war brides following World War II and the formation of the ethnically related Bicentennial committees, however, have prompted a resurgence of British awareness. Scottish culture, in particular, has gained new attention, a prominence traceable to its games, dancing, and celebrations. And food is an integral part of all such festivities. Thus the renewed interest in heritage has resulted in an increased appreciation and enjoyment of British foodways.

NOTES

[1] Sarah P. Rubinstein, "The British: English, Scots, Welsh, and British Canadians," in *They Chose Minnesota*, ed. Holmquist, 111–18, 123–25.

[2] Iva A. Dingwall, "Pioneers' Dinner Table," *Minnesota History* 34 (Summer 1954): 54–58; Marjorie Kreidberg, "Corn Bread, Portable Soup, and Wrinkle Cures," *Minnesota History* 41 (Fall 1968): 105–16.

[3] Interviews of Jean Macrae, Duluth, August 24, 1983, Myra Meittunen, Hibbing, October 11, 1983. The British Festival of Minnesota, a six-week-long celebration held in the Twin Cities in the fall of 1985, on the other hand, featured very little of contemporary British cuisine. A local restaurant offered a series of King Henry VIII feasts, and one of the closing events was a seven-course medieval banquet. A Winona woman produced a cookbook that featured mostly newly created recipes, several organizations and restaurants held teas, and a number of articles appeared in local papers explaining the eti-

quette and customs surrounding teatime. Bette Hamel, "Tea, A Changing Social Institution," in Bette Hamel, ed., *The British Festival of Minnesota Official Commemorative Magazine* (Edina: Group 7 Inc., 1985), 67, 102–4; *Minneapolis Star and Tribune*, September 11, 1985, p. 3T; *St. Paul Pioneer Press and Dispatch*, September 11, 1985, p. 1C, 2C.

[4] For an overview of English cooking practices, see Molly Harrison, *The Kitchen in History* (New York: Charles Scribner's Sons, 1972).

[5] Interviews of Rowland Nelson, Duluth, July 20, 1983, Don Pearce, Duluth, January 26, 1984; Lizzie Boyd, ed., *British Cookery: A Complete Guide to Culinary Practice in England, Scotland, Ireland and Wales* (New York: Overlook Press, 1979), 43–52.

[6] Interviews of Marybelle Johnson, Duluth, August 10, 1983, Charlotte Turner, Duluth, August 5, 1981.

[7] Nelson interview.

[8] Here and below, see interview of Selina McCracken, Duluth, October 5, 1983; Boyd, *British Cookery*, 379–85; John F. Mariani, *The Dictionary of American Food and Drink* (New Haven, Conn.: Ticknor & Fields, 1983), 321; Adrian Bailey, *The Cooking of the British Isles*, Foods of the World (New York: Time-Life Books, 1969), 12, 149–57.

[9] Interview of Joyce Cowling, Hibbing, September 1, 1983; Nelson and McCracken interviews.

[10] Here and below, see interviews of Helen Blain, Pengilly, October 11, 1983, Jean Spencer, Duluth, October 18, 1983; McCracken interview.

[11] Here and below, see interviews of Reverend Gordon MacLean, Ely, September 1, 1983, Jean Gibson, Duluth, August 26, 1983. Rutabagas and turnips reportedly grew so large in the British Isles that people frequently hollowed them out at Halloween time and carved faces in them.

[12] Interview of Margaret Tulloch, Duluth, July 25, 1983; MacLean interview.

[13] Meittunen and Tulloch interviews; Marina Polvay, "Saffron," *Gourmet: The Magazine of Good Living* 41 (January 1981): 30.

[14] McCracken interview; "Miscellaneous Notes," Grace Lee Nute Papers, University of Minnesota-Duluth Archives.

[15] Here and below, see interview of Mary Fleming, Hibbing, September 1, 1983; Blain interview.

[16] Here and below, see interviews of Mildred Koschak, Ely, October 12, 1983, Madge Matilla, Ely, October 12, 1983; Meittunen interview.

[17] Spencer interview.

[18] Interview of David Bouschor, Duluth, July 26, 1983; Macrae interview.

[19] Here and below, see interview of Ada Koski, Hibbing, November 20, 1983.

[20] Interview of Virginia Kirby, Virginia, September 2, 1983; Cowling interview.

[21] Here and below, see interviews of Janet Petersen, Duluth, September 13, 1983, Marlys Peterson, Hibbing, August 30, 1983; Macrae interview.

[22] Interview of Marguerite Bourassa, Duluth, August 11, 1983.

[23] Bouschor and Macrae interviews.

[24] There are many versions of how and why the Scots developed haggis as a national symbol. Here and below, see Janet Warren, *A Feast of Scotland* (New York: Little, Brown, 1979), 14–24, 156–57, 163; F. Marian McNeill, *The Scots Kitchen: Its Traditions and Lore: With Old-Time Recipes* (London: Blackie & Son, 1930), 27–41; L. Patrick Coyle, *The World Encyclopedia of Food* (New York: Facts on File, 1982), 299–300; Bouschor interview.

[25] Here and below, see Nelson interview; interview of Jean Sinclair, St. Paul, July 31, 1984.

[26] Here and two paragraphs below, see Cowling, Gibson, and Macrae interviews. See also Margaret Costa, "The Highlands of Scotland," *Gourmet: The Magazine of Good Living* 32 (August 1972): 17–18, 60–66.

[27] "Miscellaneous Notes," Nute Papers. For more on pasties, see Finnish chapter, below.

[28] Rubinstein, "The British," in *They Chose Minnesota*, ed. Holmquist, 114–17.

[29] Telephone interview of Mary M. Mergenthal, St. Paul, July 11, 1984.

[30] Here and below, see interviews of Rowena Olson, Duluth, September 20, 1983, Irene Maio, Duluth, September 12, 1983; Dorothy Gladys Spicer, *From An English Oven: Cakes, Buns and Breads of County Tradition* . . . (New York: Women's Press, 1948), 62–64.

Pauline Mueller, St. Paul, using an innovative spätzle maker (a ricer) to produce quanti-ties of the tiny noodles, 1983

THE GERMANS

For four decades, 1917–57, German-American foodways have been a private matter. The period that encompassed two world wars and their aftermath was a time of intolerance, censure, and in some areas, censorship. Minnesotans with roots in Germany emerged from that era with an ethnic culture very different from that of their forebears. And much of that culture, learned and transmitted through foodways, is today expressed in a very self-conscious way.[1] There is, however, no one German experience in Minnesota; there are many, depending upon an individual's place of origin, social class, religion, and time of emigration. Modern Minnesota has Germans from Russia or Russländer, Prussians, Berliners, Swabians, and Bavarians, descendants of Ruhr and Rhine dwellers, immigrants from what are today the Federal Republic of Germany and the German Democratic Republic, Roman Catholics, Protestants, including Mennonites and Amish, and Jews. The image of Minnesota's largest ethnic group, furthermore, has been determined more by Hollywood and commercialized ethnic bazaars than by German Americans themselves. If the wartime stereotypes of German farmers and German-language newspaper editors were vicious, the representation of a complex of German cultures in strudel, bratwurst, and beer is banal.[2]

More recently, German Americans' tendency to mask their heritage seems to have been reversed. The celebration in 1983 of three hundred years of German immigration to America was announced on a poster that read: "A slice of American life has a German filling"; the accompanying illustration showed a German torte, its layers the colors of the flags of the two German republics, its icing resembling the Stars and Stripes. The message was clear: Despite economic, social, and political assimilation during forty years of emotional nationalism and military crises, German-American culture today is not only intact but is also an integral part of American life. Moreover, the popularity of German restaurants, three successful conferences on the German experience in Minnesota (1979–83), and a thriving German-American Volksfest Association of Minnesota are proof of this new, public pride.

Food has occupied a prominent place in this German-American revival.

The Volksfest Association, for example, was begun in 1958 (coinciding with Minnesota's centennial celebration) with a picnic. In addition to language and cultural events of all kinds, the organization currently offers members a dozen festive meals throughout the year, some presenting traditional holiday fare and others featuring foods from a specific region of Germany or Austria.[3]

German cooking has always been carried on in the home. (This private pursuit of ethnicity was the obvious alternative for German Minnesotans during the war years.) Nineteenth-century German immigrant farmers had found the land a willing partner to their foodways. Before World War II, when diversified farming was still practiced, German-American farmers raised nearly everything they ate, buying only staples such as sugar and coffee and certain "American" products such as corn flakes, ice cream, or oysters at a local market. In those days few rural markets sold ethnic foods. But like farmers everywhere, German Americans were thrifty, utilizing every scrap, much as their forebears had in the villages of Bohemia, Württemberg, or Saxony.[4] They made headcheese from otherwise unusable scraps from the hog's head. They pickled pig hocks and feet and preserved them as delicacies. Relatively young Minnesotans with German roots recall that brains, tripe, blood sausage, and chicken feet were served as favored dishes. Potatoes — whether fried, boiled, mashed, or as dumplings in chicken soup — extended nearly every meal. Despite technical innovations and the growing specialization of farming, many, although not all, rural German Minnesotans continue these traditional foodways today.

One man who grew up on a farm near Osakis, in rural Douglas County, for example, regularly enjoyed home-cured hams, smoked sausages, headcheese, and blood sausages. In the fall of each year, his mother roasted meats and cold packed them in their juices in fruit jars. She stored cabbage with spices in stoneware crocks under a stone press to make kraut and prepared cottage cheese, beer, and even root beer. Noodles were never purchased but were made by hand and hung to dry on the backs of chairs. This mode of food conservation required extensive storage areas until rural electrification changed preservation methods. Ice houses stood on every farm, and each winter farmers worked cooperatively to saw ice and haul the blocks on sleds to farms where they were packed in sawdust or, in the Red River Valley, in flax straw.[5]

Other cooperative enterprises deepened and strengthened the bond already created through food sharing. A Carver County woman recalled that her father-in-law, a barber in town, was part of a group of men who butchered together each fall. Although he raised no animals, the barber, perhaps in return for his skills, always brought home a portion of the meat for his own use. Another woman living in rural Wright County remembered joining other farm women to collect wild horseradish. At one person's home, they ground the roots and mixed the pulp with sugar, vinegar, and milk to concoct a seasoning for meats, usually ham, and boiled eggs. Still another woman enjoyed accompanying her mother and other women as they contributed fresh milk from their cows to the making of Christmas cheeses, first at one home and then another. "We never had enough for more than one cheese at any one time, but by chipping in, we could make a cheese for one family and still visit."[6]

Giving food to the poor and in payment for services is a standard rural practice that sometimes continues into the present. One German-American family remembers that when farmers in southern Carver County brought their produce to town, they left unsold items on the porch of the Lutheran pastor, who, in turn, distributed it to needy families. In Stearns County, another German area, veterinarians tell of being paid in maple syrup, blood sausage, headcheese, or vegetables.[7]

There is nothing distinctively ethnic about these gestures of social bonding and good will. They are as typical in Michigan and Indiana as they are in Minnesota. Yet German Americans recall such acts as part of a foodways heritage that they interpret as ethnically German.

As Minnesota moved into the second half of the twentieth century, food marketing became more sophisticated in response to the demands of a better informed and more inquisitive public and due to the development of the trucking industry and refrigeration techniques. By the late 1960s, when affluence became pronounced, international cooking emerged as a major cultural force in a new American society. German foods grew increasingly commonplace in public. Acknowledging that cultural pluralism was an alternative to Americanization for Minnesotans, German Americans in urban areas returned to their food customs and menus, but found themselves without traditional, localized food sources. In addition, food preferences had changed during the middle decades of the century, and entire generations had matured without tasting authentic German cooking. Many women, mothers and grandmothers today, were diverted by the circumstances of those midcentury years. Some, for example, worked in factories during the 1940s; consequently, they did not learn and thus could not pass on the German-American foodways they knew as children.[8]

In larger cities, German foodways continued in the face of war hysteria and the influence of American mass-produced, commercialized products. Despite the growth and influence of large chain stores, some family-owned sausage markets have survived rather well, often expanding their facilities to offer customers frozen food locker storage and services. One such establishment in the Rice Street area of St. Paul, an old German neighborhood surrounding St. Bernard's Church, provides a large variety of fresh and preserved meats, many in the German style. It offers headcheese, roulade (beef roll, a very special German dish), summer sausages with or without garlic, and Thüringer, a unique smoked wurst originating in east central Germany, along with pepperoni, Polish sausage, and Swedish korv.[9]

Of all the sausages associated with German foodways, blood sausage is probably one of the most traditional and best liked among older German Minnesotans. Bratwurst, however, is what outsiders think of first. "Brats," traditionally made from pork, veal, and eggs, can be bought with a crunchy brötchen (hard roll) at a vendor's stand, a restaurant, or a gasthaus anywhere in Germany. But in Minnesota "brats," made in rural households during the early twentieth century and still prepared today (although in larger casings to save time), were late in catching the general public's fancy. When the Volksfest Association began to expand its picnics and its food presentations at the Festival of Nations in 1961, some members

Ben Steinberg, co-owner of the Pioneer Sausage Company, St. Paul, loading braunschweiger onto a rack amidst headcheese, wieners, ring bologna, beef sticks, and other delicacies in the store's cooler, 1986

attempted to sell bratwurst but found no customers. It took several years before other members, not to mention an uninitiated public, began to pick up the taste. The gray color, perhaps, makes bratwurst less interesting to Americans who often buy the darker smoked variety for picnics, parties, and football tailgating.[10]

A somewhat more sumptuous dish which Americans readily associate with German foodways is sauerbraten. A fairly subtle degree of variety exists in German versions of this item. In the north, ginger is one of the spices included. Some cooks use varying amounts of vinegar while others use different wines for the marinade. Basically, sauerbraten is a beef roast, marinated in wine or vinegar with peppercorns, juniper berries, cloves, a bay leaf, onions, salt, and pepper. The meat must soak for several days, being turned every day, before being browned and then cooked in the juices for three to four hours. The juice can be thickened with flour and made into gravy. At a traditional dinner, the meat might be preceded by mark kleussuppe, a clear bone-marrow soup garnished with chopped chives, and accompanied by side dishes such as vegetables either in a souffle or creamed, potatoes or spätzle (a soft, curly noodle), and a sweet-and-sour green salad.

If roasted meats, creamed vegetables, and potatoes are dishes easily incorporated into the American image of German cooking, the green salad is not. Many restaurants that tout a "German" menu do not prepare this simple cold dish, which has remained popular in German families over the years. Common garden lettuce or even dandelion greens are combined with finely slivered onion and cucumbers and then covered with a mixture of vinegar and sugar. Usually, tiny bits of fried bacon (not the commercially prepared synthetic substitute) and the pan drippings are also added. Thick cream may replace the bacon. A similar combination of vinegar, sugar, oil, and onion is found in the traditional German potato salad, which, unlike the American version, is served warm and uses unpeeled small and very tender potatoes.

The frequent use of vinegar in German-American households startles some outsiders. One woman of Swedish and English background, for example, found it peculiar at first, but later felt that "I loved coming into my husband's grandmother's house. She cooked on a wood stove and that stove and the vinegar, fresh bread out of the oven, and supper simmering on the stove were fond memories."[11]

Commercial canned goods, refrigeration, automobile travel, and the communications revolution have changed the self-reliant and insular world of the nineteenth century. Today a German-American family may eat Jap-

Helga Parnell slicing sauerbraten in the Volksfest Haus kitchen, St. Paul, 1983

anese sushi one night and potato dumplings the next. New interpretations of proper nutrition have led many away from an ethnic diet considered too heavy, high in calories, and lacking in fresh or raw fruits and vegetables. Contemporary German Americans have lived through what one historian has called "Leveling Times and Places," and "homogenizing the regions and seasons, toward democratizing the national diet."[12]

In addition, some young people of German background who lack a long association with their ethnic foods reject traditional dishes — such as blood sausage, grützwurst (oatmeal sausage), tongue, headcheese, soup made from chicken feet, and liver dumplings — because of their visceral connotations or because they appear bland or unappetizing. Many prefer commercial sausage and other meat products, soup mixes, and bread that contains food coloring. For this generation, texture, appearance, and ease of preparation seem more important than rich taste or food value. But more importantly, younger generations, unlike their grandparents, no longer need to use every scrap of food they raise. And few are able to draw upon folk recipes to do so in a tasty manner.

Three couples, each with partial German heritage, are examples of a recent kind of adjustment to a multicultural, convenience-oriented environment. Bringing Polish, Norwegian, and German ancestry to the marriage, one couple in rural Douglas County attends church dinners where a potluck meal may consist of Polish sausage, fried chicken, "kraut slaw," and apple pie. At Christmas, Norwegian rosetter show up with peanut brittle, oyster stew, and cabbage cooked with caraway seeds.[13]

In urban Minneapolis a working couple — a Norwegian husband and a German wife — claim they are too busy "to cook ethnic," yet their day-to-day food patterns are stylistically reminiscent of their heritages. Frequent creamed vegetables, generous helpings of milk, butter on nearly everything, and lefse distinguish the husband's taste from that of his wife, who prepares fried potatoes, pork chops, steamed red cabbage, and chicken.[14] The couple's rural ties have faded, and they now rely upon quick shopping, which does not always allow a stop at one of the local, reliable German-style sausage shops. Both couples illustrate a common trend in contemporary foodways among younger people — eclectic tastes and hurried preparations.

A third couple, each partner with many generations of German ancestry in Minnesota, lives in Forest Lake. Each grew up in a household with German-style cooking, especially the wife whose father and grandfather ran a prosperous St. Paul meat market and who attended German-language services at church. Childhood foodways included blood sausage, pfeffernüsse (cookies), Christmas stollen, marrow soups, Limburger cheese, and traditional German-style vegetables such as green beans cooked with onions, bacon, sugar, and vinegar. But she also lived in a time of pressure cookers and boiled dinners, Jell-O, and chocolate-chip cookies. Although she has time to introduce some of these traditional dishes into her own young family's diet, her family prefers a more undistinguished American style.[15]

A fourth couple in the same generation presents a contrasting case. The wife's grandparents were Germans from Russia, the Russländer who were so numerous in North Dakota. The husband's people are German and "Pennsylvania Dutch" — German Anabaptists. Each grew up with and continues to prepare what is accepted as German food: homemade noodles for soups, pork roasts with sauerkraut, salad greens with the characteristic sweet-and-sour dressing. Christmas sees them baking decorated cookies and preparing oyster stew for Christmas Eve, a dish also traditional among Scandinavians. But they live in Benson, a western Minnesota town dominated by Norwegian Americans. Norwegian tastes are publicized during the pre-Christmas sales of meatball mixes, herring, and sausages. The German-American couple incorporates some of these foods into its diet: fish, breads, and even rømmegraut, the traditional Norwegian cream porridge. In their own words, theirs is "a relaxed and comfortable, mixed diet." It is their opinion, though, that Norwegians eat more sweets than Germans who prefer a "sour" diet, and they find Norwegian food generally more spicy than German.[16]

Perhaps most interesting is this couple's style of entertaining. A recent Christmas Day buffet for friends and neighbors (from mainly Scandinavian and German backgrounds) consisted of stuffed mushrooms, guacamole and shrimp dips, herring, barbecued meatballs, wieners, baked ham, and popovers with honey and butter. It is nearly impossible to find a German theme in this public presentation of food. But, as people from various ethnic groups have suggested, "When offering food to people who may not like your own cuisine, give them something totally foreign and out of a gourmet magazine! If they don't like it, it's not you. It's neutral territory!" Cost or status may determine which "neutral" food will be served: roast beef is prestigious, fried chicken is not.[17]

Serving nonethnic food seems to be the practice at many German-American wedding and funeral dinners. The latter are often accompanied by hasty and efficient meals; for some people, in addition, elaborate eating is a joyous gesture inappropriate for mourning. At wedding receptions, which often include large numbers of people from mixed backgrounds, economy and taste often dictate a neutral menu: roast beef or ham, an innocuous salad, champagne, and cake. More often private occasions such as quilting bees or afternoon coffee in the home are appropriate places to display or share truly ethnic foods. It would seem that, more than specific holidays or social events, the size of an event, how public it is, and who attends influence the expression of German ethnic foodways.[18]

In many ethnic communities today, churches, clubs, and schools are the agents that maintain or revive traditional foodways. Recently sauerkraut suppers have become a well-established modern custom in most German-American communities and are usually fund raisers and social get-togethers. The typical meal is simple: ham, pork, or wurst, sauerkraut flavored with caraway seeds or apples, rolls, and coffee. Lions clubs in St. Michael and

Albertville, for example, hold summer dinners that feature a comfortable mixture of traditional German and American foods: pork, headcheese, krautsalat (slaw), corn on the cob, and baked potatoes. Pig roasts and church chicken dinners in those and other communities were once events to which individuals brought home-grown contributions; today the hosts make bulk purchases from stores or even hire local caterers to supply the trimmings.[19]

Specific ethnic organizations are also often entrusted with the task of presenting Old World foods. Members who recently emigrated are invaluable in this pursuit; for instance, the Volksfest Association includes war brides and émigrés who have helped the organization maintain language and food, as well as other cultural concerns. These new Americans with modern views of what is "German" and with recent exposure to European foodways can refresh an ethnic food pattern that, after four or five generations in Minnesota, may be slipping toward convenience.[20]

In addition to institutions, less formal urban social networks have always helped individuals maintain their ethnic foodways. An interested cook need not learn traditional foodways solely in a home setting; friends, neighbors, or other acquaintances often contribute their help. Why one person in a family develops a commitment to preserving foodways is a major, unanswered question, yet this pattern is not unusual. One woman, for example, grew up in a German–American enclave along St. Paul's Marshall

Trudy Mahady set the table for a traditional meal at St. Paul's Volksfest Haus, 1983.

Avenue. Her siblings all eventually married persons of Scandinavian heritage. With no children of her own, she found reward and growth in continuing what her mother had taught her and passing those traditions on to her nieces and nephews who acknowledge two ethnic affiliations.[21]

From her German-American neighbors and her mother, this woman absorbed a basic ethnic food pattern. She learned how important it was to keep chicken and beef broth in the house as staple ingredients. Combined with wirsingkohl (a savoy cabbage) and other vegetables including potatoes, the broth became a thick and nourishing soup. Her mother baked rye bread every Saturday morning and occasionally zwiebelkuchen (onion pie). On Saturday nights the family, like many of their neighbors, dined simply on cold sliced German sausage, bread and cheese, fruit kuchen, and homemade beer. Sunday dinner was usually quite special — a roast, chicken, or wienerschnitzel, dumplings or spätzle, and a sweet-and-sour salad. Warm potato salad accompanied schnitzel, since there was no gravy. Sometimes tomatoes, a new commodity for German Americans, were served, often stewed. On Sunday evening, a time for socializing with friends, the family had a simple array of foods, similar to Saturday night's. For the special Christmas dinner, goose, roasted and served with a bread dressing, was her family's choice, a traditional one with most German families.

Maultaschen, a Württemberg regional delicacy resembling giant Italian ravioli in form, was a special family favorite. Noodle dough was rolled out to a thickness of about one-eighth inch. Tablespoonfuls of ground smoked ham mixed with onions, eggs, and parsley were placed along half of the dough, then the other half was folded over the top. The covered dollops of meat filling were then separated into individual dough-wrapped pockets with a knife, sealed, and dropped in boiling broth. The resulting maultaschen, nearly four inches long and half as wide, were served with a green salad. Sometimes the family had maultaschen with spinach filling as a simple, pre-Christmas dish or for Maundy Thursday before Easter Day, a meatless day for Roman Catholics.

Another traditional family holiday treat was Silvesterkrapfen, a deep-fried, cream-filled cake served on New Year's Eve and occasionally on Shrove Tuesday, in order to use up butter and dairy foods before Lent. Prominent at the festive breakfast that marked the conclusion of Lent was hefenkranz, an extra-rich coffeecake sweetened with raisins and traditionally shaped into a wreath. In this particular family, however, the mother made one long braid that she glazed with egg and cream.

Kuchen, a sweet dough filled with fruit and covered with a rich custard, was a cake that this family, like its neighbors, enjoyed throughout the year. Traditionally, the filling changed with the season: kuchen made in the spring contained early ripening fruits, summertime versions took advantage of an array of available ones, while in fall apples were the most common filling. (This seasonal progression is no longer necessary, as canned and frozen products enable bakers to choose a favorite filling any time of the year.)

In Minnesota, German Americans began their Christmas baking soon after Thanksgiving, and, before the days of large home freezers, the order in which things were made depended upon how well they aged. It was not unusual to prepare a half-dozen different types of cookies and other pastries. First came the molded cookies, such as spekulatius, and cut-out cookies, some in the shape of people, upon which certain families fastened paper pictures of St. Nicholas using an edible paste. Next, many Württemberg women made another traditional delicacy, springerle, formed in wooden molds and flavored with anise. These nearly white cookies carry

Leigh Kessel, Minneapolis, arranging kuchen on cooling racks, 1986

the mold's clear imprint of birds, houses, animals, or flowers. Children took turns producing these delights, which were favored as gifts. At the same time, schnitzbrot, a yeasty, heavy bread flavored with brandy or schnaps and sweetened with dried fruits and nuts was baked. Last was the spiced lebkuchen, sometimes shaped into hearts and hung on the Christmas tree.

Most, but not all, families in the Marshall Avenue neighborhood also baked stollen, probably the best-known German holiday bread. This sweet yeast dough, studded with blanched almonds, raisins, grated lemon rind, citron, and candied cherries, is baked, frosted with a sugar icing, and finally decorated with shaved toasted almonds and dried fruit. Today it is also imported from Dresden and sold in specialty shops.[22]

Clearly, the foodways originally brought from Germany to Minnesota are widely varied today. Many traditions are peculiar to specific families or German-American subgroups. The Old Order Amish at Canton, for example, follow a diet similar to that of the Amish in other states. Unlike other Germans, they ignore Christmas but celebrate weddings with two festive meals. The first, following the ceremony, usually consists merely of chicken, mashed potatoes, and a dessert. The evening meal may include

Pauline Mueller making spätzle in the traditional manner, 1983

homemade Amish-style bologna, fried potato pancakes made from the left-over mashed potatoes, noodles in chicken broth (also leftover), and tapi-oca pudding, a community favorite.[23]

Members of the one-hundred-year-old Mennonite community in and around Mountain Lake have managed to perpetuate many traditions, in-cluding a distinctive low-German dialect and foodways. Their foods carry names in both their dialect and the Russian language, a holdover from the group's residence in Transcaucasia during the nineteenth century. Such pas-tries as the flaky, buttery schnetke, papenate (called pfeffernüsse or pep-pernuts in high German), and tweback (zwieback, literally "two baked"), are made weekly and offered to guests, especially at the traditional Sun-day afternoon coffee gatherings called faspa. Other delicacies make an an-nual appearance and include such items as portzilke (New Year's cookies), without which the holiday would not be complete.[24]

Mountain Lake Mennonites do not live cloistered lives; as a rule, how-ever, they are unaware of the foodways of their ethnic neighbors, just as the latter are unaware of theirs. While everyday meals are the typical, sub-stantial meat-and-potatoes affairs found on many Minnesota farm tables, frequently the homemaker will also prepare borscht (soup) in the Men-nonite version (without beets) or serve perischki, a dessert made from dough filled with apples, prunes, cherries, or other available fruits.

Foodways are also interwoven in the traditional observance of the Sab-bath, beginning with preparations the day before. In Mountain Lake the Mennonite Sunday schedule starts with church in the morning, followed by a noontime dinner and a nap or family socializing and, later, a faspa at someone's house at about half past four. At this gathering coffee, bolo-gna or German sausages, fried potatoes, cherry moos (a pudding similar to fruit soup), homemade bread, pastries, and cheese usually accompany conversation. One woman's comment underlines the way in which food traditions are an integral ingredient of the working week as well as holy day: "We always look forward to a faspa on Sunday and we do our bak-ing on Saturday. In fact, it's not Saturday if you don't make tweback!"

Individuals, too, make personal adaptations of traditions. One man who grew up in a Russländer household in North Dakota, for example, remem-bers nephle, tiny triangles of dough that his grandmother mixed with sauer-kraut or put into broth. While he does not make nephle, he consciously carries on a single but persistent German food tradition for his Minneapolis family by turning out a dozen kuchen each month with apples, prunes, apricots, cherries, or California green grapes placed in the custard.[25] For other contemporary German Minnesotans, the traditions emerge only in haute cuisine, such as when they occasionally bake an elegant walnusstorte (walnut torte) or a cream-filled nussroulade (nut roll), which uses no flour, only ground almonds, sugar, and nuts.

Traditional technologies are also adapted to suit individual needs. Among those German Americans who still make spätzle, for example, preparation methods are changing. The dough for this special noodle of unbleached flour, eggs, and water was traditionally mixed and spread on a cutting board with a knife. Then the cook, using the knife's cutting edge, worked the sticky dough to the end of the board and scraped strips of it off into boiling broth. Today most people simply squeeze the dough through a ricer, but some traditionally minded cooks still stir up the batter with a quirl, an instrument with lateral prongs attached to the end of a long handle.

It is evident that German-American ethnicity is reemerging in contemporary Minnesota. Currently, a popularized version of certain traditional foods is presented at festivals and other public occasions. But many of the complex foodways, their meanings, and their historical significance remain part of a rich but relatively private culture.

NOTES

[1] For a detailed overview of this traumatic period, see Clarence A. Glasrud, ed., *A Heritage Deferred: The German-Americans in Minnesota* (Moorhead, Minn.: Concordia College, 1981), especially Colman J. Barry, "Religious and Language Experiences of German-Catholic Americans," 80–89, and Carl H. Chrislock, "The German-American Role in Minnesota Politics, 1850–1950," 104–17; Hildegard Binder Johnson, "The Germans," in *They Chose Minnesota*, ed. Holmquist, 153–84; La Vern J. Rippley, *The German-Americans* (Boston: Twayne, 1976).

[2] Rachel A. Bonney, "Was There a Single German-American Experience?" in *A Heritage Deferred*, ed. Glasrud, 20–31; Rippley, *The German-Americans*, 193.

[3] Interview of Mary Ann Hauser, Trudy Mahady, Pauline Mueller, and Helga Parnell, St. Paul, October 1983.

[4] See Johnson, "The Germans," in *They Chose Minnesota*, ed. Holmquist, 154.

[5] Interview of Mr. and Mrs. Clarence Drexler, Benson, December 1983.

[6] Interview of Nora Lindenfelser, Albertville, January 26, 1984.

[7] Interviews of Ruth Bettendorf, Minneapolis, December 1983, Marla Jean Hermann, Richfield, January 1984.

[8] Hermann interview.

[9] The Pioneer Sausage Company opened in 1949; in 1971 Robert Weik, who grew up in St. Bernard's parish, became a co-owner. "We have over two hundred years of sausage-making experience in this shop with all these older men," said Weik, who prides

himself on the German heritage of his recipes. The market also caters to hunters who wish to have venison steaks preserved.

[10] Interviews of members of the Volksfest Association, October-December 1983. In Germany and Austria today, bratwurst is made without preservatives and sold daily.

[11] Interviews of Marla Jean Hermann, January 1984, Mr. and Mrs. William Hetrick, Benson, December 1983, Pauline Mueller, November 1983.

[12] Daniel J. Boorstin, *The Americans: The Democratic Experience* (New York: Random House, 1973), 307, 327.

[13] Interview of Mr. and Mrs. Bruce Ferris, Osakis, December 1983.

[14] Interviews of Peggy Schatzlein and her sister, Jeanne Eibisch, Minneapolis, November 1983.

[15] Interview of Shirley Washolz, November 1983. Women's roles in German-American families differ somewhat by generation. Those born in the 1920s or 1930s often remark that they followed their husbands' food preferences and cooked to suit them, whatever their own traditions. Younger women tend to be more assertive in their culinary activities.

[16] Here and below, see Hetrick interview.

[17] Interview of Rene Holzer, Minneapolis, October 1983.

[18] Interviews of Marla Jean Hermann, Richfield, January 1984, Fay Sandven, Milan, and Pat Hetrick, Benson, December 1983.

[19] Lindenfelser interview. While cabbage cooked with caraway seeds is typically German, baked potatoes are never found on traditional menus.

[20] For more on the effects of new immigration on established ethnic foodways, see Willard B. Moore, "Metaphor and Changing Reality: The Foodways and Beliefs of the Russian Molokans in the United States," in *Ethnic and Regional Foodways*, ed. Brown and Mussell, 91–112.

[21] Here and four paragraphs below, see Mueller interview. For a contrasting view, see Norval Rindfleisch, "In Loveless Charity," in *The Minnesota Experience: An Anthology*, ed. Jean Ervin (Minneapolis: Adams Press, 1979), 355–75. In many respects, the tradition Mueller shares is Württembergian, not pan-German. Interethnic marriage, generally along religious lines, is an increasingly common pattern, one that deeply affects ethnic life and foodways.

[22] Recipes for stollen are found in many American cookbooks, but its association with German ethnicity remains firm.

[23] Willard B. Moore, "A Recent Immigration to the Upper Mississippi River Valley: The Amish of Canton, MN," in George E. Bates, Jr., et al., *Historic Lifestyles in the Upper Mississippi River Valley* (Lanham, Md.: University Press of America, 1983), 347–68. On the foods of another ethnic group, some of whose members emigrated from Germany, see Jewish chapter, below.

[24] Mennonite tweback, unlike the zwieback that many Americans know as rusks or teething biscuits, is not baked twice. Rather, the term refers to the form of the roll, which is made from two round pieces of dough, the smaller of which is pressed on top of the larger. Here and two paragraphs below, see interviews of Maryann Harder, Butterfield, and Eva Harder, Joyce Bucklin, and Sam and Elva Quirling — all Mountain Lake, February 26, 1985. See also Mountain Lake Gopher Historians, *Off the Mountain Lake Range: A Collection of Old Recipes and Customs Brought to this Country by the Early Settlers of this Community*, rev. ed. (Mountain Lake, Minn.: Mountain Lake Gopher Historians, 1958).

[25] Interviews of Leigh Kessel, Minneapolis, December 1983, January 1984.

Bitten Norvoll putting final touches on a kransekake to be decorated with Norwegian, Danish, and Swedish flags, at a Sons of Norway class, Minneapolis, 1986

THE SCANDINAVIANS

Images of Scandinavian ethnicity for most Minnesotans derive largely from the field of entertainment. Viking football promotions, seasonal festivals such as "Æbleskiver Days" in Tyler or Walker's Scandinavian "Christmas in July" bazaar of decorations and gifts, dance groups, church dinners, and media stories about Norwegian bachelor farmers and record-breaking giant lefse — all set ethnicity apart from the serious world of work.[1] Unfortunately, this superficial and misleading cluster of images has crystallized certain stereotypes that dominate public thinking about Scandinavian foods.

Yet food images reveal much about assimilation, expressing the cultural visibility either experienced by each immigrant group or sought by today's descendants. For example, Swedish meatballs, economical and simple, are well known and commonly eaten by all kinds of Americans, in part because their taste, form, and texture so closely resemble other items in the mainstream American diet. Swedish Americans, like their meatballs, appear to be less separate from the mass of Minnesotans, although their cultural contributions have been enormous. By contrast, whereas the name and basic form of Danish open-faced sandwiches are somewhat familiar to most Americans, the contents and the details of preparation lend this delicacy an air of complexity, sophistication, and elegance. Likewise, the Danes, less numerous than their northern brethren and having immigrated under less severe conditions, maintain a general image of haute cuisine and a deliberate and highly sociable approach to food events. Norwegian Americans seem indelibly linked with lutefisk, a boardlike, salt-preserved, imported codfish which is treated with lye, repeatedly rinsed, and boiled. The result, sometimes flaky but often gelatinous, is a feast that tends to polarize those who discuss it: One either loves lutefisk or detests it; either reaction reinforces a relatively visible Norwegian-American ethnic profile. A "survival food" for Norwegian immigrants and early pioneers, lutefisk continues to lend that group an image of cultural tenacity in the face of hardship.[2]

Scandinavians seem to hold two views of what constitutes ethnic foodways and, similarly, two views of the role foodways fill in real life. One view holds that hard-working, marginally subsistent immigrants and their children used what was available from their environment and followed as well as they could a traditional diet that they knew to be reliable. Some Minnesotans attribute the intake of fats, starches, and meats in their forebears' diets to people laboring long hours and needing lots of calories. They observe that the old diets lacked variety, even in Minnesota, and one was obliged to eat a great deal in order to benefit at all.

Others, remembering the Great Depression, insist that ethnic cooking required too much time and ingredients too dear for their budgets. Not until the 1950s did these persons feel comfortable enough to buy, or even make, the delicacies they consider ethnic. Which set of conditions, then, strengthened the folk cooking of the Scandinavians in Minnesota: hardscrabble or affluence?

Early adversity led to the establishment of ethnic organizations which assumed the Old World functions of the village. Fraternal orders and insurance programs, for example, established networks that helped new Americans survive and maintain their Old World identity and values. Yet today these cultural institutions would not exist without some degree of affluence among the members. And with affluence comes, at least for some, leisure time which, if only at Christmas, can be bent toward learning about and preparing the traditional foods. Ethnic affiliation is kept alive and adaptive in a changing world through educational programs and seminars, charter flights, and tourism.[3] In the end, ethnic identification is some mixture of the romantic and colorful but expensive foods, on the one hand, and the meager and earthy one-pot meals that continue to be popular today.

The image of a pan-Scandinavian foodways tradition in Minnesota was established and accepted early on. Documents from the nineteenth century show that writers, and therefore their readers, saw a less-than-distinctive diet among the Swedes and Norwegians. By the mid-1940s, a reporter characterized a Minnesota Christmas Eve: "Lutefisk would be there in big portions with butter or cream gravy, potato sausage and Swedish meat balls, pickled herring and a dozen other piquant appetizers, brown Swedish beans with their sweet-sour sauce, rice pudding and lingon berries, cakes and cookies in so great a variety that it is hardly possible to eat a sample of each — spritz, rosettes, smorbakelse [*sic*], kringler, pepperkakor and many more. Feasting would go on far into the evening."[4]

A more recent magazine article described "A Scandinavian Thanksgiving in North Dakota," a portrait of two rural families of the pre-World War II era — one Norwegian and the other Swedish — visiting and sharing their food at Thanksgiving. In a sunny dining room with windows looking south to an endless, snow-covered prairie, "Places for fourteen were laid with white china on a white damask tablecloth. There was no color on the table except a luscious ribbon of translucent jellies, relishes, and preserves that ran down its length and caught the sun — like a feast spread out in the snow. In the center was a glorious tomato aspic crown, and streaming down on either side were grape and chokeberry jellies, rhubarb jam, plum preserves, pickled beets, spiced crab apples, and watermelon pickles."[5]

To this exercise in counterpoint was added, after prayers, the *pièce d'occasion*, "diaphanous steamed *lutefisk*. . . . glistening with drawn butter" and served with mashed potatoes, köttbullar (Swedish meatballs), creamed carrots and peas, scalloped corn, and lefse, followed by a hazelnut meringue cake and, finally, fancy cookies: fattigmann, krumkake, pepparkakor, and many others.

Within such scenes are many important clues to patterned borrowing among Scandinavians and to the subtle ways in which each group, through conscious commitment or instinctive loyalty, preserves its distinctiveness. To begin with, Norwegian lutefisk is called lutfisk by the Swedes. A small matter, to be sure, but in addition Swedes prefer a cream gravy on their fish instead of glistening butter. Danes would never offer lutefisk — even at Christmas. Norwegian Americans today never mention Swedish brown beans.

Norwegians claim that Swedes make their fruit or sweet soups from "lighter" ingredients — golden raisins, pears, peaches, and so forth — while the Norse version calls for prunes, black raisins, and other darker fruits. Swedish Americans reply that they have no fixed preferences. Danish Americans toss any fruit in the household into their sødsuppe: home-canned, dried, or store-bought, without distinction. All groups agree, however, that this soup, nearly a compote, can serve as a one dish meal.

Perhaps more important than the differences are the underlying similarities linking all Scandinavians. Colors and textures are contrasted in culinary pairings: lutefisk and meatballs, sweet relishes and jellies with hearty meats or delicate fish, and the brightly colored condiments and berries against the white or subdued major colors. Unmentioned is another set of rules for all Scandinavian pastries: cookies are never overly sweet but are rich in cream; they are never garishly colored but are traditionally served undecorated, unless a bit of powdered sugar is sprinkled on top. Their quality (and, perhaps, their ultimate symbolic message) has to do with substance and control. The forms of the Scandinavian fattigmann, rosett, sandbakkels, brunekage, and certainly krumkake and goro are unique and precise. They are perfectly achieved only with much practice and patience.

The ubiquitous Norwegian kransekake (kransekage in Danish, kranskaka or mandelringstårta in Swedish), a popular festive pastry consisting of layers of baked rings, is a good example of a food prepared by Scandinavians and adapted to various settings. Made of almond paste, sugar, and egg whites, each succeeding ring is somewhat smaller than the one below it, thus forming a pyramid usually about eighteen inches high. Decorated with loops of white sugar-syrup icing, flags designating the national heritage of the honored guest, snappers, flowers, a crown, medallions for silver or golden anniversaries and even costumed figures for weddings, the kransekake requires two persons to serve — one to lift the cake (for servings are always begun at the bottom) and a second to remove each ring and then ceremoniously break it into pieces for each guest. As a rule, each Scandinavian community has a dozen or more persons, usually retired or widowed, who specialize in the time-consuming task of making the cakes, which are usually ordered for weddings, confirmation luncheons, anniversaries, and senior citizens' birthdays.[6]

There are many other patches of common ground. Norwegians, Danes, and Swedes share each others' sausage styles (although only the Norwegians eat blood sausage with cream), puddings, soups, certain traditional preserved items such as headcheese (sylte in Norwegian, sylta in Swedish), herring, torsk (cod), and boiled potatoes. Less visible to outsiders are the Swedish and Norwegian traditions of boiling potato dumplings in water flavored with pork or ham or the way some but not all Swedish communities now serve Norwegian lefse with their lutfisk, while most but not all Norwegians prefer to eat flat bread with this meal. Although the Danes are the acknowledged superiors in making open-faced sandwiches, both Norwegians and Swedes follow the same general style: thinly sliced dark rye bread (never Swedish limpa that most consider too sweet), squared corners with no crusts, butter spread to the very edges, and a generous portion of topping.

Currently in Minnesota the preparation and distribution of ethnic foods can be a money-making proposition. As noted above, informal specialists supply most Scandinavian communities with festive pastries. This tradition has roots in Norway, at least, where itinerant bakers prepared certain breads and cakes, sometimes only twice annually. In Minnesota, this folk system is supported and enhanced by the prime suppliers of ingredients — the ethnic markets.

One of the most unusual phenomena in the state is the extent to which nonethnic food markets, even locally operated chain stores, cater to Scandinavian customers. In the small town of Dassel, the local supermarket stocks homemade Swedish sausage from the manager's own smokehouse, as well as lutefisk, headcheese, fresh potato sausage, and lefse. For those who prepare sausages at home, the store also sells the casings, and for those who have no time to give to ethnic food preparation, it offers "Scandinavian" meatballs — already formed and covered with a spicy sauce.

Minneapolis Scandinavians (and those who drive in from outlying towns for periodic replenishment) frequently shop at a combination food market and gift shop that offers a variety of specialty implements for preparing Scandinavian pastries. Also for sale are a wide range of imported and domestic spices, meats, fish, and baked goods, imported Swedish knäcke-bröd (crisp bread), Danish dry mustard for fish sauces, fresh and canned lingonberries, almond paste for baking, cheeses such as gammelost and gietost, and even reindeer meatballs. The store also prepares a long list of holiday foods which are unique to Scandinavians and generally available only if prepared in the home: fruit-soup mix, rullepølse, spekekjøtt (cured meat), and pinnekjøtt (steamed or roasted mutton). This store, like many others in the state, offers annual autumn sales of Swedish meatball mix for the approaching holidays; each store's recipe, including spices, is somewhat different.[7] Half-page newspaper advertisements usually announce these sales; thus the state's newspapers, especially those in small towns where Scandinavian immigrants settled more than a hundred years ago, are signposts of continuing ethnic foodways.

Less visible and less effective in the grass-roots ethnic foodways tradition are restaurants. Visitors to the state invariably ask about Scandinavian dining, and the lack of such restaurants is erroneously attributed to a diminishing interest in these groups' foods. The absence of "Scandinavian," much less Norwegian, Danish, or Swedish dining, however, is probably best explained by ethnic group members. They suggest that regional differences within any ethnic group, the difficulty of maintaining high quality in dishes that require much time to prepare, and the relatively narrow range of entrees in the Scandinavian tradition discourage restaurateurs.

Nevertheless, an ethnic influence exists. In Austin a restaurant whose owner is part Swedish and part British offers generous appetizers of pickled herring and features dark rye bread. The napkins carry the Swedish phrase, "Var så god" (loosely translated, "Eat well!"), and the corned beef is served with a distinctly Danish mustard sauce introduced by a Danish-American pastry cook over a decade ago. From time to time, the owner prepares his mother's Swedish chicken and "heavy noodles," traditionally cut with a knife and dried over a chair back.[8]

In western Minnesota's Red River Valley ethnic fare is more subtly announced but heartily pursued. A stranger entering a roadside cafe in Benson might scan the menu and never see a Scandinavian dish. But above the cash register or taped to the door near the pay telephone is a crude sign: "Klubb. Wed. 11 a.m.," announcing what everyone in town already knows — the establishment will serve the Norwegian potato dumpling on Wednesday. What is understood, further, is that on Thursday the klubb not consumed on Wednesday will be sliced, fried, and served with syrup and butter for breakfast or lunch. The dish has long had a strong following in this region. High-school boys in Watson, Milan, and other towns have been known to abandon school lunches on days when klubb is served in their towns' cafes.[9]

A more ostentatious approach is employed at a Willmar motel whose rosemaling-decorated "Hardanger Room" offers torsk with its sirloin steaks and schedules a lutefisk dinner each December. But the profit motive does not stop with commercial enterprise. Rotary clubs, Masonic lodges, and, in those areas where Scandinavians are densely settled, even public schools prepare and sell foods at annual dinners, bazaars, and fund raisers. Churches founded by bands of Swedish immigrants and those primarily attended by Minnesotans of Norwegian ancestry still serve their own versions of Christmas holiday dinners: lutefisk (lutfisk) and meatballs, boiled potatoes, fruit soup, pastries, and coffee. More often than not, teen-agers from the congregation help with both preparation and serving. In this manner, a sense of commitment and identity is instilled in the young, and techniques are passed from one generation to another.[10]

Large-scale events such as these require sources where bulk quantities can be purchased at the lowest cost. Minnesota entrepreneurs have risen to the occasion. Lutefisk and torsk, for example, can be obtained from outlets in Duluth, Minneapolis, and Glenwood. The distributor in the latter town completes the process of soaking and rinsing the fish and ships it throughout the Upper Midwest. Accompanying his shipments to churches and other institutions are complimentary placemats telling the story of the fish's passage from capture near the Lofoten Islands of Norway to Minnesota.[11]

For meats and meat products, Scandinavians, mostly in rural areas, use a modern equivalent of the farmer's smokehouse — the town frozen food locker plant. At this centrally located facility, informal groups of farmers carry on the folk customs of slaughtering and gathering fresh blood. Thus they are still able to prepare the all-but-extinct blodklubb (blood dumpling) and blood sausage. This method of storage, too, allows Scandinavian Americans to maintain their thrifty traditions of using flank cuts for rullepølse and preserving ham hocks and pig's feet. They have also adopted the more modern practice of putting up game and fish by freezing.[12]

By the late twentieth century, Minnesota's citizens of Norwegian, Danish, and Swedish heritage had much in common with Americans of other ethnic backgrounds. They also shared foodways that have come to be called simply "Scandinavian." Yet in addition each group maintained traditions that distinguished it from the others as well as from the more unrelated American ethnic groups. The sections that follow explore both these similarities and differences.

THE NORWEGIANS

The humble lutefisk is not the sole reason for public awareness of Norwegian-American foods. Nordics themselves are often enthusiastic promoters of their ethnic identity and the entire range of foods that are so strongly retained in their Minnesota diets. Irrepressible in their zeal, the Norwegian Americans of Starbuck, for example, sought both quality and quantity as they attempted in July 1983 to produce the world's largest lefse, made with an old binder roller. Quality and quantity also abound at the annual julebord, a holiday feast held each January at Mindekirken (Norwegian Lutheran Memorial Church), Minneapolis, where two dozen different dishes suggest that the term be translated "groaning board."[13]

The remarks of Norwegian immigrants are a revealing commentary on Minnesota's early foodways. Many of the staples of the midwesterners' pioneer diet were unfamiliar to the immigrants. Their distrust was echoed in one man's diary in 1843: "Food here is not the right sort for the newcomers, since the usual food here is pork, beef, and wheat bread, whereas in Norway they were accustomed to coarse rye bread, milk, and cheese."[14]

Slowly the immigrants adapted. Housewives delighted in the American flour that yielded bread and cakes unheard of in their native villages. Wild and domestic fowl, considerably plumper and generally larger than found in the Scandinavian countries, enriched their larders.[15] Kjøtboller (meatballs) made from beef and pork, American-style bacon, sweet corn, and a strange delight called watermelon all appeared on the immigrants' tables, and the process of growing from immigrant to ethnic began.

Randi Johansen, Minneapolis, garnishing trays of open-faced sandwiches to be served at the Mindekirken's annual rømmegraut fund raiser, 1983

If the Norwegian immigrants missed their North Atlantic cod (until it could be imported) and suspected the plentiful but unfamiliar vegetables might be noxious, there were certain foods that were both known and reliable. Potatoes, for example, had been introduced to Norway in the nineteenth century to alleviate food shortages, and their virtues had even been praised from the pulpit by what came to be known as "potato priests." This worthy tuber, dried peas, and a few other vegetables became a solid part of the diet. Abundant midwestern dairy products, mutton, and the lush profusion of American berries and fruits were all embraced in the frontier diet.

By the turn of the century, purely Norwegian meals had all but vanished, and cooks concentrated their efforts on high celebration in the Christmas season. One daughter of immigrants recalled the entire process of yuletide food production, beginning with cookie baking and followed by the preparation of rull (a rolled flank of beef or lamb, stuffed with pork; see also Danish section), headcheese, and lutefisk, bought in long strips that hung outside the meat market in freezing weather. Preparing lutefisk was a process in itself. For three days hardwood was burned in a clean stove. The ashes were then used in a lye solution to clean the fish before it could be boiled on top of the stove.[16]

In many rural and urban communities today, Norwegian Americans have either incorporated a lively foodways program into the meetings of already established institutions or have inaugurated clubs or activities that are in some measure concerned with eating and socializing. In Minneapolis, post-World War II immigrants founded Kontakt, a social club that organizes get-togethers and sports activities, always including a well-planned repast of Norwegian favorites. Better known are torskklubbene (codfish clubs) whose members gather periodically to enjoy each other's company as well as imported North Atlantic cod — poached, boiled, or baked and served with butter and akevitt. In some small towns such as Dassel, the function of the torskklubbe is assumed by a local fraternal order or lodge with so many Norwegian members that there is little difference ethnically between such gatherings and a club founded solely by Norwegians. Churches, too, organize dinners and luncheons, usually to raise funds. As many Norwegians testify, the interest in food runs unusually deep in the church context.

For the Norwegian immigrant, the parish church in America continued to be a focal point of community activity. Parish life, however, developed in a manner far different from that in Norway. While that country's pastors are part of the state administrative system, Norwegian-American ministers are employed by, and therefore closer to, the community; social

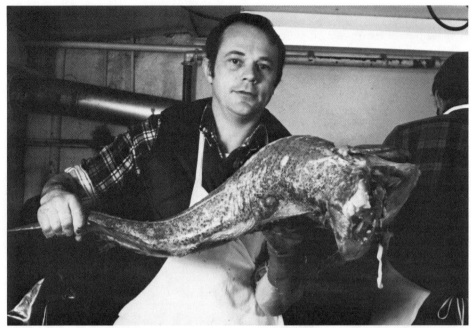

A volunteer worker helping clean and prepare the fish for the Sons of Norway annual torsk dinner in Minneapolis, 1979

life at the church is more intensely and directly connected with community interests. Norwegian pastors in America have generally had to face, if not accept, the phenomenon that ethnic expression is indelibly linked with the church. Norwegians readily accepted the nineteenth-century advent of church kitchens and used theirs to preserve and develop ethnic cooking. Sometimes today pastors jokingly complain, and congregation members agree, that Norwegian Americans are more interested in food than in theological discussions. "If one could get to heaven by eating, our congregation would be first!" testified one church supporter. "We come to church more for the coffee pot than for prayers," confessed another. Yet the vital and supportive network of services to the elderly and the caring programs upheld by volunteers belie this image. Nevertheless, if nineteenth-century Norwegian pastors in America had to accept cultural pluralism, including English-language services and "American" morals, modern clergy must consider the continuing role of the church as a vehicle for ethnic expression.[17]

For many young Norwegian Americans who leave their homes and communities for college, foodways patterns continue. Interviews in Minnesota's most densely populated Norwegian-American communities revealed that a large number of college-aged people enjoy cultural continuity through the periodic ethnic dinners at Augsburg College in Minneapolis or at St. Olaf College, Northfield. The latter's annual Christmas smørgåsbord for students, their families, and any devotee of Norwegian food, is sold out early. It provides what has come to be a standard ethnic (and not necessarily authentic) feast: lutefisk, meatballs, rømmegraut (a cream pudding), søtsuppe (sweet or fruit soup), lefse, and the traditional rich cookies, which at this event are sometimes colored with red and green sugar sprinkles. In this and other ways, colleges founded through Norwegian Lutheran churches extend the ethnic network in which members can meet potential marriage partners, strengthen their values, and continue to sample the foods of their cultural heritage.[18]

Norwegian Americans celebrate the Christmas holidays much as they enjoy their food — intensively and extensively — carrying the holiday well past the usual twelve days of Christmas to tjuendedagen, the thirteenth day of January.[19] Traditionally Advent, the beginning of the Christmas season, is also the quiet period following the harvests. In colder climes it is a time for visiting and sharing (or displaying) the fruits of the year's labor. Food that is offered at this time should represent the highest possible quality, whether out of personal pride or as a sacred symbol of love and the nourishment one gains from love.

In old Norway, Christmastide was a time for brewing beer, house cleaning, and celebration. Some Norwegian Americans today still remember lillejul, or Little Christmas, on December 23, a day of supreme effort to clean, scrub, and bake. As one Norwegian-born woman testified, "For Americans, Christmas morning is the end of things and a letdown. For Norwegians, it is only the beginning!"[20]

In Norway each region and valley had its own variation of Christmas festivities. Foods also differed somewhat from family to family, as they do today in Minnesota, although certain dishes are typically served and eagerly anticipated. In Norway, the family will often eat hastily and frugally on St. Thomas's Day, December 21, on lillejul, and right up until dusk on Christmas Eve, the time of the holiday's most luxurious meal. For many, that main course consists of a pork roast or ribs cooked with juniper berries and served with fårikål (mutton and cabbage stew). This entree is preceded by warm fruit soup (to be served next day as a cold dessert). The meal concludes with a delicate rice pudding in which one almond has been hidden; whoever finds it is rewarded with a special gift.

For many Norwegian Americans, lutefisk is obligatory, although it is usually served with meatballs in consideration of those whose tastes are less staunch. Boiled potatoes are also required, and sometimes lefse or flat bread, the latter usually preferred with lutefisk as a contrast in texture.

Some families choose to follow what is considered the American custom of having a large meal on Christmas Day and a lighter menu the evening before. In that case, oyster stew, served with lefse and flat bread, is a Christmas Eve favorite in many households. Particular dishes aside, the traditional pattern finds Norwegian Americans in Minnesota eating simply — klubb, soups, or porridge — before whichever Christmas dinner inaugurates the holiday. Some Nordics reserve December 26 as the day for lutefisk, celebrating the main day with American-style turkey, usually with meatballs as an additional main course.

Better known to the world at large is the Norwegian tradition of baking cookies. Many hours of kitchen work in mid-December result in a profusion of delicacies — both Scandinavian and American. Norwegian cookies come in many distinctive shapes, but all have a rich, buttery texture and are available in every home. Eaten with coffee throughout the day as guests drop in, given to children, munched while watching television — the cookies are a tradition of indulgence without regret.

In Minnesota, for members of Mindekirken, the annual julebord signals the end of the holidays. This Christmas table, like the season itself, holds a rich array of traditional dishes, authentically prepared, and, very clearly, deeply appreciated. The buffet includes pork roast, meatballs, and

Kari Foss pouring coffee, a symbol shared by several ethnic groups, at the Mindekirken's annual rømmegraut fund raiser, 1983; the coffeepot reads (in Swedish) "Coffee drops are the best of all earthly drinks."

medisterpølse (pork sausage), pickled herring in several different sauces, boiled potatoes, a traditional pease porridge, Norwegian-style sauerkraut with caraway seeds, fiskecabaret (a fish-based mousse), ham, headcheese, rull (mutton roll), a variety of pickles and relishes, cranberries, lingonberries, homemade white and dark breads, American caramel rolls, lefse, and flat bread. At a separate table, guests help themselves to the usual holiday pastries: fattigmann, rosetter, sandbakkels, krumkake, Berlinerkranser, or spritz, and then bløtkake (a sumptuous layer cake topped with thick whipped cream), rice pudding with raspberry sauce, a caramel pudding, and finally, kransekake, the tall tower of baked rings, decorated with white sugar icing and Norwegian flags. Coffee is served continuously, and a special European touch is added through artfully folded cloth napkins and the painstakingly prepared pyramids of molded butter balls.[21]

"Praise the Lord and Pass the Lutefisk: The Joys of Being an Ethnic Christian" was the title of an address delivered in Northfield some years ago by a Lutheran bishop visiting from Seattle. Not only does lutefisk stand as a complex symbol in Norwegian-American foodways, but it is also one of many dishes about which young Norwegians, visiting this country for the first time, know little or nothing. Many Americans are surprised to learn that lutefisk does not enjoy in Norway the attention it receives on this side of the Atlantic. And it probably never did. Disdained today as "peasant" or "fisherfolk" food, it is available in Norway's major cities and comes in plastic "boil bags" that can be put in microwave ovens, thereby avoiding one of the dish's major faults — the lingering smell in the kitchen.

Initially, Norwegians in America went without lutefisk. Then salted cod was shipped from Massachusetts and the pioneers began their own luting — the process of soaking and rinsing. Minnesotans of Norwegian ancestry insist that their forebears brought lutefisk with them on the ships during emigration. Others believe that lutefisk is all they had to eat at first on the frontier. In any event, the fish is linked symbolically with hardship and courage in Minnesota.[22]

Cod are caught in the North Atlantic mainly in January and February, processed over a three-week drying period, wrapped in burlap, and shipped in one-hundred-pound bales. Upon arrival or upon order from domestic clients, the boardlike cod undergo a second three-week process, consisting of alternate lye and fresh-water soaks and rinses, designed to soften and swell the flesh. Some distributors attempt to shorten the processing period by using caustic soda to dissolve the lye, but the results are not consistently satisfactory.[23]

Norwegians, wherever they reside, always eat lutefisk doused with melted butter and serve it with boiled potatoes. While some lutefisk lovers enjoy the dish throughout the year and a few stores stock it regularly, for most Norwegians lutefisk is a holiday specialty. Cold, leftover lutefisk may be eaten wrapped in lefse, but there is generally little enthusiasm for it after its initial appearance at a holiday table.

The favorites of Norwegian Americans, especially at Christmas, are fattigmann, sandbakkels, krumkake, Berlinerkranser, goro, rosetter, kringler, and julekake. Most cookbooks print a variety of recipes for these cookies and cakes, and bakers may even pencil in suggestions from close friends whose results seem tastier than those produced from the printed version. Flour, butter, eggs, sugar, and cardamom are the basic ingredients for each. Fattigmann require sweet cream, goro use cognac or vanilla, and kringler call for anise oil. Sandbakkels are a simple, year-round favorite; almond extract and finely chopped almonds give them a rich and "sandy" texture, thereby explaining their name.

If these delicacies are uniformly rich, each is also unique in form, a feature which adds to the fun of making them. Goro, krumkake, and rosetter are shaped on baking irons, which once were stove-top implements but today are often electric. Goro are rectangular and usually depict a religious scene impressed upon the dough. Krumkake are thin, round, and flat but are then rolled, usually into cones for easy stacking. Rosetter are dipped and deep fried to become crisp, delicate wheels or flower shapes. Berlinerkranser are shaped like wreaths. Sandbakkels are baked in fluted tins. Fattigmann are more complex: a slit is cut longways in a generously sized diamond shape of fresh dough; one end corner is pulled through the slit and tucked fast before the cookies are deep fried. Julekake, a Christmas cake, calls for yeast and citron and is basically a sweet bread baked in loaves. Many Norwegian Americans who take the time to bake cookies will not bother with a julekake but purchase one at a reliable bakery.

The festive kransekake has a macaroonlike taste. Seldom seen at Christmas parties unless the gathering is unusually large and of some special importance, it is the one Norwegian pastry that will most likely appear at a wedding. One Minneapolis Norwegian who bought the delicacy from a local specialist flew to her son's wedding in New York City with the boxed kransekake on her lap.[24]

Equally festive is the bløtkake (similar to a Danish delicacy), which contemporary ethnic cookbooks sometimes call the sunshine cake. Popular at birthdays and other parties, it is a five-egg layer cake, light, fluffy, and laden with whipped cream. Between the layers one places generous portions of thickened fruit pudding.

In Norway today lefse is omitted from full meals, as are all breads except flat bread; in Minnesota, however, lefse appears regularly as a unique ethnic specialty at community dinners, bazaars, and family meals. There seems to be an infinite variety of lefse produced in the villages, valleys, and regions of Norway, but in Minnesota the item is fairly predictable. Specifically referred to as "potato lefse" in Norway, the usual Minnesota version calls for mashed potatoes, salt, shortening, and flour. The ingredients are combined while hot, then chilled, rolled into thin flat rounds, and baked on a stove top or a large griddle. The most typical lefse in Norway, especially from the western regions, is here called "Hardanger" or "Norwegian" lefse. Three egg yolks, baking soda, and buttermilk replace the potatoes. When baked, this lefse is extremely crisp and must be softened before serving by being placed between two damp towels. Kept dry, it may be stored indefinitely; in fact, rural Norwegians bake lefse only a few times a year, storing the accumulation in an outbuilding called a bryggehaus.[25]

The modern Norwegian American's lefse grill might be sold as a "Heritage Grill" or a pancake griddle and is usually thought of as an all-purpose

Margaret Overland, Minneapolis, flipping lefse to brown its second side, 1979

cooking surface.[26] The "lefse stick," a flat two-foot by three-quarter-inch wide wand, is an indispensable utensil that the cook slips under the lefse, deftly turning it to brown on both sides.

Minnesota lefse is somewhat thinner than a commercially prepared tortilla but is much larger and softer. Traditionally, the surface is a mottled brown and white, a result of uneven cooking due to variations in flour, potatoes, or other ingredients. The younger generations of Norwegian Americans, especially those who learned to cook lefse in church kitchens, are more demanding of consistency. In order to achieve an even-colored lefse and eliminate brown spots, they use commercially prepared potato flakes and rely on one brand of flour, which the community has agreed is the best.

Lefse is served plain, with butter, butter and sugar, or wrapped around a filling. Many think of lefse when they want a snack and sometimes use it as a vehicle for herring, goat-milk cheese (jokingly called "Norwegian peanut butter" because of its color, consistency, and popularity), cold mashed potatoes, sliced meatballs, or even cold lutefisk.

Traditionally, Norwegians eat the kinds of bread Americans know — white, dark rye, or whole-wheat loaves — at breakfast, with snacks, and as a sandwich base, but never with main meals. Flat bread is preferred with fish, especially herring, and most native Norwegians have a liking for crumbled flat bread in a bowl of tettemelk, which resembles stringy yoghurt. In Norway, too, the consistency of flat bread varies widely with region, family, and type of flour — rye, wheat, or oatmeal. All of these recipes prevail throughout Minnesota; in Milan, families make flat bread from graham flour and a sweetener, with results surprisingly close in taste to the American commercially made graham cracker.[27] Most Minnesota food stores carry some version of flat bread, usually a wafer-thin, rectangular crisp bread of a consistent beige color, imported from a Scandinavian country. Similar flat bread is served in Scandinavian restaurants.

Klubb, like lefse, varies greatly, depending upon the Norwegian area of origin. Less widely appreciated than lefse, this dumpling is made from a mixture of grated raw and boiled potatoes, flour, salt, water, and, occasionally, cream. Two types prevail: blodklubb combines fresh pork blood, sugar, and rye flour. A more popular version in Minnesota is a white klubb that omits the blood. For extra flavor, a piece of suet or salt pork is pressed into the center of each before cooking. Both types are boiled in a pot of water in which a ham hock has simmered to add flavoring. Seldom eaten here but remembered as a staple in Norwegian seacoast towns is a white klubb that is cooked in water flavored with simmered fish heads.[28]

Graut means "porridge," of which there are many kinds in traditional Norwegian cooking. In Minnesota's Norwegian ethnic churches and clubs, rømmegraut has emerged as another of the ethnic dishes that, like lefse and lutefisk, are as much symbols as they are food. Rømmegraut calls for sour cream of the type available on Norwegian farms. In Minnesota, an extra-heavy sweet cream, approximately 35 percent butterfat, is combined with a little flour, warm milk, salt, sugar, and some fresh lemon juice. The ingredients are cooked for several hours and stirred with a whisk, a sturdy spoon, or, in keeping with tradition, a tvare. This handy implement is made from the top of an evergreen tree, the end branches of which are clipped short to form "teeth" or tines, dried, and stripped of bark. It is an excellent example of a folk tool in Norwegian ethnic culture.

As a result of the long cooking, butterfat rises to the surface of the mixture and is periodically spooned off into a bowl. When the graut is done, the reserved melted butter is poured over each serving, on top of which Norwegian Americans like to sprinkle sugar and cinnamon. But they seldom use the graut as a dessert, despite its puddinglike quality. Today it often serves as the main dish of a special luncheon, but traditionally it is a first course in a larger meal. As a drawing card for a fund-raising luncheon, rømmegraut, served in huge, steaming bowls, is paired with small sandwiches of cheese or spicy sausage slices and coffee. The basic recipe in Norway is the same, although instead of cinnamon and sugar some top it with chopped, boiled eggs. In both countries, Norwegians, as a rule, prefer to accompany the rømmegraut meal with akevitt, believing that the alcohol will counteract the cholesterol in the cream.[29]

Rømmegraut is frequently referred to in Norwegian folklore, usually as a gift for the nisse (barn spirit) or a bribe for the trolls.[30] Folk medical beliefs dictated that new mothers consume continual dosages to aid digestion or the flow of breast milk. In modern times, the custom has been continued, and Minnesotans of Norwegian heritage recall taking rømmegraut as a gift to the mothers of newborn babies. In Norway this rich porridge or something akin to it was also served to field hands, often as a symbolic gesture toward the richness of the harvest. And a Norwegian exchange student at Augsburg College relates that rømmegraut is sometimes served at midtsommer (midsummer) celebrations in June, on fetetirsdag (Shrove Tuesday), and at the beginning of Advent.

Clearly, rømmegraut is more than a rich porridge for Norwegians and Norwegian Americans; it seems to symbolize fertility and productivity in many forms. This connection is not new, for in a letter to his family over a hundred years ago, a Norwegian immigrant wrote that the soil in

*Hanna Solheim stirred
rømmegraut for the
Mindekirken's annual
fund raiser, 1983; her
husband Martin made
the tvare from the
top of the family
Christmas tree.*

southern Minnesota was so rich that "One could make rommegraut of it!"[31]

Norwegian Americans do not have a highly elaborated tradition of preparing meats. Sausages such as pølse and rull (rolled flank of beef or lamb) are a pan-Scandinavian manner of using all cuts of meat to full advantage. Norwegian rull is identical to the Danish, although seasonings sometimes vary. In Minnesota, however, Norwegians alone seem to prefer blood sausage lightly fried and then doused with cream or syrup.

Nearly every Norwegian-American family still consumes the popular lapskaus. Similar to a Danish recipe and sometimes considered a hash or a stew, it is a hearty, one-dish meal of meat, onions, and potatoes. Cold lapskaus sometimes reappears in lefse as a snack. A few Norwegian Americans use the term to refer to leftover meats and vegetables combined and served over boiled potatoes. (A similar dish is plukkfisk made from leftover fish fillets, potatoes, onions, and seasonings in cream sauce.) Lapskaus is usually eaten at home, although some of the older members of St. Olaf Lutheran Church in Austin remember it being served at church suppers twenty years ago.[32]

Whether in the home or in public settings such as church suppers and ethnic festivals and whether for holiday celebrations or routine, secular meals, Norwegian foodways have been adapted to life in contemporary Minnesota. In fact Norwegian edibles have, to some degree, transcended their ethnic boundaries and contributed to the popular image of the state, where lutefisk and lefse are practically household words.

THE DANES

Danish Americans view their foodways with enormous pride. Eating is time set aside — a relaxing social event. In their own words, Danish cuisine is characterized by thrift, yet graced with a certain elegance of style. This style is perhaps a result of the circumstances of immigration, generally devoid of poverty and serious adversity. The Danes' transition to American life was less traumatic than the experiences of other Scandinavians; consequently the Danish-American network of mutual-aid institutions was less strongly developed than those of other ethnic communities.[33]

In many ways, Scandinavian foods in Minnesota reflect eating preferences in Europe of fifty years ago. Yet the cuisine of Denmark seems to have remained fairly stable. Minnesotans visiting relatives in the homeland, a common practice since World War II, frequently remark that the food there seems very much like what they found on their parents' table and their own: "We knew as kids it was special, but we didn't know it was Danish until we left the community and got to see what other people ate!"[34]

Thrift has always been a means to stability for Danes, both in their early, rural settlements at Tyler, Hutchinson, and Askov or in a contemporary condominium in suburban Minneapolis. Regardless of background or income, Danes confide that an economical attitude toward food is a virtue in family life. Research shows that this concern is a pervasive cultural pattern, one that may be manifested in any meal, traditional or otherwise. When asked what a typical Danish meal consists of, the responses quickly flow back: Meat, potatoes, gravy, and pickles! Tuna casseroles! Soup! Frikadeller (Danish meatballs)! While these substantial, thrifty foods convey the realities of contemporary foodways, the special Danish style is apparent only in the complete context of their cooking in Minnesota: time, place, and occasion as well as food.

Christmas among Danish Americans, as for other ethnic groups, is a

Diane Larsen, St. Louis Park, rolling up rullepølse, 1983

special time of year for traditional cooking. A favorite meal on Christmas Eve is pork roast, cooked so that the rind is crisp, served with red cabbage stewed with apples, caramelized small potatoes, and a vegetable. This entree is introduced, in typical Danish fashion, with a soup, and inevitably is followed with ris à l'almande with cherry sauce, a holiday dessert enjoyed by other Scandinavians as well. The Danish tradition of a large and somewhat sumptuous meal on Christmas Eve is explained, in part, by the need to have leftovers for the nisse (barn spirit) who, in turn, will bring in the holiday gifts during the night.

Variations on the meal, however, abound. Goose and turkey are frequent favorites, and Danes claim that they have never heard of anyone else stuffing the birds with prunes, apples, and dried fruit. Two menus, collected from a husband and wife, attest to the continuity of Danish taste as well as the way it was adapted in Minnesota farm kitchens. The husband, born in Denmark, remembers Christmas Eve dinners as soup, frikadeller, a beef roast or chicken, red cabbage, dark pumpernickel bread, wine, and ris à l'almande, followed by coffee. His wife recalls from her childhood in Donnelly chicken soup with dumplings, a baked chicken loaf, dark pumpernickel bread, milk, coffee, and ris à l'almande.[35]

Christmas Day is a time for visiting, and one's table might offer guests several kinds of herring (including a curried variety), sausages, liver pâté, rullepølse, headcheese, shrimp, wine, beer, akvavit, and smørrebrød, the Danish open-faced sandwiches. Danish cheeses, a well-known commodity outside ethnic households, are also on hand. They are usually sliced thin and served on Danish kiks or Swedish knäckebröd, a crisp, rye, cracker-like bread either imported or made in the home. Cheese is always served last at formal dinners.

At Christmastime, too, the Danish cookies appear, many of them resembling cousins from Norway or Sweden. Rosetter, krumkage, and klejner, a Danish diminutive variant of Norwegian fattigmann, are all in abundance, as are a variety of unadorned cookies made from sugar, butter, and cream, such as pretzel-shaped Danish kringler and round, cardamom-flavored cookies and the spicy pebernødder.

But the essence of the Danish style is also apparent in most everyday foods, whether served for lunch or to guests. This style is probably most evident in what Danes choose as preferred ingredients. Their use of vegetables, for example, especially in soups, is unique to Danish food preparation. Parsley pervades their cookery, not only as a garnish but also as a flavoring in cooked dishes, soups, and spreads. Older Minnesota Danes remember grandmother's kitchen garden where large patches of parsley, carrots, peas, and usually kale grew in abundance. Potatoes are common to European tables, but Danes in the homeland and Minnesota prefer to serve new potatoes boiled and seasoned with butter and parsley. Cucumbers were and still are a prize that appear in home-canned pickles seasoned with mustard seed, sugar, celery seed, onions, and fresh dill. These pickles are essential with meats and on certain sandwiches.

In Minnesota, traditional Danish soups exist in great diversity. Vegetable soups are often thick, almost porridgelike, in consistency. Kale, for example, is the principal ingredient in the widely loved grønkålsuppe; cauliflower went into blomkålsuppe, a creamy favorite. Pea and celery are other common varieties. Meat, fish, or chicken broths are considered thin or kødsuppe and are usually served with boller (dumplings), sliced vegetables, or meatballs. A third and very important category is vælling or milk soup thickened with rice, barley, or buckwheat. The best remembered is kærnemælkvælling, which is made from buttermilk and served warm. Called clabbermilk or buttermilk soup today, it is thickened with tapioca and seasoned with fresh lemon and frozen orange-juice concentrate. Some younger Danish Americans have innovated further, concocting a milk-shakelike drink seasoned with cardamom and thickened with rusks and cooked raisins and sometimes grated dark pumpernickel bread. In general, hot soups are customarily served with dark rye bread, and this is the only time when bread is appropriate with a hot meal.[36] A fourth soup, shared with other Scandinavians, is sødsuppe (fruit soup), which may be eaten hot as a first course in a formal dinner or cold as a dessert or a snack. For Old Country Danes, it was sometimes a traditional gift to a new mother.

Older Danish Americans who have a little more time (or simply take more time) continue the custom of preparing homemade soup at least once a week. Grown children request it when visiting parents or grandparents, and if the pattern common to many ethnic groups prevails, the younger generation will begin to make homemade soup and other traditional dishes when their families request it and time allows.

The Danish diet also depends on both fish and red meat, one a product of the country's historic seafaring traditions, the other a result of its rich and carefully conserved agricultural resources. One of the oldest examples of this Danish thrift is rullepølse, a food popular among Norwegians as well. Preparation is often a family event. Danes in Minnesota select a lamb flank, usually approximately twelve by twenty-four inches, and thoroughly scrape it to remove any excess fat. Then they layer thinly sliced pork loin on the flank to a thickness of three-quarters of an inch. The meat is dosed with a mixture of saltpeter and salt and seasoned with pepper, freshly grated cloves, and finely chopped onions. Then it is rolled (thus "rulle") tightly, the end flaps of the roll folded over, and the entire affair

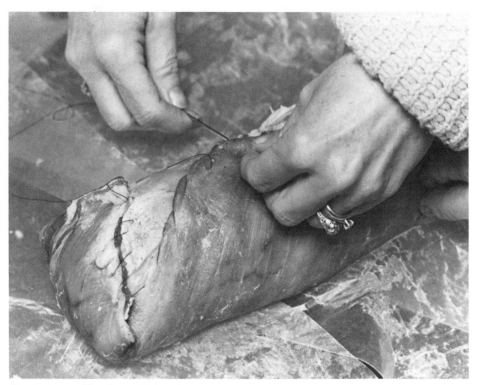

Sewing up rullepølse, 1983

sewn up with cotton thread. Once again the surface is liberally rubbed with saltpeter and salt before the roll is placed in a pan and stored in a dark and cool spot, usually a cellar, for ten days. During this period the amount of salt, aided by frequent turning of the roll, releases meat juices, which are stored for later use as a marinade. When properly drained, the rullepølse is boiled until tender and then pressed, either in a specially designed utensil or under a large stone, to extract excess moisture. The result of this ancient process, carried out on Danish farms and brought to Minnesota in the nineteenth century, is a delicate meat roll that is sliced thin and served with mustard on dark rye bread, accompanied by beer. While some Minnesota Danes continue to prepare it, rullepølse is also available at most urban Scandinavian butcher shops. It is frequently part of a light holiday dinner with a cream soup and ris à l'almande or as festive fare for guests on Christmas Day.[37]

The traditional Danish sausage, medisterpølse, is also very popular with other Scandinavians in Minnesota. Unlike the distinctive Swedish potatiskorv (potato sausage) or the Norwegian version that uses grains, Danish medisterpølse is made either entirely from pork or sometimes from pork and veal. Somewhat spicier in Minnesota than in Denmark today, medisterpølse continues to occupy an important place in the common diet. It is another example of Danish Americans' continuing reliance on meat products.

Fish dishes are also extremely popular among the state's Danes. Perhaps because of the major place it occupies in traditional Danish diets, fish in Minnesota is judged more stringently than some other foods. Danes insist that their fish be fresh. They tend to prefer ocean fish but never, as a rule, dally with the Norwegian and Swedish lutefisk (lutfisk). (In Copenhagen today, street vendors sell live torsk and rødspætte, a flounderlike fish.) Residents of rural Minnesota during the 1930s testify that they never bought frozen fish, both expensive and "foreign" to their taste, although they readily ate fresh-caught fish from nearby streams and lakes. Often, these were smoked and put away to be used in future smørrebrød.

Today, Danish Minnesotans serve torsk boiled, simmered, or prepared in a microwave oven and topped with a cream sauce or with the traditional sennep saus (mustard sauce). Fish fillets, rolled and stuffed with parsley, oysters, and mushrooms, are a typical weekend treat. Herring of every variety and seasoning and anchovies are eaten at any meal, even breakfast. Eel, prepared in a variety of ways and extremely popular in Denmark, is but rarely as available as it was several years ago when the Great Northern Market was open in Minneapolis. But it is not forgotten, at least among the older Danish Americans. Whatever seafood is served is usually accompanied by ample quantities of beer and akvavit because, as the "happy Danes" are prone to remark, "The fish has to swim!"[38]

Thrift and simplicity with a Danish flair also appear in hearty everyday food and in the treatment of leftovers. One Danish version of a supper omelet is æggekage, eggs and cream poured into the frying pan over cooked bacon, not stirred but moved around so that the eggs cook entirely, served with yet more bacon, and garnished with parsley. The most frequently recalled dish and one of continuing popularity, however, is labskovs or biksemad, referred to in the Danish vernacular as ruskomsnusk. Originally this food (similar to the Norwegian lapskaus) was a method of using leftovers — meat and potatoes — with carrots added. It was served over cooked rice with pickles as an accompaniment. Today Danish Americans in Minnesota carefully prepare fresh peas and carrots, tiny new potatoes, and possibly some leftover pork roast and serve it all with a cream sauce. This meal, in form and content, is so close to the American hot dish that the only things to mark it as ethnic are the cook's and consumers' perceptions that it is traditional Danish food.[39]

Desserts such as rabarbegrød (rhubarb pudding) and many other fruit puddings are still another example of Danish frugality. Upon cooking the rhubarb, Danish Americans strain off the syrup for the pudding, saving the fibrous material to garnish a pork roast or to thicken the gravy.[40]

The Danish touch can subtly affect even the common hamburger patty. Danes select the leanest beef or have it ground several times in the shop. At home, they mix in finely chopped onions, parsley, and capers and then fry the mixture gently until it is just done. The juices, with a little butter and flour added, are whipped into a savory brown gravy and poured over the patty and the entire affair is served as bøf med løg (beef with onions).

Morning memories bring out recollections of the famous Danish æbleskiver. In Minnesota, this round pancake has become popular as a breakfast treat on cold winter mornings, although in Denmark they are exclusively an afternoon snack, served with coffee, or sometimes as a second course at formal dinners following the sødsuppe. Æbleskiver require specially designed skilletlike pans with seven cup-shaped wells; a dollop of rich batter is dropped into each and cooked briefly on the stove top. Sometimes a skive (sliver) of apple is added, although the pancakes are usually made plain and served with powdered sugar and fruit jelly or preserves. An even more radical departure from pure Danish custom occurs when Minnesotans serve æbleskiver with maple syrup and bacon or ham.[41]

Despite its low profile, Danish-American ethnic cooking is a major vehicle of cultural expression. And the Danish perspective on quality remains an essential, if not a major, element in this expression. The case of the currently popular rødspætte dinners in St. Paul is a good example. In the mid-1970s, in response to the good-natured chauvinism of the ubiquitous torskklubbe organized by the lively Norwegian Americans, a handful of Danes planned and organized a series of dinners to take place annually during the winter months. With typical Danish epicurean aplomb, they chose as the centerpiece the famous rødspætte, a flounderlike ocean fish served in the best restaurants of Denmark. There are many ways to prepare this delicacy, but the Minnesota Danes prefer it deep fried and served with boiled potatoes, cabbage slaw, and a fancy Danish dessert. Singing and numerous toasts with beer and akvavit make for a lively occasion. Begun in a modest fashion, the rødspætteklub grew and eventually moved to the German-American Volksfest Haus in St. Paul, which offers a large dining room and catering service. Enjoying professional preparation and a relaxing atmosphere, the club remains at a fixed number of members with a

Esther Sorensen, Marie Miltersen, and Edna Flint of Askov preparing for a mid-morning snack of æbleskiver, 1983

lengthy waiting list. The elegant rødspætte serves now as an effective symbol of Danish pride; the fact that it is prepared by German Americans is no hindrance.[42]

Danish and American tastes have influenced each other. The Danish penchant for baked delicacies is demonstrated as much by the dozens of home-made doughnuts Danish-American mothers prepared for hungry children returning from school as in their traditional holiday cookies. The Waldorf and Jell-O salads they carried to community gatherings also show the influence of life in America.[43]

But within this mix of things, the one question Danes always raise is whether or not the world knows that the "Danish pastry" sold in American coffee shops is not the authentic item. Danish desserts in their true forms are a far cry from the commercially packaged snacks which have been so labeled. The real "Danish," called kringle, is made with butter-rich dough that, upon baking, is very light and flaky and encloses a filling of fruit or almond paste. The difference lies, essentially, not in the form, but in the quality of the ingredients and in the time and care given to their union.

When the Minnesota Orchestra held a lavish fund-raising buffet a few years ago, the centerpiece among the sweets was citron fromage which, despite its French name, is a highly esteemed Danish dessert. But the dessert that most distinguishes Danish baking from American is blødkage (a layer cake). Somewhat similar to the Norwegian bløtkake, it is laden with thick whipped cream and filled, between the half-inch-thick layers, with thickened fruit compote or jam and custards. The cake's layers should, however, remain visible. The details of the finished product vary from one region of Denmark to another, and those stylistic details are carried on in Minnesota with a rather intense pride that sometimes provokes good-natured arguments. Some prefer to embellish the cake top with marzipan; others insist upon cream and fruit. In no case would an American frosting be used. The towering dessert is served at birthday parties, special anniversaries, weddings, and always at the annual Danish Constitution Day picnics on the Sunday nearest June 5. The blødkage concludes the picnic feast that includes smørrebrød in dozens of varieties, herring, kringler, a kransekage decorated with Danish flags, beer, akvavit, and, of course, coffee.

The Danish-American institutions in Minnesota all use traditional foodways from time to time to entertain members or to raise money for some worthy cause. The Society Dania, basically a social club, has an occasional prime-rib dinner with a nod to its cultural inheritance through akvavit and a Danish dessert. At least once a year St. Peder's Lutheran Church, Minneapolis, serves the congregation æbleskiver for breakfast and a torsk dinner. Danish language camps for youngsters usually employ Danish-born cooks and attempt to serve authentic meals as often as possible, frequently engaging the students in the preparation.[44]

But the most intense and popular institutional support is directed toward perpetuating the Danish tradition of smørrebrød, which are as important in Danish tradition as lutefisk and meatballs are in the Norwegian and Swedish. Requiring some skill and time to prepare, smørrebrød are generally reserved for special occasions and small gatherings. The Danish American Fellowship of Minneapolis holds classes in the art of composing smørrebrød, and Minnesotans, with or without a Danish heritage, flock to the sessions to learn the time-consuming but rewarding skills. The classes are every bit as much a social experience as a culinary adventure.

In discussing their smørrebrød tradition, most Danish Americans will make it quite clear at the outset that a certain protocol attends the creation and eating of the delicacy. Only the finest foods are used, and bread must suit the ingredients. All components must be thinly sliced, and butter and other subsequent toppings must be spread or layered to the very edges of the sandwich. Breads with a minimal crust are preferred; otherwise the crusts are cut off. The combination of ingredients is flexible only within certain limits, and sandwiches must be eaten in a given order from herring to fish, to chicken or egg salads; next, meats, pâté, sausages, and frikadeller; and finally cheeses, with Havarti, bleu, and Camembert being the most commonly used. Most important, Danish open-faced sandwiches

Arol and Herta Hansen, Askov, with their table set for a Danish meal: smørrebrød and imported beverages, 1984

must never be eaten with the fingers but approached with knife and fork, preferably in the European manner. It is also customary to serve akvavit with the first and final courses and beer with each intermediate one.[45]

Breads for the sandwiches are strictly assigned: rye pumpernickel for most sandwiches, but white bread for shrimp, salmon, and cheese. Cheeses may also be served on kiks, rye crisp, or knäckebröd. Artistically and culinarily, the sandwich becomes more complex at this point. The range of toppings is broad, running from smoked eel, flaked crab, and raw scraped T-bone steak to scrambled eggs, leftover, cold frikadeller, and the dependable rullepølse. Certain sandwiches require a special selection of garnishes: a lemon twist on herring, aspic on salami, beet pickle, bacon, or cucumber slices on liver pâté. Garnishes for cheeses are necessarily delicate, such as a grape cut in half or a sliced mandarin orange. Finally, in addition to garnishes, one may use a dressing on certain sandwiches: remoulade made with mayonnaise, sweet relish, curry, sugar, or other seasonings including horseradish and whipped cream.

What appears to be a lively and popular tradition, at least in urban areas where Danish Americans are relatively numerous, is at something of a disadvantage in small towns. Because the Danish smørrebrød are so time-consuming to prepare (and no short cuts or compromises are sufferable), they are served at ethnic events less and less frequently. In Tyler, for example, heartland of Danish settlement and site of the famous folk school (now a summer institute), the Danebod Lutheran Church has had to discontinue the traditional annual smørrebrød dinners. Young working mothers, in the past the core of the food preparation team, can no longer commit the time to the extensive details of the task.[46]

Yet such lapses of tradition are sometimes but temporary setbacks. In fact, the perception that customs are being lost may prompt a renewed effort to maintain Danish-American foodways. Such connections are often difficult to see or predict, but sometimes a new interest in foodways is linked to an old one that has faltered. Formal classes in which students are taught, outside the home, to prepare traditional dishes show how a perceived threat can generate action.

Danes have a traditional saying, common in other Scandinavian languages as well: "Tak for sidst," or "Thanks for the last time." This phrase is used to greet someone who entertained or acted as host at a previous get-together, no matter how long ago it was; with these words Danes express their appreciation and remembrance of that earlier generosity immediately upon saying "hello." Surely the Danish-American tradition will persist in Minnesota, and generations to come will address their forebears with "Tak for sidst."

THE SWEDES

Scholars have argued that Minnesota's Swedish Americans exhibit a considerable degree of assimilation. The lively visibility of other Scandinavians, who tend to use foodways more dramatically than do the Swedes, may have contributed to this image. In fact, much of the traditional Swedish diet brought to this country in the nineteenth century closely resembles Norwegian food choices. The two countries, situated side-by-side, draw upon the sea and their dairy resources for many of their foods.

In large measure, the Swedes were refugees from poverty and adversity, conditions they but slowly overcame in initial settlements in Chisago

Lucia (Valerie Lancello), holding a plate of lussekatter and ginger cookies, and members of her procession gather around a formal table at the American Swedish Institute, Minneapolis, Lucia Day celebration, 1985.

County, then Carver and Meeker counties, and still later, the Twin Cities. Their descendants testify that the core of the pioneer diet — as much rural as ethnic — consisted of homemade soups from the Swedish tradition, potatoes, fish, and various uses of grains, more often than not cooked as gröt (porridge) or mush. Some of these foodways, ingrained in current Swedish-American tradition, are completely unknown to visitors from Sweden.[47]

There are, of course, some exceptions and anomalies in this pattern of New World retention. Lucia Day, December 13, is a widely celebrated and intensely emotional holiday in Sweden. According to legend, Lucia, an Italian saint, appeared to a starving Swedish community and saved it from disaster by providing food.[48] The tradition carried on today in Swedish households dictates that the eldest daughter, symbolizing Lucia, prepares and serves breakfast to her parents that day. Over the years this custom has evolved specific forms: lussekatter (Lucia buns), baked in a traditional S shape and flavored with saffron, are served with coffee and sometimes with ginger-flavored cookies called pepparkakor.

This symbolic gesture — sharing food and paying respect to those who provide sustenance throughout the year — is interpreted in various ways in the Swedish-American communities and institutions of Minnesota. In Lindstrom the day is typically acknowledged with an open house for neighbors and friends who drop in to enjoy coffee, cookies, and pastries prepared, as a Swedish proverb directs, "with butter and love." The ceremony at the American Swedish Institute, Minneapolis, is somewhat closer to traditional practice, although it is a public event. Institute members and an interested public gather to watch a chosen Lucia queen lead a procession of her peers, all carrying candles. After a brief program of song, the young people and the adult audience, with scores of preteens in tow, enjoy the traditional buns and pepparkakor with coffee. St. Paul's First Covenant Church holds a widely attended Lucia Day ceremony during the second week of December; in other communities the celebration is marked with a lutfisk dinner. Many families, however, do not observe the day at all.[49]

Swedish foodways are in evidence in other institutional events. Lutherans of Swedish origin, usually in the Covenant churches, are strong supporters of traditional foods, particularly at Christmas. First Covenant Church of Minneapolis, for example, the first church in the city with Swedish roots, holds noon concerts in December followed by a buffet of cardamom bread, skorpor (rusks), fruitcake, American-style cookies, and coffee. The annual Svenskarnas Dag observance of midsummer is uniquely Swedish, although the Minnesota celebrations are not as festive as those in the homeland. At the event in Minnehaha Park, Minneapolis, Swedish delicacies

abound side-by-side with American picnic foods, all brought from individual kitchens.[50]

Institutional dinners serve as fund raisers for activities, but they are also
a way for members and friends to visit and for adults to involve youngsters in food-related activities. Each group and institution must face shift-
ing tastes and trends and do what it can to blend the old and the new.
The American Swedish Institute, a leader in bridging generations, brought
together the following menu at a recent dinner: pickled herring, boiled
potatoes, anchovies, homemade headcheese, pickled cucumbers, meatballs,
and sausage — all from the older tradition. New additions included dev-
iled eggs and omelets with ham and bacon.[51]

Integrating old and new, exploring innovation, and coming to terms
with what is currently acceptable are problems every institution must re-
solve. In past decades colleges founded by Swedes served some Swedish
dishes, but as the schools grew, food services became more complex and
tradition was challenged by economics and modern nutrition. Still, Swedish
menus appear from time to time at Gustavus Adolphus College in St. Peter.
It is said that the former head of food services there helped finance a new
wing to the building by selling limpa (rye bread) to donors.[52]

Markets that serve Swedish communities offer clues to customers' food
preferences. A modest Lindstrom grocery, for example, exhibits a rich ethnic flavor. There, unannounced from the street, is a wealth of Scandinavian and particularly Swedish-American foods, including bruna bönor
(brown beans), grown, shelled, and carefully packaged in Stacy by an immigrant's granddaughter. Popular with the immigrants, the beans are
cooked today in a sweet-sour sauce, sometimes flavored with nutmeg, or
are simply prepared with molasses, salt, and pepper. Potatiskorv (potato
sausage) is a well-stocked item, and the supply needs replenishing several
times each week. Pork cuts of every variety, headcheese, and ring liver
sausage are offered with the more ordinary steaks and chops.

The market sells a steady amount of "Swede food" throughout the year,
but as Christmas approaches, buying intensifies. Sill (herring), ordered in
huge wooden tubs, doubles in sales. Lutfisk, anchovies, and whitefish are
more popular than ever. Cartons of lingonberries, direct from Sweden and
Nova Scotia and selling at four dollars per jar, never languish on the shelves.
And everywhere there are food items, mainly imported, which will help
Swedish Americans celebrate the holidays properly: huge, round knäckebröd (hardtack) in red, white, and blue wrappers; pumpernickel bread
and limpa; cheeses such as Bondost or caraway in huge bricks from Wisconsin or Scandinavia; and even homemade lefse from local ovens.

From this storehouse, food is also purchased by local Masonic lodges, churches, and other organizations staging annual dinners of lutfisk, Swedish meatballs, lingonberries, sill, and the appropriate breads. But not all Swedes can attend these feasts, and the market also sends out "care packages" of Swedish foods to retirees residing in Florida. According to the proprietor, institutional cooking has declined in recent years, yet his sales continue to rise. "So there must be some Swedish cooking going on out there someplace!" he surmised.[53]

As is typical in Scandinavian households, the Christmas holidays are preceded with a flurry of cleaning, decorating, and baking. Traditional straw figures and plain white lights usually adorn the Christmas tree, and smörbakelser (puff pastry), pepparkakor, and lefse are made in ample quantities. Many modern Swedish Americans, both urban and rural, make headcheese at home only at Christmastime. Swedish-American Christmas dinners generally follow the pattern found in other Scandinavian households: light eating on December 24 until the great Christmas Eve feast. The noon meal is simple — perhaps dopparedagen soppa (a clear meat broth from beef and pork bones) poured over fresh-baked bread, risgrynsgröt

Vivian Bergstedt, Prior Lake, making mazariner, a rich little cookie similar to shortbread with an almond-paste filling, for Christmas, 1985

Soaking lutfisk in preparation for the seasonal rush, Lyons Food Products, Golden Valley, 1971

(rice mush cooked in milk until thick and eaten with sweet cream, sugar, and cinnamon), or oyster stew and fresh lefse.[54]

Christmas Eve dinner has many variants. Lutfisk is a general favorite, usually accompanied by potatiskorv or meatballs, possibly ham, headcheese, lefse, and lingonberries. Some families prepare pig's feet or herring, while others feel that Christmas without bruna bönor or a molded aspic flavored with fish would be incomplete. As with Norwegians and Danes, Swedes like to conclude their holiday dinner with ris à l'almande. Many admit to contriving that one of the children finds the single hidden almond, but in some families adults participate in the custom as well. Sometimes the lucky nut is hidden in the Christmas morning porridge, usually risgrynsgröt which might be served with limpa and coffee. Swedish pancakes, very much like French crepes but sweetened with lingonberries, are also a Christmas morning favorite. After breakfast, Christmas Day repasts are sometimes a buffet or smörgåsbord for guests and family. Or, contrary to mainstream American practice, there may be no plan or specific menu at all: "Almost an afterthought," suggested one Swedish American.[55]

Most Minnesotans claim that Swedish foods appear in the day-to-day diet at Christmastime alone. But further probing reveals that Swedish foods are prepared almost unconsciously for any festive occasion. One family, for example, invited friends to watch a postseason football game and served herring with flat bread, smoked fish, limpa flavored with raisins and anise, and a variety of beverages, yet at first claimed that nothing "Swedish" was served after Christmas.[56] A less special occasion might warrant kroppkaka (similar to Norwegian klubb), a dumpling made from potatoes and flour and boiled with salt in ham-flavored water. A variation is fiskbollar (fish balls) in which fish is blended with flour and water.

Many of the dishes Minnesotans serve derive from specific regions of Sweden. For example, a hot dish from the Stockholm area, popularly called "Jansson's Temptation," combines anchovies, potatoes, sausages, onions, cream, butter, and breadcrumbs to make a baked dish that some Minnesotans compare to scalloped potatoes "Swedish style."[57] Another family with relatives from different parts of Sweden prepares lutfisk for Christmas but serves it with three sauces representative of the north, central, and southern areas of Sweden: mustard gravy, butter, and cream sauce.[58]

Because of unusual ingredients people remember many special dishes that are seldom, if ever, served today. Since few Swedes keep a family cow any more, they are unable to obtain the colostrum or "first milk" produced immediately after the birth of a calf, and thus cannot make kalvdans, a rich pudding. Similarly cherished but seldom served is ostkaka, a kind of cheesecake with the whey removed.

Many Swedish-American ethnic foods in the mid-twentieth century are strongly influenced by what rural families with Swedish roots could afford to feed themselves. Farm families with easy access to wild berries and other fruits, for example, continued to make Swedish kräm, a thickened fruit pudding served with cream. But later, in urban neighborhoods, cooks who prepared the dish resorted to canned grape juice, cornstarch, sugar, and any fruit at hand—wild plums or chokecherries, store-bought currants or gooseberries. Traditional Swedish soups are still a mainstay: pea, cabbage (sometimes with a little meat added), ox-tail, chicken, usually with noodles or dumplings, and fruit soup, a one-dish meal in many Scandinavian homes.

Another popular staple of years past was mush or gröt, which consisted mainly of rice cooked in butter and milk and flavored with syrup and cream. Rye mush, according to an early cookbook, required "newly harvested and threshed rye, or otherwise gleanings from the barn floor. Put an iron pan with water over the fire, and when it has become hot, place the rye in it and stir steadily until it begins to crack and the rye assumes a light brown color. When dried this way, grind it in a hand mill, but not fine, about the size of small rice. This done, stir it into boiling water already salted. Boil for 1 hour and eat with cream and milk. When cold this mush is hard, and can be cut in slices and fried in butter."[59]

This nineteenth-century recipe represents an early phase of Swedish foodways in Minnesota. In the ensuing years, cooks delighted in their discovery of American white flour, only to be confronted by their children who "discovered" the nutritional merits of whole-wheat bread in the schoolroom health classes of the 1920s. In the years before and after World War II, more and more European breads and rolls were sold in American stores. This phenomenon, in turn, renewed Swedish Americans' interest in baking their own wheat and rye breads at home.

During these same decades, American social agencies assumed an ag-

Vivian Bergstedd with traditional Swedish Christmas cookies: rullrån (rolled cookies), pepparkakor (ginger hearts), smørkringlor (pretzels), mandelmusslor (shell shapes), and lussekatter (Lucia buns), 1985

gressive role in teaching newcomers "American" cooking. In Swedish-American homes recipes for snacks like oatmeal cookies from newly published American farm-extension and Four-H club cookbooks began to take priority over the traditional, plain varieties. By the 1960s, however, the mood had shifted, and the same extension programs taught Scandinavian cooking to Minnesotans eager to learn Swedish ethnic baking.

The Swedish language is no longer so widely spoken as it was in the early twentieth-century days of "Snoose Boulevard," "Swede Hollow," and "Swede Alley." Yet Swedes of all ages remember their food heritage in the original Swedish names, or a close approximation, and "Tak för matten," or "Thanks for the food," is still the approved way to express one's appreciation at the end of a meal.

In 1983 a Norwegian television producer visited Minnesota to document traditional Norse cookery and found that the ethnic food tradition had changed less over the years in the state than in its native Norwegian setting.[60] Since the immigrants' departure for America, tastes in Norway, Denmark, and Sweden have modified, becoming more international and more aware of balanced diets at the expense of traditional food patterns.

This is not to say that Scandinavian foodways in Minnesota have not changed. Lutefisk cooked in microwave ovens, æbleskiver for breakfast, and eclectic holiday menus that combine American and traditional Old Country dishes testify that they have. In Minnesota, furthermore, Scandinavian foods, however authentic, are but a small percent of one's day-to-day consumption. In the end, it is the Scandinavian-Americans' perception of what is best or worth remembering from their individual traditions that will determine a future sense of their ethnic foodways. In this process family and regional heritage will play a major role.

NOTES

[1] Some of the more humorous articles in the popular press include *Minneapolis Tribune*, December 17, 1980, p. 3B, 6B; Bob Ehlert, "Lutefisk in the 1980s," *Minneapolis Star and Tribune*, December 8, 1985, Sunday Magazine, p. 6–11. Literary references include Art Lee, *The Lutefisk Ghetto: Life in a Norwegian-American Town* (Staples, Minn.: Adventure Publications, 1978). For Scandinavian food references in music, see Don Freeburg, "The Lutefisk Lament," performed by Charlie Boone and Roger Erickson (Minneapolis: Skan-

disk Music, 1981); this song is also included in the album by Mike, Else, and Mari Sevig, *Scandinavian Smørgåsbord* (Minneapolis: Skandisk Music, 1982). References to shy Norwegian bachelor farmers are legion on Garrison Keillor's weekly radio program, "A Prairie Home Companion," broadcast nationally from St. Paul; none of the Norwegian Americans interviewed for this study acknowledged or knew about Keillor's remarks. The foreign-language terms in this chapter are transcribed in modern Swedish, Norwegian, and Danish spelling, which may differ from the many dialect variants currently spoken and written in Minnesota.

[2] Because of their austere roots, lutefisk and some other foods viewed as "primitive" are sometimes called "Norwegian Soul Food." Similarly, the pan-Scandinavian liquor called aquavit in Swedish, akevitt in Norwegian, and akvavit in Danish, distilled from grains or potatoes and flavored with caraway seeds, has been referred to in the newspapers as "Norwegian Drāno." The overall connotations of these food items is strong, harsh, earthy, and barely palatable.

[3] In a recent survey of persons who completed classes in Norwegian cooking offered by the Sons of Norway, Minneapolis, over half said they enrolled because of their heritage. The time and money, although minimal, for these classes would not have been available earlier in the century.

[4] *Minneapolis Tribune*, December 24, 1944, p. 6. See also Theodore C. Blegen, *Norwegian Migration to America*, vol. 2, *The American Transition* (Northfield, Minn.: Norwegian-American Historical Assn., 1940), 188–206, 215–20; Ethel J. Odegard, *A Norwegian Family Transplanted: The Genealogical Writings of Ethel J. Odegard* (Decorah, Iowa: Anundsen Pub. Co., 1974), 130–34.

[5] Carrie Young, *Gourmet: The Magazine of Good Living*, 43 (November 1983): 36, 192, 194, 196, 198–208.

[6] On occasions such as weddings, a bottle of wine or champagne is installed inside the rings. At one point in the serving, the bride and groom must grasp the bottle by the top and lift it clear of the bottom rings. Tradition has it that the number of rings that come away with the bottle indicate the number of children the couple will have. The baker can influence this prophecy by producing many thin rings of small diameter. Interviews of Rev. Arden Haug, Den Norske Lutherske Mindekirken (Norwegian Lutheran Memorial Church), Minneapolis, October 1983, Arna Njaa, Minneapolis, November 1983, Verna Nielsen, Minneapolis, January 1984. Many of the kransekake makers also prepare and sell large batches of Christmas cookies, principally through their churches.

[7] Proprietors of most markets claim that providing sausage is a valuable part of their service to the community. The recipes are jealously guarded, since it took years to perfect them, and faithful customers are now satisfied with the results. Interviews of Charles Swenson, Ingebretsen's Scandinavian Center, Minneapolis, Peter Nelson, Community Market, Lindstrom, and clerks at the Pioneer Sausage Company, St. Paul – all November 1983.

[8] Interview of Jerry Kellogg, Oakleaf Restaurant, Austin, November 1983.

[9] Interviews of Leroy and Fay Sandven, Milan, December 1983, staff at Cindy's Cafe and Delmonico's Cafe, both Benson, December 1983.

[10] Holiday Inn, Willmar, "Hardanger Room" menu, 1983, copy in Minnesota Ethnic Foodways Project files, MHS. Interviews of staff, secretary, and members of the congregation at Bethlehem Lutheran Church, Minneapolis, November 1983. Generally, parents of teen-aged children are most active in these food events, providing supervision as well as a gesture of care and respect for elderly members who are the majority of the diners. Some churches have had to dispense with such dinners as commitment waned and younger

members, even those with strong ethnic affiliations, could not find time to assist.

[11] Telephone interview of and correspondence with Richard "Mike" Field, Glenwood, December 1983.

[12] Interviews of Leroy Sandven, Milan, December 1983, Cindy Flaaen, Minneapolis, January 1984, Harold Gjerset, Watson, December 1983.

[13] For the attempt at making the world's largest lefse, see *Minneapolis Star and Tribune*, July 4, 1983, p. 2B. Julebord literally means Christmas table.

[14] Søren Bache, Diary, December 4, 1843, cited in Blegen, *Norwegian Migration*, 190. See also Einar Haugen, *The Norwegians in America, 1825–1975* (1967; rev. ed., Oslo: Royal Ministry of Foreign Affairs, 1975), 17, 20.

[15] Here and below, see Haug interview.

[16] Odegard, *Norwegian Family Transplanted*, 131.

[17] For a theoretical discussion of this subject, see Randall M. Miller and Thomas D. Marzik, eds., *Immigrants and Religion in Urban America* (Philadelphia: Temple University Press, 1977), and Timothy L. Smith, "Religion and Ethnicity in America," *American Historical Review* 83 (December 1978): 1155–85. See also Carlton C. Qualey and Jon A. Gjerde, "The Norwegians," in *They Chose Minnesota*, ed. Holmquist, 234. Some American Lutheran pastors now serving in Norway have tried to introduce their native, popular foodways patterns to their host congregations. Efforts are not always successful, given the European styles and eating patterns strongly connected with home and occupation and the schedules that they impose upon individuals. Interview of Randi Johansen, Minneapolis, October 1983; Haug interview.

[18] Interviews of Gwen Morem, Astrid Earl, Lois Paulson, and Lee Ann Sheggeby, Austin, and Lois Dokken and Marie Sanbo, Minneapolis — all November 1983.

[19] In Norwegian folk tradition, Christmas is "driven out" by a figure called "Knute" or "Tjuendagsknute" on the twentieth day; interview of Randi Johansen, Minneapolis, January 1984.

[20] Interview of Liv Dahl, Minneapolis, December 1983.

[21] In modern Norway, the julebord is a pre-Christmas social event. Since churches there never support foodways, it is generally hosted by an employer at a hotel or restaurant; interviews of Randi Johansen, Anna Bateman, and other congregants of Mindekirken, Minneapolis, November 1983.

[22] Blegen, *Norwegian Migration to America*, 195.

[23] Field interview.

[24] Interview of Anna Bateman, Minneapolis, October 1983. At certain parties and especially on national holidays, Scandinavians attach snappers or noisemakers to the kransekake.

[25] For example, lefse from Nordland, far up in the northern region of Norway, calls for wheat or rye flour and potatoes, as well as thick cream. They are baked to a thickness of approximately one-quarter inch. In Norway today, potato lefse is always eaten fresh and never stored; interview of Randi Johansen, November 1983.

[26] In areas densely settled by Norwegian Americans, the local hardware store is the place to find these grills, which usually include a lefse stick; see OK Hardware, "Holiday Gift Ideas," 1983, p. 17, copy in Minnesota Ethnic Foodways Project files, MHS. Most sticks, however, are homemade and are inherited from mothers and grandmothers with a degree of pride.

[27] Interview of Fay Sandven, Milan, December 1983.

[28] Interview of Rev. Carroll and Mary Hinderlie, Minneapolis, October 1983.

[29] For example, rømmegraut is served at the annual fund-raising luncheon of Vesterheim, the Norwegian-American museum in Decorah, Iowa, and at many of the luncheons prepared at Mindekirken, Minneapolis.

[30] See Reidar Thorwald Christiansen, ed., *Folktales of Norway*, trans. Pat Shaw Iversen (Chicago: University of Chicago Press, 1964).

[31] Interviews of Elizabet Rudjord and Andy Hovland, Norwegian exchange students at Augsburg College, Minneapolis, November 1983, Einar Johansen, Minneapolis, December 1983. The letter is in the possession of Rudjord family.

[32] Interview of Sigrid Stordalen, Minneapolis, January 1984; Paulson interview.

[33] Ann Regan, "The Danes," in *They Chose Minnesota*, ed. Holmquist, 277.

[34] Interview of Sine Duus, Minneapolis, January 4, 1984.

[35] Interview of Kristian and Lorlee Thusholt, Bloomington, November 22, 1983.

[36] Interviews of Caroline Olsen, Minneapolis, December 1983, Inger Larsen, Fridley, January 1984.

[37] Interviews of Marvin and Diane Larsen, St. Louis Park, November 21, December 11, 29, 1983. Marvin Larsen's recipe is from his Danish immigrant grandparents. His mother also preserved farm eggs in brine to tide the family through the nonlaying season.

[38] Interview of Inge Nathan, Edina, December 6, 1983. On the "happy Danes," see Regan, "The Danes," in *They Chose Minnesota*, ed. Holmquist, 282.

[39] No Dane interviewed knew the origin of the word ruskomsnusk, and only one person spelled it with confidence. The casserole is not widely in evidence at Danish ethnic gatherings, except funerals, to which, for any ethnic group, a hot dish is easily transported.

[40] Here and below, see interviews of members of Virkelyst (a women's welfare club of the Danish American Fellowship), Minneapolis, January 4, 1984.

[41] Æbleskiver pans are usually available in hardware stores in Danish areas or in urban gourmet shops. Interview of Karen Muller, Edina, December 8, 1983.

[42] Virkelyst interviews.

[43] Interviews of Marvin and Diane Larsen.

[44] These include camps at the old Danish settlement in Tyler and at Skovsøen (Lake of the Woods), one of the International Language Villages sponsored by Concordia College (Moorhead).

[45] A local guide to this art is published by the Danish American Center under the title *Danish Sandwiches: Recipes from Inge Nathan* (n.d.). Many Minnesota Danes who have visited Denmark have brought back the four-foot-long menu from Oskar David & Sons Restaurant, now closed; it describes dozens of combinations. See also Åsta Bang and Edith Rode, *Open Sandwiches and Cold Lunches: An Introduction to Danish Culinary Art*, trans. Kris Winther (Copenhagen: J. Gjellerup, 1948), and St. John's Lutheran Church, Annex Club, *From Danish Kitchens* (Seattle: The Club, 1941), popular among Minnesota Danes.

[46] Telephone interview of the secretary of the Danebod Lutheran Church, Tyler, January 1984.

[47] John G. Rice, "The Swedes," in *They Chose Minnesota*, ed. Holmquist, 253–58, 264; interviews of Karen Humphrey, Dassel, January 1984, and Anne Rudeberg, St. Peter, December 1983.

[48] Kristina Carheden, *Food & Festivals Swedish Style* (Minneapolis: Dillon Press, 1968), 22.

[49] Interviews of Greta Swenson, Fargo, December 1983, January 1984, Mary Rhodes, Plymouth, January 1984. Swedish Minnesotans who remember Lucia Day in the 1930s recall that they celebrated with beauty pageants or, at home, carols in the morning, tricks played all day, and glögg (hot spiced wine) in the evening.

[50] Interviews of Eric Erling, Edina, January 1984; Rhodes interview.

[51] Interview of Beverly Schilleman, Minneapolis, November 1983.

[52] Humphrey interview.

[53] Peter Nelson of the Community Market in Lindstrom does not pregrind his meatball mix but fixes it to suit each customer's taste. Seven grindings seems to be the average request; Nelson interview.

[54] Interviews of Marianne Rodning, New Sweden, January 1984, Anne Marie Swenson, Center City, January 1984; Humphrey and Rhodes interviews.

[55] Greta Swenson interview, January 1984.

[56] Rhodes interview.

[57] Interviews of Sandra Johnson, Lindstrom, November 1983; Anne Marie Swenson interview. The dish is listed as "Janssons Frestelse" in American Swedish Institute, *Var Så God* (Minneapolis: American Swedish Institute, 1980), 9.

[58] Here and below, see Anne Marie Swenson interview.

[59] Interview of Minnie Osterholt, Nelson, December 1983; Greta Swenson interview, December 1983. See also *Fullständigaste Svensk-Amerikansk Kokbok: Swedish-English Cookbook* (Chicago: Engeberg-Holmberg Publishing Co., 1897), 219–20. Frequently a one-dish meal of rice pudding was cooked on the stove alongside the water heating for washday.

[60] Johansen interview, October 1983.

Preparations for Little Christmas Eve dinner at the International Institute, St. Paul, 1985; Raija Wietzke stirring egg-butter topping for piirakka (foreground), Maiju Hongell displaying prune tarts, and bowl of rosolli in background

THE FINNS

"Simple foods," "plain," "basic," and "earthy" are words most Finns in Minnesota today use to describe their traditional cuisine. "Bland" is another common adjective, one shared by food enthusiasts and detractors alike. So simple and unadorned is traditional Finnish food, in fact, that some Finnish-American cooks fear it lacks distinction; its rutabaga and potato casseroles, rice pudding, canned berries, and fish soups, they believe, have blended right into the American diet.

It is true that the recent surge of popular interest in ethnicity, in displaying one's roots, has caused traditional Finnish-American cooks to regard their foods in a new light. Finnish food has much in common with that of the Scandinavian countries and, to a lesser extent, with that of the Soviet Union, Finland's neighbor to the east. This fact, combined with the Finnish reliance on common foods, simply prepared — boiled or mashed potatoes or rutabagas, coffee, hot cereals, whole-grain breads, soups, and stews with little seasoning — has made it hard for Finnish Minnesotans to project a distinctive image of their cuisine to others. Women who have organized food booths at St. Paul's Festival of Nations, for example, found, "There hasn't been a distinct something you could say was Finnish. The Germans can serve bratwurst for one hundred and fifty years, and they'll sell thousands. Baklava will always be popular . . . the beautiful Norwegian bakings will always be, the Danish open-faced sandwiches. . . . We have served a beet-herring salad, but the Swedish and the Norwegians serve it too. Pickled herring bridges all Scandinavian countries."[1] Food demonstrators at the Iron Range Interpretative Center, Chisholm, have had similar experiences; in one case, a Slovenian woman claimed that Finnish squeaky cheese was "invented" in her homeland.[2]

The active desire to find "a distinct something" Finnish has added an interesting twist to traditional foodways. While some cooks are currently looking to their history and attempting to revive customs long out of practice among their families, others are experimenting with contemporary Finnish cuisine. Thus from a mix of modern European gourmet foods and historic peasant dishes, innovative Finnish Minnesotans are creating a hybrid system of foodways.

The earliest Finnish immigrants in Minnesota homesteaded in the south-central part of the state in 1864. Subsequent newcomers established the still-Finnish settlement of New York Mills in the west-central region, but the last and greatest influx settled in and around Duluth and the iron range towns. There they combined homesteading with work in the lumber and mining industries.[3] Thus the Finnish settlement pattern in Minnesota has been both rural and urban, a fact that has significantly influenced foodways. In general, Finnish Minnesotans in ethnic enclaves like New York Mills and the Palo-Markham area of northern Minnesota have retained traditional foods as an intrinsic part of their daily regimen. Those living in multiethnic urban environments, on the other hand, seem to treasure their foodways more as unique symbols of their heritage than as daily sustenance. They tend to prepare Finnish foods for holidays or special events. Thus rural and urban experiences have not necessarily produced different kinds of Finnish-American foods; rather, the same foods seem to possess a different status in different settings.

The foods and foodways of Finland, like those of almost any other country, exhibit considerable regional variation. Climate, geography, and the vicissitudes of history contributed to the development of localized cuisines. Centuries of cultural and political domination by Sweden, as well as a period of Russian rule, have undoubtedly left their marks on Finnish culture. Most of the Finns who emigrated to Minnesota were from the western part of Finland which looked to Sweden; consequently, their food traditions are most widely represented in the state. Only in more recent times, with the publication of Finnish cookbooks and a general interest in the foods of the homeland, have a number of eastern — especially Karelian — dishes gained widespread popularity in midwestern households.

In addition, most of the immigrants left Finland before the time when technology and mass imports made fresh foods available year round to common folk. Thus the cuisine that evolved into Minnesota's Finnish foodways was distinctively seasonal, derived from a pattern of eating fresh fruits and vegetables in late spring, summer, and early fall, fish and game in season, and other fresh meat at slaughtering time. The staples were hardy root crops and salt fish that would last through a long winter. What would not keep in a root cellar was preserved by such methods as salting, brining, or canning.

In much of Finland, traditional foodways were part of a hand-to-mouth life style based on subsistence agriculture and fishing. Minnesota, especially its northern reaches, presented a similar environment, with its birch woods, lakes, and short growing season; as a result, Finnish foodways transplanted with relative ease. The great majority of the early Finnish immigrants were lone men — either bachelors or husbands who temporarily left families behind. Many of the newcomers sought out Finnish boarding-houses where they could converse in their own language and eat familiar food, but those who lived apart found it reasonably easy to fend for themselves. While cooking and baking were traditionally women's tasks, almost all men were able to make the simple stews and breads that are a mainstay of the Finnish diet.

Thrift, as well as simplicity, was a hallmark of Finnish immigrant foodways. In their homeland, Finns were accustomed to supplementing their own provisions with whatever they could glean from the wild. Besides fish and game, this meant a good variety of berries — blueberries, raspberries, strawberries, cranberries, cloudberries, and the arctic mesimarja — and mushrooms. While Minnesota lacks some of Finland's diversity of wild berries and mushrooms, immigrants still were able to pursue their customs of fishing, hunting, and berrying, especially in the northern part of the state.

Late summer was a busy time for immigrant women, who canned, at the very least, copious amounts of berries. Some families, especially during depression years, preserved fish, venison, and beef as well. Minnesota's Finns, unlike their Slovenian, Italian, and German neighbors, are not noted for sausage making; nevertheless, families made use of virtually all of a slaughtered animal. While some people today shudder at the memory of blood pudding, blood pancakes, and blood bread (basically a mixture of blood and rye flour) floating in hot milk, others remember such dishes with fond nostalgia.[4]

Many Finnish Minnesotans today claim that the virtues of thrift and simplicity also guided the development of their traditional style of cooking. The soups, stews, and casseroles for which the Finns are so well known are all derived from a standard list of hearty ingredients, common foodstuffs like rutabagas, potatoes, rice, milk, and fish, combined with minimal seasoning. But there is room for flexibility and creativity within these traditional guidelines. Given the format of a casserole, for example, the cook is free to choose ingredients, mixing and matching them to produce a familiar dish, a variation thereon, or to experiment with something new. And for thrifty cooks, such a process can also be a good way to use up a little bit of this and a half bowl of that.

The great variety of Finnish breads supports the anthropological maxim that the more examples of a given item in a culture, the greater its significance. "The bread was the important part of the meal. If you had the bread, you go on from there. . . . Fish and bread and viili [sour, clabbered milk] and you'd get along just fine," reflected a descendant of Finnish homesteaders in northern Minnesota.[5]

In fact, bread is a definitive element in Finnish and Finnish-American foodways: a meal without bread is not considered to be a meal. Furthermore, in Finland bread types represented in microcosm the differences between western Finland and western Karelia, which had been part of the eastern border of Finland under Russian rule since 1721 and part of independent Finland since 1920. In western Finland, the standard bread was rieska, a sour rye, baked into a crusty, flat, round loaf with a hole in the center. Unlike the Karelians who baked rye bread as often as twice a week, these westerners originally produced their bread about twice a year. They threaded the loaves on a pole that they placed in the rafters. There the bread hung to dry out before being stored. When the Soviet Union annexed western Karelia in 1940 many residents fled and were resettled in Finland. Then, in the words of one woman who was in Finland at the time, "Everybody saw how much different was the food the other people make!" The Karelians found the western bread tough and the westerners felt strongly that the crusty bread was, among other things, good for one's teeth. At present both varieties coexist in the stores and are served in the folk high schools.[6]

Although most Finnish immigrants in Minnesota were from western Finland, they baked smaller quantities of rieska more frequently and ate

Rieska, the crusty rye bread, stored on a pole in the traditional manner at the Loon Lake Museum, Palo, 1986

it fresh; nevertheless, they retained its traditional shape, punching it down after one rising, pricking the top with holes, and baking it almost immediately to create a low, solid loaf. The Finns made other breads in a diversity of shapes and sizes, from a variety of ingredients, depending on region of origin and the occasion for which the bread was to be used. Rye and barley, which will ripen in Finland's short growing season, were the flours they were accustomed to using. Wheat flour was virtually unknown in Finland before the 1900s, so many immigrants to Minnesota would not have used it. Even today wheat flour is imported to Finland and is reserved mainly for special breads served on holidays. But contemporary Finnish Minnesotans seek out stone-ground, whole-wheat flour as well as rye and barley.[7]

Hardtack, the flatter, crunchier, crackerlike bread eaten in the Scandinavian countries, was a Finnish favorite as well. While Finns in Minnesota

Alex Hietala,
Embarrass,
grinding wheat in
his garage, 1978

concede that it is possible to make hardtack at home, none remembered seeing it done. Instead, their parents or grandparents bought the flat bread out of barrels at grocery stores.

In Minnesota, thrifty Finnish women also used leftover food to create mixed-grain breads. Cooked cereals such as oatmeal or farina, as well as mashed potatoes, were common additions to the dough. Since women, especially those with families of any size, tended to bake often, saving the leftovers — even the water in which vegetables were cooked — until baking time was no problem. Asked what people did before the days of home freezers, one woman answered simply: "Bake, bake, bake, bake!"[8]

Pulla, called "biscuit" in northern Minnesota, is a basic sweet "coffee bread," distinctively flavored with crushed cardamom. Although made with white flour, eggs, and butter in addition to the spice, in Minnesota the bread has always had common, everyday status. Pulla and coffee might be a quick breakfast. It was also a staple for "coffee" — the midmorning, afternoon, or evening snack. Leftover pulla made good toast or bread pudding; some women used slices of the stale bread as a crust for a casserole-type dessert.[9] For special occasions like holidays or Christmas celebrations, bakers often dressed up everyday pulla with raisins, dates, or nuts. They could either choose to stay with the traditional braided shape or bake it in regular loaf pans, in the shape of Santa Claus with raisins for features, as buns swirled with cinnamon or caramel, or otherwise iced or decorated.[10]

In Finland, essentially a peninsula with fifty thousand lakes, fish of both salt and fresh water have remained an important part of the diet to the present day. Fish markets operate daily in towns of any size, and dried, salted, and packaged fish is available in the stores. Silakka (Baltic herring or sprats) was a staple item; in Minnesota, immigrants could buy it pickled or salted from grocery-store barrels. While fresh red salmon was the prerogative of the rich, many of the immigrants occasionally cooked with salt salmon — "Finnish gold." And those who had access to Minnesota's lakes usually supplemented store-bought fish with smelts (similar in size, at least, to the fresh silakka), walleye, and northern pike.

Fish is a versatile ingredient in Finnish cooking. Some families fried fresh fish, but many more used it to make kalamojakka, a Finnish-American dish that, in the 1980s, generates some controversy. This fish stew, or soup, is a simple dish of onions, potatoes, and fresh fish in a water- or milk-based broth seasoned with either whole allspice or pepper. By most accounts, fish mojakka is the American equivalent of kalakeitto (fish stew). But nobody knows the origins of "mojakka." Some believe it to be a dialect term, others think that on the iron ranges Finnish speech blended with the Slavic languages to produce this hybrid, and still others claim that it is simply a "made-up word." For some, mojakka has overtones of being a dish of leftovers, not "good, expensive meat with good, fresh vegetables!"[11] Nevertheless, mojakka has been a standby for generations of Finns in Minnesota.[12]

Herring, whether the traditional silakka or the bottled, pickled variety more readily available in the United States, was another common dinner item for Minnesota's Finns. Traditional accompaniments included pitkäpiimä (buttermilk) and hardtack or rye bread. Salt herring or even anchovies were also incorporated into salads and casseroles. The most common salad was rosolli, a colorful mixture of beets, apples, carrots, potatoes, and the chopped fish, which seems to have been included primarily for its salty flavor. As in most Finnish cooking, the list of ingredients for rosolli was flexible; individuals felt free to add or delete almost anything but the beets and still call the salad rosolli. In recent years, Finnish Americans have even left out the fish!

Laxlada, essentially scalloped potatoes made with bits of salt salmon for flavor, is a dish second- and third-generation Finnish Minnesotans remember fondly. Although salt salmon was never as affordable as herring, it was within the means of most of the immigrants; in addition, when used in a casserole, "a half pound went a long way to serve a lot of people."[13] Today many women substitute canned salmon for the more expensive salted variety in laxlada.

"Of things that are really quite Minnesota Finn, if I had to take one item, it would be milk."[14] This statement of a third-generation woman accurately portrays the esteem in which this one ingredient is held. Sweet or soured, eaten, drunk, or used in cooking, milk was and is basic to both Finnish and Finnish-American foodways. Homesteaders in Minnesota, following a traditional Finnish pattern, usually kept a few cows. Calving times were staggered so there was always a supply of fresh milk. Many Finns who lived in town had friends in the country; thus some urbanites carefully maintained access to the "first milk" necessary for some of their traditional dishes. On the other hand, Finns who lived in town and bought all of their milk in grocery stores were more likely to stop making foods, such as cheeses, which required gallons and gallons of milk at a time.

Finns drank quantities of milk and put it on their hot breakfast cereals and sometimes in their coffee. They also cultivated sour, clabbered milk products, viili and piimä. The first resembles yoghurt and is made in much the same way — by adding a tablespoon of starter to fresh milk that must

Squeaky-cheese mold and cheese

stand in a warm spot, like on a kitchen or pantry shelf, overnight. Finns and Finnish Americans enjoyed the thickened, slightly stringy or stretchy milk with a meal (good with fish and hardtack) or whipped up and drunk as piimä, or "stretchy buttermilk."

That second- and third-generation Finns today still maintain viili cultures illustrates nicely how traditional foodways depend on a social network. In America, starter is not available commercially. People who ate viili had to "keep it up." If one "lost" the starter, forgot to reserve some, or had it go irretrievably sour, the only way to begin again was to find another aficionado. Thus viili eaters formed a sort of loose social chain; sometimes it was necessary to go through several of the links before finding someone with a good starter.

Uunijuusto (oven cheese), or "squeaky cheese," was a favorite food found more commonly among Finns who kept cows than among town dwellers. Not only does it take three to four gallons of milk to make one cheese, but also the best uunijuusto requires colostrum—the rich "first milk" of a cow that has just calved. Again, urbanites with country contacts could either obtain the milk or buy the cheese from a rural acquaintance. A snack food, although it can accompany a meal, uunijuusto is soft, white, and round. A few minutes under the broiler produces golden flecks on its surface. Coffee is its natural companion; some of the immigrant generation floated cubes of the cheese in their beverage, simply to warm it up.[15]

Finally, dairy products were important ingredients in many of the most traditional of Finnish dishes: kalamojakka, maito keitto (a dessert of hot, sweetened milk poured over zwieback), riisipuuro (rice pudding), and pan-nukakku (oven pancake), a rich, baked concoction that resembles a large popover. In addition, whipped cream took a prominent part in many Finnish desserts which, bakers claim, are not sweet but tend to be very rich.

Though many Finnish Americans today consider theirs a "meat and potatoes" diet,[16] their immigrant ancestors ate relatively little meat. American-style steaks, roasts, or chops were generally a rarity reserved for special celebrations. More often meat would be cut, ground, chopped, or otherwise extended with grains or vegetables. Like members of many other nationalities, Finns ate cabbage rolls filled with a mixture of ground beef and rice. Meat mojakka, the stew made of short ribs or cubed beef, carrots, potatoes, rutabagas, cabbage, or whatever other vegetables were on hand, was common. So too was pasty, a specialty that Finns seem to have learned from the Cornish in the mining regions of Michigan and Minnesota.

As with mojakka, there is no one recipe for pasty. The kinds of ingredients — either ground beef or pieces of an inexpensive cut of steak, rutabagas, carrots, potatoes, onions, salt, and pepper — are standard, but the combination and proportion depend on the individual cook. Some made their pasties like pies, to be cut into servings. The majority, however, made them in the Cornish style, as individual turnovers. Finnish miners supposedly carried pasties wrapped in paper in their lunch pails. By mealtime, the pasty would still be warm, thereby providing the worker with a "hot lunch" that included meat, vegetables, and bread all in one piece. Families also dined on pasties, which, originally Finnish or not, fit nicely with the Finnish style of combination dishes.

The Finns who left their homeland for Minnesota in the early years of the twentieth century did not bring with them an elaborated tradition of vegetable preparation.[17] Most of the species of wild mushrooms that they were accustomed to gathering and preserving did not grow in Minnesota. There is little evidence that they continued to garnish foods, including breakfast sandwiches, with cucumbers as was customary in the homeland. The immigrants did, however, continue to grow or buy and prepare rutabagas, potatoes, carrots, onions, and beets. Cooks valued these items not only because they kept well, but also because they were versatile ingredients, the building blocks for soups, stews, casseroles, pasties, and pickled and raw salads.

New potatoes and rutabagas stand out as the favorites of the Finnish immigrants and their descendants. When the new potatoes were big enough to dig, many families enjoyed them boiled in the skin, then peeled and sprinkled with dill. But, more than potatoes, "Rutabagas were really, for vegetables, a treat."[18] The sheer number of rutabaga recipes attests to the food's importance among the Finnish immigrants. A good rutabaga tasted delicious in raw strips. Boiled rutabagas, mashed, cubed, or browned rutabagas, and rutabaga or rutabaga-potato casseroles frequently appeared on Finnish-American tables. In fact, lanttulaatikko, a casserole of mashed rutabagas combined with egg, milk, and maybe nutmeg, salt, and pepper, was a specialty, often reserved for Sunday dinners and traditional at Christmastime. "Make a souffle with some breadcrumbs and bake it with nutmeg. It's delicious. . . . It's one of our favorites," declared one Finnish-American woman.[19]

Finns today claim for themselves the distinction of being a people traditionally "not much for sweets." Cakes, tortes, puddings, cookies, and breads, while rich with cream and butter, relied mainly on natural substances like fruit and berries for their sugar. Traditionally, the day held two distinct kinds of occasions for eating sweets: dessert, which followed the meal, and "coffee," a more flexible snack time that could occur in midmorning or midafternoon, as well as late evening. Usually light and simple affairs, favorite desserts included fresh berries, fruit, or kiisseli (sauce) made from cooked berries or rhubarb with a little cornstarch or potato flour added. Sometimes the women made fruit soup, a thickened mixture of dried fruits such as prunes, raisins, and apricots seasoned with a cinnamon stick.

Puddings were another category of common desserts. Bread pudding was a tasty way to use up leftover, stale bread, especially pulla. In addition, like people of Scandinavian descent, Finns enjoyed rice pudding either made on top of the stove or baked like a custard in the oven. Some families even made a light midday meal of rice pudding and fruit topping. With fruit soup or berry sauce spooned over the top, rice pudding took on new meaning, becoming a special dessert to be eaten after Sunday or Christmas dinner.

Of all pudding desserts, ilmapuuro (air pudding) elicits the most mixed reactions from Finns today. Pink and fluffy, it consists of farina cooked in fruit juice (usually cranberry). When thickened, the mixture is cooled and beaten rapidly, so that it virtually triples in volume. There are Finns in Minnesota today who love ilmapuuro and make it fairly often; however, more people remember it as a unique dish whose novelty quickly wore off. It was difficult to make a little bit, novice cooks were frequently surprised at its volume, and beating the stuff by hand could be a real challenge. "I was telling Mother I remember probably the first time she ever made it," said a third-generation Finnish-American woman. "I had to be less than nine years old. She used to make her biscuit [pulla] in a great big pottery bowl. So, she decided to make this cranberry pudding. It was the first time she ever made the recipe. It just kept getting bigger! We had a big bowl of this cranberry stuff yea high!"[20] One woman, who today makes ilmapuuro in her food processor, remembers her mother sitting in a snowbank, cooling the mixture while whipping it by hand.

Finns traditionally have prided themselves on the amount of coffee they can consume in a day, and they rarely drink coffee alone. "Coffee" or "coffee table" was and remains a true Finnish and Finnish-American institution. Depending on the economic circumstances of the host and the importance of the occasion, coffee might include any of a number of cakes, filled and topped with berries and whipped cream, pastries, cookies (such as almond or ginger), pulla, cheeses, and breads. Coffee for family members was a simple, informal affair, usually including only pulla and cookies. When travelers or guests dropped in, however, it took on another quality.

One rarely went visiting, for one thing, without bringing a sweet to the host. "Finnishness" was not important; bakery cookies would do as long as the visitor brought something along. As soon as they arrived, guests were served coffee. A meal or snack could then follow at the appropriate time. The responsibility for hosting, however, dictated that company be treated to a profusion of sweets, regardless of what they might have brought

Members of the Ladies of Kaleva, Duluth, displaying traditional ginger cookies, pulla, rice pudding, piirakka, and viili, Depot Food Fair, Duluth, 1985

along with them. Women remember that their mothers "Emptied the cupboard. . . . There was everything on that table! And one was going to outdo the other. They were all in there for competition. They'd serve the best!"[21]

The meal patterns of the Finnish immigrants were closely tied to the occupations and economic circumstances of individuals. Few ate three big meals a day. Breakfast, especially among poorer people, might be bread and coffee; others might add hot cereal, viili, milk, or even open-faced sandwiches to the menu. There was little to distinguish lunch from dinner, except that the evening meal tended to be a more formal one with family members gathered together to eat a greater quantity of food. Any of the basic foodstuffs of the immigrants might appear at either meal. The elaborateness and frequency of interim snacking or "coffee," too, depended on individuals' circumstances. Men who punched in at a time clock or carried their lunches, for example, did not have the choices available to those who worked for themselves or close to home.

The Finnish immigrants, like members of most other ethnic groups, wove food into their celebrations of religious and calendar holidays. Their preparations for Christmas, probably the most elaborate of all holidays from a culinary point of view, showed three categories of traditional foods: "more of the same," or a profusion of common dishes such as casseroles, present all at once; everyday dishes prepared in a fancier, more elaborate way, such as iced, swirled, fruit-studded pulla; and holiday specialties that cooks would not be likely to make at any other time of the year.

Many families began the Christmas Day meal with an appetizer of lipeäkala (lutefisk), the boiled cod dish also popular among Swedish and Norwegian immigrants. But lipeäkala, the smell of which is reputedly far worse than its taste, has always evoked strong reactions — both positive and negative — and sometimes both within one family. Many would agree with a second-generation woman who said, "I never cared for it, but my husband likes it. . . . It's got a terrible, terrible odor when you cook it . . . but it doesn't taste like it smells. . . . I think if you didn't put anything on it [like] melted butter, it would be very blah."[22] Its popularity has declined with the aging and death of the immigrant generation.

Ham was the traditional centerpiece for Christmas dinner (and Easter, too), although some families had chicken instead. Rutabaga casserole was de rigueur, as was rice pudding and fruit sauce for dessert. Later in the evening, when it was time for coffee, nibblers could choose from an array of holiday cookies or pastries, as well as several versions of pulla and limppu, a molasses rye bread with white raisins and mashed potatoes in the dough. Prune tarts, however, were the chief Christmas specialty. Like

Pulla in its everyday form

many foods reserved for particular occasions, these took time and skill to make. The dough was a buttery, flaky pastry that required cool temperature and a light hand, and the filling and folding process was time consuming, if not difficult. "You start in the morning with the dough," stated a Duluth Finnish woman. "You roll it out, spread it with butter and put the dough in the refrigerator. You do this all day long. . . . All that work — and one mouthful and it's gone!"[23]

Aside from Christmas celebrations, Finnish Minnesotans did not cultivate or maintain many specific foodways for special occasions. Easter was mainly a religious event, and on Midsummer's Day (juhannus or St. John's Day), according to interviews conducted in the 1930s, "the food is seldom typically Finnish except for an abundance of buttermilk and rye bread."[24]

Laskiainen ("sliding down hill"), traditionally celebrated on Shrove Tuesday, however, presents an interesting study in the revival of ethnic traditions, including foods. This festival in Finland was meant to ensure good luck and abundant crops in the coming year; it was also a last fling before the onset of Lent. In St. Louis County, early immigrants apparently continued the festival, but by the 1930s it was no longer celebrated. But in 1937 the county schools' social workers decided to revive the festival in the Palo-Markham school district and to focus on winter sports. Almost fifty years later, Laskiainen was still going strong; so popular had it become, in fact, that in addition to the community-based event at Palo, a public celebration was added at the Iron Range Interpretative Center in Chisholm. Hernekeitto (pea soup made with ham), pannukakku, coffee, and pulla have always been the foods for Laskiainen. Like those linked to other celebrations, however, these dishes, while being absolutely traditional for the festival, may also be eaten at any time throughout the year.[25]

From immigrants to the second or third generations, two kinds of changes are evident in traditional Finnish foodways: changes in the foods themselves and changes in the way that they are integrated into daily life. Technology is responsible for alterations in both arenas. And technology receives both praise and blame for its role. For instance, blenders and food processors greatly alleviate the work of those who wish to make air pudding and avoid the tedium of whipping by hand. Microwave and convection ovens speed, if not simplify, the baking of pannukakku.

More than any other appliance, however, the freezer has made it easier to produce and maintain a stock of certain favored dishes. Numerous women confide that they bake pulla only when they have time. But then they bake it in quantity and store loaves of it in freezers, thereby maintaining an almost constant supply. Other women freeze leftover foods that they can later incorporate into casseroles or breads. Almost anything that is time consuming — pasties, prune tarts, even soups — can be made in advance and stored for future use. Freezing has also replaced canning, to a degree, although some families prefer the taste of canned berries to frozen ones.

On the negative side, commercially canned foods, while liberating cooks from many steps of food preparation, cannot approach the taste of fresh or home-processed items. Tuna fish in kalamojakka is a palatable timesaver, but no substitute for the real thing. Likewise, although commercial distribution makes rye flour readily available, the texture and freshness cannot compete with locally milled grains. One woman, who thought boil-in-the-bag lipeäkala would be a great timesaver found the cooked fish "gelatiny . . . a flop. A mess!"[26]

In recent years, the revived interest in ethnicity has added a new dimension to traditional Finnish foodways in Minnesota. Through the early 1970s, Finnish-Minnesotan foodways followed a pattern common among most ethnic groups: where contemporary life styles resembled those of the immigrant generation — in rural settlements like the Palo-Markham and New York Mills areas — traditional dishes and practices continued to occupy a place in the daily lives of the ethnic community. In 1970 almost half of Minnesota's Finns lived in St. Louis County; one-fifth of them in Duluth and the rest presumably spread around the iron range towns and rural set-

Elsie Wierimaa and Edna Johnson, Aurora, hold cubes of squeaky cheese; these women represented Minnesota Finns at Finn Fest '85, Hancock, Michigan.

tlements.[27] Preliminary interviewing indicates that retention of traditions is stronger among Finns still on their homestead land or in small towns than among those concentrated in Duluth. And likewise, in the urban or suburban settings of the Twin Cities where traditional "plain, basic foods" face competition from a variety of other, often alluring, cuisines there has been less retention of traditional foodways on a daily basis. Thus by and large, Old Country Finnish foods, or even the Finnish immigrant cuisine, has evolved to the status of isolated dishes served only on special occasions.

Through the mid-twentieth century, as the gap between rural and urban life styles narrowed and as farm children moved to the cities, traditional Finnish foodways appeared to be on the decline. Fresh blood and "first milk" have become rarities even in rural areas as fewer people keep or butcher animals. Silakka, an immigrant staple, is increasingly hard to find in any form. Pickled herring is a substitute for Baltic sprats and lox (for those who can afford it) for salt salmon. It is an irony that in the cosmopolitan urban environment of the 1980s, some of the basic ingredients for traditional dishes have become exotic and unavailable. While residents of Palo or Aurora, for example, can still buy the potato flour that makes a prettier, unclouded berry sauce, Finns in Duluth and the Twin Cities must settle for cornstarch.

Several individuals and events, however, have intervened, halting what seemed to be the slow, if inevitable, eradication of food traditions. As a result, Minnesota's second- and third-generation Finns stand as a good example of the ways in which traditions may be resurrected or rejuvenated. In St. Paul, for instance, the need to maintain a food booth at the annual Festival of Nations has prompted committees of women to delve into their memories and into cookbooks — both old and contemporary, Finnish and Finnish American — in search of distinctive foods. While some of the members of these committees customarily prepare a few traditional foods, others have joined in hopes of learning more about their heritage. Thus the Festival of Nations, as well as events at the Finn Creek museum in New York Mills and at the Iron Range Interpretative Center, have reminded Finnish Minnesotans of forgotten aspects of their foodways. In the aftermath of such festivals numerous participants as well as observers have begun to cook at home the foods they saw on display. In this manner, through public events, some nearly abandoned foodways have regained vitality in private settings.

Festivals and other public events, however, do not bring about the revival of completely authentic Old Country foodways. A certain blending and modernizing influence appears when food demonstrators, for instance, choose to present foods from many eras and different regions of a country. Thus, the Karelian uunipaisti, a lamb-pork-beef ragout also from eastern Finland, for example, has entered the ethnic foodways of Finnish Americans with no connection to Karelia or other eastern regions of their homeland.[28]

Another factor altering the shape of Finnish food traditions in the state has been the infusion of contemporary Finnish gourmet foods, a trend most noticeable among urban Finnish Minnesotans who are interested in "authentic" foods with a distinctively Finnish image. Features in gourmet food magazines promote sophisticated, as well as country, foods. Dinners with Finnish visitors and the catered foods at public embassy functions further promote elegant dining. Recent immigrants and returned travelers have also introduced modern Finnish recipes that Minnesota's cooks have added to their repertoires.[29]

A final influence on foodways that is especially strong among Finns in Minnesota comes from the cookbooks and newspaper columns written by Minnesota native Beatrice A. Ojakangas. Her publications function as reference books in many homes. They are sources of new recipes and a treasure trove for the curious who wish to learn and experiment with new foods; they also supplement memories, providing a place to track down the exact measurements or procedures of a recipe learned long ago and only partially remembered.

Thus through festivals, recent immigrants, and published works, the traditional foodways of Minnesota's Finnish population have become a synthesis of tradition and innovation, a blend of old and new.

NOTES

[1] Interview of Marlene Bantarri, Roseville, February 1, 1983.

[2] Interview of Geraldine Kangas, Aurora, August 23, 1983.

[3] Timo Riippa, "The Finns and Swede-Finns," in *They Chose Minnesota*, ed. Holmquist, 296, 298–304.

[4] Cooking with blood is a good example of the clear link of foodways to life style and historical context. Access to fresh blood was essential for these dishes, which consequently were more prevalent in rural areas. Town dwellers, as well as farmers who kept no cattle, sometimes bought blood from acquaintances; interview of Helen Jacobson, Maplewood, February 10, 1983. When Finns ceased to keep and slaughter their own cattle, blood cookery began to wane. In Finland today, however, blood products reputedly are readily available commercially, and homemade dishes such as blood pancakes are common items; interview of Mary Latola and Geraldine Kangas, Palo, August 23, 1983; Bantarri interview.

[5] Kangas interview; interview of Pamela Leino, Minneapolis, February 18, 1983.

[6] Interview of Lilja White, Palo, August 23, 1983; Beatrice A. Ojakangas, *The Finnish Cookbook* (New York: Crown Publishers, 1964), 15; Leino interview. Mrs White was born in Aurora, returned to Finland with her parents at the age of seven, and remigrated to Palo in 1948.

[7] Ojakangas, *Finnish Cookbook*, 16.

[8] Interview of Geraldine Kangas, Lilja White, and Hilda White, Aurora, August 23, 1983.

[9] Leino interview.

[10] Interviews of Mary Latola, Palo, August 23, 1983, Jennie Kuiti and Helen Hepokoski, both Duluth, November 4, 1982, Marianne Brown, Minneapolis, January 6, 1984.

[11] Interview of Sylvia Wirtanen, Duluth, August 24, 1982; the quote is from her mother.

[12] Data on the Finns in Minnesota, Nute Papers. Lihamojakka, also known simply as mojakka, uses beef instead of fish and often includes carrots and rutabagas. Some Finnish Americans also make a salt-pork mojakka; Kangas, Hilda White, and Brown interviews.

[13] Interview of Natalie Saari Gallagher, St. Paul, February 1, 1983.

[14] Gallagher interview.

[15] Bantarri interview.

[16] Interview of Kielo Eila Eilers, Duluth, August 24, 1983.

[17] As late as 1964, a cooking teacher and author was able to say, "One of the greatest challenges to Finnish home economists today lies in thinking of ways to make vegetables more appealing to the public"; Ojakangas, *Finnish Cookbook*, 166.

[18] Latola interview.

[19] Interview of Lois Nelson, White Bear Lake, February 9, 1983.

[20] Gallagher interview.

[21] Latola interview.

[22] Hepokoski interview.

[23] Kuiti interview. On traditional Finnish Christmas foods, see also Data on the Finns in Minnesota, "Festivals," Nute Papers.

[24] Data on the Finns in Minnesota, "Festivals," Nute Papers.

[25] Data on the Finns in Minnesota, "Festivals," Nute Papers; Kangas and Lilja White interviews.

[26] Jacobson interview.

[27] Riippa, "The Finns," in *They Chose Minnesota*, ed. Holmquist, 299, 300, 303.

[28] Brown interview.

[29] For a discussion linking foodways, change, and prestige, see Jack Goody, *Cooking, Cuisine, and Class: A Study in Comparative Sociology* (Cambridge: Cambridge University Press, 1982).

THE GREEKS

F amily custom, religious ritual, and the current public interest in international cuisine all contribute to the stength of Greek cooking in contemporary Minnesota. Ethnic dinners are well attended, cookbooks and recipes are in demand, and food at folk festivals sells readily. Non-Greek people find that their ideas about "terribly heavy and fattening" foods "swimming in olive oil" disappear as they become more familiar with the great variety of Greek dishes.

Greek people have long maintained that their diet accounts for their vigorous health, and nutritional studies bear them out. The Greeks' subtle use of seasonings and herbs, of vegetables, fish, and poultry fits the modern dietary trend away from beef, pork, and high-fat foods; their customary reliance on soup as a main course and fruit for dessert likewise corresponds to the latest medically endorsed food plans. Traditionally Greek food is simple; only on holidays or other festive occasions is the table laden with a variety of special dishes.[1]

There is no single, easily defined Greek cuisine in Minnesota because in Greece every region, every village, and in some cases, every family, had a different way of creating a given dish using foods locally available. Stifado (stew) incorporated whatever meat was plentiful and whichever vegetables and herbs grew best in a particular climate. Greeks who lived near the sea ate fresh fish and shellfish while those living inland and in northern areas used an abundance of dried codfish. Nuts for pastries varied from almonds to walnuts, pecans, or a combination of all three, depending on the supply. The lemons and oranges basic to sweets in one area of Greece were not used in other districts where kumquats, apricots, or cherries were more easily grown. Residents of the mountain regions ate more goat and lamb than did city dwellers. In fact, northern Greeks — the Macedonians — who settled in the northern Minnesota towns of Deer River, Hibbing, Virginia, and Duluth retained this love of lamb and goat, and today their descendants obtain the meat from area farmers or local markets.[2]

Early Greek writings record the use of many of these same foods. The Epicurean, Hesiod, wrote extensively about foodways in 500 B.C., and in 350 B.C. Archestratus produced his great work, variously translated as

Gastronomy or *Gastrology*. Aristotle explained that the Greeks when they visited Egyptian cities as tradesmen had learned about beekeeping and the varieties of honey. During this period, seafaring merchants founded colonies in Spain, North Africa, southern Italy, Sicily and other Italian coastal islands, and what is now Marseilles, France. In all these places they introduced their native cuisine.[3]

When the Romans conquered Greece in 250 B.C. they removed many of the Greek chefs to Rome to teach the Greek art of food preparation. Almost six hundred years later Greece became part of the Byzantine Empire with Constantinople, an international city, as its capital. Trade flourished, and Persians, Armenians, Egyptians, and Indians who came to the city introduced their spices and foods, as well as customs, to the Greeks. In 1453 Constantinople fell to the Turks, and Greece became part of the Ottoman Empire for the next four hundred years, finally re-emerging as an independent nation in 1830. For more than a millennium, the basic Greek fare was greatly influenced by those who extended their empires — and their culinary tastes — over Greek lands.[4]

Greece as a cultural entrepot faces both east and west, and its cuisine is identified sometimes as Mediterranean and sometimes as Middle Eastern. Middle Eastern elements include rice, lentils, chick-peas, yoghurt, lamb, cinnamon, nutmeg, and strong coffee, while the Mediterranean influence is apparent in the use of seafoods, citrus fruits, tomatoes, leafy vegetables, pork, and wine. The resulting cuisine can draw upon one or many traditions and still be lavish or thrifty, plain or imaginative.

Significant numbers of Greeks began emigrating to Minnesota around 1910, although several hundred — mainly bachelors who joined the state's floating labor force as railroad or lumber workers — had arrived in preceding years. Most of the later immigrants were from the Peloponnesos; some, however, had left central Greece and Macedonia. Among the Greek people who flocked to St. Paul, Minneapolis, and Duluth in 1913–14 were families with young children, single women, and more bachelors. Poverty, along with political and religious discrimination, was the primary reason for emigrating. Although many Greeks hoped to save their wages and return home, they found they could adapt to the new land where jobs were available and altered their plans. They became citizens and started businesses and families.[5]

The immigrants brought their food habits with them to the United States, and their descendants have maintained many of these customs with few changes. In new neighborhoods, Greek families lived side-by-side with non-Greek Europeans and native-born Americans. Many men and women worked in boardinghouses, restaurants, bakeries, or school and hospital

Coula Perros, Duluth, holds prosforon (bread) and sfragida (seal) bearing symbols of the Greek Orthodox church, 1985; the bread is integral to the religious service.

kitchens where they learned new recipes and food ideas. But at home they continued their Greek ways.[6]

Maintenance of traditional diet patterns, induced by a genuine love of the food, was simplified by the relative ease of obtaining familiar ingredients. Grocery stores in Minnesota operated by Greek, Slavic, or Italian merchants imported a variety of commodities from Europe. Vegetables, fruits, dried codfish, octopus, and canned goods were shipped from Chicago. Although it was necessary to experiment with new varieties of fish, Lake Superior and other inland waters throughout Minnesota provided an ample supply. Farmers' markets in several locations in the larger cities sold fresh seasonal foods. Whenever possible families planted gardens as soon as they arrived, filling the yards around their homes with vegetables, herbs, and grapevines. Mining companies provided plots for their employees in the towns located on Minnesota's iron ranges.[7] The immigrants used garden produce in season, and canned, pickled, dried, or stored food in sawdust or sand for the winter months.

Good times with family and friends and the resulting memories also contributed to the continuation of national foodways. In the 1920s the Duluth community organized Twelve Holy Apostles Greek Orthodox Church, the only one of its kind in the area, which was attended by Greeks from Hibbing, Chisholm, and Virginia.[8] Duluth families, always glad to have visitors, outdid themselves preparing an abundance of traditional foods for these occasions, beginning days before an event. Leg of lamb, chicken, and fish would be partially cooked the night before and finished during the church services to be ready for the happy gathering afterward.[9]

Living in Minnesota, however, required some adjustments in traditional recipes and cooking methods, and a few techniques were destined to disappear. Greek women no longer cooked on open hearths or baked in beehive-shaped ovens in their yards or in the central ovens in their village square. Waiting until the oven became hot and white from the wood fire built under it and using long, flat, wooden utensils to push pans of food in and out became a fond memory. Many of the immigrant women, however, found it difficult to do without the traditional round pans, which are still used in Greece, to bake all of the pitas (pies made with layers of phyllo dough), cakes, and many of the sweets. They employed local tinsmiths to make these pans in a variety of sizes, some with a rim for bread, roasts, and deep-dish cookery. Food baked in the round pans was always cut into diamond shapes, and even those cooks in Minnesota who changed to square or rectangular ones continued this custom.

In Macedonia the men in the lumber camps had done their own cooking over open fires and, later, had incorporated their favorite dishes into

Baklava, cut into diamond-shaped pieces, each pinned with a clove

family menus. These recipes plus those cooked over the open hearth at home were the origins of the one-pot and single-pan meals. Immigrants found such foods practical and easy to prepare in Minnesota kitchens. Many Greeks still savor these stews, hearty soups, bean and lentil dishes, pilafi (rice combined with vegetables, meat, or poultry), pastitsio (baked macaroni and meat topped with a rich sauce), and moussaka (a layered vegetable, meat, and sauce casserole).

Immigrants also continued to prepare cheese, yoghurt, phyllo dough, and bread in much the same way as they had in the Greek villages. Bread was the first food that young girls learned to make by watching and questioning older, experienced cooks. One woman remembers her question: "How will I know if I have kneaded the bread long enough?" and her grandmother's reply: "If you have sweat all over your body, the bread is kneaded enough."[10] Very large families baked many loaves of bread during a week, often starting after an evening meal. The women would make the bread dough, put it to rise, and then go to bed, setting the alarm clock to awaken them about midnight to place the loaves in the oven to bake, after which they would return to bed.

Phyllo, the thin pastry used for many traditional Greek dishes, was usually the next food a young cook would attempt. On a kitchen table or other large surface she would roll the dough with a dowel or plasti (an old broom handle), until it became thin. It was then lifted from the floury table onto a bed, which had been covered with a clean sheet, and was gently pulled even thinner. Pans were placed over the dough so the cooks could cut pieces to size. Few women undertake this process today,

Sisters-in-law Chris (left) and Anna Regas, Duluth, make baklava for their restaurant, 1986; Anna holds a sheet of phyllo while Chris sprinkles on filling.

preferring to buy frozen phyllo at the grocery store in packages of precut sheets.

Many Greek Minnesotans, however, still make their own yoghurt. The butterfat content of the milk and the methods of preparing and of keeping the mixture warm while it thickens vary with each family. Some wrap blankets around the container to keep the temperature constant; others use the heat from the pilot light on a gas stove. Those who like thick yoghurt drain it in a piece of cheesecloth until it reaches the consistency of sour cream. It can then be spread on bread, used to top pilafi and other dishes, or mixed with broken pieces of bread and eaten from a bowl.

The immigrants were accustomed to eating khorta (greens), which, in Greece, they gathered on hillsides and at the edges of fields.[11] In Minnesota mustard and dandelion greens were plentiful in the undeveloped areas of the cities where these people settled. Around Duluth the best greens grew at the end of the Woodland streetcar line, on the hills to the west of the city where Enger Tower is now located, or at many locations along the north shore of Lake Superior. Gathering them was a real social event for families and friends, and everyone in a foraging party carried a small knife to cut the youngest and tenderest leaves. The rewards were both immediate and long range: at the end of the day some greens were steamed and served with oil and lemon juice. The women processed the rest for winter storage. First they washed and thoroughly dried the leaves, tied them into small bundles with string, and then tied the bundles to a cord hung across a back room. After the bundles were completely dry, they were placed in brown paper bags, which were given a tight twist, and stored in a dark, cool place for winter consumption. Steamed and served, the dried greens tasted as though they had just been been picked. [12]

Immigrants grew grapevines in great abundance primarily for use in dolmades, stuffed grape leaves. Today leaves in brine are available in specialty stores; however, some Greeks, especially residents of the iron range towns, have retained the tradition of growing their own. Just as their grandparents did, they select leaves for their size and tenderness — the third, fourth, and fifth on a branch — and parboil them in preparation for canning. The parboiled leaves are piled, rolled, tied with string, and canned in brine. Jars are stored in a cool place for winter use. Today some women freeze the raw leaves between layers of plastic wrap and then parboil them when they want to prepare dolmades.

Because the growing season in most Minnesota areas is too short to produce any grapes, Greeks who wanted to make wine bought fruit, usually Tokay, Concord, or Malaga grapes, from local merchants. During Prohibition many Greeks returned to making wine since they could not buy it; others secretly purchased it from Italian neighbors because selling homemade wine was illegal.

Everyone grew herbs. Where there was insufficient garden space, plants were raised in outdoor pots that could be brought inside for the winter. Families gathered herbs continually during the growing season to ensure an ample supply all year long. Carefully washed leaves were dried either at room temperature, covered with cheesecloth in the sun, or in a slightly warm oven. When completely dry, they were lightly crumbled by hand and stored in tightly covered glass jars. Today, as in the past, some cooks mix dried parsley and dill for storage because they frequently use them together in cooking.

Parsley, dill, oregano, mint, and basil seem to be favorites. Dill is characteristic of the cooking in the Peloponnesian village of Sparta where many Minnesota Greeks had their origins, while Macedonians seem to prefer cinnamon and allspice. Oregano is everyone's favorite, especially when used in a tomato sauce for fish or chicken. People new to Greek cuisine often express surprise at the use of mint, cinnamon, and nutmeg in meat dishes; others may pause when they recognize the basil flavor in some sweet syrups that saturate pastries.

"Sweets" is the name Greeks give to all cookies, pastries, and cakes used for desserts, for entertaining at special times, or for treats taken to shut-ins. They are seldom eaten at daily meals but are served to guests, usually in individual fluted cupcake papers. Now, as in years past, families sometimes enjoy them with coffee around three o'clock in the afternoon. Midafternoon visitors are served a sweet accompanied by a glass of cold water or strong Greek coffee or, if the guest is a man, probably a liqueur or brandy. Friends who come later than the normal coffee hour receive the usual sweet and beverage, but the family does not join in.[13]

An early custom that, as far as anyone knows, has disappeared from northern Minnesota is glyka tou koutaliou, or "sweets of the spoon." A dollop of this combination of fruits thickened to the consistency of a preserve would be served to guests on a small plate with a spoon and accompanied by a glass of cold water. Some households offered it stirred into the water as a sweet beverage, occasionally followed by liqueur, brandy, or Ouzo—the famous Greek drink distilled from raisins, fennel, and anise. Glyka was made from lemons, oranges, cherries, grapefruit, kumquats, or even rose petals, depending upon what was available in the area and what the family traditions in Greece had been. While no one seems to make it now in Duluth, Hibbing, or Virginia, Greeks in Duluth say that relatives in Chicago and eastern cities have retained the custom. Many older women remember the honor of being chosen to serve guests their plate of glyka and water.

Immigrant families served various beverages. Many today remember wine on the table at most mealtimes. Children learned how the various types—Retsina, Mavrodaphne, or the dry white wines—enhanced the flavors of food. Today wine is served for holidays, celebrations, and often at Sunday meals. A liqueur, a cordial, or the Greek brandy, Metaxa, were and remain favorite alcoholic beverages, and the tradition of serving guests Ouzo at room temperature with an accompanying glass of water is still maintained. Whatever the occasion, however, the beverage offered is always accompanied by food.

Although strong American-style coffee is found at mealtimes in homes today, the Greek (actually Turkish) variety is still commonly served as a refreshment in the afternoon, when guests drop in, or in the late evening. One of the tastes acquired during centuries of Turkish domination, this finely pulverized kafe is ritualistically prepared in a pot called a briki. It always leaves a fine silt at the bottom of a cup.

The immigrants enjoyed telling fortunes from these grounds, a pastime seldom practiced today. A drained coffee cup would be upturned, and the pattern that emerged held the drinker's fortune. Interpretations varied from person to person, but in general a trip was ahead if the grounds ran in streams down the sides of the cup, and a marriage was forthcoming if rings formed. Grounds that stayed at the bottom of the cup foretold lots of money, and if the rim of the cup became covered trouble lay ahead.

Traditionally men did not prepare food in the home, but there were many families where the father had his own specialty, such as roasting lamb for special occasions, making mageritsa (Easter soup), or baking the family's supply of sweets. In addition, there are homes where everyone participates in the preparation of holiday foods, and still others where all the members of the family cook entire meals. Some immigrant parents felt it was so important for children to do well in school that they excused them from any work in the kitchen, leaving only the mothers and often fathers who willingly did all the food preparation. Surprisingly enough their children, as adults, have kept an interest in Greek food, retaining many of the old family recipes, and if the fathers cooked, the sons continue the tradition.[14]

The foodways of second- and third-generation Greek women vary from maintenance of the immigrant cuisine to preparing special dishes for holidays only to complete neglect of Greek food. Diverse forces may cause a drift from traditional patterns. When Greeks marry non-Greeks, for example, the emphasis on ethnic foods often changes, or women who work away from home may not have time for the various steps required by the traditional dishes. In some kitchens, olive oil has given way to corn oil because of price and availability, lemons to bottled lemon juice, and quarts of homemade chicken or beef stock to cubes or cans of bouillon. Family menus are influenced by children who learn about pizza, chili, spaghetti, and hamburgers from their peers. Many women who do not cook traditional foods on a daily basis, however, may prepare special dishes on weekends, holidays, and vacations. And even those with limited time at home continue certain customs, such as growing grape leaves, raising herbs, or making yoghurt, cheese, breads, or sweets.

Advances in cooking technology frequently offer short cuts in preparing traditional foods. With the introduction of pressure cookers in the late 1920s, for instance, some women found a quick way to make dinner after church services. Meat or fish was readied the night before or early in the morning. After the service, greens were fixed in the cooker, then put aside in a marinade while potatoes were cooked. Finally beans or other vegetables were added, and in a short time dinner was ready.[15]

Although mixers, blenders, and food processors may now be used to shorten the steps described in traditional recipes, many Greek women still prefer to use their own two hands for food preparation. Hands have always been a prime cooking utensil, one which no modern device seems to replace. They take the place of a brush, for example, to spread melted butter or oil on phyllo leaves. Kourabiedes (tender, buttery cookies) are traditionally mixed entirely with the hands, a process that takes at least two hours.

Menu patterns — as well as some of the foods and technologies — have changed radically over the years. Breakfasts in Greek homes today are much the same as anywhere else, and only a few families have the traditional olives, toast, and feta cheese. Unlike their ancestors who ate their main meal at midday, most Greek Minnesotans have a light lunch — yoghurt, toast, and fruit, perhaps — with a heavier meal in the evening. A typical menu, however, still includes meat about twice a week; most of the main meals feature rice, bean, or lentil dishes, vegetable stews, soups, or fish. Various pitas — eggplant, squash, or spinach combined with cheese — a salad, bread, and fruit complete the meal. During the Great Depression this largely meatless cuisine was more than a tradition; it was an economic necessity.[16]

Easter is associated with more food traditions than any other holiday, in part because it follows seven weeks of Lenten fasting. During this time no animal product — meat, eggs, fish, or milk derivatives — can be eaten. On Wednesdays and Fridays and the whole week before Easter, wine and olive oil are also ruled out. Women cook many bean and lentil soups as well as various combinations of rice and vegetables such as spinach, cauliflower, artichokes, or eggplant. In the early years members of the Greek Orthodox church strictly observed this ritual, but now Lenten fasting varies with individuals and usually occurs only on Wednesdays, Fridays, and the entire week preceding Easter.[17]

Most of the symbols and rituals for Easter weekend remain intact. The Good Friday observance commemorates the crucifixion and entombment of Christ. On Saturday the midnight service lasts for several hours and is followed by a dinner to celebrate the resurrection and the breaking of the Lenten fast. In Duluth church members prepare and serve a meal for any who wish to attend — often the elderly, as well as others, without families. Many stay briefly and then go home to further festivities. Large families may continue celebrating until Easter Day sunrise, following dinner with live or recorded music.[18]

Red eggs are central to Easter rituals both at home and in church. (The egg is the symbol of the renewal of life, and the red color signifies the blood of Jesus.) In most homes they are hard boiled and dyed on Maundy Thursday — the Thursday of Holy Week. At that time women of the church also dye dozens of eggs for the Saturday night resurrection service, when the priest blesses and passes the eggs out to the congregation.

Young people play traditional games with their eggs, trying to break each other's with end-to-end blows. As the contest continues, participants declare "Christos Aneste" (Christ is risen) and "Alethos Aneste" (He is truly risen), each hoping to keep his own egg unbroken and thus have good luck in the year ahead. In another custom brought from Greece and still practiced in Minnesota, one of the blessed dyed eggs is kept on the family icon where it stays until the next Lenten season.[19]

The long awaited Saturday night (Sunday morning) dinner brings out the very best of Greek cooking. The first course is mageritsa (the Easter soup), made of the head, liver, lungs, and heart of a lamb, seasoned with celery and onions, and cooked with rice. Some cooks add pieces of beef to the broth at the end of the simmering period; others flavor it with an avgolemono (egg-lemon) sauce. Leg of lamb is the traditional meat, accompanied by pan-cooked vegetables, a dish using manestra (also called orzo, a small oval pasta), salad, and lambropsomo (the Easter bread), which is adorned with a cluster of red eggs. Spinach or cheese pitas are sometimes added to the menu. The favored sweet, found in all homes, is koulourakia (a cookie); some women also bake galatoboureko (layers of phyllo pastry with a custard filling), diples, baklava, and kourabiedes. The wines and beverages served depend on family traditions.[20]

At Easter and other festive occasions when a whole young lamb was served, it was traditional at the end of the meal to hold the blade bone to the light and examine it. If the bone was fairly transparent, good luck would come to the family that year; if blemished or dark, it forecast "a bad year ahead." Although this is a custom infrequently practiced today, Greeks occasionally remember the old ways and test the blade bone of a young lamb.

After Easter, namesdays are the most elaborate holidays in Greek culture. They are marked with services at church and festivities in the home and far outshine birthday observances. Children named for a patron saint celebrate that saint's day, and those not so named are assigned a Sunday, so everyone has a yearly observance. In the 1920s the church service was followed by an all-day buffet and party at home. Greeks progressed from

Women of Twelve Holy Apostles Greek Orthodox Church, Duluth, frying diples, 1984

dwelling to dwelling where namesday festivities were held, relishing the food and drink. A cordial or glass of wine, brandy, or Ouzo started the celebration and was followed by a cup of Greek coffee. Next the hostess passed appetizer trays laden with sliced lamb, meatballs, feta cheese, or a variety of other foods she chose to prepare. Last came a traditional sweet tray containing diples, kourabiedes, karidopeta, or melomakarona. Today the church observance is the same but a late-afternoon buffet or sit-down dinner has replaced the day-long celebration.

Christmas Eve and Christmas Day are less important Greek holidays, although currently, as a result of Americanization, they command large family gatherings and, of course, favorite foods. Christmas Eve prompts an array of dolmades, salad, avgolemono soup, spinach and cheese pitas, and a variety of sweets. Some families might vary this with leg of lamb, pastitsio, or pasta with brown butter. The routine for Christmas Day includes an early dinner and, later in the afternoon, appetizers and drinks — Ouzo, wine, or brandy. Christmas has supplanted New Year's as the traditional time for exchanging gifts. Bachelors, the elderly, and shut-ins customarily receive fruit and sweets at Christmas and often on other holidays as well.

On the first of January Greeks in the Orthodox church celebrate St. Basil's Day, honoring the patron saint who was known as the granter of wishes and bestower of blessings and who also established orphanages and homes for the poor. Vasilopita, a soft bread in which a coin is hidden, is a central feature of this holiday in all Greek homes. The top of the loaf is always decorated with rounds and twists of dough. Many families begin serving freshly baked Vasilopita around Thanksgiving, thus allowing several members to share in the joy of finding the coin, which brings good luck in the coming year. In some homes the first visitor on St. Basil's Day receives a coin as a symbol of welcome and good fortune. Many Greek Orthodox

Father Constantine Aliferakis, Twelve Holy Apostles Greek Orthodox Church, offering bread to congregants during Vasilopita ceremony, 1986

churches in the United States also hold benefit dinners and send the proceeds to St. Basil's Orphanage in Garrison, New York. In Duluth community leaders of all denominations are invited to this event where they are given slices of the bread and their organizations are blessed.

Foods for St. Basil's Day vary from household to household. Leg of lamb, again, is a favorite although some families prefer roast turkey or pork. A typical meal includes mageritsa ("too good to eat only at Easter"), leg of lamb baked with vegetables, pastitsio, salad, an orzo dish, and Vasilopita, with sweets and black coffee to conclude. Thus the New Year is welcomed in "with good luck of the bread and the sweetness of the pastries."

A special round loaf of bread, prosforon, is part of the communion service every Sunday and on special occasions. Each week one of the women in the congregation bakes two loaves. Before setting these aside for rising, she places on top of each loaf her family's sfragida, a flat wooden seal carved with Greek letters that stand for "Jesus Christ conquers" and symbols of the church. The letters and symbols are thus imprinted into the bread as it rises and become part of the baked loaf. The priest cuts them from the loaf, and they are eaten as part of the communion service. At

Prosforon bearing the imprint of the sfragida

the end of the ceremony, the rest of the bread is divided and passed out to all in attendance as antidoron ("instead of the gifts"), that is, blessed bread, but not the body of Christ. For generations it has been a favorite of children, and uneaten portions are sent to those who could not attend church. The bread left from namesday services, however, is carefully wrapped and taken home by the celebrant.[21]

Traditional foods are also typically associated with rites of passage — funerals, weddings, births, and baptisms. Following the graveside service, for example, mourners return to church for a dinner that always includes fish and a bean dish. Sweets are never served during the mourning period; instead families have paximade, a bread which is sliced after baking and toasted in the oven. Likewise, guests in the home of the bereaved do not receive the traditional sweets but are served paximade with coffee.

Closely related to the funeral service is the kolivan (or kolyvan) or wheat service that is held as a memorial at various times after the funeral — forty days, six months, one year, or as an annual observance thereafter. Whole or cracked wheat is cooked and drained and mixed with toasted crumbs, sesame seeds, raisins, walnuts or almonds, pomegranate seeds, fresh parsley, Jordan almonds, cinnamon, and sugar. This mixture is mounded on a tray by a family member who then, using a cutout pattern, decorates it with sifted powdered sugar and nuts, making a cross and the initials of the deceased. Everyone in attendance takes and eats a portion. Traditionally leftovers were given to the poor; however, in Minnesota today money is sent to a needy Greek village in memory of the deceased.

Food — served for ritual, social, or nutritional purposes — plays an important part in other celebrations even when tradition dictates no specific dishes. Weddings usually include a sit-down dinner at the church or in the home of the bride, and the food reflects the family's favorites. No one knows just why, but at each place setting there is customarily a packet called a boubouniera, containing Jordan almonds, usually wrapped in something as plain as a piece of tulle or as fancy as a hand-crocheted square.[22]

Births are observed by offering sweets such as loukoumades (sweet, deep-fried puffs) to all who visit the home. Each person present at a baptism receives a token that is symbolic of having witnessed the ceremony. This memento is usually a small packet containing Jordan almonds and a special medal or the baby's picture. The infant's family then serves a post-baptism dinner either at the church or in the home.

Family custom bolstered by religious ritual provides a perfect environment for the preservation of foodways. Observed one woman, "If we can keep our churches going, our traditions will stay."[23] And, indeed, it seems that those Greeks most active in church affairs are also the most traditional in their foodways. Surviving recipes are associated with religious holidays. Many have been passed down through the generations intact; others reflect changes in ingredients and cooking methods that have emerged over the years. All, however, are authentic versions of traditional Greek cuisine.

NOTES

[1] Ancel Keys and Margaret Keys, *How to Eat Well and Stay Well the Mediterranean Way* (Garden City, N.Y.: Doubleday, 1975), 38–40.

[2] Interview of Evdoxia Gerogeorge, Duluth, February 16, 1982. Macedonians live in northern Greece as well as in southern Yugoslavia; see also the South Slav chapter, below.

[3] Here and two paragraphs below, see Vilma Liacouras Chantiles, *The Food of Greece* (New York: Avenel Books, 1979), ix–xv, 3–38; *The World Atlas of Food: A Gourmet's Guide to the Great Regional Dishes of the World* (New York: Simon and Schuster, 1974), 192–95; Betty Wason, *The Mediterranean Cookbook* (Chicago: Regnery, 1973), 1–17; Betty Wason, *Cooks, Gluttons, & Gourmets: A History of Cookery* (Garden City, N.Y.: Doubleday, 1962), 150.

[4] In the twelfth century many artists, philosophers, and important cooks escaped persecution by fleeing to monasteries. These Greeks, as they worked with the black-hatted monks to create the daily repast, were given white hats to wear. It is from these white hats that the chefs' hats of today emerged.

[5] Theodore Saloutos, "The Greeks," in *They Chose Minnesota*, ed. Holmquist, 472–77.

[6] For more on Greek-American foodways in an urban setting, see Gregory Gizelis, "Foodways Acculturation in the Greek Community of Philadelphia," *Pennsylvania Folklife* 20 (1970–71): 9–15.

[7] Interview of Efthimia Gerodimos, Hibbing, November 4, 1981.

[8] Before the Duluth church was founded, Greeks from the range cities had been attending St. Vasilije of Ostrog Serbian Eastern Orthodox Church, which was organized in Chisholm in 1910; Saloutos, "The Greeks," in *They Chose Minnesota*, ed. Holmquist, 477.

[9] Here and below, see interviews of Christine Kontonikos, June 23, 1981, Mary Andrews, November 19, 1981, and Coula Perros, January 22, 1982 — all Duluth.

[10] Gerodimos interview.

[11] Ernestine Friedl, *Vasilika: A Village in Modern Greece* (New York: Holt, Rinehart and Winston, 1962), 29.

[12] Here and four paragraphs below, see interviews of Margaret Apostole, Duluth, November 17, 1981, Helen Fotopolous, Hibbing, November 5, 1981.

[13] Here and four paragraphs below, see interview of Mary Bitsiannes, Hibbing, November 4, 1981; Gerogeorge interview.

[14] Here and below, see interview of Kathy Bougalis, Hibbing, November 4, 1981; Bitsiannes interview.

[15] Kontonikos interview.

[16] Interviews of Teddi Bovis, Cloquet, and Emily Regas, Duluth — both December 3, 1981.

[17] Greek Orthodox Holy Week celebrations are based on the Julian calendar, which was devised during the reign of Julius Caesar in 46 B.C. As a result Greek Holy Week is later than the Protestant or Roman Catholic celebrations, which are determined by the more widely used Gregorian calendar.

[18] Interview of Father Ted Trifon, Duluth, December 13, 1981.

[19] Interviews of Coula Perros, November 17, 1981, and Father Ted Trifon, April 8, 1982 — both Duluth. An icon stasion (icon stand) is a place of reverence in the home, containing a vigil light (a votive candle) and icons (pictures) of patron saints, Jesus, Mary, or other images of religious significance. The icon stasion either rests on shelves or on the wall in the dining room or in one of the children's rooms. Other items which have been blessed and given out at church — the red egg, bay leaves and palm leaves on Palm Sunday, flowers from various services, or basil branches handed out on September 14 (the Elevation of the Holy Cross Day) — may also be displayed.

[20] Here and five paragraphs below, see Perros, Regas, Gerogeorge, Andrews, and Bovis interviews. For more on the use of Vasilopita at benefit dinners, see *Minneapolis Star and Tribune*, January 1, 1986, p. 3T.

[21] Trifon interview, April 8, 1982. For more on antidoron, see Robert T. Teske, "Votive Offerings and the Belief System of Greek-Philadelphians," *Western Folklore* 44 (July 1985): 221.

[22] Here and below, see interview of Gloria Maras, Duluth, December 12, 1981.

[23] Interview of Coula Perros, Duluth, March 30, 1982.

Delmonico's Italian Foods, Minneapolis, 1986

THE ITALIANS

Italians and food — the association is almost automatic. In Minnesota the connection reaches back to the last century and transcends the stereotype of the Old World mama stirring a vat of spaghetti sauce on the back burner of her stove. In the 1850s some of the Italians who emigrated to Minnesota's urban areas began their careers peddling fruits, vegetables, ice cream, cigars, and confections.[1] Home gardeners sold surplus produce to raise spare cash. In 1889 the Italian Macaroni and Vermicelli Company was established in St. Paul, and in 1909 the Duluth Macaroni Company began marketing its pasta throughout northeastern Minnesota.[2] Today the Stella Cheese Company in Wisconsin, largest producer of Italian cheeses in the United States, and the Mondavi winery in California are the results of enterprising Minnesota Italians.[3] Descendants of some of the early peddlers and shopkeepers run wholesale and retail produce businesses in the Twin Cities. And the success of Jeno's, Totino's, and Mama Vitale's frozen foods reveals more than a love of convenience. According to a recent *Wall Street Journal* report, Italian is the favorite ethnic food of Americans in the East, Midwest, and South.[4]

Authentic Italian foods, however, far exceed in number and variety the offerings commercially available to the American consumer. Italy is a country of strong regional cultures, each with its own distinctive cuisine. It stretches from the Alps to the Mediterranean Sea. One major culinary difference divides the country, separating the rice and corn eaters of the north, who generally make rich sauces of cheese and butter, from the pasta eaters of the south, whose sauces depend on tomatoes and olive oil. While wheat is grown in both regions, the soft-grain flour of the north requires eggs for binding; hence, the local ravioli and other egg pasta.[5] The hard wheat of the south, on the other hand, produces semolina flour which, with the addition of water, makes the familiar varieties of noodle. Since the majority of Italians both in the United States and in Minnesota emigrated from southern Italy, theirs is the dominant Italian-American cuisine. From southern Italy come not only spaghetti but also pizza, said to have been created in Naples.

But even within the two broad areas, climate, topography, soil quality, access to waterways, and, of course, historical influences make for great diversity. Thus few of the largely valid generalizations often made about Italian food hold true across the board. Garlic, for example, is a staple seasoning in many Italian regions yet is "regarded with some suspicion by cooks of many other[s]";[6] likewise hot peppers. Said a woman whose parents emigrated to Hibbing from the Italian region of the Marches, "Maybe a little garlic, hardly any oregano. . . . You just don't have all those spices, and it's [the food's] not really hot."[7]

Minnesota posed a culinary challenge to most Italian immigrants regardless of region. Although to the outside observer their settlements often resembled "a village of southern Italy transported as if by magic,"[8] residents could only approximate life in the Old Country. Minnesota was a far cry from their native environments. Where would a poor Sicilian find squid for Christmas dinner? With a growing season too short to produce grapes, how would the immigrants make wine? While solutions to some such problems were not long in coming, some changes in life style and foodways were inevitable.

Although merchants, artists, and skilled craftsmen were among the earliest Italians in Minnesota, the great majority of the immigrants were poor men who hoped to accumulate enough capital to return home and buy land. They settled almost exclusively in urban areas and worked at industrial jobs. As their dream of return to Italy faded, they sent for wives, sweethearts, or families, adding stability and substance to the budding communities. By the early 1900s St. Paul had two distinct Italian neighborhoods, while Minneapolis, Duluth, and most of the towns on the iron ranges had one each.

Italian regional loyalties at first prevailed in Minnesota, as friends and relatives from particular villages or areas clustered together in the new urban neighborhoods. Even boardinghouses frequently followed a pattern of voluntary regional segregation. The semi-isolation of these Little Italies helped sustain traditional culture, including the language, customs, and foods.

The immigrants' foodways subsumed customary ways of obtaining and serving food, as well as preparing it. They relied heavily on what their heirs today call "peasant food" — some form of starch accompanied by vegetables and occasionally graced with a bit of meat. Polenta — corn meal boiled in water and then either cooled on a board, baked, or sliced and fried — was a staple for northern Italians. So were rice-based dishes such as risotto: rice cooked with herbs, small pieces of vegetables, and occasionally meat. Southern Italians ate quantities of pasta in a multitude of shapes.

Dried beans, a rich source of protein, were a common staple for all Italians. Sometimes served as a side dish, the beans more often appeared as a main ingredient in soups such as minestrone or in dishes such as pasta fagioli — pasta and beans.

Pizza, a traditional by-product of bread baking, was another pan-Italian food with regional variations. Extra bread dough would be placed in a pan to form a thick crust. Northern Italians typically topped their pizzas with green peppers, onions, olive oil, salt, and pepper, but no cheese. Southerners opted for crushed fresh tomatoes, parsley, garlic, oregano, and grated cheese. Maybe some salami. Sometimes anchovies, but no one ate pizza with "the works." Even today Italians adamantly state that while there may be a great variety of possible ingredients, there are also correct and incorrect ways to combine them. Cheese and anchovies just do not mix.[9]

When the immigrants ate meat it was most likely pork, preserved in some form of sausage or ham. Chicken and even veal were more common in their diets than beef. Dishes such as chicken cacciatore relied on herbs, white wine, and sometimes tomatoes to add zest and a distinctive Italian style to inexpensive poultry. While ground beef was a chief ingredient in meatballs and sauces, other cuts of "steak" were seldom used. An exception was the round or flank steak needed for braciolis, a company dish for which the beef is wrapped around a filling of ham or pork, cheese, and chopped vegetables. Fish or seafood were still more common than any meat among those who had lived near Italy's rivers, lakes, or seacoasts. Sicilians and mainlanders from southernmost Italy were accustomed to eating squid and octopus, especially on holidays. Desserts were reserved for special occasions, often religious celebrations.[10]

Food-getting consumed a good deal of the immigrant families' energy, for the majority were as self-sufficient as was possible in an urban setting. The areas in which they lived, even by the 1920s, were not densely populated. Once established on a small plot of land, the immigrants quickly re-created facets of their traditional food system. They gathered mustard and dandelion greens by the banks of the Mississippi River, on vacant hillsides, or in empty lots. They raised gardens of tomatoes, squash, peppers, beans, and herbs at the very least. Some kept small barnyard animals. Others bought meat but made their own sausages. Families or neighborhood groups built outdoor ovens for bread baking. The women made fresh pasta. And if the garden did not yield enough food for the annual canning, they bought bushels of produce from peddlers. They also dried their own herbs and bought grapes to make wine. No doubt poverty initially motivated many to produce staples such as the bread and

Filomena and Luciano Cocchiarella with loaves of bread baked in an outdoor earthen oven on Hopkins St., St. Paul, around 1940

pasta that by the twentieth century were readily available in groceries or Italian specialty stores. But beyond that motive was a genuine preference for the homemade.[11]

Men, women, and children were all involved in providing food. At an early age, girls learned to help their mothers, aunts, and grandmothers in the kitchen. Making bread, pasta, and sauces and canning produce were typically female tasks. Men and boys were more likely to take a hand in gardening, gathering greens, and making wine. But such roles were not absolute. Several women interviewed for this book learned to cook from their fathers who had cooked for railroad gangs, presumably because they exhibited some prior culinary flair. "Every Sunday in our house my father would get up early and make the sauce. It lasted us for an entire week," remembered a man who today cooks almost all of his family's meals. One woman recalled that her father always prepared the family's entire Palm Sunday dinner, beginning by making the special egg noodles.[12]

Given this background, it comes as little surprise that Italian Americans today associate traditional food almost exclusively with family life. And the more Americanized third and fourth generations feel this bond as vividly as did their parents and grandparents. "Cooking Italian — you have to do it with your family or some people in the house . . . maybe because [of] the whole Italian tradition of cooking in big families and enjoying and sharing the food. I never make it just for myself."[13] Spoken by a woman in her thirties, these words were echoed by women more than twice her age. This statement of traditional values, however, is fraught with implications for the future of traditional Italian cooking. What will become of it as intermarriage, geographical mobility, death, or divorce — to cite a few possible social forces — dilute the customarily tight Italian family structure?

The present is a good time to study traditional Italian foodways in Minnesota, for the past is still readily accessible. The children and grandchildren of the earliest immigrants are still active in the communities. Memories of their parents' experiences coupled with those of subsequent generations cover virtually the entire history of Italian-American cuisine in the state.[14]

From the vantage point of the present we can see in progress a gradual evolution, not a deliberate break with the past. But almost a hundred years of gradual evolution have produced great, albeit slow, changes in food patterns.[15] Few if any of Minnesota's Italians today subsist solely on Italian food. Fewer still have maintained a strictly regional cuisine. Reasons for these changes vary. Throughout the twentieth century as immigration steadily diminished, the Italian communities became first more regionally and then ethnically integrated. Thus we might expect that the longer a family lived in the United States, the less Italian their cooking would become. The passing of time alone, however, does not explain change, for some Italians who emigrated forty years ago are still very traditional cooks. Contact with other Italians and Americans and constraint on or abundance of time, money, and available ingredients have influenced traditional foodways. So, too, have individuals' conceptions of what is healthy and tasty and family requests for specific dishes.

Aside from such changes, no one today is willing, let alone able, to cook as one would have in Italy or Minnesota a hundred years ago. Advances in technology have made preserving, preparing, and serving food faster and easier. Gone are the outdoor bread ovens that baked the enormous loaves of bread with great, thick crusts. Changes in the urban landscape have limited the places to gather wild greens or mushrooms, and zoning codes have curtailed the practice of keeping small barnyard animals.

Nevertheless, striking examples of continuity with tradition remain. Better incomes and modern conveniences have not outdated the virtue of self-sufficiency. Despite urban development, some women still gather dandelion and mustard greens each year. They carefully monitor the springtime growth in unsprayed park lands, on florists' lawns, and similar undisturbed areas, for the plants should be picked before they flower.

Rose Corbo, St. Paul, making various Italian and "American" Christmas cookies, 1985

Italians enjoy greens in salads dressed with oil and vinegar, boiled and served with meat such as pork chops, cooked with a little olive oil and fresh pepperoni or bacon, or floated in chicken soup.[16]

Most Italians, be they first, second, or third generation, still raise gardens, although they invariably remember that their parents' were bigger and better than their own. In the words of one, "I keep a small garden — eight or a dozen tomato plants, some basil — just for tradition."[17] Tomatoes, peppers, beans, parsley, and basil are still the basic crops. Some families grow enough food to preserve for winter, some share their bounty with children or friends, while others grow "just enough to have during the summer."[18]

Many second-generation women and later immigrants have continued to can quantities of fried or roasted peppers, tomatoes, tomato sauce and paste, and antipasto, which in its authentic form is a colorful combination of pickled vegetables, olives, and fish such as anchovies and tuna. Freezing is a newer technology that has been adapted in different ways by various women. It has liberated some from what they consider to be the drudgery of canning. Others have accepted it as an addition to canning. They might freeze either foods that need minimal processing, like tomatoes, or foods that require great care in canning, like peas and beans. Aside from preserving vegetables, freezers have also made it possible for cooks to prepare quantities of time-consuming foods at their leisure and store them for future use. "I make two or three thousand cookies every Christmas — about ten different kinds," declared one woman. "I start at Thanksgiving, and I freeze them. I have two big freezers. Matter of fact, I still have cookies I use all summer. When fall comes, I get to the end."[19] Not only do freezers ease the cook's task, they also enable families to defrost and eat traditional foods more often than they otherwise might.

Italian cooks have mixed opinions on the many other available kitchen aids. Most feel microwave ovens are a luxury, good mainly for reheating foods. "If you want to take pride in your cooking, you have to really take the time and cook it."[20] Many Italian women have steadfastly continued to make their own pasta, unaided until recently by pasta machines. Some still do not own a machine; others have received them as gifts from children. While the new technology has won some converts among the "old timers," many contend that the machines cannot produce all of the pastas as nicely as one can by hand.

Few Italians make use of prepackaged Italian convenience foods. Some of the frozen entrees are pronounced passable, but only as a last resort. As a rule, processed foods that are ingredients, not finished dishes, are the only acceptable shortcuts: instant polenta, canned chick-peas, or frozen

*Michelina Frascone,
St. Paul, shaping
cavatelli, 1986*

fish. Tomato sauce, even more than pasta, seems to be one ingredient that Italian cooks simply will not purchase. And it is not just supermarket tomato sauce that they reject. As an Italian grocer in Duluth who sells his wife's homemade sauce said, "Most Italian people won't buy her sauce. . . . That's because most Italians think their [own] sauce is the best in the world. But everyone else will love it."[21]

In order to maintain the authentic taste of their foods, many Italians patronize specialty shops, buying the frequently more expensive, imported versions of cheese, meat, olive oil, and pasta. Breads may be purchased at Italian bakeries and sausage or ham at Italian groceries or butcher shops. Families or friends may band together to order wheels of cheese or cases of oil from out-of-state suppliers. Travelers return with quantities of food from Italy or larger Italian-American communities. The expense of these ingredients, however, has led several cooks to serve the food less frequently, while keeping the taste authentic. Others experiment with alternatives, such as using only half the olive oil called for and making up the rest with corn or sunflower oil.[22]

Today most of Minnesota's Italians enjoy a pan–Italian cuisine. This blending of regional traditions was an almost inevitable result of friendships and marriages within Italian communities. One woman's experience, irrespective of geography, was typical: "My family was from northern Italy, my husband's from farther south. He learned to like my Italian cooking, and I learned some from his mother."[23] Neighbors and friends commonly traded recipes. A more recent phenomenon are the cooks who actively seek diversity. A search for minimally processed, healthy "peasant" dishes has led some to experiment with all Italian — and, indeed, all ethnic — foods. Others are avid cookbook collectors who simply like to try new things. And in still other instances marriage to a non-Italian, who loves Italian food without regional distinction, has introduced new elements to the daily diet.

In fact, intermarriage has made a surprisingly small impact on Italian cooking traditions. There is no satisfactory explanation for this phenomenon. The claim that Italian food can be inexpensive, delicious, healthy, and easy to prepare could be made for selected foods from virtually any ethnic group. Furthermore, this retention of foodways does not seem to depend on the primary cook's being Italian; rather, it seems to rest on the traditional prerogative of the man of the house to select what his wife will cook. In the words of one woman, "My mother's full-blooded German and my father's Italian, but she cooked to please my father."[24] The other side of the coin is the Italian-American woman married to a German American: "He likes Italian food. I don't cook much German stuff."[25]

Walk into an Italian home today and you are still likely to find pizza, pasta and sauce, ciambotta (stew), polenta, frittata (a baked custard of eggs, cheese, milk, and vegetables), fried peppers, or a side dish of cooked vegetables with cheese. A glass of wine may accompany the meal, but there will probably be no sweets. Many of Minnesota's Italians, despite a fondness for a variety of other ethnic cuisines — including standard American — tend to cook some traditional food on the average of one or two times a week. This average, however, masks a variety of individual decisions about what and when to cook. Several women who emigrated to Minnesota in the 1950s, for example, cook Italian food far more frequently than the norm; furthermore, their nontraditional dishes, such as beef stroganoff, all tend to have "an Italian flavor."[26]

While the frequency of cooking traditional foods also varies among the second generation, most prepare Italian food at least twice weekly. Many of these women have taken an active role as tradition bearer, making recipe files or books for their children and teaching family members and friends how to cook difficult dishes. While quite a few of these second-generation Minnesotans now live alone or, at most, with a spouse, their family food networks did not dissolve when grown children left home. Commonly, women have continued to garden, can, freeze, and even cook enough to distribute to all family members. As a result, many younger women have not learned to can and they maintain minimal gardens.[27]

Members of the third generation, most of whom are aged approximately thirty to forty, prepare traditional foods both less frequently and less consistently than their parents' generation. "I don't do a lot of Italian cooking, but when I get urges I definitely go all out,"[28] is one common pattern. Another approach is to make a big pot of sauce on the weekend and use it with different pastas, meats, or vegetables during the week. Some weekend cooks prepare a number of dishes for later use. At least one woman who uses this method to maintain her ethnic foodways, however, claims that while she prepares a respectable amount of Italian food, the variety of traditional dishes is declining. She does not prepare certain complicated pastas like ravioli, or soup, bread, and desserts. Time constraints have limited her repertoire.[29]

Religious holidays and other festive occasions, on the other hand, call forth a great variety of traditional foods. Even those who infrequently cook Italian foods agree with one woman's opinion: "The holidays are when I get nostalgic and have to have Italian food. That's when the traditional recipes come out."[30] For many Italians, holiday meals are distinguished by an increased number of dishes and by the addition of dessert.

Meals for Christmas Day and Easter Day, for instance, commonly follow a pattern: antipasto, soup, pasta, meat, salad, and finally, dessert. "Separate courses and separate dishes also!"[31] Families usually have their own traditional foods for each course. The soup could be chickarina (chicken broth with tiny meatballs and green beans) or chicken with cappelletti (stuffed pasta), homemade noodles, or chick-peas. Spaghetti, lasagne, ravioli, and pasta with sausages are common choices for the pasta course. In Italy roast kid or lamb was the traditional meat; in Minnesota most people have adopted the ham and turkey tradition, although not without some trauma. Several women related similar stories of transition. "When we first got a turkey for my little brother, my mother almost went crazy. She made it with [spaghetti] sauce until we decided to learn to make dressing. It's hard when you don't know."[32]

Christmas and Easter are also times for special desserts, many of them served on both holidays. In keeping with the American Christmas cookie phenomenon — the production and exchange of an abundance of sweets — many of Minnesota's Italians have expanded their traditional repertoires. Regional specialties like the turdiddi or tordillas (glazed, deep-fried wine balls) of Calabria, tarrales (hard rings of sweet dough good for dunking, sometimes also served at Easter) of central and southern Italy, and the panettone (yeast cake studded with raisins and candied fruit) of Lombardy are joined by pan-Italian favorites like zeppole (deep-fried puffs, sometimes filled with ricotta cheese), biscotti (nut slices), struffoli (small deep-fried dough balls glazed with honey and stuck together to form rings, wreaths, or trees), and nocches or cenci ("bow knots" — more deep-fried morsels). In addition there are "the American brand of cookies": Russian tea cakes, spritz, chocolate chip, butter horns, Croatian filled horns, peanut-butter cookies with a Hershey's chocolate kiss on top, and more.[33] Other Christmas treats include oranges, nuts, roasted chestnuts, and, for southern Italians, lupines — beans that must be boiled then soaked for a week, changing the water frequently. On Easter, some fami-

Anna Vigliotti, St. Paul,
preparing to fry the pastry shells
for cannoli, a holiday treat
in her family, 1986

lies from northern Italy may serve a yeasted cake flavored with citrus rind and rum.[34] Easter pie, a ricotta cheesecake also served on Christmas, is a more widely known dessert.

Another Easter pie, also called pizza rustica or pizza pasquale, was originally a seasonal dish that has come to be associated with the holiday. Traditionally this savory pie was made from a combination of eggs and fresh cheese, such as ricotta or farmer's, basket, or hoop cheese, poured into a crust formed from bread dough. The sprouted wheat berries that are included in some crust recipes as well as the fresh cheeses and eggs all symbolize rebirth and renewal, themes common to both springtime and the Easter celebration. Some contemporary Minnesotans add pieces of cooked Italian sausage to the filling, making a dish they find more flavorful and substantial. Others have substituted Romano, mozzarella, even American and Monterey Jack cheeses for the fresh ones, although the latter are sometimes available in specialty stores in the spring. Crusts made from packaged biscuit mix are a time-saving alternative for busy cooks, but few women rely solely on this substitution. Despite such changes, which actually negate the food's symbolic value, this pie remains a holiday dish, one associated primarily with Easter but prepared as well for occasions such as birthdays and graduation parties.[35]

Besides these foods, the Catholic requirement that Lenten and Christmas Eve meals be meatless has added a second dimension to traditional holiday cooking. Once again, some regional differentiation in food choice still remains. Sicilians and Calabrians traditionally have served squid, lobster tails, scallops, shrimp, baccalà (salt cod), herring, eels, or swordfish. Although fresh eels, lobster, and shrimp are available in gourmet food shops, most of these foods are both expensive and difficult to obtain in Minnesota. Frozen squid (from Oriental groceries), baccalà, and "fine quality fish" of necessity have become the traditional staples. Baccalà prepared in a variety of ways turns up in the meatless meals of most Italians; other meatless dishes such as cece e pasta (pasta and chick-peas) from southern Italy, and rice and pasta, from farther north, have a narrower constituency.[36]

The Feast of San Giuseppe or St. Joseph's Day, March 19, is another food-oriented Italian holiday. Its purpose — to feed the poor — has been accomplished in a variety of ways. As late as the 1940s Italians in one St. Paul neighborhood celebrated with bonfires and food for all. The women would prepare a meal of pasta in orange sauce. Children went door-to-door offering bowls of the food to their neighbors.[37] Elsewhere, a meatless dish, traditionally cece e pasta, would be served to all who came. Simple foods like baccalà and macaroni might fill out the menu. Sfigni di San Giuseppe, a ricotta-filled pastry puff, is the traditional dessert.

Currently, however, celebration of the saint's day depends on individuals. Several women in the Twin Cities annually hold feasts, the formats of which range from simple tradition to an elaborate menu and innovative approach. Minneapolis restaurateur, Giovanna D'Agostino, known to many Minnesotans simply as "Mama D," annually hosts a meal for St. Joseph's Day at her restaurant. Although the food is free to all, some people make "substantial donations," which D'Agostino channels to various charities. Another woman who feeds from thirty to forty people, mostly friends and relatives, in her home asks diners for a donation that she sends either to Italy or to the education fund of an American religious order. And since her crowd has come to include many non-Italians who do not like such traditional foods as chick-peas and pasta, she has expanded her menu to include meatballs, sausage, ham and cheese, pasta alfredo, and lasagne.[38]

But if "American" tastes have influenced traditional cooking, the reverse is also true. The current popularity of ethnic food in Minnesota is dramatic proof that acculturation can be a two-way street. Whether or not the recent American fascination with pasta machines, pesto, and food al fresco lasts, authentic Italian-American cooking will continue to evolve. While it is difficult to predict what — or even how — the fourth and fifth generations will cook, we can say for the present that Italian foodways in Minnesota remain as a well-loved source of nutrition and a powerful ethnic symbol, undiluted by frozen pizza and canned spaghetti sauce.

NOTES

[1] Rudolph J. Vecoli, "The Italians," in *They Chose Minnesota*, ed. Holmquist, 450; Jacqueline Rocchio Moran, "The Italian-Americans of Duluth" (master's thesis, University of Minnesota-Duluth, 1979), 5–20.

[2] Moran, "Italian-Americans," 42.

[3] Vecoli, "The Italians," in *They Chose Minnesota*, ed. Holmquist, 455–57.

[4] *Wall Street Journal*, August 12, 1982, p. 1.

[5] Ada Boni, *Italian Regional Cooking*, trans. Maria Langdale and Ursula Whyte (New York: Dutton, 1969), 83.

[6] Boni, *Italian Regional Cooking*, 11.

[7] Interview of Lillian Repesh, Duluth, November 4, 1982.

[8] Here and two paragraphs below, see Vecoli, "The Italians," in *They Chose Minnesota*, ed. Holmquist, 451–54.

[9] Interview of Anna Vigliotti, St. Paul, March 17, 1982; Repesh interview.

[10] Interviews of Michelina Frascone, St. Paul, May 27, 1982, Dominic Greco, St. Paul, July 7, 1982, Theresa Inzerillo, Minneapolis, June 7, 1982.

[11] Interviews of Michelina Dreyling, May 10, 1982, Mary Anzevino, July 12, 1982, Rose Corbo, June 8, 1982 — all St. Paul; Carmen Cardini, Chisholm, August 23, 1982; Frascone and Repesh interviews.

[12] Greco and Frascone interviews.

[13] Inzerillo interview.

[14] This chapter is based on interviews with Minnesota's Italians from St. Paul, Minneapolis, Hibbing, Chisholm, Coleraine, and Duluth. For a case study of Italian-American foodways in another state, see Toni F. Fratto, "Cooking in Red and White," *Pennsylvania Folklife* 19 (1970): 2–15.

[15] For a thoughtful discussion of contemporary Italian-American foodways, see Janet Theophano, " 'It's Really Tomato Sauce But We Call It Gravy': A Study of Food and Women's Work among Italian-American Families" (Ph.D. diss., University of Pennsylvania, 1982); Judith Goode, Janet Theophano, and Karen Curtis, "A Framework for the Analysis of Continuity and Change in Shared Sociocultural Rules for Food Use: The Italian-American Pattern," in *Ethnic and Regional Foodways*, ed. Brown and Mussell, 66–88.

[16] Frascone and Anzevino interviews.

[17] Anzevino interview.

[18] Repesh interview.

[19] Corbo, Cardini, Frascone, Greco, and Vigliotti interviews. See also interview of Louisa Andretta, St. Paul, May 17, 1982.

[20] Corbo, Inzerillo, and Frascone interviews.

[21] *Duluth News-Tribune*, April 22, 1982, p. C1.

[22] Interview of Anna Rosati, Coleraine, August 23, 1982; Repesh, Louisa Andretta, Inzerillo, and Greco interviews.

[23] Interview of Vicki Costanzi, Chisholm, August 23, 1982.

[24] Interview of Linda Andretta, St. Paul, May 17, 1982.

[25] Dreyling interview.

[26] Linda Andretta interview.

[27] Frascone, Corbo, Cardini, and Repesh interviews.

[28] Inzerillo interview.

[29] Repesh interview.

[30] Inzerillo interview.

[31] Frascone and Repesh interviews.

[32] Rosati, Frascone, and Dreyling interviews.

[33] Corbo, Frascone, Linda Andretta, Louisa Andretta, Dreyling, Inzerillo, and Greco interviews. It is interesting to note that cookies not originally from the Italian tradition are categorized "American," including Croatian horns and Scandinavian butter cookies.

[34] Louisa Andretta and Linda Andretta interviews.

[35] Waverley Lewis Root, *The Cooking of Italy*, Foods of the World (New York: Time-Life Books, 1968), 59; Corbo, Greco, and Anzevino interviews.

[36] Inzerillo, Greco, Frascone, Repesh, and Corbo interviews.

[37] Dreyling and Linda Andretta interviews.

[38] *Mama D*, Minnesota Living History videorecording (Osseo, Minn.: Independent School District No. 729, 1980), copy in Minnesota Historical Society Audio-Visual Library; Corbo interview. See also Giovanna D'Agostino, *Mama D's Homestyle Italian Cookbook* (New York: Golden Press, 1975).

Festive meal following the wedding of Lena Friedman and Rabbi C. David Matt, Min-neapolis, 1913; note individual challahs at each guest's place

THE JEWS

For many Minnesotans the mention of Jewish food conjures up images of steaming bowls of chicken soup, golden braids of challah (egg bread), and perhaps the mouth-watering aroma of a kosher delicatessen. A more complete list, however, would include such delicacies as polo (crusted rice), falafl (ground, seasoned, deep-fried chick-peas), a surprising array of doughy wrappers, and a mélange of fillings. The question "What is Jewish food?" is easier to pose than to answer, for traditional Jewish cuisine has been shaped by a blend of religious and cultural factors. While religious law specifies what may be eaten and, to some extent, how it must be prepared and served, the diversity of Jews' historical experiences, countries of origin, local customs, and interpretations of the dietary code have created a cuisine notable for its variety.

Minnesota's Jews or their ancestors emigrated from a great many European, Asian, and Middle Eastern countries, often making several stops before settling in the state. As a result, the broad outlines of their foods are as traceable as postmarks: the influence of Russia is evident in borscht (soup), kasha (buckwheat groats), and blintzes (filled eggy pancakes); that of the Middle East in grains, dried fruits, and spices. The considerable German contributions include latkes (potato pancakes) and many sweet-and-sour dishes. While Sephardic (Middle Eastern) Jews have lived in the state since its territorial days, they have always been outnumbered by their Ashkenazic cousins (primarily from the German, Austro-Hungarian, and Russian empires), whose traditions and European-style foods have come to be identified in the United States as quintessentially Jewish.[1]

The earliest Jews in Minnesota Territory were predominantly of middle-class German backgrounds. Most of these men were merchants, salespeople, or peddlers. They settled in St. Paul, Minneapolis, and Duluth, later migrating with their families to almost all of the territory's (and later, the state's) market towns. These residents were different in language, dress, and culture from the influx, beginning in the 1880s, of eastern European Jews who were fleeing Russian oppression. Until the

United States' entry into World War I curtailed immigration and again, for about four years after the armistice, these refugees poured into Minnesota, overwhelming their Germanic cousins. They eventually formed networks, communities, and religious and social institutions of their own.[2]

Through the middle years of the twentieth century, refugees from Hitler's Europe and displaced persons, as well as small numbers of European and Israeli students and professionals, migrated to Minnesota. Then, in the 1960s and 1970s, a new trickle of refugees began to arrive. Like their eastern European predecessors they, too, fled religious oppression — this time of the Soviet Union and of Iran. Unlike earlier immigrants, however, these latest arrivals were mostly urban and some were university educated.

What all of the Jewish immigrants to Minnesota held in common, save, perhaps, the Israelis, was the finality of their break with the homeland. While not all chose to remain in Minnesota, few had any notion of saving money in order to remigrate and establish themselves in their Old Country villages. This intention differentiated them from the thousands of other Europeans who swelled Minnesota's population at the turn of the twentieth century.

In Minnesota European regional or national cuisines tended to blend as Polish, Russian, Romanian, Hungarian, and Baltic Jews, for example, intermarried. Status barriers among the German, eastern European, and Sephardic contingents were slower to dissolve, but by the mid-twentieth century these, too, began to give way.[3] In the 1980s foods from the many Jewish traditions could be found at a single table, sometimes alternating with Chinese, Mexican, American, or other ethnic dishes. This culinary state of affairs has led some Jewish Minnesotans to conclude that "Jewish food is just food that Jewish people eat or serve."[4]

This somewhat radical conclusion can be tempered, however, by religious, cultural, and environmental factors that allow us to isolate a core of "Jewish" foods — dishes intrinsic to the group's ethnic identity — from the huge catalog of "what Jews eat." The kosher dietary laws, which exclude many commonly available foods and combinations of ingredients, are the basis of the cuisine. As given in Deuteronomy XIV and summarized here, they stipulate that meat must come from animals that have cloven hooves and chew the cud, from birds that do not prey on others, and from fish that have fins, scales, and backbones. By-products of forbidden species are also taboo. Animals and birds must be slaughtered in a particular way by a ritual specialist; creatures that die of their own accord are unclean. Milk and meat products may not be mixed together in a dish or combined in a meal.

These rules are meant to be inflexible; according to a Minneapolis synagogue cookbook, "The term 'Kosher-Style' to designate any food, however prepared but not meeting the traditional Dietary Laws, is a fraud and is a desecration and exploitation of the historic term." In practice, however, contemporary ethnic cooking does not always follow religious dictates. There are probably as many modifications of the laws — such as buying kosher-type cuts of meat from nonkosher butchers — as there are Jewish cooks. Thus, "kosher-style" cookery — ethnically correct but religiously taboo — flourishes in Minnesota along with strictly kosher cuisine. Deviation from the religious standard, however, is limited. While chicken soup made from nonkosher poultry still tastes like chicken soup, chopped chicken liver flavored with bacon drippings instead of schmaltz (rendered chicken fat) is not chopped liver — it is pâté.[5]

A strictly kosher regimen, on the other hand, does not necessarily produce traditional Jewish foods. How do we classify the chow mein made with leftover Sabbath chicken, or the "lobster" salad of haddock and hot sauce? Furthermore, modern convenience foods such as nondairy creamer and soybean-based cheese and meat substitutes allow the cook to circumvent religious prohibitions against mixing milk and meat. Kosher cooks could seize the opportunity to add cheeseburgers, chicken Kiev, or artificial bacon to their repertoires, but it will be a long time before these become ethnic specialties. Thus religious and ethnic factors alone do not account for Jewish cuisine.

Environment — place, time, and individuals — is a vital part of what makes food Jewish (or any other ethnic label). Many Jews, lacking a definitive culinary style and always conscious of their minority status — whether in European ghettos, the Middle East, or New World enclaves like North Minneapolis in the twentieth century — evolved the feeling that Jewish food was whatever they were eating that their Christian neighbors were not. For example, a mundane peanut-butter sandwich made on leftover Sabbath challah instead of the pervasive white bread was perceived as Jewish food when eaten among Christians in a school cafeteria. Conversely, any food served in a Jewish context could take on ethnic significance. For many Jewish Minnesotans both memories of traditional food and current ethnic cooking center on the holy days. Surely the association of foods with religious or cultural traditions helps explain why such undistinguished dishes as roasted chicken or beef brisket are so commonly cited as the cornerstones of Jewish cuisine. Through a combination of environmental, religious, and cultural factors common foodstuffs may come to be regarded as ethnic specialties.

There is yet one more key ingredient in the essence of Jewish — or any other — ethnic food, and that is tradition. Tradition is implicit in all the factors listed above. It is a powerful determinant even though its original motivations, if remembered at all, may appear outdated or insignificant. Tradition says that Jewish food is not just food that Jews eat — it is the food that they have eaten and will continue to eat. It is food that has withstood the test of time. Jewish chow mein may be a flash in the pan; recipes from a recently advertised "kosher-creole" cookbook may or may not survive in Jewish kitchens. Many of the foods discussed in this chapter were, at one time, adopted from outside sources or invented out of sheer necessity, but they have been prepared, served, and eaten by Jews for decades, generations, and even centuries. Flexibility has always been a hallmark of Jewish cooking. If today's traditions depend heavily on the central and eastern European and Middle Eastern foods of former homelands, might not tomorrow's bear the mark of Minnesota's multiethnic environment?

The foodways that immigrant Jews brought with them to Minnesota formed the baseline of their descendants' ethnic cuisine. Most, although not all, of the first generation followed the dictates of the kosher laws. They supported kosher butchers, bakers, and grocers. The foods they at first ate were largely the foods they had known in their native lands. Increased contact with members of other ethnic groups, however, had two effects on their cuisine: the Jews first became aware of their foodways as "ethnic" or "traditional," instead of taking them for granted as everyday sustenance. At the same time, they began integrating into their diets the new foods that they saw around them. Ground beef, for example, was formed into hamburgers instead of sweet-and-sour meatballs; macaroni and cheese took its place alongside blintzes or cheese knishes as an acceptable dairy dish. Jews learned to love Chinese and Italian food.

This gradual kind of change always begins with members of the first generation — be they the Polish Jews of the 1890s or Iranian and Russian refugees in the 1970s. The degree and speed of innovation depends, of course, on individuals' commitments to tradition, desire for change, time, skill, and other resources available for learning and experimentation. Typically, it has been the second and third generations who have initiated the most radical departures from traditional Jewish foodways.

At the very heart of Jewish tradition are those foods linked to special occasions. These are dishes consumed for their symbolic as well as nutritional value. And they are the foods that generations of Jews, regardless

Sophie Frishberg and Josephine Berg baking hamentaschen for the St. Paul Talmud Torah fund raiser, 1963

of their everyday commitment to ethnic foodways, have always consumed. On Rosh Hashanah, the New Year, foods such as honey cake, honey-glazed cookies, or tsimmes (honey-coated vegetables) are eaten to ensure that the coming year will be a sweet one. Hamentaschen, the triangular, filled cookies eaten by Ashkenazic Jews on the holiday of Purim simulate — depending on whom you ask — the three-cornered hat, pockets, or ears of Haman, the story's villain.[6] And on Hanukkah — the Festival of Lights — Jews eat food fried in oil (typically latkes — potato pancakes — among the Ashkenazim and sufganiyot — similar to jelly doughnuts — among the Sephardim) to commemorate the miracle of the tiny vial of holy oil that burned for eight days, allowing time to purify a new supply of oil for the rededication of the temple that the Romans had defiled.

Passover is a holiday particularly rich in symbolic foodways. All foods, commemorating the Jews' sudden release from slavery in Egypt — an exodus so swift that there was no time for their bread to rise — are made without leavening. Matzoh, a crackerlike sheet, is substituted for bread, matzoh meal for flour, and any attempts at cakes or rolls must depend on quantities of beaten eggs for a modestly airy quality.

On the first two nights of this eight-day holiday of Passover, observant Jews hold Seders. The Seder (which means "order") is traditionally a home-based service, although some synagogues host public ceremonies. Food provides the central metaphor: participants gather around the Seder table to read the Haggadah, which tells the story of the exodus, in part, through food symbols. Prominently displayed on the table are a bowl of salt water, a platter holding three matzohs, and the Seder plate, which holds karpas (greens, such as parsley or lettuce), maror (a bitter herb such as fresh horseradish root), haroses (a mixture of chopped apples, nuts, cinnamon, and wine), a roasted lamb shank bone, and a roasted egg. At specified times in the service, participants eat the karpas dipped in salt water to remember the tears the Jews shed while enslaved, maror to commemorate the bitterness of slavery, haroses to symbolize the mortar the slaves used to build the pyramids, and matzoh, sometimes called "the bread of affliction." The lamb shank represents the thank offering the fleeing slaves made to the Lord, and baytzah, the egg, is a sign of renewal. Four cups of kosher wine (or four sips, before each of which the cup must be refilled) are drunk at appropriate times in praise of the Lord, and at one point in the service,

Scott Zuckman, Lisa Savitt, and Susan Hoffman taste matzoh at a children's seder, St. Paul Talmud Torah, 1960; each child's plate also holds other symbolic foods.

each participant spills ten drops of wine onto a plate, one for each of the plagues inflicted on the Egyptians, as a sign that one's cup of joy cannot be full when others, even one's oppressors, suffer.

Many of these culinary traditions tend to be preserved even by normally nonobservant, contemporary Jews, and these are the kinds of foods most commonly and emphatically cited as "Jewish." No matter how well liked, they are rarely eaten out of their holiday seasons. As one woman put it, "I think it's the association with the holidays and my understanding of its [the food's] traditional meaning that gives it the Jewishness. We try to preserve that by not eating the foods at other times of the year. . . . If matzoh brie (matzoh scrambled with seasoned eggs) is so good, why must we wait until Passover to eat it? We decided that because it was so good we had to wait until Passover to eat it; that it would just be something that we would look forward to. . . . It would become non-Jewish if we had challah on Thursday!"[7]

Unlike the annual holidays, Shabbat (Sabbath), which begins every Friday at sundown and lasts until sundown Saturday, has no symbolic foods peculiar to it, but a cup of kosher wine is blessed as a symbol of joy to bring in the Sabbath. The challah, which is blessed and divided before the meal, is a ritual part of many other holidays, as are the standard Ashkenazic entrees, chicken and brisket, or the Persian Sephardic polo and khoresht (a stewlike sauce). Accompanying dishes are a matter of individual choice. Nevertheless this weekly holiday is a vital part of the Jewish culinary calendar. The Friday night meal is more elaborate than any ordinary weekday dinner, traditionally including soup (often chicken), an appetizer, and main and dessert courses. By and large, foods that are considered special — by varying, highly personal criteria — are served. In the words of one woman, "I don't serve meat loaf on Shabbat. It's just not something that we do."

Similarly, foods for ritual events that mark an individual's passage through the life cycle are usually special in some way, but few dishes are unique to a particular occasion. The feast following any wedding, baby naming, brit (circumcision), or funeral that is celebrated in a sacred ceremony will open with a blessing over wine and challah. So, too, will the meal following a Bar or Bat Mitzvah, the service that marks the entry of a thirteen-year-old boy or girl (respectively) into the Jewish covenant. But menus for such events leave great room for individual self-expression. Often foods from a family's Old Country heritage — such as pickled herring, kishke (stuffed intestine), chopped liver, ash (soup) — appear as appetizers before a main course of chicken or beef. But the entree might also be shish kabob or Oriental-style meat and vegetables. Desserts, especially at a buffet meal, may include traditional Jewish pastries along with popular gourmet

Phyllis Brody, St. Paul, rolling up kamish bread to be served at a Bar Mitzvah party; Goldie Schachtman, grandmother of the boy to be honored, shaping cookies in the background, 1986

foods. Many families hire caterers to prepare large ceremonial meals and then negotiate an appropriate menu based on cost and the caterer's options as well as their own notions of what it is proper to serve. Some families supplement commercially prepared food with homemade desserts, ranging from traditional cookies like mandel and kamish breads to "American" bars and cookies. Others prepare all foods themselves, often calling on friends or relatives to help with the cooking. In most instances, the menus reflect each family's multicultural identity as Jewish Americans.[8]

Not all Jewish food, of course, is holiday food. Soup is a versatile element of Jewish cuisine. It may appear as a first course for a holiday dinner, as the central attraction of a more casual meal, or even as light refreshment. Recipes are generally little more than guidelines that invite personal embellishment. Substitutions of ingredients and adjustment of quantities "to taste" are an inevitable part of the process. Chicken soup — in its pure, clear form or dressed up with carrot slices, matzoh balls, kreplach (a filled dough), or other additions — is famed for its powers to nourish, comfort, and cure. But other varieties are also notable, ranging from the cold soups (beet, spinach, or cherry, for example) favored in the summertime to the more hearty combinations, popular among Sephardic and Ashkenazic Jews, that are almost meals in themselves. Main dishes such as sweet-and-sour stuffed cabbage, falafl, or blintzes; accompaniments such as kugel (pudding, usually of noodles or potatoes), knishes (flaky dough filled with potatoes, cheese, or meat), polo, soup, and kreplach; and desserts like kamish bread, cookies, and filled pastries are theoretically all part of a cook's weekly repertoire. In fact, however, many second-, third-, and fourth-generation Jewish Minnesotans seem to be preparing these dishes only "when the spirit moves" — and it moves them less frequently than it did their parents.[9] Time, dietary restrictions, and expanded culinary horizons are major deterrents.

As part of this departure from tradition, however, a curious transition has evolved. Formerly common foods have taken on heightened significance for a younger generation, becoming specialty items when served in a cosmopolitan culinary context. These dishes are made for their good taste, nostalgic value, and ethnic associations on special occasions — when children return home for a visit, for weddings, parties, or even as part of Jewish celebrations. Thus the old line between holiday food and daily fare is blurred. A dessert like kamish bread, for example, is a New Year's treat for some families and an ordinary cookie for others.[10]

Other kinds of changes in Jewish ethnic cooking are readily apparent in Minnesota's communities. Considerations of time and health seem to be the major factors modifying contemporary practices. The declining use of schmaltz, once a favored ingredient for spreading, frying, and flavoring, is a case in point. Formerly common delicacies, well loved among the immigrant and second generations, are relegated to the status of fond memory. Foods such as helzl (the skin from a chicken neck stuffed with a mixture of schmaltz, flour, and salt, sewn up, and roasted along with the rest of the bird) or gribenes (chicken skin crisped by frying it with onions in schmaltz) are lovingly recalled as "those fatty little things that have probably taken years off of our lives!"[11] Low-cholesterol, low-sodium substitutes for traditional ingredients are an answer for some cooks in some instances: corn-oil margarine for butter in pastries, unsaturated oils, synthetic sprays, or treated cookware for other fats in baking, frying, and flavoring. When there is no substitute for the real thing, a recipe is abandoned or granted special-occasion status. As one woman said of her chopped-liver recipe: "I use a tenth the schmaltz my mother did [on a daily basis], but when I make those traditional dishes, I make them authentic. I don't make them that often. . . . I know some people who . . . just add a little hot water to keep it moist . . . [or] some people put in Mazola oil, *but it doesn't taste the same.*"[12]

Dietary concerns also seem to have dictated reduced quantities of food. Although the stereotype of the food-fixated Jewish mother remains healthy, Minnesotans have reported eating and serving less at a time. Remaining mostly in memory are the five-course meals cooked by grandmother in her tiny kitchen for the fifteen-to-twenty-member extended family.[13]

If some foods have dropped out of common use, however, others have entered the tradition. Several women in their thirties have cited what one called "ladies' luncheon foods" — carrot-loaf rings and molded Jell-O salads — as examples of Jewish foods. That older cooks vigorously deny this claim on the grounds that "those recipes we acquired quite a bit later"[14] only points to a tradition that is constantly evolving. That non-Jewish Minnesotans view these same foods as essential components of church suppers might demonstrate that multiethnic Minnesota is already making an impact on Jewish cuisine.

Recent Jewish immigrants to Minnesota, on the other hand, present a different picture. Their numbers are not large; in 1985 it was estimated that 306 Russian-Jewish families had been resettled in Minneapolis and 181 in St. Paul since the exodus from the Soviet Union began in 1973. While almost one-third of these families subsequently relocated elsewhere, still others have moved to Minnesota from the east coast, hoping to rejoin relatives and find work. Members of the Iranian-Jewish community in 1982 guessed there were some fifty persons in the Twin Cities and a few in school in Mankato and St. Cloud. Nevertheless, these recent arrivals add a different dimension to Jewish foodways in Minnesota.[15]

For reasons largely economic and sociological, Russian Jews, especially the older women, have continued to "cook Russian," a term that covers a great latitude of culinary styles. Former residents of the Soviet Socialist Republic of Azerbaijan, which borders Iran, for example, cook what Americans would call Middle Eastern food. Like recent Iranian-Jewish immigrants, the Azerbaijanis were accustomed to eating a variety of locally grown fruits and vegetables in season and to flavoring their foods liberally with herbs and spices, some of which are either unavailable or prohibitively expensive in the United States.[16]

Jews from the western republics (like the Ukraine), who comprise the majority of the Russian-Jewish immigrants to Minnesota, had less variety in their diets. Theirs was a cuisine built around a few staple foods, and they evolved numerous dishes from potatoes, cabbages, beets, turnips, and similar vegetables. They generally stretched meat by including it in pies like pierog, extending it with rice as in stuffed cabbage leaves, or using it in thick, hearty soups such as borscht.[17] Bread, a subsidized item in the Soviet Union, was both cheap and plentiful, and immigrants miss the high-quality, dark loaves.

Keeping kosher was out of the question in a country where "You could ask for beef and they might give you pork." In a context that made strict observance impossible, different people made different adjustments, ironically similar to those of American Jews who can keep strictly kosher but choose not to. One woman, for example, never combined milk and meat products at a meal. Although the ingredients were not strictly kosher, she baked her own matzoh for Passover (it was forbidden to sell matzoh) and kept the other holidays as best she could.

Under the circumstances in the Soviet Union, maintaining Jewish food-ways was a purely symbolic act in the richest sense of the word. Most of the foods that the immigrants in Minnesota today consider Jewish, rather than Russian, are linked in their minds to the Jewish holidays. These foods, identical to those made by contemporary American descendants of nineteenth-century immigrants, show a continuity in traditional cookery: honey cake and tsimmes for Rosh Hashanah, potato latkes for Hanukkah ("Potatoes we had!"), gefilte fish and challah for appropriate holidays.[18]

In traditional Russian-Jewish foodways, dinner is not considered a meal unless it begins with soup, whether a cabbage-vegetable borscht based on a meat stock, chicken soup, or a broth. The meal then proceeds in courses: meat in some form if it is affordable, or a kasha, noodle or rice dish, or potatoes. Compotes made from dried fruits are a common dessert. Most Russians continue to prefer tea to coffee. It is interesting to note that some of the foods that they do not single out as Jewish — kasha, stuffed cabbage (or grape leaves in Azerbaijan), kasha and varnishkes (a kind of noodle), and borscht — are considered distinctively Jewish by third- and fourth-generation American Jews.

Those immigrants who can afford the time and money to experiment with new foods do so. American social workers have observed that especially the younger couples "adore good American food" and want to add new dishes to their repertoires. Cooking classes at the St. Paul Jewish Community Center on subjects such as American-Jewish holiday foods, doctoring packaged cake mixes, and making appetizers from frozen foods have been popular, mostly but not exclusively with the younger members of the immigrant community.[19]

Iranian-Jewish immigrants, too, have tended to maintain their foodways as faithfully as possible. These foodways differ markedly from those of Ashkenazic Jews, partly because they derive from Sephardic tradition and partly because of the influence of regional cuisine in Iran. Some Sephardic holiday foods, like the custom of eating squash on Rosh Hashanah, are based on ingredients that have mystical significance; these principles are spelled out in the *Zohar*, a cabalistic treatise on the Pentateuch introduced to Spain in the thirteenth century. Sephardic Jews also follow different rules for what is kosher for Passover; unlike their Ashkenazic cousins, for example, they are permitted to eat rice and certain beans. But all rice must be cleaned and checked, grain by grain, to make sure no impurities are intermixed. It is then ground into flour for baking, in addition to being served as a grain. Recent immigrants, in Minnesota as in Iran, also eat matzoh as ritually prescribed, but only for its symbolic meanings. During the holiday, they subsist on other bread substitutes.[20]

Other Jewish holiday foods derive more from regional tradition than Sephardic belief systems. Qabali, in which split peas, carrot slivers, and raisins are layered with seasoned beef and rice, seems to come from northern Iran, bordering on the Soviet Union. In Minnesota, immigrants from that region continue to serve this dish for the fall festival of Sukkot, which

Sandra Dudovitz, Joel Rutchick, and Ken Kozberg, St. Paul, decorating the Temple of Aaron's sukkah, as is traditional, with fall harvest fruits and vegetables, 1967

commemmorates the huts that housed the Jews in the desert after their exodus from Egypt.[21]

Ash (soup), bearing a strong Persian influence, is also a cornerstone of traditional cookery. Porridgelike varieties are served on Sabbath day, because they can simmer unattended for twenty-four hours without violating the proscription against working on the Sabbath. And when a baby cuts its first tooth, it is traditional to hold a party and serve a special ash, usually prepared by the child's grandmother from a combination of beans, rice, bulgar, barley, and meat.

While school-aged children and sometimes men, who have more contact with American ways, may request spaghetti, steaks, or pizza for dinner, the women of the community, who are the cooks, are resistant to change. Food embodies their cultural identity: "We grew up with these, so you can't stop eating them!" Furthermore, cooking those foods is an integral part of the self-definition of these women, who, in Iran, usually did not work outside the home. In Minnesota to date, even those who hold outside jobs continue to prepare traditional foods virtually every day. This task often includes baking the varieties of flat breads that they bought in Iran but are not available in the state. With time, however, these same women have gradually begun to relax their strict attitudes. They may start by cooking an "American" cut of meat in a traditional manner, such as slowly simmering a roast for hours with stewed fruits or cooking spaghetti so that it achieves a Persian-style crust on the bottom.

But even in maintenance of traditions there is often a degree of change. Certain crucial herbs and vegetables used by Iranian Jews, for example, are not available in Minnesota. Other key spices such as saffron and cumin ground with rose leaves are prohibitively expensive. Substitutions are made where possible: turmeric for saffron in all but the most special dishes; parsley or green-onion tops for unavailable leafy vegetables. Families keep gardens, and women dry their home-grown herbs for winter use. Cooks depend on traveling relatives to return from New York or California with hard-to-find items or on family still in Iran to mail them other delicacies. Newcomers were delighted to discover the Twin Cities' system of food co-ops where they can buy the familiar beans, grains, and some herbs and spices in bulk.

Much of traditional cooking — and this surely is not limited to Jewish cuisine — requires a good deal of time and some training. There are noodles and pastries to be made from scratch; legumes to soak, boil, and mash; pounds of potatoes to grate; vegetables to dice; doughs to roll, fill, seal, and boil, bake, or fry. As a result of these requirements, some foods have faded from everyday use, and others have been lost to traditional reper-

Lois Brand rolling up potato knishes, Shirlee Freeman (background) preparing stuffed cabbage for a sisterhood meeting at Temple of Aaron, St. Paul, 1986

toires entirely. In the words of one woman, "One thing I learned to make and have never made since is gefilte fish. I spent the entire day. . . . It was really fun. . . . but it was such a job that I'll never do it again."[22] (Gefilte fish in its most common form is made by skinning, boning, and grinding several kinds of fish with onions, cracker meal or breadcrumbs, and seasonings. The mixture is shaped into balls and boiled with sliced carrots and celery tops for several hours. Originally the fish was skinned whole, processed as above, and then returned to the skin for boiling; hence "gefilte" — stuffed.)

Interestingly enough technology, often painted as the foe of things traditional, has encouraged ethnic cooks to carry on. Frozen pastry dough is seen as a more-than-adequate substitute for knish skins; Greek phyllo dough doubles for strudel leaves. Commercial preparations such as noodles, poppy-seed filling, potato latke, falafl, or soup mixes, sauces, and even schmaltz are readily available. Specialty stores and some supermarkets carry fully cooked, frozen items such as blintzes and kugels for those intent on eating, if not preparing, traditional foods.

The process of freezing has been a boon to traditional cooking in more ways than the above. For decades the ability to stock up has encouraged cooks to prepare traditionally time-consuming foods in greater-than-average quantities. The excess is frozen for future use, allowing families to enjoy these dishes more frequently than they otherwise might.

But more than anything else it has been the mechanical gadgets — mixers, blenders, grinders, and food processors — that have helped preserve and perhaps even occasioned a small renaissance in Jewish traditional cooking by minimizing the drudgery. Care must be exercised to achieve proper textures in some mechanically processed foods, but given the savings in time and energy, most cooks are willing to experiment. While machines have merely allowed seasoned cooks to update their techniques, they have inspired novices to make first or more frequent attempts at traditional dishes.[23]

Does the food taste the same? As good? Some say yes, others disagree. Change is an emotional issue when it comes to traditional cooking and eating habits. "My mother has told me I'll never make a good potato kugel if I don't grate potatoes by hand," stated one woman; according to another, "The Cuisinart [to grate potatoes] makes all the difference in the world. We have latkes a lot now because it's so much easier to make them." There is no reconciling different individuals' tastes and needs![24]

On thing, however, is certain: the variety of opinions represented in Minnesota's Jewish communities will ensure both the maintenance and evolution of traditional foodways.

NOTES

[1] So few were the Sephardim that none of the literature on Jews in Minnesota takes explicit notice of them. On one territorial family with descendants still living in the state, see the entries on the Cardozos in W. Gunther Plaut, *The Jews in Minnesota: The First*

Seventy-five Years (New York: American Jewish Historical Society, 1959). It has been estimated that easily 95 percent of the approximately thirty-five thousand Jews in Minnesota in the 1980s were Ashkenazim; telephone conversations with Kim Marsh, executive director of the United Jewish Fund, Rabbi Bernard Raskas, Temple of Aaron congregation (St. Paul), and David Cooperman, Department of Sociology, University of Minnesota — all March 4, 1982. The author wishes to thank Marjorie Kreidberg, author of *Food on the Frontier: Minnesota Cooking from 1850 to 1900 with Selected Recipes* (St. Paul: Minnesota Historical Society Press, 1975), for sharing her knowledge of Jewish foodways.

[2] Hyman Berman, "The Jews," in *They Chose Minnesota*, ed. Holmquist, 489–92.

[3] On the genesis and maintenance of intraethnic barriers, see Berman, "The Jews," in *They Chose Minnesota*, ed. Holmquist, 491–93, 498.

[4] Interview of Rolla Unowsky, St. Paul, November 22, 1981. A recent Russian-Jewish emigrant agreed that pinpointing the Jewish elements of cuisine is difficult: "Jews are all over. They take the recipes and they become Jewish." Interview of Helen Gurevich, director of New Americans program, Jewish Community Center of Greater Minneapolis, Minneapolis, October 24, 1985.

[5] Women's League of Beth El Synagogue, *Let's Cook for the Holidays* (Minneapolis: Women's League of Beth El Synagogue, 1955), 9. For an anthropologist's analysis of the dietary code, see Mary Douglas, *Purity and Danger: An Analysis of Concepts of Pollution and Taboo* (London: Routledge & Kegan Paul, 1966), 41–57; for more on some Minnesotans' modifications of the dietary laws, see Anne R. Kaplan, "Ethnic Foodways In Everyday Life: Creativity and Change Among Contemporary Minnesotans" (Ph.D. diss., University of Pennsylvania, 1984), 194–96.

[6] Purim commemorates the downfall of Haman, vizier to the Persian king, who advised hanging all the Jews, and the bravery of Queen Esther, the Jew who opposed Haman's plot. Iranian Jews traditionally eat halvah, made from rice, sugar, cinnamon, and saffron, and a cookie made from rice flour; interview of Soheyla Amrami, St. Paul, February 22, 1983.

[7] Here and below, see interview of Lisa Schlesinger, St. Paul, November 10, 1981.

[8] Interviews of Kimberley Amrami (an American married to an Iranian immigrant), St. Paul, January 11, 1982, Lois Brand, Phyllis Brody, Goldie Schachtman, St. Paul, January 21, 1986, Evelyn Grosby and Cynthia Unowsky, St. Paul, November 12, 1981. On kosher caterers and menu choice, see Leslie Prosterman, "Food and Celebration: A Kosher Caterer as Mediator," in *Ethnic and Regional Foodways*, ed. Brown and Mussell, 127–42.

[9] Kimberley Amrami interview.

[10] Interview of Shira Schwartz, Minneapolis, January 28, 1982; Rolla Unowsky, Schlesinger, and Cynthia Unowsky and Grosby interviews.

[11] Interview of Martha Schmitz, St. Paul, December 23, 1981.

[12] Grosby in Grosby and Cynthia Unowsky interview.

[13] Interview of Marjorie Kreidberg, St. Paul, October 20, 1981; Rolla Unowsky interview.

[14] Interview of Janice Goldstein, St. Paul, December 28, 1981; Grosby in Grosby and Cynthia Unowsky interview.

[15] *American Jewish World* (Minneapolis), August 16, 1985, p. 3, 6; Kimberley Amrami interview.

[16] Interview of Felicia Weingarten, director of Russian program at the St. Paul Jewish Community Center, St. Paul, October 24, 1985; Gurevich interview.

[17] Here and below, see interview of Dora Hack, St. Paul, October 25, 1985; Gurevich interview.

[18] Hack, Weingarten, and Gurevich interviews.

[19] Weingarten interview.

[20] Kimberley Amrami interview.

[21] Here and three paragraphs below, see Kimberley Amrami and Soheyla Amrami interviews.

[22] Interview of Shoshana Hoose, St. Paul, Janaury 7, 1982.

[23] See, for example, Schmitz, Rolla Unowsky, Soheyla Amrami, and Kreidberg interviews. Mechanization is not confined to the United States. Soheyla Amrami noted that her family was delighted to discover that pasta makers, which they find expensive, could be made to substitute for an Iranian device unavailable in Minnesota and used to produce a particular cookie.

[24] Kreidberg and Schmitz interviews.

John Kalsich family garden, Ely, 1922

THE SOUTH SLAVS

Food for lean times" could well be the theme of a chapter on South Slav food. Soups, stews, and combination dishes have long sustained South Slav families, whether in the regions of Yugoslavia or during their first months in the United States. Having few resources with which to begin a new life, immigrants brought to Minnesota only their Old Country food customs and hopes for a more prosperous future. Their traditional, simple ways of cooking proved useful again when the Great Depression hit Minnesota, enforcing a back-to-basics style of living. More recent depressed times have witnessed the revival of some of the immigrants' foodways.

Croats, Slovenes, and Serbs are the principal groups of South Slavs that settled in Minnesota. Most arrived between 1900 and 1920. While many had been farmers in Yugoslavia, the majority settled either in the St. Paul area to work in the meat-packing industry or in northeastern Minnesota towns where they found jobs in the iron mines and related industries. Some, however, established small farms around St. Cloud or farther north near Hibbing, Chisholm, and Ely.[1] For most immigrants, regardless of location, the early months were difficult until they found housing, started gardens, and purchased some livestock.

From their gardens, pigs, and cows, the South Slavs were able to supplement their meager incomes. The immigrants also foraged for game, berries, and greens. Some of their favorite garden crops would not grow in the harsh Minnesota climate, but the South Slavs soon learned from their neighbors what might be successful. Accustomed to having fresh fruit, they planted apple, cherry, apricot, and olive trees. Apple and cherry trees seemed to take hold and thrive, but the others managed with only indifferent success. So, like others before them, the South Slavs learned to use the wild blueberries, raspberries, chokecherries, and pin cherries that grew in profusion in northern Minnesota.[2]

South Slav cooking has always adapted readily to new foods and new methods of preparation. Living in mine-location towns with Swedish, Irish, Scottish, German, Finnish, English, and Italian neighbors, many women traded specialties and recipes. One, for example, learned to make scones and in return taught her friend to make strudel. Lasagne, Finnish fish soup, and baklava soon found their ways to South Slav tables. In larger towns such as Chisholm, Hibbing, Gary, and New Duluth, however, South Slavs usually congregated in neighborhoods, thereby ensuring a continual reinforcement of their cookery. Americanization workers employed by public schools and other local and state agencies managed in their goodhearted way to introduce immigrant cooks to such items as lemon and apple pies, marble and angel food cakes, and Jell-O.[3]

The early history of the South Slavs parallels that of many other East European groups. For centuries, central and eastern Europeans migrated in search of work or better farmland, often settling among people of dissimilar background. Conquerors and rulers came and went, and the countryside frequently was overrun. The land that is now Yugoslavia was ruled by the Ottoman Empire for more than four hundred years and was under the suzerainty of the Austro-Hungarian Empire from 1878 until the end of World War I. Yugoslavia, formed in 1918 from parts of the defeated Austro-Hungarian Empire and other lands, contained six political divisions: Slovenia, Serbia, Croatia, Montenegro, Macedonia, and Bosnia-Herzegovina. It was called the Kingdom of the Serbs, Croats, and Slovenes until 1929 when the name was changed to Yugoslavia, "the country of the South Slavs." In 1945 it became the Socialist Federalist Republic of Yugoslavia.[4]

When the treaty makers created Yugoslavia, they drew boundaries that included people of different nationalities, distinctive foods, and varying traditions. As a result South Slav recipes blend Turkish and classic eastern European cookery so subtly that few are aware of the mixture. The Turkish influence is most apparent in the dishes using stuffed vegetables, soured milk, yoghurt, and cheese curds and pastries using thin, paperlike dough. (German, Austrian, Hungarian, Russian, and Polish cooks, as well as South Slavs, have been influenced by the Turkish cooks, specifically in the use of a delicate pastry dough to make strudel.) The central or eastern European presence includes soups, stews, sauerkraut dishes, sausages, hearty vegetable combinations, meats grilled on skewers, and filled pancakes; Greece, Hungary, Romania, Bulgaria, Austria, and Yugoslavia share these elements of cuisine. The regional Mediterranean influence shows up in dried codfish dishes, pasta, polenta (corn-meal mush), browned butter, garlic sauce, and baked dishes using eggplant, zucchini, or potatoes.[5]

The three predominant religions in Yugoslavia — Roman Catholic in Croatia and Slovenia, Eastern Orthodox in Serbia and Montenegro, and Islam in Dalmatia and Bosnia-Herzegovina — also contributed to the diversity in national food habits. Islam prohibits eating pork, and both the Eastern Orthodox and Roman Catholics have numerous fasts that exclude meat and all by-products such as lard and dairy foods. Finally, in addition to cultural and historical differences, Yugoslavia's geographical and agricultural variety has also influenced its foodways. South Slavs who live by the sea use fish, olives, figs, and other fruits. Those inland on the fertile plains cook with the available grains, while those in the mountainous areas raise and eat lambs and goats.[6]

Because of all this diversity, it is difficult to identify a set of recipes and customs in Minnesota that are peculiar to only the Slovenes or Serbs or Croats. These South Slav groups are like members of a family. Each feels unique, yet to an outsider, their individual qualities are less apparent than the family resemblance.

In immigrant times, the kitchen was the center of the South Slav home. Women worked almost continually to feed their large families and the many boarders they often took in. Preparing hearty meals as cheaply as possible demanded creativity with whatever foods were on hand or in the garden. Meats were limited to what could be raised or hunted, vegetables were lightly seasoned to enhance their natural flavors, and fruits were served raw, stewed, or sometimes baked in a light crust. Menus expanded on holidays, however, no matter how poor the times. For special occasions, a woman might serve two or three meats, several vegetable dishes, salads, and breads along with favorite desserts.[7]

Many South Slav women became boardinghouse operators. Often a family member would welcome a newly arrived relative; later, immigrants from the same Old Country village were invited to stay, and suddenly a wife was in the boardinghouse business. Remodeled rooms or lean-tos provided added space. There are records of such establishments in Gary, New Duluth, and Morgan Park, on the iron ranges, and in St. Paul and Minneapolis — most having homelike conditions, traditional foods, and a friendly, supportive environment that surely helped large numbers of single men adjust to a new land. Around 1910–15 men usually paid between five and ten dollars a month for room, laundry service, and daily meals — two at the boardinghouse and a lunch pail of hearty food. It was not uncommon for an establishment to house twenty-four or more residents, although the average operation had ten to twelve. When one shift of workers left in the morning for the day's work, another was returning from the night shift.[8]

Cooking for so many was hard work, and most women had only their own children to help. In some instances a neighbor's young daughter was hired or an unmarried sister from the family's South Slav village came to help with the work. It was in boardinghouses that many young girls learned their way around the kitchen, watching and copying the cooking methods.[9]

The day started early — five o'clock was the latest anyone arose. Some women slept in their clothes so that not a moment would be wasted. The first task was to ready the lunch pails, which had two compartments, the bottom one for tea, coffee, or lemonade and an insert for meat, bread, fruit, and cake or strudel. (Women, lacking time to raise their own pigs, frequently purchased whole pork loins that they cooked and sliced themselves, not only obtaining the quantity of meat they needed but also serving juicier, more flavorful portions.)

Next the women prepared breakfast for both shifts. Four typical menus listed these combinations: pork chops, potatoes, eggs, and fruit; scrambled eggs, bowls of homemade cottage cheese, and pork chops or ribs; eggs, two kinds of meat (probably ham and steak), potatoes, hot cereal, and fruit; potatoes, steak with catsup gravy, and lots of coffee with boiled milk and crushed soda crackers added. Another favorite breakfast food was jeladija (pig's feet in aspic), cooked many hours the day before and allowed to stand overnight, and then eaten with generous amounts of pepper. The cheapest meal consisted of potatoes and cooked cereal.

With breakfast over, women did the bulk of their cooking, preparing meats, baking bread, and rolling the dough for desserts such as potica or strudel. The evening meal regularly began with soup, followed by potatoes, vegetables, salads, and "always two meats." Stews of beef, onions, and either potatoes or rice were popular. Slovenians particularly enjoyed goulash, usually prepared with cubed pork, veal, or beef, and distinctively seasoned with paprika and red pepper. Some people added sauerkraut while others served the dish over polenta. Veal, pork chops, and chicken — all usually breaded — were served often with salads, vegetables, fruit, and bread. Fruit or fruit desserts usually completed the evening meal. Except in the very largest boardinghouses, the families ate with the boarders at one long table with benches running down the sides; however, a few families remember eating in the kitchen, finishing the leftovers from the boarders' meals.[10] Boarders enjoyed all the traditions of the family when holidays were celebrated; in fact, some were members of the family, and others had become "family" through long, close association, or through marriage to a daughter of the family.

Generally, food preparation methods have changed little since the immigrant and boardinghouse era. In the 1980s some families still garden, preserving the produce and making sauerkraut and wine, and it is not uncommon to find men who butcher and barbecue whole animals at holiday

*Katie Bruich, Duluth,
slicing potica, 1984*

times or women who make their own sausage. Very few of these people remember ever seeing their mothers use a cookbook. Lard and butter were measured in pieces "the size of an egg", other quantities included the pinch, handful, or fistful. Although lately some recipes have been recorded in church and organization cookbooks, many exist only in the heads of the first-generation women and their daughters, who leared to cook by watching and helping.[11]

Potica is one such handed-down favorite among all South Slavs. Slovenians call it potica and Serbians, povitica; regardless of name, this special bread is an integral part of traditional cooking. Originally the word referred to anything rolled up in dough — apples, cheese, nuts, or even sauerkraut and meat. More recently it has come to mean yeast dough, rolled or pulled extremely thin, covered with a walnut mixture (and sometimes dates or raisins), rolled up jelly-roll style, and baked in long bread pans. Immigrant women baked potica frequently, placed it on the table at all meals, and treated it as daily food. Today this time-consuming delicacy is generally available only at bazaars, luncheons, or other money-raising affairs or from women who sell homemade potica at prices ranging from eight to ten dollars a loaf. Many cooks who no longer have time to make the traditional recipe still enjoy the flavors by baking a cake with similar ingredients.[12]

Strudel, like potica, is a thin, rolled-dough pastry that is filled with apples, cheese, berries, sauerkraut, or other vegetables, but the dough has no yeast. Practically every cook has her own recipe as well as definite methods and techniques for preparing the perfect strudel; nevertheless, most agree "everything must be warm — the room, the dough, the bowl." Whatever the procedure, the mention of strudel brings a smile to everyone's face. Along with potica, it is always made for special occasions and is frequently sold at fund-raising events.

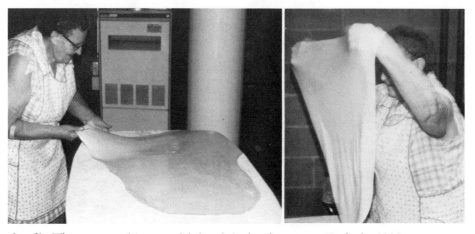

Amelia Thomas stretching strudel dough in her basement, Duluth, 1983

Watching women make strudel is like seeing an age-old ritual, one passed down for generations from mother to daughter. There is a harmony and a oneness between the dough and the woman as she coaxes and pulls it into a three-by-four-foot rectangle. Ultimately stretched to size, it is thin enough "to read a newspaper through," with "not a hole in sight!" For the cook new to the process, it will take time and practice to master the art, and a few holes may appear.

Weddings, baptisms, communions, and confirmations typically bring out the best in South Slav cooking, and pastries are featured prominently. According to an old saying, "Every Slovenian wedding has walnut potica, flancati, and krofe." Serbians and Croatians would add strudel to that list.

Flancati, called pohaney by some South Slavs, is a thin piece of sweet

*Frances Krainik,
Chisholm, frying
flancati, 1983*

dough, shaped, pulled, and fried in hot fat. The resulting puff, similar to
the Norwegian or Swedish fattigmann (poor man's cookie) and the German schweinsohren (pig's ears), is either sprinkled with sugar or eaten plain.
Slovenian women still make bushel baskets of flancati for weddings,
decorating the baskets with ribbons and lining them with their finest
tablecloths.[13]

Krofe, called krapi in some areas and similar to the Serbian ustipke,
resembles a yeast doughnut without the hole. Only practiced bakers know
precisely when to flip it over as it fries in hot fat, leaving the mark of an
authentic krofe — a horizontal, bisecting white stripe. Krofe may be served
plain or sprinkled with sugar; children love to dip them first in water so
that more sugar will stick to the surface. Raisins are added if the krofe
is to be served at breakfast. Like potica, this delicacy is popularly served
with sliced ham.

A task equally as time consuming as potica or strudel making was sauerkraut making — a nostalgic childhood memory for most South Slavs but
still an annual ritual for others. In earlier days it was not unusual to prepare from five hundred to eight hundred pounds of cabbage, although contemporary families typically store from one to six crocks of kraut. Families harvested cabbages after the first frost, and the woman of the house
prepared for the ensuing task by covering the kitchen floor with clean

cloths, setting out large tubs, and washing and halving the cabbage heads in preparation for grating. A variety of graters, including a large model that fit over the tub and had a place for a person to sit at one end, were available. The grated cabbage, layered with salt in fifty- or sixty-gallon crocks, had to be pressed to extract the juice. Families used one of two methods: either pounding with a wooden mallet or placing a child with well-washed feet in the crock to stamp the mess down. When the pounded cabbage became juicy, they added more layers of cabbage, pressing these down until the crock was full. Currently, kraut makers use wooden mallets or potato mashers to compress the cabbage. From that point on, they follow traditional technology.[14]

The next step was to place a clean cloth, a clean birch board, and a rock on the kraut in each crock to hold everything firm. Some South Slavs wrapped a blanket around the crock while the cabbage fermented in a warm place for two to six weeks, depending on the temperature. Each week someone skimmed the foam off the top and carefully washed the cloth, board, and rock. After curing, the crocks of sauerkraut were stored in a cool place, such as a basement or dirt cellar, to slow the fermentation, thus preventing the cabbage from becoming too sour. Later, often in the winter, women canned the kraut. Sauerkraut juice, straight from the crock, was a favorite drink, often declared a "physic better than milk of magnesia" or more recently "penicillin number one."

In addition to turning cabbage into kraut, South Slavs also preserved some whole as sour heads. Sour heads were used to make sarma (rolled cabbage leaves stuffed with a mixture of meat, rice, and seasonings). While sarma was also made from fresh cabbage with a layer of sauerkraut on the bottom of the pan, many people who have tasted both kinds favor the sarma made from sour heads. To can sour heads cooks separated the leaves, rolled each one tightly, and packed as many as possible into a jar. Currently some women freeze the heads whole; traditionalists claim that freezing toughens the leaves.[15]

Sauerkraut, a staple food in immigrant homes, is prepared less frequently today, although it still appears either as a plain dish or in various combinations. Some South Slavs make a sauerkraut strudel, while others brown kraut with onion in oil or lard and serve it with potatoes. Sauerkraut-and-bean dishes, often combined with sausage, pork pieces or ribs, or ham and seasoned with garlic, green pepper, onion, or caraway seed, are also popular.

During the first quarter of the century nearly every South Slav family made its own wine, starting with dandelions in the early spring. Local merchants also sold grapes — muscatel for white wine, concord for red — by the crate or ton, depending on the needs of the buyer. Juices extracted from cherries, blackberries, and grapes were also used to make brandy. Wine making continued during Prohibition, and many stories tell of informers and the subsequent raids of federal agents.[16]

Wine making was a family project since the process required many hands — and feet. Adults cleaned and washed the grapes and placed them in large barrels where barefooted children stomped them into a juicy pulp. Three wines could be obtained from the crushed grapes: the first from the juice only and the second and third from the residue with sugar and water added. The wine, labeled first, second, or third wine, was stored in a cool place, sometimes in bottles but more often in small kegs. Today the traditional art is still practiced, albeit by fewer people.

Wine and brandy held prominent places in immigrant foodways. Wine was on the table at most mealtimes, and the popular plum brandy, slivovitz, was enjoyed in morning coffee, before a meal, or any time when family or friends gathered. Women made hot mulled wine with cinnamon sticks as a remedy for a cold or an upset stomach, sometimes adding a little plum or apricot brandy. Brandy was a common treatment for stomach aches, and many families joke today about certain members who repeatedly came down with this ailment. Children were accustomed to small amounts of plain or mulled wine, and even babies were quieted by sucking on a finger dipped in wine.

Using the products from their huge gardens, families produced a variety of vegetable salads. Leaf lettuce dressed with oil and vinegar, salt and pepper, and perhaps a little diced onion was popular. Cooked vegetable salads were also favorites, varying as crops in the garden changed. Green or wax beans, beets, cabbage, cooked dried beans, potatoes, and turnips were all used, but seldom combined. Preparation was the same for each: cook and drain, combine with oil, add vinegar, salt, pepper, and minced onion or garlic, and serve at room temperature.[17]

A number of bean dishes have remained mainstays of the South Slav diet. In earlier times, many families planted Roman, pinto, or kidney beans specifically for drying. A favorite light lunch consisted of kidney beans, salt, pepper, and oil mixed with chopped leaves and cores from sour heads and served with homemade bread. Green beans, fresh from the garden, were a favorite among the immigrants, and quantities of green beans were eaten daily. The rest of the harvest was canned or even allowed to mature for drying.

A wealth of other garden vegetables graced the immigrants' tables. Cabbages, potatoes, beet greens, and spinach were often fried. Peppers were commonly stuffed with a meat-and-rice filling, using beef or pork or mixtures such as beef and ham. Women canned, dried, or otherwise stored garden produce such as potatoes, onions, carrots, rutabagas, turnips, and beans. Frugal housewives saved the peeled skins of rutabagas and turnips, dried them in a pan at the back of the stove, and stored them in airtight containers for use as flavorings in soups and stews when the supply of fresh vegetables was exhausted.

The South Slavs seasoned hot vegetables with browned butter, buttered breadcrumbs, or the cook's favorite — a brown roux, which Slovenes call prezganje, Serbians and Croatians, ajmpren. Although it may be made as needed, women usually keep a bowlful on hand to season soups, stews, and vegetables. Today many cooks make roux with low cholesterol vegetable oil, although they maintain that lard gives the best flavor.[18]

Browned breadcrumbs or small bread cubes are another characteristic South Slav touch. Partially dried, homemade bread, crumbled or cubed by hand and, in true South Slav tradition, browned slowly in butter, oil, or lard, makes the very best crumbs. These may be tossed with noodles or vegetables to give the dish a crunchy, zesty flavor. Slovenian women sprinkle them on top of a favorite dumpling, štruklji. Other South Slavs encase them in dumpling dough or include them in strudel.

Fall was a busy season for the immigrants as that was the time to slaughter the piglets or porkers that had been fattening since spring. Usually each family killed two, saving a third for Christmastime. Neighbors helped each other, and on fall weekends "pigs were squealing all over town." One man held the animal, another slit its throat, and the woman of the house collected the blood in a pan that contained salt. Constant stirring kept the blood from clotting until the mixture could be used for making blood sausage.[19] After slaughtering, the workers removed the hair from the animal's hide and stripped out the intestines and other parts for later use.

If the porker was to be roasted whole, it was skewered on a pole. Otherwise, men cut the meat into hams, ribs, and bacon slabs, soaking these in brine salty enough "to float an egg" and seasoned with pickling spices, garlic, sugar, or whatever suited the family's taste. Hams and pork pieces that were to be smoked were first soaked from one to six weeks, depending upon personal preference. Then the meat cured in the smokehouse for two days to two months. The finished products were hung either in a cold attic or were tightly packed with grain in containers and placed in a cool cellar.[20]

Families consumed smoked meats in a variety of ways throughout the winter. Bacon was frequently eaten at breakfast and also seasoned sauerkraut, beans, and vegetable dishes. A whole baked ham graced the table at holidays or special occasions, while bones and bits of leftover ham added flavor to soups. South Slavs commonly snacked on uncooked slab bacon, usually accompanied by pogača (a flat bread), a little wine, and sometimes peeled garlic. Currently people use less bacon in response to cautions about excess amounts of animal fat.

Nothing was ever wasted in the immigrant kitchen where people prided themselves on using "everything but the squeal." They soaked intestines for sausage casings or dried, smoked, and cut them into small pieces that they consumed by the handful or used to season bean and sauerkraut dishes. A few families smoked the pig's head, but most simmered it long and slowly, later using portions in sausage, dumplings, or soup. They learned to make headcheese from their Scandinavian neighbors.[21]

Women cut pork fat into one-inch pieces and rendered it in large copper kettles. They sprinkled cracklings, the small, crisp pieces left from the rendering, in bread dough and dumplings, included them in sausage, added them to vegetables and corn-meal dishes, and ate them "just . . . by the handfuls." Cooks used to store large amounts of cracklings in crocks with lard for later use. Those who no longer butcher today but still long for that taste buy pork fat, render it, and use the cracklings in family recipes.

Kidneys from the pig have always been considered a delicacy. While most people preferred them fried or grilled and served with fried onions, kidney stew was also popular. Even the pig's tail was smoked and used to season various dishes or to flavor soup. The stomach was washed inside and out and stuffed with bread or a mixture of bread and meat. Slovenes filled the stomach with garlic sausage, making a dish called žlodtz, often prepared for Easter dinner. Some family members did not always know what they were eating, and "mothers never told." In later years children were often surprised to learn how a favorite dish had been prepared.[22]

As for the bladder, parents used to clean it well, tie one end securely, blow air into the other, and tie it off. This balloon, made for a small child to bat about, became a kick ball for older children when it was well dried. A handful of dried corn or beans inserted in the balloon created a rattle. The liver was usually fried on butchering day and served with other foods at a special dinner after the slaughtering was finished. Neighbors traditionally passed a bottle of wine from hand to hand, adding a festive touch to the day.

South Slavs, like the Swedes and Finns, put the blood collected at slaughter time to good use in sausage. Slovenians and Serbians combined cooked rice with the blood; Croatians used corn meal. Usually, cooked head pieces and lungs were included together with salt, pepper, and cinnamon; Slovenes added a touch of mint or marjoram.

Cleaning the intestines for sausage casings was a smelly and time-consuming job, but every family member took a turn. The casings, soaked first in salted hot water and then in salted cold water, were turned inside out and scraped to remove any fat. The sausage stuffer then inserted three fingers in the end of an intestine to hold it open while forcing in the sausage mixture. Some used a cow's horn with its tip cut off as a funnel. The stuffed intestines, carefully tied to prevent bursting and splitting, were then boiled until they rose to the top of the water; once drained they were ready to eat. Depending on custom and taste, families also prepared liver, garlic, or potato sausage. Today, pork casings are available at many grocery stores, and metal funnels or commercial sausage stuffers have replaced the older methods. Friendly rivalry continues to exist among Slav families as to who makes the best sausage.

To this day, South Slav families maintain parts of their ancestors' holiday traditions. The Christmas season is perhaps the biggest time of celebration. Serbians, for example, observe not only December 25 but also their traditional Eastern Orthodox date from the Julian calendar, January 7: "What [gifts] we don't get on the 25th we get on the 7th." Earlier in the century, preparation began during the first days of December when families planted wheat in dishes and judged the prospects for new life and good luck for the coming year by the height of the new growth. In those years, Serbs, Croats, and Slovenes alike fasted for several weeks before the Christmas Eve church services. Now, however, people fast for varying lengths of time, but most South Slavs adhere to a Christmas Eve dinner with no meat or meat by-products. The main course is customarily bakalar (codfish) with potatoes, onions, vegetable oil, and vinegar, served either hot or at room temperature. Traditional accompaniments include flat bread prepared without milk or animal fat, bean soup, and quantities of fruit. In addition, some family traditions call for potato soup, homemade noodles, plates of garlic, bread dipped in honey, or other simple fare. Preparations for Christmas Day must be completed by midnight.[23]

For special occasions such as Christmas Day, men traditionally butchered piglets to roast over an open fire, a practice that many continue in the present. So that all flavors would blend together, the women seasoned the meat with salt, pepper, and garlic the night before roasting. The next morning, the men built a fire in a pit and carefully skewered the animal on a pole to be laid across two Y-shaped supports. Either children or men turned the spit by hand, basting the meat from time to time with a cloth attached to the end of a stick and dipped in a mixture of fat, water, and seasonings. Today a small motor keeps the skewered animals turning, but the preparation of the pig remains unchanged.[24]

Roasted piglet played a prominent part — decorative as well as culinary — in South Slav Christmas Day celebrations. After being removed from the pole, its head was cut off, placed on a platter, and brushed with pan drippings or some coloring to brighten it up. Preparing the pig's head for a centerpiece, the women inserted peanuts, chestnuts, or candy into its ears and an apple or short wine glass into its mouth. Sometimes they wrapped the teeth with foil. They placed mixed nuts and fruit or candy on the platter around the base of the head. Flanked by candlesticks on the dining table, the centerpiece was complete. As the family and guests gathered for dinner, it was customary to fill the pig's wine glass and pass the head from person to person. Each offered a toast, raised the head, and drained the glass. Sometimes the platter went around the circle several times in this way. Although the wine-drinking custom is no longer widespread, several iron range Croatian and Serbian families still roast a piglet. During the ensuing three days of the Christmas celebration, family members eat their favorite parts of the head — jowls, tongue, or ears. Whatever is left is made into soup.[25]

On Christmas Day, children still receive apples, oranges, bananas, nuts, and chewing gum to supplement other gifts. The dinner this day with its roast suckling pig has always been very special; this feeling remains, although roast ham may replace the suckling pig. Most South Slavs also serve several kinds of strudel and the ever-popular potica. Croatian families prepare apple pita, a rectangular type of apple pie with sweet-pastry crusts. Some women bake kifli, a rolled crescent with a walnut filling, or a bar cookie with currant jelly. The bread of the day is česnica, a loaf with a hidden coin. Since finding the coin guarantees good fortune for the year ahead, some mothers place several coins in the dough so that each child might find one. Česnica, traditionally broken into pieces, is now often sliced.[26]

Roman Catholics — Croatian and Slovenian alike — and the Serbian Orthodox celebrate the Easter season in much the same way. While many do not adhere to the Lenten fast preceding Easter as strictly as in the past, they still fast on Fridays and the day before Easter. Individual families also may honor particular days. Menus for the fasting period are like those for Christmas Eve.[27]

South Slavs, regardless of faith, use eggs both as a decoration and a food in remembrance of the ones Mary Magdalene brought to the tomb of Christ on Easter morning. On the Saturday before Easter or on Easter morning itself, Slovenes always took a basket of eggs (usually colored), bread, potica, sausage, slivered or whole horseradish, and other favorite foods to church. After the priest blessed the basket, the food became part of the family's Easter feast.

The highlight of an Easter celebration has always been janjitina (roast lamb). The animal is skinned, and seasonings are poked into slits that run through the fat into the meat. Some cooks use whole cloves of garlic while others chop and combine them with salt and pepper. For a dinner at two o'clock in the afternoon, barbecueing begins at five or six o'clock in the morning. Before the meat is sliced and placed on serving platters, the koza (browned fat) is eaten still warm and crunchy.[28]

Patron saints' days are celebrated in Serbian homes, often with festivities more elaborate than exist at Christmastime. Every home has its own patron saint, the one given to the father on his christening day. There are ceremonies at church as well as one at home when the priest blesses the house using wine, koljivo (a dish of cooked wheat), and the festal bread, kolač. This bread has been proudly prepared by the woman of the house, who braids strips of dough and then pats them into a round baking pan. She decorates the top of the loaf with strips of dough that form a cross

Katie Bruich braiding kolač, 1983

and places a "C" in each of its four corners. These forms symbolize Serbian words that can be translated "Only unity will save the Serbs." In the past families celebrated their patron saints' days with elaborate, all-day open houses; today, however, only the immediate family usually gathers for a splendid meal. Although the traditional barbecued lamb is still served in some homes, many have replaced it with roast pork, chicken, or even a lamb roast.[29]

Recollections of depression days are vivid among the South Slavs who lived in Minnesota during the 1930s. Money was scarce; only the chickens, pigs, cows, and produce from their gardens kept many families from extreme privation. Residents on the iron ranges hunted game birds, deer, rabbits, and other wild animals and caught fish; all types of food were canned, and some meats and fish were smoked. Church cookbooks from this era often included recipes for rabbit served with corn-meal mush and tomato sauce. Sauerkraut served with beans or potatoes or tomatoes or onions — or whatever was on hand — was a staple dish. So were potatoes — in salads, soups, stews, or served alone with a spoonful of thick soured cream.[30]

Soups helped stretch the family food budget. A "poor man's soup" of vegetables thickened with brown roux was part of all families' menus, the roux substituting for the flavor of meat. Another low-cost variety combined boiling water, brown roux, and a whipped egg or two, to which some people added vinegar to produce the slightly sour taste they preferred. Recipes still abound for beef soups using meaty ribs and bones and veal broths from stew meat and knuckles. Other popular soups included split pea, bean, lentil, barley, bean and sauerkraut, cucumber with wide noodles, and wax bean or cabbage seasoned with garlic or onion. Oftentimes butchers gave away bones, hearts, livers, and lungs. A versatile cook could combine these into a broth, to which she might add noodles or liver dumplings made with buckwheat flour. Despite memories linking soup to the Great Depression, it is still a popular part of the South Slav diet.[31]

Northeast Minnesota provided a variety and an abundance of berries. In the Hibbing and Chisholm area, families spent entire days picking the "blueberries that hung like grapes on the bushes." Many people recall eating boiled potatoes with wild blueberry sauce during the worst days of the depression: "Good when you are hungry." Blueberries and raspberries were canned as malinovač (a fruit drink), and prunes or plums were commonly stewed or used in dumplings. Most of the fruit was canned, but some was bartered at the grocery stores.[32]

Corn-meal dishes have long been a South Slav staple, and during hard times families relied on them even more heavily. The preparation of corn meal was almost ceremonial in nature; through the generations families passed down techniques as well as particular utensils and methods for cooking and serving this stand-by food. Cooked corn meal went by several names: polenta, žgance, or cicvara, depending on how different South Slavs prepared it. Polenta was cooked in salt water, stirred vigorously with a wooden spoon, and served as a mush with buttermilk, cheese, or yacina (a sauce made from the cooking water). Men were usually called to the kitchen to stir these large kettles of cooking corn meal. Žgance referred to thickened corn meal taken spoonful by spoonful from the cooking pot and dropped into a bowl. The resulting soft, egg-shaped morsels were sometimes arranged carefully in rosettes on a platter. Cicvara was the basic corn-meal mixture into which cream, cottage cheese, or grated hard cheese was folded and baked. Many South Slavs

Molly Fredrick, Sara Howard, Katie Bruich, and Mary Petrich rolling dough for cheese triangles, Duluth, 1984

liked browned butter poured over corn-meal dishes; others ate it with cottage cheese or topped it with a cooked egg. Fried bacon pieces, cracklings, or mashed potatoes were sometimes mixed in.[33]

South Slavs also consumed more milk products, long a traditional part of their diet, during the depression years. Just as families had milk cows on small farms in Yugoslavia, immigrants to Minnesota's iron ranges also kept the animals until city ordinances expelled livestock from the towns. People drank milk and buttermilk, made cheese, and soured milk for cooking or topping corn-meal dishes, potatoes, stews, and even some desserts. In Gary, New Duluth, and iron range towns women often sold surplus milk door-to-door.[34]

Milk was usually boiled and allowed to stand so that the cream would rise to the top. The thick top layer was a popular snack, either spread between two slices of homemade bread or on a single slice and sprinkled with sugar. The second, thinner layer of milk was dipped off and used in baking. For example, palačinkes (thin pancakes) were filled with jam or cheese, then covered with the milk and baked for a short time.

The remaining milk was used to make cheese. In one process, the milk, with a piece of rennet added, was heated slowly until curds resembling cottage cheese formed. The curds could then be combined with brick cheese, eggs, and sugar to make presnac, a baked dish similar in flavor to palačinkes. Or, to make a whole cheese, the women placed the curds in a colander under a weighted plate or scooped them into a cheesecloth bag and hung it up to drip overnight. This "squeaky cheese" could be used immediately or left for several days to compress and dry until suitable for grating. For additional flavor, some people placed the rounds in the smokehouse for a few days.

Bread was another mainstay. Europeans were accustomed to a coarse, dark loaf, but in the United States they "weren't going to use dark bread any more." Women baked white bread several times a week, and young girls learned to make it during their first cooking lessons. For variety, the cook might roll dough into a long strip about nine inches wide, sprinkle it with bacon pieces, pork cracklings, or cheese, and roll it up to bake in a bread pan. When caught without bread for a meal, women quickly mixed up a batch of white bread, patted the dough into a flat, round loaf, poked the top all over with a fork, and slid it into the oven of the wood-burning stove on a sprinkling of corn meal. Families loved this crusty pogača, and many women made it regularly along with their other breads.[35]

Other traditional breads baked regardless of economic conditions were potica; česnica, made for the Serbian Orthodox Christmas on January 7; kolač, a decorated Serbian bread used for patron saint celebrations; and nafra, unleavened communion bread. A depression stand-by was deva (wild angels); made of bread and sugar, it was an inexpensive noontime treat for children. Pieces of dough were pulled long and dropped into hot fat where they puffed out to look like angels' wings.

Economic conditions have fluctuated since the 1930s, and family menus reflect the prevailing times. Even during periods of relative prosperity the traditional dishes or "foods for leaner times" find their way to the table. But the question remains: Are holidays and economic depressions enough to maintain the vitality of South Slav foodways? Although church and other women's groups help to keep some traditions alive, older citizens worry that their customs and foodways will be lost: "Traditional foods will be a thing of the past if our young ones don't learn how to make them." Cookbooks available in local communities contain traditional recipes, and grandmothers who had discontinued many of the Easter, Christmas, and other holiday foods and practices are reviving them again for grandchildren. Second- and third-generation children call home for recipes, and mothers frequently mail strudel and potica to those away from home.[36]

It is true that changes have occurred. South Slavs are marrying non-Slavs. New foodways are incorporated and old ones forgotten. Some tried-and-true ingredients and processes have been replaced. Bakers may use hot-roll mix in potica, make strudel dough in a food processor, or simply substitute packaged phyllo sheets for homemade dough. Many people feel sad that family life, too, has changed in recent years and miss the days when the entire family joined together in activities. They remember when South Slav groups visited back and forth, attended church and social events in other towns, and food was the focus of hospitality. Today it continues to evoke pleasant sentiments and fond memories, providing a common bond that unites families and friends in happiness, comfort, and gratification.

NOTES

[1] June D. Holmquist, "The South Slavs," in *They Chose Minnesota*, ed. Holmquist, 381–83.

[2] Interviews of Christine Kappa, Mildred Orlich, and Mary Nordin, Chisholm, September 28, 1982, Mary and Joseph Milkovich, Virginia, November 5, 1982.

[3] Interview of Mary Palcher, Ely, September 15, 1982, Mary Nornberg, Chisholm, August 12, 1982; "Americanizing the Immigrant Woman Through the Home Teacher," Nute Papers.

[4] Thelma Barer-Stein, *You Eat What You Are: A Study of Canadian Ethnic Food Traditions* (Toronto: McClelland and Stewart, 1979), 568–83; Coralie Castle and Margaret Gin, *Peasant Cooking of Many Lands* (San Francisco: 101 Productions, 1972; distributed by Scribner), 83–86; Jane Grigson, ed., *The World Atlas of Food: A Gourmet's Guide to the Great Regional Dishes of the World* (London: Mitchell Beazley, 1974), 194–203; Joel Martin Halpern, *A Serbian Village* (New York: Columbia University Press, 1958), 1–36. For more on the Macedonians, see Greek chapter, above.

[5] Jinx Morgan, "Step By Step To The Perfect Barbeque: Rosa Rajkovic Creates a Special Summer Menu," *Bon Appetit*, July 1982, p. 45–56; Kay Shaw Nelson, *The Eastern European Cookbook* (Chicago: Regnery, 1973), ix–xi, 179–87.

[6] Interview of Father Peter Pritza, Hibbing, September 29, 1982; Fred Singleton, *Twentieth-Century Yugoslavia* (New York: Columbia University Press, 1976), 66; Spasenija-Pata Marković, *Yugoslav Cookbook*, trans. Vukosava Kojen (New York: L. Stuart, 1966), 14–15, 36–40, 185–95.

[7] Interview of Elizabeth Smolniker, Duluth, May 26, 1981; Orlich and Nornberg interviews.

[8] Interviews of Millie Belich, Duluth, July 14, 1982, Frank Blatnik, Duluth, April 13, 1983.

[9] Here and two paragraphs below, see interviews of Katie Bruich, Duluth, July 7, 1982, Amelia Thomas, Duluth, July 30, 1982; Nornberg and Milkovich interviews.

[10] Interviews of Helen Berklich, Hibbing, September 28, 1982, Mary Hutar, Ely, September 16, 1982.

[11] Smolniker, Orlich, and Nornberg interviews.

[12] Here and two paragraphs below, see interview of Frances Danko, Duluth, September 23, 1982; Bruich and Thomas interviews.

[13] Here and below, see interviews of Frances Krainik, Chisholm, August 12, 1982, Pat Mestek, Hibbing, September 29, 1982, Marion Dellich, Duluth, July 29, 1982, Violet J. Ruparcich, Chisholm, August 4, 1982.

[14] Here and below, see interview of Veda Ponikvar, Chisholm, July 21, 1982; Dellich, Bruich, and Milkovich interviews. Sliced or shredded turnips or rutabagas were often prepared in the same way as cabbage.

[15] Here and below, see interview of Mrs. Mike Miskovich, Pengilly, September 29, 1982; Smolniker interview. Sarma is sometimes called "pigs in the blanket" or stuffed cabbage rolls.

[16] Here and two paragraphs below, see interview of Rose and Tony Crnkovich, Hibbing, October 14, 1982; Belich, Milkovich, and Thomas interviews.

[17] Here and two paragraphs below, see interview of Mrs. John Puhek, Hibbing, August 11, 1982; Danko, Krainik, Mestek, Nornberg, and Thomas interviews.

[18] Here and below, see Miskovich, Krainik, Danko, and Blatnik interviews.

[19] Interview of Thomas Vukelich by Joe Drazenovich, May 14, 1975, tape in files of Iron Range Research Center, Chisholm; Smolniker interview.

[20] Here and below, see interview of Mary Prebich, Hibbing, November 17, 1982; Milkovich and Blatnik interviews.

[21] Here and below, see Kappa, Mestek, Thomas, and Prebich interviews.

[22] Here and three paragraphs below, see interview of Sonja Ulvi, Duluth, September 22, 1982; Kappa, Blatnik, Prebich, Milkovich, and Ponikvar interviews.

[23] Interview of Father Luzar Kostur, Duluth, September 10, 1982; Pritza, Prebich, and Miskovich interviews.

[24] Belich and Milkovich interviews.

[25] Crnkovich and Ulvi interviews.

[26] Hutar and Ulvi interviews.

[27] Here and below, see Kostur, Pritza, Blatnik, Danko, and Ruparcich interviews.

[28] Bruich, Milkovich, and Miskovich interviews. Roast lamb is also served at Fourth of July celebrations.

[29] Kostur, Pritza, Blatnik, Danko, and Ruparcich interviews.

[30] Palcher, Thomas, and Danko interviews.

[31] Milkovich, Orlich, Belich, and Blatnik interviews.

[32] Belich, Hutar, and Orlich interviews.

[33] Ruparcich, Krainik, and Thomas interviews.

[34] Here and two paragraphs below, see Bruich and Dellich interviews; interview of Mimmie Boben, Duluth, July 10, 1981.

[35] Here and below, see Palcher, Belich, and Blatnik interviews.

[36] Here and below, see Danko, Puhek, Belich, and Palcher interviews.

THE HMONG

At the close of the war in Vietnam, the Hmong people of northern Laos began a journey from their mountain villages into neighboring Thailand's refugee camps. From there, aided by various organizations, the first Hmong families arrived in Minnesota in 1976. After a series of population shifts to and from other major resettlement points such as San Diego and Fresno, California, and cities in Rhode Island, Iowa, and Ohio, there remained in the mid-1980s a fairly stable population of approximately ten thousand Hmong in the Twin Cities and a couple dozen other families in Rochester and in Duluth. Smaller pockets have been settled in Rice Lake and other Minnesota towns where individual and organizational sponsors have managed to accommodate the refugees.[1]

The Hmong are unique for several reasons. With obscure origins in China, they have always been a highly individualistic, mobile, and energetic minority group, surviving stubbornly amid a dominant culture. As a result, they are adept at achieving a functional biculturalism in which they maintain their own language, customs, and cosmology. Yet they assimilated sufficiently to be valuable and productive members of the host society. An example of this skill is their facility with languages. Most Hmong adults speak or at least understand Laotian and some Thai as well; however, until the mid-twentieth century they had no written language. Instead they developed a strong oral tradition of legends, songs, and myths, through which they passed on their narrative history. In wartime Laos, the Hmong preserved their traditional ways even while fighting as members of the Royal Laotian Army with the encouragement and logistical support of the American Central Intelligence Agency. If a decade of close contact with Americans precluded their safety in the postwar Laotian society, it also gave them a modest beginning at learning about life in the United States.[2]

The Hmong came to the United States with some knowledge of its military technology and behavior, some suspicion of American medical and agricultural programs abroad, and some slight familiarity with its language, culture, and foodways. They knew that Americans could be generous since many Hmong in Laos had survived on rice dropped from United States

Air Force planes. They knew about American convenience foods and particularly the soft drinks, both available from military post exchanges in Laos. These foods intrigued them but left their appetites unsatisfied. Furthermore, rumors about skeletons in hospitals circulated among some of the refugees, suggesting that Americans ate their patients upon decease. Thus, despite the need to escape camp conditions and to find a new life, the Hmong had serious doubts about finding their traditional and preferred cuisine in a strange land.[3]

In their mountain villages of Xieng Khouang, Sayaboury, and in other provinces, the Hmong had pursued a farming life characterized by annual clearing and burning of forest plots in February, planting in May, harvesting in October-November, and eventually moving to yet another dormant and productive field for replanting and continuation of the slash-and-burn agricultural cycle. Extended families clustered in villages of virtually identical, traditional houses. Adults and nearly grown children walked to the fields at dawn after arising somewhat earlier to feed and care for domestic animals and to prepare the family's morning meal. The Hmong unanimously equate this life with a hearty diet. Breakfast in rural Laos consisted of freshly cooked rice, eggs, and meat. Rice, wrapped in banana leaves and easily carried to the fields, was the core of the midday meal. Evenings found the people tired and hungry at the family hearth, sharing a dinner of rice accompanied by chicken or pork cooked with vegetables and seasoned with hot green peppers, garlic, cilantro (fresh coriander, also called "Chinese parsley"), ginger, chives, or other combinations of seasonings.

Within this pattern of life, the Hmong learned to cook just as they learned many other things: by observing and participating. A common response to the question, How did you learn to cook? confirms the pattern. Both girls and boys watched and assisted their mothers in the preparation of food. When adults went to the fields, however, younger children remained at home, the preadolescents serving as baby-sitters for toddlers and responsible for their own food as well as for beginning the evening meal. "I just would try it," said a young Hmong in St. Paul. "I tried several times and burned everything or the food fell into the fire, but finally I got it right and I could cook!"[4]

Today the Hmong do not see these patterns evolving in the same way. Both males and females will fix food for the family, but youngsters seem less interested in preparing for their customary role in the family's food patterns. Adults complain constantly that the children do not know the traditional recipes and beliefs about their foods.

In urban America, Hmong live quite different lives, and their foodways

Kao Yang, Minneapolis, serving sticky rice, 1985

Shopping at St. Paul's Country Store, a discount supermarket, 1982

have had to be adjusted accordingly. Whereas they once resided in spacious, rectangular houses built of bamboo and thatch, they now crowd into housing project apartments or, if less lucky, into poorly maintained flats in sometimes unfriendly neighborhoods.[5] While substantial predawn meals fortified Hmong adults for field work in Laos, their daily schedule in American classrooms, shops, or at home caring for grandchildren requires considerably fewer calories. Many Hmong insist that two meals a day are sufficient. In fact, most Hmong have observed that, by their native standards, American foods are too expensive, too widely varied, too ample at each meal, and "too heavy." By contrast, they describe their own food as "light but strong." Most, therefore, continue the traditional breakfast of rice and some protein, but some, especially the youth, compromise by eating American cereals or having no breakfast at all. School-aged children are nearly all following dual foodways. A ten-year-old might eat a bowl of cereal for breakfast, pizza and salad from the school cafeteria for lunch, and a family evening meal of chopped pork, hot green peppers, Hmong herbs and greens, and a bowl of rice. In such a case, the family breaks with historic foodways that were devoid of dairy foods by providing milk for the cereal. High-school students may purchase soft drinks at lunch with their pizza but drink plain, cool water, the preferred beverage of all Hmong, with dinner.[6]

Traditional Hmong foods in Laos should not be viewed as "primitive."[7] Their slash-and-burn agricultural techniques, together with concentrated livestock maintenance, yielded the Hmong a balanced diet consisting of rice, corn and other grains, vegetables, an enormous range of meats from domestic animals and wild game, fish, and easily obtainable fruits, nuts, and roots. Much of this pattern is continued in Minnesota. Many Hmong in Laos also raised buckwheat, millet, barley, and three kinds of corn, much of which was chopped each morning by hand and fed to animals. They also grew soybeans from which they made tofu, a practice carried on in Minnesota as well.

The central staple of their diet is still rice, which is cooked fresh for each meal. In Laos, the Hmong were distinctive for growing rice in dry, upland farms instead of in paddies as is done in lowland regions by Laotians and other Asians. They invariably identify their culture and themselves with a particular type of rice that they term mov txhua, or fluffy rice. While they admit that some Chinese also eat this rice, they are quick to point out that others, such as their former neighbors, the Laotians and Vietnamese, prefer mov nplaum, or sticky rice. Moreover, they stress that Hmong always eat their rice separately from meats and vegetables while others, especially Chinese and Indians, mix rice, meats, spices, and vegetables in a single dish. As rice is set apart from other dishes in the meal, so, too, do the Hmong feel set apart, and the position of rice in their diet symbolizes this perception. After extended contact with lowland Laotians, the Hmong incorporated sticky rice into their diet but only for certain holidays, a pattern that they maintained in the United States.[8]

Hmong in Laos raised water buffalo, oxen, pigs, chickens, and sometimes cows, each of which played a special role in their foodways. Pork and chicken are still probably the most popular protein sources, but Hmong never serve pork roasts and chops. Meat and chicken is usually removed from bones. Sometimes chunks of meat are served in soups or stewlike dishes, but more often it is shredded and chopped to the consistency of hamburger. It is then cooked with spices and, finally, combined with vegetables and served in a deep bowl as a soup or as a stir-fried companion to the ever-present rice. Hmong believe that all meats must be thoroughly "attended to" — that is, thoroughly chopped and seasoned — by the host so that guests may eat with minimal exertion. The only exception to this pattern is in the preparation of suckling pigs at rare holidays or for religious offerings. Chicken parts or bones are never boiled to prepare broth; however, chicken feet, well scrubbed and boiled in herbs, are considered a delicious snack or lunch. In Laos cows and water buffalo were infrequently slaughtered for food. Because of their monetary value, such animals were usually set aside for special holiday meals or as principal offerings to ancestors, especially at the New Year.[9]

The central herb-vegetable in Hmong cooking is zaub ntsuab, a leafy plant resembling mustard greens but not native to Minnesota. Most Hmong brought these seeds with them or had relatives send them from Laos, and today zaub ntsuab occupies a major portion of backyard gardens or of planter boxes in apartments. In addition, the Hmong in Laos raised white cabbage, onions, two kinds of tubers that resemble American sweet potatoes, squash, pumpkins, cucumbers, green beans, and snow peas. From the surrounding forest, they gathered papaya, coconuts, bananas (which are eaten only as snacks since fruit is never included with meals), bamboo shoots, large mushrooms similar to the "Chinese mushrooms" sold in America, and an enormous variety of plants and herbs for which there is often no English or other easily recognizable name. Bitter melon, sold in most Asian markets, is usually a flavoring for pork or chicken. Less familiar to Americans is tauj dub (lemon grass), which can be identified by its long, thin green leaves and its distinctive scent which resembles citronella. Zaub txhwb (cilantro) is used in nearly every dish from scrambled eggs to steak tartare.

In Laos, the forest and its mountain streams were a handy source of food. Several species of deer were hunted but so were tiger (which was smoked), bear, and wild boar. Some Hmong also hunted and ate monkey, but because of its peculiar odor not everyone enjoyed that meat.[10] Occasionally, Hmong ate elephant meat but only as a token gesture of appreciation to the spirit world after killing the beast for its valuable tusks. Squirrel, like monkey, was popularly hunted, especially since both these animals preyed upon the family's vegetable gardens.[11]

Obviously, several of these favorite foods have now vanished from the Hmong diet in Minnesota, and many are sorely missed. Instead of wrapping rice in banana leaves or packing it in a woven basket to take to work, Hmong now use aluminum foil; plastic containers are seldom employed since rice sealed off from the air develops an unpleasant odor and taste. Tripe or spleen, delicacies in Hmong native villages, are infrequently eaten now, but availability of ingredients is not the issue. Rather, the problem lies with the time-honored technique of preparation: tripe, made from hnyuv npua (pigs' intestines) was traditionally taken from the slaughtered animal and carried directly to a nearby mountain stream where it could be thoroughly washed and rinsed in the swift waters. In America, the Hmong insist, one cannot pursue this reliable mode of cleaning; the quality of store-bought tripe is too doubtful for most to enjoy. Those Hmong, however, who have access to a farm where they can select and slaughter a pig, carry home buckets of intestines along with the meat.

The Hmong are generally delighted with the availability of many of their preferred foods in Minnesota. Rice is bought in one-hundred-pound sacks on a regular basis, usually monthly for a family of six to nine persons.[12] A few Hmong-owned markets handle this important commodity, but their customers are equally as likely to buy their rice from a Korean or Vietnamese store if the shipment is sure to be fresh or of a particularly desired type. These markets also carry other necessities: fish sauce, canned bamboo shoots, rice paper for making egg rolls, durian or "jack fruit," and txiv quav miv (tamarind), the latter two also being ingredients in Hmong candy. The markets sell various kinds of noodles made from rice and the popular mung bean thread noodles that the Hmong have adopted from the Laotians. One shelf is always laden with brightly colored "prayer money," which is used in ritual offerings to ancestors. Another shelf holds dozens of the aluminum rice steamers popular among Asian Americans; these two-piece cookers resemble double boilers but have tiny holes in the bottom of the upper pan through which steam rises to cook the rice. Some Hmong managed to bring their old steamers from Thailand,

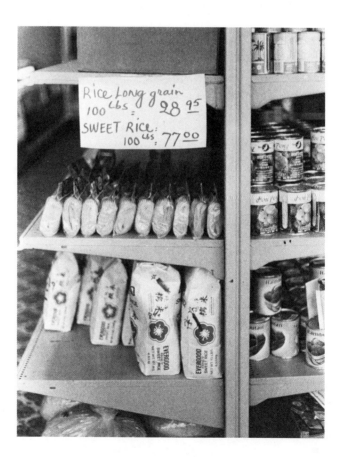

Shelves at Vietloss Oriental Foods, St. Paul, 1980

another sign that they were unsure of what gastronomic adventures awaited them in this country.

Not only is the need for imported goods minimal, in many cases food adaptations and innovations are both convenient and felicitous. For example, families now savor chicken cooked with broccoli, a totally new vegetable at Hmong tables; American apples and peaches are close enough to certain forest fruits of Laos to be acceptable substitutes; yams or sweet potatoes take the place of native tubers, qos liab; sunflower or corn oils replace lard, although the latter is still preferred. Sugar is used sparingly in cucumber salads, holiday rice cakes, and one soup dish but is generally avoided. Other new foods include carrots, canned pineapple, and lettuce, which is boiled like cabbage. The Hmong learned to use monosodium glutamate from the Laotians and Cambodians and now seldom omit it from their Minnesota cooking.

American styles of preparation have been incorporated into the Hmong diet. Stuffing peppers and tomatoes with meat and rice noodles, making meatballs, and rolling ingredients in cabbage leaves have become common ways of fixing foods. They seem to like omelets, pizza, sweet corn, and oranges. Many enjoy venison from autumn kills in northern Minnesota, and pan fish from nearby rivers occasionally are a family meal — more frequently than in Laos. Babies are fed canned formula, and older children relish Ovaltine, both products introduced by American medical advisors to the Hmong in the refugee camps. And while nearly all adults avoid American sweets, the children will dash to parents for change when an ice cream vendor's bell rings down the block. Finally, the Hmong, unlike other Asians, brew no beverages such as tea to accompany meals. A few herbal teas are employed as cures, but the Hmong simply prefer water with their foods. Yet with their limited and somewhat naive understanding of American foodways, they always serve carbonated soft drinks to American guests and sometimes drink these beverages themselves.[13]

Utensils comprise one of the most interesting parts of Hmong material culture. Most impressive are their kitchen knives, which average eighteen inches in length and are often hand-fashioned from old car parts by a traditional blacksmith or even the father of the family. The knife serves to peel, slice, and finely chop vegetables and to bone and mince meats. Watching a tiny Hmong woman slip the knife handle under her arm and grasp the broad blade as she peels a cucumber is an awesome sight. Then, she will squat over a chopping block on the kitchen floor and cut up a chicken, removing most bones with a flick of the knife point.[14]

The knife's partner in much of this work is a log cam, a slab of wood cut across the grain from a certain tree in Laos valued for its hardness.

Slicing onions with a handmade knife, Minneapolis, 1985

These chopping blocks were carried to the United States as part of a limited hoard of household goods as the Hmong had to leave many of their implements behind when they emigrated. Adults can still draw detailed sketches of rice and corn grinders, tofu mills, or the ingeniously crafted knives. In place of these instruments, Hmong have adapted their foodways to available utensils. They make chopping blocks from local woods, and they have chosen new items for their kitchen counters: blenders, toaster ovens, and an occasional electric can opener. Freezers are a popular way of extending the use of communally purchased and butchered pork and beef, and refrigerators and stoves are now common kitchen appliances. The basic tools for making spicy sauces—a mortar and pestle—are easily available here.[15]

The adaptation to such conveniences was rapid but not without some misgivings. Hmong women had traditionally cooked over a qhov cub, a three-legged ring that supported a cooking pot above a fire. Literally translated as "hearth," this arrangement was maintained in the same spot in all traditional households, where it symbolized the social center of the home.[16] In another area of the house was a qhov txos, a second and larger stove somewhat like a small brick outdoor barbecue, used almost exclusively for steaming rice. Both stoves also served as heat sources.

When the Hmong fled to the Thai refugee camps, the limited resources and crowded conditions forced them to modify their cooking patterns. Some Hmong who had managed to bring their three-legged rings continued to use them. Most, however, had to use a different stove that resembled a bucket lined with fire bricks and had draft holes near the bottom. In one or, if lucky, two such cooking devices, Hmong families — and sometimes several families together — had to manage all food preparation. By careful planning, the rice was not too cool by the time the other dishes were ready.

Unlike so many other Asian people, the Hmong, with few exceptions, prefer to use spoons rather than chopsticks. Some utensils are plain flatware; others are Oriental-style ceramic soup spoons. Forks and knives are seldom provided except to guests and then only in those households that have had prolonged and frequent contact with westerners.

Americans invited to a Hmong home must learn to follow prescribed behavior if they hope to demonstrate "good manners" and to communicate appropriate appreciation for their hosts' efforts. Male and female guests are expected to sit and engage in formal conversation for about fifteen minutes, after which the hostess excuses herself and disappears into the kitchen. Soon children stream out of the kitchen with bowls, spoons, and tableware and begin to set the table. Guests are invited to wash their hands. On more formal occasions, the host may bring a basin and towel to the living room and hand-washing is "performed" — more a traditional gesture than a necessity. If there are several guests, they will sit down to dinner with the host and begin; the wife and children will withdraw and eat later. Sometimes when but one or two guests are present, the entire family will join them, and all will be seated around a large table. American female guests are included with males, but in Laos only males ate together in such formal circumstances.

It is appropriate that guests thank their host before eating, and there are several levels of remarks, the most formal being those offered, for example, by a traveling merchant who, in Laos, was probably Chinese and had brought his wares to the village. Somewhat less formal are thanks offered by nonrelatives, and least formal are acknowledgments of the hostess's efforts offered by kin.

As soon as this formality has been discharged, eating may begin. One must always turn first to the rice, scooping out several spoonfuls from the main bowl into the smaller, personal bowl that has been placed at each setting. One is further expected to eat several mouthfuls of plain rice, thereby acknowledging that this is the central or most valuable dish of the meal, the dish one anticipates and turns to first. With these preliminary steps behind them, the guests may now contemplate the array of meat and vegetable dishes on the table. When the gathering is large and the table equally commodious, two or more bowls of each dish are set down so that, again, guests will not be unduly inconvenienced as they taste each preparation.

There is a seemingly infinite variety of combinations of chicken, pork, and beef, mixed with the many vegetables the Hmong learned to use in Minnesota. One might find a stir-fry of pork, onion, cabbage, and cilantro. And there may be a dish of pork, bamboo shoots, and lemon grass in a very soupy preparation. If the weather is warm, a cool salad may be served, consisting of slivered green papaya, carrots, garlic, peanuts, lemon, fish sauce, and monosodium glutamate. Sometimes a simple dish of cucumbers, sweetened with honey and iced, is prepared instead. One might find Hmong-style meatballs, some variety of egg rolls if the meal is considered "fancy," baked chicken, or a combination of mung bean thread noodles, cilantro, onion, mint, garlic, hot green peppers, and finely chopped pork. Frequently, the hostess prepares a bowl of zaub tsuag (literally, vegetables without salt) and reserves the broth or cooking water. Adults consider this broth the main and indispensable beverage of their meals and drink it in addition to plain water.[17]

Good manners at a Hmong table dispense with extensive asking and passing, though a minimum is unavoidable at large gatherings. Instead, one simply tastes one dish and then another, dipping into the nearest bowl and conveying the food directly to the mouth. One never pours the meat-vegetable combinations over the rice, and one should always be careful not to drip the spoon's contents into the other dishes. The easiest manner is simply to bring the spoon to the mouth by passing it between bowls. As each diner busily sees to the dishes at hand, the host will exhort each please to eat more and will apologize that "Everything is too far from you!" Actually, bowls crowd your elbows, but it is the host's obligation to assure you that you are welcome and to be certain himself that he has done his utmost to provide adequate hospitality. In Hmong culture, a host's status is judged by his skill, warmth, and generosity. Guests are always fed without question when they appear, even when they arrive unexpectedly. As many Hmong have explained, "One cannot tell from your guest's face if he is hungry," or as a Hmong proverb says, "To be a person is not (necessarily) to show hunger." Only by offering food can one protect one's reputation. The goal is simple: to provide enough for all.

One of the things that makes Hmong meals unique is their nearly total absence of desserts or sweets of any kind. Fresh fruit may be offered at the meal's end, but this practice is rare and, in some cases, traceable to French influence. Steamed and sweetened rice cakes have, in the decade of the 1970s, been adopted from Laotian cuisine.[18] Traditional Hmong rice cakes, by contrast, are somewhat less firm and are never sweetened.

As veteran survivors within a dominant culture group, the Hmong have taken on a number of foods which they now prepare superbly and to which they lend their own distinctive style. In some cases they have also borrowed the Laotian name for the dish. Egg or spring rolls are the best example of this assimilation, but others include a kind of steak tartare that the Hmong call nqaij liab, or, literally, "red meat." As with European versions, raw pork, beef, or chicken is finely chopped and heavily seasoned with herbs. Food scholars have argued that steak tartare, sushi, or carpaccio and other raw meats must be "transformed"; that is, they must undergo some culinary process, such as smoking, curing, salting, or pickling, in lieu of cooking in order to remain within the code of what is edible in any given society. This is true also for nqaij liab.[19] Prepared only for the most formal and festive occasions — when special guests are present or at New Year's — it would but rarely appear in a workaday meal. It is never shared with children and is not appropriate food for a ritual offering to the ancestors. Raw meat, like egg rolls and sticky rice, is set apart from common Hmong fare in form and in degree of intricacy that is necessary for its preparation.

Egg rolls, requiring thin rice paper, would have been exceedingly difficult to prepare in a mountain Hmong village and, more importantly, would have taken up more time than deemed worthy unless an ostentatious display of effort was required. Once the Hmong established frequent contact with urban Laotians and Cambodians who produced the rice-paper wrappers commercially, however, supplies could be carried easily. Egg rolls were then incorporated into the holiday home diet. Even the word employed by the Hmong for this delicacy, kab yaub, is Laotian.

As with rice paper, the Hmong use of Thai rice noodles and other types of pasta has been intensified in Minnesota where these foods are readily available. Thus, interethnic borrowing is a demonstrated trait among the Hmong. But it is even more important to note that the Hmong rely upon these foods to establish a public identity with Americans and to negotiate social status through them. These borrowed foods, utilized as "Hmong" delicacies in public contact with non-Hmong, are favorites whenever food-sharing is called for. So, at New Year's dinners, special entertainments, church suppers, and for honored guests, these foods are preferred because they are more intricate, more demanding in their production, and, therefore, they impute more status to the host.[20]

Making a food offering to ancestral or other spirits is yet another dimension of Hmong foodways. Traditional animists with a rich pantheon of spirits invested in trees, rocks, animals, and other objects and beings, the Hmong are obligated on pain of sickness or other misfortune to maintain good relationships with these spirits and particularly with those of departed ancestors.[21] Illness, then, might be interpreted by a shaman as caused by a dead relative's desire to be fed an ox or a water buffalo.

As believers in reincarnation and the movement of souls into and out of people's bodies, the Hmong have developed a myriad of curing ceremonies that aid them in achieving equilibrium. For example, when a shaman determines that an offering to the spirit world is required, it may be because his patient's soul has been displaced and needs to be enticed back into the body. The curing method employed includes killing a chicken as an offering of food to the spirit, coaxing it to return to the world of the living and into its proper place. Inevitably, food offerings, together with a complex pattern of taboos or avoidance behavior, are the principal solutions to these problems.

The spirits of deceased parents often demand that an ox be killed and communicate this request for tso plig (ancestral offerings) to an elder son, usually in a dream. He then draws his brothers and other male family members together who frequently will pool their resources to offer the best sacrifice they can. In Laos, a water buffalo was a typical offering, but in Minnesota a pig will do as well. At such a ceremony, a head of household will offer a token of cooked meat and rice at an altar. Afterwards, the entire family group partakes of a feast that includes the usual variety of highly seasoned dishes containing chile peppers and onions. If, for some reason, the food supply is small and the gathering large, the meat may be extended by brewing a broth, but every family member present must partake of the shared offering. The food offering prepared for the ancestors is plain and unseasoned for a logical reason. Highly spiced food is deemed necessary for good health among the living, and green chile peppers, it is believed, contribute to good eyesight and healthy blood. Clearly, the dead have no need of these benefits.[22]

The celebration of the Hmong New Year in early December is the most propitious time to perform tso plig. With the harvest behind them, the Hmong set aside this time for visiting, entertainments, courting, feasting, and relaxation. A festive New Year's meal is much like an everyday meal except that it is more varied. Having killed one or more large animals, the cooks prepare a wide range of pork, chicken, and beef dishes, each seasoned slightly differently.

In Minnesota, the Hmong celebrate their New Year at any convenient time near the end of the calendar year, usually mid-November or early December. Frequently a large public auditorium or school is used for an all-day gathering that begins early and ends late and which draws crowds of Hmong from all over Minnesota and beyond, as well as their American guests. In many ways, the celebration has begun to take on the form of other ethnic festivals, including dances or skits presented by organized groups, silver-ornamented costumes, worn especially by young women, and festive food, if possible. In some large civic buildings only the food from concession stands is permitted.

In some ways, too, the uniqueness of traditional Hmong culture is preserved here, particularly those ethnic activities that have somehow gained positive recognition from the non-Hmong community at large. The traditional lines of boys facing girls are formed, and the youths toss a ball back and forth, talk, and use the ancient arrangement as an opportunity to meet other young people and, perhaps, a future spouse. The graceful performance on the qeej, a wind instrument, of a Hmong musician is another example of cultural sharing with Americans; the music is increasingly being presented as an entertainment at public New Year's celebrations. Rarely do Americans see the qeej played in its serious contexts of communicating with ancestral spirits at funerals or other rituals.[23]

The new year is the one time during the year when all must return home, a time when all the living and all the spirits and souls are joined in one place. Since there are so many spirits present, an abundance of food must be provided. In Laos, wealthy Hmong sacrificed a chicken for each living person in the family. Less fortunate persons offered one or two chickens for the entire family, collectively, and the poorest offered eggs for each household member. To call the souls, the head of the household stands before the sacrificed chickens and the joss sticks (incense) inside the house facing out the door and says:

> Today is New Year. The old year is going to pass, all souls please come home, come to have the food. We have plenty of food for you. Please don't believe people who are trying to persuade you to go elsewhere. Come and stay home until you are old, until your hair has become white as silver. All the souls of horses, oxen, pigs, and chickens please come home. . . . If you cannot come this chicken will go to bring you. If you miss the way back home, you can follow the smoke of the joss sticks. If you get any disease before you come home, throw it away. Don't bring it into the house. Post spirit and door spirit, please pull them to help them into the house.[24]

To ensure success, the head of the family calls all the family names and walks about the interior of the house. Then to conclude, he throws the kuam, two divining sticks usually made from water buffalo horns that are inscribed with special markings much like those on dice, until the flat sides of both are turned down. This position means that all spirits have returned. He further divines the coming year by removing the tongues from several of the sacrificed chickens and examining them for omens, good or bad. If bad fortune looms, a shaman is called to intercede.

Of all the animals used in ritual offerings, the water buffalo or the ox represents the greatest monetary value and therefore the most generous gesture to the ancestors. It is the chicken, however, that is more frequently used, both as the offering per se and as a means of divining the will of the gods for the welfare of the family or the clan.

It is believed, in general, that the chicken knows a great deal about the world. The rooster, for instance, knows beforehand that the sun will rise and announces this to the Hmong and to the other beasts on the farm. According to one myth, the rooster lived underground and called the sun each morning to rise. At sunset, he crowed once more to tell the sun that she could now go, to return again on the morrow. As a symbolic extension of human roles, a rooster and a hen are served at a wedding feast, the rooster to the men and the hen to the women.

A chicken used in an ancestor ceremony should be bought live and have black plumage in order to resemble as closely as possible the fowl raised in Laos. These are held to be the tastiest type and therefore are the most persuasive offering. After the chicken is killed, it is thoroughly examined. The tongue, the feet, and possibly the bones are inspected by any adult male but usually by heads of households or by a shaman. It is understood that, after the spirit has eaten, certain marks on the bones indicate its approval of the family's plans. Similar diagnosis can be made from a chicken's tongue, skull, thigh bones, and toes. Several Hmong remember that during the war in Laos, divination by examining chicken parts allowed them to implement successful strategies against Communist forces in their battles. But, whatever the dilemma, once the ritual has been properly performed and the message discerned, the chicken is merely food and all present will partake.[25]

The chicken plays one other major role in Hmong life that can also be documented in Minnesota. Pregnant women and mothers of newborn infants, as in most cultures, are considered highly vulnerable to dangers from the spirit world as well as from the physical environment. Women in early or middle stages of pregnancy, for example, may not cross streams for fear that labor will begin immediately. In the Hmong communities of Minnesota, new mothers follow a strict diet of warm foods: rice and very fresh chicken cooked in some half-dozen herbs that their families grow in their gardens or on apartment porches. They may also eat a little cabbage or broccoli but no spicy foods such as hot peppers, no cucumbers, and no other meats. Sweets and cold foods must be avoided; otherwise the women's skin will bruise easily when they are older.[26]

Some general taboos concern persons of different generations or the opposite sex. Others mark the special condition of people in transitional stages. For example, it is widely and strictly understood that nursing mothers must guard against the possibility of their breast milk "contaminating" the foods of anyone except their own infants. Women must carefully cover their breasts when preparing food for the family or even if they are feeding domestic animals. Should a pig, for example, consume food that contains a woman's breast milk, the pig, in turn, will "contaminate" all who eat it. In one case, a family's house mysteriously burned down, and the cause was attributed to violation of this taboo.[27]

A different avoidance has to do with hot green peppers that are so liberally added to most dishes. Children are generally not offered such spicy condiments or raw foods. Hot peppers usually are not served to a young couple at their wedding feast, for they create a burning sensation in the mouth, akin to hot words. Such "burning" in later life would signal a marriage not going well, one full of arguments and incompatibility. To encourage a union harmonious and calm, the foods at a wedding should be as bland as possible, yet interesting for guests. Some Hmong insist that fried foods should be avoided at these occasions as well. Qhuav, the Hmong word for "fried," also means "plain" or "dry" (as in not spicy) and can also connote "sterile." To eat fried foods might suggest that the bride and groom will not love each other (or the woman will not love the man). No one at a wedding wants even to imply that the couple's life might be unadorned (as rice is plain and unadorned), sterile, or, worst of all, childless.

More particularized food taboos are laid down along clan lines. For example, members of the Yang clan should not eat sour fruit on pain of becoming blind. The males of some families of this clan are also prohibited from eating the heart of any animal, for according to a myth:

Some men from the Yang family in the grandfathers' time were hunting and killed an animal. In the process of preparing it for food, they misplaced the heart. Lost it. So they had this prisoner who was dumb [could not talk] and they killed him and took out his heart and ate it so the meal was complete. And then they were told that they shouldn't do that thing, and ever since that time, they do not eat any heart of any kind of animal or anything.

Other stories explain why some Lee families should not eat pancreas, why some Vang families must avoid bones, or why some Her families must

American soft drinks mingled with a wide variety of traditional Hmong food at a wedding reception in St. Paul, 1981

not carry rice and fruit on their backs in the same basket. But these taboos are in no way debilitating; rather, they reinforce clan identity, especially within the Hmong community at large where they serve as guides for political and marital behavior.[28]

In Laos, Thailand, and Minnesota, Christian Hmong generally observe other food prohibitions. They are exhorted to avoid eating blood from any animal, partaking of any animal or fowl used in a ritual by a traditional shaman or priest, and wearing and utilizing the Hmong "life rings," necklaces given to and worn by Hmong after a shamanistic ceremony is performed for their family. A more celebrative example involves the Hmong traditional drinking games during marriage negotiations. Male representatives from both families participate in a series of challenges during which one may either drain his cup or dip his hand into a stew of pork fat and juices and consume as many pieces as he can hold in his fingers. This game is called "fishing" and is considered a hilarious part of the traditional ceremonies. At Hmong weddings, eight rounds of whisky accompany the ceremony from entering the bride's home to its formal conclusion. Since Christian Hmong usually refrain from drinking alcohol during this ceremony, the intraethnic schism is particularly dramatic. These restrictions on Christian Hmong drive a small but nevertheless noticeable wedge between them and their non-Christian clan members, specifically limiting their contact at meal-sharing occasions in spiritual or secular contexts.[29]

The foodways of the Hmong, from a nutritional and medical point of view, have been the subject of much study, especially in the early stages of residency in the United States. An attempt by the Minneapolis Health Department in 1980 to examine their traditional diet revealed that the Hmong were incorporating the least nutritious American "junk foods" into their daily diets and that they were having trouble adjusting traditional Hmong food preparation methods to the American urban environment. That is to say, raising and slaughtering pigs and chickens in backyards was not only disturbing to neighbors but also was prohibited by law. After a year's study, nutritionists concluded that the original Hmong diet, pure and simple, was best. They began to reinforce this message among the youth, hoping to persuade them that their three basic food groups (contrasted to five in the standard American diet) were not something to be ashamed of in their parents' culture but could be validated by American nutritional standards. It was shown that staples (rice), body-building protein sources, and protective foods like vegetables and fruits were superior to many popular processed foods.[30] Today, however, Hmong youth are still heavy consumers of American packaged foods. Indeed, when asked if they have tried American restaurants, they invariably respond that, yes, they have been to McDonald's or tried a frozen pizza!

Another ongoing problem in the Hmong dietary patterns in Minnesota has to do with child-rearing practices. In rural Laos, a fussy child was immediately given the breast or something at hand to nibble on. But in Minnesota, such oral gratification tends to be less nutritious than in the old cultural setting. Some young Hmong children suffer from obesity, tooth decay, and stomach problems, conditions exacerbated by ice cream, candy, and low-quality breads that comprise the bulk of commercial and easily available baked goods. While many Hmong teen-agers have managed to find things here and there to eat in their high school cafeterias, others now in technical schools testify that they spent four long years with upset stomachs while attending public schools. Of course, these young people were born in Laos or Thailand, and we have yet to learn what will develop among the American-born generations.

The careful observer of Hmong foodways must document a number of tangential behaviors that are seldom of interest to the casual visitor or journalist. For example, in a collection of forty-one Hmong proverbs (called paj lug or "flower language") fourteen had to do with eating in a literal or metaphorical manner of speaking. For example:

> Noj tsis noj kuj tuav diav,
> Luag tsis luag kuj ntxi hniav
> (Whether you eat or not, at least hold a spoon.
> Whether you laugh or not, at least force a smile.)

This proverb is introduced when one is inviting guests to eat even though they refuse. By contrast, in a dispute, someone might repeat a proverb borrowed from the Chinese:

> Yeej kom tshij xas looj cib
> Pem kom puj yawb chib.
> (The accuser has eaten three baskets of chickens,
> But the defendant has not gotten up yet — is in no hurry to go to trial.)

Or, to illustrate traits of caution or even xenophobia:

> Zaub tsib tsis yog ntxuag,
> Nciab tsis yog luag.
> (Bitter vegetables are not suitable to eat with rice,
> Or strangers are not good companions.)[31]

These Old World sayings explain a fair amount about traditional Hmong culture. But what of the Hmong experience in Minnesota? One Hmong elder summarized his fatalistic Hmong world view about adapting to yet another dominant culture by saying: "When you live on this side of the heavens, you have to learn to eat their kind of rice."[32]

The Hmong resignation to American ways extends beyond their foodways. As they have bought and come to employ modern American technology in the home, they have also, to some extent, forsaken some of the traditional cures of shamans and folk medicine for the local clinics and medical centers. In 1983, a brief flurry of news revealed that elderly Hmong often received opium from Thailand through the mail to relieve arthritis and other discomforts of old age. Although law enforcement officials soon came to understand that the practice was traditional and never pursued outside this particular context, they nevertheless had to ask community leaders for help in persuading older generations to use approved American medical techniques. The subject remains a sensitive issue as the Hmong strive to become exemplary citizens in a new land.[33]

Similarly discouraging were the observations of one anthropologist. In reviewing the factors that sustain the Hmong sense of identity in San Diego, California, he noted external forces included, contrary to other patterns, a resistance to class identity and a reinforcement of Hmong identity as "foreign" or at least "ethnic." Initially optimistic, the Hmong soon after arrival became discouraged by the wide gap between their abilities and their needs to fit into American society. He observed two things in the Hmong-American experience so far; despite their willingness and toughness: "(1) their condition will probably not get better in time, and (2) adversity does not seem to bring out the best in their people."[34] A University of Minnesota psychiatrist who has worked extensively with Hmong patients, added, "Their problems are not all clearing up. The majority are making the adjustment, but they still have high rates of disability — depression, family problems, suicide, intergenerational strife, you name it . . . it takes a fair amount of stress for little old grandmothers to be opium smugglers."[35]

In their attempts to "take care of themselves," the Hmong have striven toward those modes of life that they know and survive in best: farming and livestock work. But the Hmong farming experiences have, for the most part, been limited to backyards or to plots of land that have been donated by local institutions. The Wilder Forest near Stillwater, for example, has offered Hmong families dozens of acres of excellent land, but those plots lie some thirty-five miles from their St. Paul neighborhoods. Still, in the mid-1980s, many Hmong families made the trek to this generously allotted land to harvest traditional and American vegetables, often with the help of the preserve's farming director who also supplied current information on fertilizers and nutrition. Here, too, Hmong were able to begin raising their preferred breeds of pigs and chickens. Some of the products from this effort show up at the farmers' markets in Minneapolis and St. Paul on a weekly basis in the summer and autumn.

Larger projects have also been started. A privately organized farming experiment under the sponsorship of Church World Service in Homer failed in 1984 due to poor financial planning by its American managers. In 1985, however, based on what they learned in Homer, a number of Hmong

Blia Moua, Lu Vang, Mao Vang, and Chee Thor gardening at Wilder Forest, near Marine on St. Croix, 1984

formed their own corporation and launched a successful agricultural operation in Hugo. Another venture was begun in 1982–83 when representatives of the Agricultural Extension Service, concerned citizens, and members of Lao Family Community of Minnesota, Inc., met to develop a more integrated approach to the overall economic problems of the Hmong. The result was the establishment of the Minnesota Agricultural Enterprise for New Americans (MAENA), a four-year farming project in Farmington that will attempt to provide a transition from patriarchal to cooperative management, teach efficient and modern farming techniques, and develop short-term incentive systems for the extended family. As both a training project and a business enterprise, MAENA will lead many Hmong toward a higher level of self-sufficiency and self-esteem.[36]

With each passing day, the Hmong are developing new strategies for survival in Minnesota. They are familiar customers in urban supermarkets and have demonstrated their industry in the business and technical fields of American life. They now can chuckle over their experiences with sponsors during the early years when, hungry for their traditional foods, they had only their sponsor-family's token offering of a one-pound package of Uncle Ben's Rice.

Yet some suspicion and discomfort remain. Many Hmong are wary, even fearful, of Americans' propensity to create artificial foods, the use of steroids in stock raising for commercial foods, and America's unwillingness or inability to perceive and solve the dilemma of this new ethnic group. In characterizing the establishment's short-term approaches to Hmong food and economic problems, one elder summarized his views in the statement, "The government feeds you, but then makes you throw up."[37] This metaphorical description applies, clearly, to the Hmong feelings of disorientation over the loss of a family center in the home, the family-owned farm, and the round of seasonal, traditional observances that take place there. Without their own land, Hmong food is nourishing but tasteless in the deepest sense of that word.

NOTES

[1] In 1986 Minnesota had an estimated Hmong population of 10,500, ranking third in size after California and Texas; telephone interview of Ron Grimm, Refugee Program Office, Minnesota Department of Public Welfare, April 16, 1986. Some sixty thousand Hmong arrived in the United States between 1976 and 1980, according to "Toward Hmong Self-Sufficiency," *CURA Reporter* (Center for Urban and Regional Affairs, University of Minnesota) 14 (July 1984): 1. More complete data can be found in Sarah R. Mason, "The Indochinese," in *They Chose Minnesota*, ed. Holmquist, 586–88. The most extensive compilation of readings on the Hmong in Asia and in the United States is Douglas P. Olney, comp., *A Bibliography of the Hmong (Miao)*, Southeast Asia Refugee Studies, Occasional Papers no. 1 (Minneapolis: Center for Urban and Regional Affairs, University of Minnesota, 1981). See also Glenn Hendricks, *Indochinese Settlement Patterns in Minnesota* (Minneapolis: Center for Urban and Regional Affairs, University of Minnesota, rev. ed., 1983). A recent and particularly beautiful book about the Hmong in Asia is Paul Lewis and Elaine Lewis, *People of the Golden Triangle* (New York: Thames and Hudson, Inc., 1984), which includes chapters on five other Southeast Asian ethnic groups besides the Hmong.

[2] For more on linguistic development of the Hmong, see Olney, comp., *Bibliography of the Hmong*, 29–37. The Hmong in the United States divide themselves principally into two subgroups, named according to colors that decorate their costumes: white and blue or green. Each group speaks a slightly different dialect, and there are some subtle differences in foodways. The terms noted in this text are given in White Hmong, the dialect of the larger of the subgroups.

[3] There is evidence that getting rice from the United States government depended upon each family in a village sending one man to serve in the Hmong forces supporting the royal Laotian government, backed by the Central Intelligence Agency; *Minneapolis Star and Tribune*, April 21, 1985, p. 31A. Hmong families were also astounded by television and initially believed that they were seeing ghosts, a phenomenon not considered strange in their cosmology.

[4] Interview of Blong Thao, St. Paul, August 1984.

[5] The densest Hmong settlements in the Twin Cities are in St. Paul in the Rice Street-Maryland Avenue neighborhood and in the area south of Interstate-94 between Dale Street and Summit Avenue; see Hendricks, *Indochinese Settlement Patterns*, 9. By 1985 pockets were also established along Jackson Street on St. Paul's East Side, and on Congress Street on the West Side; interview of Marlin Heise, August 9, 1985.

[6] Hmong insisted during interviews that milk from cows was assigned to calves and never used for human consumption. A derogatory epithet in Hmong is "He's a drinker of buffalo milk!"

[7] For a review of early attempts to study and possibly revise the Hmong diet, see *Minneapolis Tribune*, March 12, 1981, p. 1T. On the dietary shifts consequent upon migration and the biological consequences of these changes among twenty-nine Hmong households in Seattle, Washington, see Marshall G. Hurlich, "Rural Hmong Populations in Western Washington State: Nutritional and Demographic Adaptations," presented to the Conference on Hmong Research, University of Minnesota, Minneapolis, October 2-3, 1981, copy in Southwest Asian Refugee Studies office, Department of Linguistics, University of Minnesota, Minneapolis.

[8] Hmong distinguish linguistically between nplej (unhulled, unprocessed rice, such as that growing in the fields), mov (cooked rice), and txhur (uncooked but processed, often bagged, rice). The phrase "to eat a meal" is translated in Hmong as "to eat rice." No Hmong interviewed was familiar with American wild rice nor had any tried American "instant" rice. Brown rice, touted by nutritionists as more healthful, is totally ignored by the Hmong. For some Hmong families in Minnesota, breakfast is now a good time to serve sticky rice because it requires less actual cooking time. The symbolic uses of rice are many, and one good example is found in the practice of placing grains of rice — a quantity equal to the number of persons in the family — on the site of a proposed new house. If, overnight, the spirits have not disturbed the grains, the house may be built without fear of interference from the spirit world or of natural disaster. See *National Geographic* 145 (January 1974): 92.

[9] Some intolerance toward the Hmong and other Asian refugees has been expressed by Minnesotans who accused their new neighbors of killing dogs and eating them; see *Minneapolis Star and Tribune*, October 24, 1984, p. 3T. The Hmong do not eat dogs.

[10] Monkey is generally singed first to remove the hair. It is then cleaned, and the meat is cut from the bones and smoked on a rack over an open fire.

[11] *Minneapolis Star and Tribune*, October 24, 1984, p. 3T.

[12] In 1984 California rice sold for $21.95 per one hundred pounds, but the sweeter and preferred Thai rice sold for $22.00 per fifty pounds.

[13] Pepsi Cola, Orange Crush, Mountain Dew, and 7-Up are favorites. Beer is not particularly popular except among assimilated young men, and whisky is reserved for

special occasions such as weddings and the New Year's celebration.

[14] As paj ntaub, the traditional Hmong embroidery, is women's work, knife making at the forge is a man's craft, and most can still remember how to do it. Each village in Laos had men who specialized in blacksmithing because of their great skill.

[15] Many Hmong in Minnesota who can afford modern appliances have bought electric rice steamers. Pressed for time in the mornings, they begin steaming rice late at night and allow the appliance to run all night, thereby avoiding an unusually early rising to prepare the traditional breakfast. This is an excellent example of how the Hmong have become "American," placing a high priority on time and using economic resources to bridge the gap between efficiency and tradition.

[16] Typically, the stove for preparing rice is kept separate from the stove for vegetables and meats, a spatial extention of the pattern at meals. Hmong spatial assignments are often highly symbolic. For example, the head of the household always sleeps by the main support post of the house. Moreover, while the placentas of female babies are buried beneath the central "hearth," those of male babies are buried just outside the main doorway to the house. Traditionally, each Hmong house has two doors, and many people have insisted that "If you didn't have two doors, no one would come to visit you!" The symbolic uses of space also are evident in courting procedures and marriage negotiations. See Timothy Dunnigan and Tou Fu Vang, "Negotiating Marriage in Hmong Society, An Example of the Effect of Social Ritual on Language Maintenance," *Minnesota Papers in Linguistics and the Philosophy of Language* 6 (1980): 28–46. Dunnigan makes frequent reference to the role of foods in these matters on p. 32–37, 43–44.

[17] There are only two differences between an everyday meal and a celebrative meal in Hmong foodways. The former will consist of but two or three dishes — probably one meat dish, a vegetable side dish, and a saltless vegetable. Essentially, the celebrative meal uses more animals, and each animal is used completely; that is, everyday food is served, but in larger quantities and in more imaginative varieties. And, a more formal dinner includes certain intricately prepared foods.

[18] *Minneapolis Star and Tribune*, October 24, 1984, p. 5T.

[19] Roger Abrahams, "Equal Opportunity Eating: A Structural Excursus on Things of the Mouth," in *Ethnic and Regional Foodways*, ed. Brown and Mussell, 29.

[20] On intricacy in foodways analysis, see Mary Douglas in *Annual Report*, 1979, to the Russell Sage Foundation (New York), 28–30; Goode, Theophano, and Curtis, "Continuity and Change in Shared Sociocultural Rules for Food Use," in *Ethnic and Regional Foodways*, ed. Brown and Mussell, 66–88.

[21] One of the best references on Blue or Green Hmong spiritual beliefs is Nusit Chindarsim, *The Religion of the Hmong Njua* (Bangkok: Sompong Press, Ltd., 1976), 29–34.

[22] There is considerable Hmong folklore on the uses of hot green peppers, of which there are several sizes and varieties. According to several Hmong men, when one goes hunting it is a good idea to leave food supplies at home but to take green peppers. Such a condition raises the possibilities of finding game; if one takes a supply of food along, however, the game is sure to be scanty. One explanation of the Hmong use of peppers lies in a tale about a father who asked his daughter-in-law to prepare some food that would please him. The young woman was unhappy with the assignment and contrived to poison the man by mixing a new-found ingredient into the food. As it turned out,

the "poison" was the spicy green pepper, and the more the father ate, the more robust he became, and the better he liked it! Some Hmong jokingly refer to the peppers, now, as "the father-in-law's poison," but, more interestingly, the tale demonstrates the traditional role of the eldest son's wife in her husband's household — that of principal cook for the family — which obliges her to wait upon her husband's parents. In general, Hmong males look for prospective wives who will be energetic and conscientious, the opposite of the wife in the tale. Interview of Foom Tsab, St. Paul, August 22, 1984.

[23] For example, the 1984 New Year's celebration was held in the Minneapolis Civic Auditorium from seven o'clock in the morning until midnight and included ball tossing, songs, a demonstration by Boy Scouts, and speeches. In midafternoon, a shaman performed an abbreviated version of six Hmong religious rituals typically expected at the New Year. All, including a variant of the offering to the ancestors, involved the presentation of a chicken as a token gift to the honored deceased or to respected living elders. The most recent and complete ethnographic study of the White Hmong New Year is Jean Mottin, *Fêtes du Nouvel An: Chez les Hmongs Blanc de Thailande* (Bangkok: Don Bosco Press, 1979).

[24] Chindarsim, *Religion of the Hmong Njua*, 138. As is true in many Hmong rituals, the family home is the preferred place for such social gatherings since it symbolizes centrality and permanence. Although it seems that most Hmong in Minnesota attend public New Year's celebrations, some carry out a modified, private New Year's observance in their apartments as well, despite their well-founded concerns that such ceremonies will seem strange to and even disturb their neighbors.

[25] Chindarsim, *Religion of the Hmong Njua*, 49–50. Shamans are accountable for all animals killed and must "release" their souls so that they may be reincarnated. At New Year's, each shaman settles this account through prayers to the spirits, one for each of the jawbones of the slaughtered animals or fowl that he has retained in his home to keep track of his obligation.

[26] According to interviews, three leaves from each of six different plants must be cooked with chicken and, or instead of, brewed into tea and administered to new mothers; the plants have no American equivalent. See also *Minneapolis Star and Tribune*, October 24, 1984, p. 4T.

[27] Interview of Gail Yang, Rochester, December 18, 1984.

[28] Interviews of Vang Chu, Duluth, September 14, 1984, Vang Shoua, St. Paul, August 26, 1984.

[29] *St. Paul Pioneer Press*, September 16, 1984, p. 1H. Many in the Hmong community believe that those who have fallen victim to the so-called "sudden death syndrome" are exclusively Christian converts; see *Minneapolis Star and Tribune*, March 12, 1983, p. 1C, 10C. To many Hmong, it seems that these converts have forsaken their traditional spirit world with its ceremonial patterns for a new one that does not sustain them in this anxious period of transition in their lives. On the other hand, some claim that their old spirit world is weak in this country because the new land is unclean, because there is too much electricity, or because they are simply too far from the homeland.

[30] *Minneapolis Tribune*, March 12, 1981, p. 1T.

[31] Ernest Heimbach, *White Hmong-English Dictionary* (Ithaca, N.Y.: Cornell University Press, 1957), 461–66.

[32] Interviews of Yua Yao Xiong and his son, Chu Xiong, St. Paul, August 23, 1984.

[33] *Minneapolis Star and Tribune*, August 23, 1983, p. 1A.

[34] George M. Scott, "The Hmong Refugee Community in San Diego: Theoretical and Practical Implications of its Continuing Ethnic Solidarity," *Anthropological Quarterly* 55 (July 1982): 146–60.

[35] *Minneapolis Star and Tribune*, August 23, 1983, p. 3C.

[36] Minnesota Department of Welfare, "Hiawatha Valley Hmong Farm Project to End," news release, May 3, 1984, and Executive Summary and Progress Report, Minnesota Agricultural Enterprise for New Americans, July 1984, copies in office of Lao Family Community of Minnesota, Inc.; see also *Minneapolis Star and Tribune*, July 7, 1982, p. 10A; *St. Paul Pioneer Press and Dispatch*, September 17, 1984, Midweek sec., p. 1, photocopy in Minnesota Ethnic Foodways Project files, MHS.

[37] Yua Yao Xiong interview.

RECIPES

THE OJIBWAY

WILD RICE AND CHICKEN WING SOUP

Yield: 10 to 12 servings

Cooks have long combined available fresh foods with wild rice to serve a hearty soup to their families. The use of chicken wings is a recent adaptation.

2½ pounds chicken wings	1 cup chopped celery
3 quarts water	1 cup chopped carrots
1 teaspoon salt	2 cups cooked wild rice (see recipe)
2 tablespoons vegetable oil	Parsley to taste
1 cup chopped onions	Salt and pepper

1. Wash wings and pat dry. Place in 6- to 8-quart kettle and add water and salt. Bring to a boil and cook for 5 minutes. Remove from heat and skim off any scum that has appeared on surface. Cover pan and simmer 1 hour.
2. Remove from heat and take out chicken wings. Set aside.
3. Heat vegetable oil in heavy frying pan over moderate heat. Saute onions, celery, and carrots for 10 minutes, stirring occasionally.
4. Skim fat from top of chicken broth. Stir in onions, celery, carrots, and parsley. Taste and adjust seasonings.
5. Remove chicken meat from bones. Return meat pieces to kettle. Add cooked wild rice. (Bones and skin can be cooked further in water for a chicken broth.)
6. Cover kettle and simmer ingredients for 20 minutes or until vegetables are cooked but still crisp.

VARIATIONS: For a thicker soup, add another cup of cooked wild rice. Other garden vegetables can be used. Dumplings are often added to this soup.

WILD RICE   Yield: 2 cups

Actually the kernel from an aquatic wild grass, wild rice remains an integral part of the Ojibway diet.

⅔ cup wild rice
3 cups water
½ teaspoon salt

1. Wash rice several times in hot water to remove all particles.
2. Place all ingredients in a 2-quart saucepan. Bring to a boil, cover, reduce heat, and simmer until rice is tender. Hand-parched rice, which is dark green in color, cooks tender in a very short time so check after 12 minutes. The darker, brown-colored rice has usually been parched mechanically and more moisture has been removed; it should be done in about 40 minutes.

FRY BREAD   Yield: 15 3-inch rounds

A favorite treat for Ojibway and non-Indians alike at all powwows and reservation events. Ingredients and shapes for fry bread vary from family to family.

2 cups all-purpose flour, spooned into cup   *⅔ cup water or milk (can use evaporated*
3 teaspoons baking powder   *milk or 6 tablespoons dry milk and ⅔*
2 tablespoons sugar   *cup water)*
1 teaspoon salt   *Vegetable oil for frying*

1. Combine dry ingredients (add dry milk now if using it).
2. Stir in liquid. Dough may be a little sticky. More flour can be worked in as dough is kneaded for about 3 minutes. Allow to stand at room temperature for about 1 hour, covered with plastic wrap. This step can be omitted but dough will not pull into shape as easily.
3. Divide dough in 15 pieces. Flour hands and flatten each piece into a 3-inch round. Cover with plastic wrap.
4. Heat at least 2 inches of oil to 340 to 350 degrees in a deep-fat fryer or heavy skillet.
5. Fry flattened round about 1 minute on each side or until lightly browned. Several rounds can be fried at a time.
6. Drain on paper towels. Serve with butter, sugar, honey, or jam.

VARIATIONS: Make a slash in the center of each round before frying. Add fresh berries to the dough.

NOTE: To reheat the next day, place in a brown paper bag. Twist the top of the bag. Heat in a 325 degree oven until warmed through.

PICKLED FISH

Yield: 1 quart

Ojibway living at Grand Portage use this method to preserve their plentiful catches of lake trout or whitefish. The brine can also be used with other varieties of fish.

2 to 2½ pounds fish fillets or pieces,
   cleaned
2 cups vinegar

2 cups white vinegar
⅔ cup table salt
Pickling Brine (see below)

1. Cut fish into 2-inch pieces.
2. In a large glass jar combine vinegars and stir in salt. Add fish pieces and cover tightly. Refrigerate for 5 days.
3. After 5 days drain off vinegar-salt solution and rinse fish well in cold water. Soak fish in cold water to cover for ½ hour.
4. Make pickling brine. Use small clean jars and pack with fish pieces. Add cooled pickling brine to cover. Cover tightly. Refrigerate at least 2 days before sampling. Can be stored in refrigerator for a month.

Pickling Brine

½ cup sugar
½ cup packed brown sugar
1 cup vinegar

1 cup white vinegar
1½ cups chopped onions
1½ tablespoons pickling spices

In a small saucepan combine all ingredients. Stir occasionally until mixture boils. Set aside to cool.

FISH CAKES

Yield: 6 to 8 2½-inch cakes

Cooked and boned fish whether from Minnesota streams or Lake Superior can be used in this recipe. Long a staple of the Ojibway diet, pieces or chunks of fish are also traditionally boiled or poached in seasoned water.

1 pound cooked trout
2 eggs, slightly beaten
¼ cup cracker meal
1 tablespoon finely minced onion

½ teaspoon salt
¼ teaspoon black pepper
¼ cup vegetable oil

1. Flake fish, making sure all bones are removed.
2. In large bowl, combine fish, eggs, cracker meal, onion, salt, and pepper. Mix lightly.
3. Shape into 6 or 8 flat cakes. Heat oil in heavy frying pan over moderate heat.
4. Fry cakes until lightly browned on both sides. Drain on paper towels.

VARIATION: Fry cakes in bacon fat for added flavor.

VENISON STEW

Yield: 6 to 8 servings

One-pot meals have long been part of the foodways of the Ojibway. The earliest recorded accounts of their lives tell of the cook fire in the center of the wigwam or in the area outside where a single large birch-bark container held stew of some kind.

2 tablespoons lard
1½ pounds venison, cut in 1-inch pieces
¼ cup flour
1 can (14½ ounces) beef bouillon
1 can water
1½ cups onion pieces

1 cup carrot pieces
⅓ cup uncooked wild rice
2 medium potatoes, cut in 2-inch chunks
2 stalks celery, cut in 2-inch pieces
1 teaspoon salt
½ teaspoon black pepper

1. Melt lard in Dutch oven or heavy 4- to 5-quart pan. Pat venison pieces with absorbent paper to dry. Dust meat with flour and brown in hot lard. Do not crowd pan. For best browning, do meat pieces in 2 batches.
2. Add bouillon and water. Cover pan. Simmer for 1 hour, 15 minutes. Add onions, carrots, wild rice, and more water, if necessary. Cover and simmer for additional ½ hour.

3. Add potatoes, celery, salt, and pepper. Cover and simmer until potatoes and celery are tender. Test meat for tenderness. May need to cook an additional 15 minutes.
4. Gravy is usually of right consistency for serving. Can thicken if desired.

VARIATIONS: Vegetables can vary as to amount and kinds. Also some cooks use more wild rice, while others use more liquid and call the combination soup.

WILD RICE AND CHICKEN　　　　Yield: 6 to 8 servings

Wild rice, which combines well with many ingredients, is used by the Ojibway to extend a main dish if there is a limited amount of meat, poultry, or wild meat or fowl.

½ cup uncooked wild rice　　　　　*¾ cup diced celery*
½ cup uncooked long-grain white rice　*1 teaspoon salt*
2 cups chicken broth　　　　　　　*¼ teaspoon black pepper*
1 cup finely diced onions　　　　　*3 cooked chicken breasts, boned*
1 jar (2½ ounces) mushrooms with juice

1. Preheat oven to 350 degrees. Butter a 3-quart casserole.
2. In casserole dish, mix the 2 rices, broth, onions, mushrooms and juice, celery, salt, and pepper. Cover dish tightly and bake for 1 hour, 15 minutes.
3. Cut cooked chicken into 1-inch pieces. Remove casserole from oven and gently stir in chicken. May need to add more broth if mixture seems dry.
4. Cover tightly and bake for ½ hour. Check for tenderness of rice and serve when done.

NOTE: Because wild rice varies in the amount of moisture it contains, check the casserole about halfway through the first baking time to be sure there is enough liquid.

VENISON ROAST

Yield: 6 to 8 servings

Venison is still preferred to other meats among most Ojibway, although Grand Portage residents are equally fond of moose meat.

3 to 4 pounds venison roast
2 tablespoons flour
2 tablespoons lard
½ pound salt pork, cut in thin slices
3 cups sliced onions

2 cups diced celery
1 cup beef broth or 1 cup water and
*   bouillon cube*
Salt and pepper

1. Heat lard in heavy pan or Dutch oven. Dredge roast with flour and brown on all sides in hot fat.
2. Arrange slices of salt pork on top of roast. Add onions and celery to pan and also to top of roast. Pour in broth. Add salt and pepper to taste.
3. Cover and bake in 325 degree oven for about 2 hours or until tender.
4. Remove roast from pan. Make a gravy with pan drippings. Adjust seasonings.

VARIATIONS: After roast has baked for 1½ hours, any one or all of the following vegetables can be added: 3 medium carrots, cut in chunks; 4 onions, halved; 2 stalks celery, cut in chunks; 3 potatoes, quartered. Or, substitute moose meat for venison.

WILD RICE MEATLOAF

Yield: 8 to 10 servings

The Ojibway often use ground venison or moose meat in this recipe, although ground beef is substituted if their supply of wild meat is exhausted.

½ cup dry stuffing mix
½ cup evaporated milk
2 cups cooked wild rice (see recipe)
1 pound ground beef
½ cup chopped onions
2 eggs, slightly beaten

¼ teaspoon ground sage
¼ teaspoon black pepper
¾ teaspoon salt
2 ounces salt pork, cut in thin strips
*   (bacon can be substituted)*

1. Preheat oven to 350 degrees. Grease a 5-by-9-inch loaf pan.
2. Combine stuffing mix and evaporated milk. Set aside.

3. In a large mixing bowl, combine wild rice, meat, onions, eggs, sage, pepper, and salt. Mix with clean hands until well combined. Add stuffing mix and evaporated milk and continue to mix.
4. Spoon meat mixture into prepared pan. Lay strips of salt pork or bacon over top. Bake for 1½ hours.
5. Allow to stand in pan for 5 minutes. Loosen meatloaf from sides of pan and remove to platter.

BREAD PUDDING

Yield: 8 to 10 servings

Except for the maple syrup, this pudding does not contain any of the traditional Minnesota Ojibway ingredients; however, the dish is made by many families, and the recipe appears in the few cookbooks that are available.

2½ cups milk
¼ cup corn meal
2½ cups stale white bread or mix of
   white and whole-wheat bread
3 eggs
⅓ cup maple syrup
⅓ cup sugar

1 teaspoon ground cinnamon
¼ teaspoon salt
½ teaspoon vanilla
¼ cup melted butter
½ cup raisins
1 teaspoon flour

1. In a 2-quart saucepan, heat milk until warm. Stir in corn meal.
2. Tear or cut bread into small cubes and add to milk. Set aside.
3. In a bowl beat eggs well. Blend in syrup, sugar, cinnamon, salt, vanilla, and melted butter.
4. Preheat oven to 350 degrees. Butter 2-quart baking dish. Place an inch or so of water in a pan larger than baking dish and place pan in oven.
5. Toss raisins in small bowl with flour. Combine all ingredients in baking dish. Set dish in pan of hot water in oven and bake for 1 hour or until custard is set. Serve plain or with cream or ice cream.

VARIATION: ½ cup chopped apple can be added or raisins can be omitted and 1 cup chopped apple included.

NOTE: Use genuine maple syrup, not maple-flavored pancake syrup.

POPPED WILD RICE
Yield: 2½ cups

Preparing wild rice in this traditional manner highlights the rich nutty flavor usually associated with the grain. Ojibway people often mix the popped rice with pure maple sugar and enjoy the blend of two natural foods.

3 cups oil
½ cup hand-parched uncooked wild rice
Salt to taste

1. Sort rice, picking out any pieces of hull.
2. Heat oil to 375 degrees in a 1-quart saucepan, using a thermometer on the side of the pan.
3. Place rice in a sieve, 1 tablespoon if using a sieve 3 inches in diameter, or 2 tablespoons in a 5-inch sieve.
4. Lower sieve into hot oil. Rice will pop rapidly for about 30 seconds. As soon as popping stops, lift sieve from oil. Drain for a minute or so over oil, and then turn out on paper towels to drain further. Repeat for remainder of rice. Salt as desired or mix popped rice with maple sugar.

MAPLE SYRUP APPLE PIE
Yield: 6 to 8 servings

Maple syrup has long been the sweetener for fruit and berry dishes among Ojibway. This recipe incorporates a traditional ingredient into a popular but nontraditional dessert.

1 cup maple syrup
½ cup boiling water
3 tablespoons cornstarch
3 tablespoons cold water
1 tablespoon butter

5 to 5½ cups apples, peeled, cored, and
thinly sliced
½ cup nuts, finely chopped (optional)
Pastry for 2-crust, 9-inch pie

1. Boil syrup and water for 5 minutes, gently. Mix cornstarch and water and slowly pour into boiling syrup to thicken.
2. Stir in butter and cook for a few seconds. Remove from heat.
3. Line pie dish with pastry for bottom crust. Add apples.
4. Pour syrup mixture over apples and sprinkle nuts on top. Lightly moisten edge of trimmed bottom crust.
5. Lay on top pastry crust. Trim and crimp edges. Cut 2 or 3 vents in top crust.

6. Bake at 425 degrees for 15 minutes. Lower oven temperature to 350 degrees and bake for 25 to 35 minutes. The length of time will depend on the type of apples used. Test apples for tenderness through one of slits in crust. Some apples cook to mush if pie is baked too long.

VARIATION: If apples are not tart, sprinkle 2 tablespoons lemon juice over pie before adding top crust. For a richer pie, 3 tablespoons additional butter can be mixed into syrup.

NOTE: Use genuine maple syrup, not maple-flavored pancake syrup.

THE BLACKS

VEGETABLE SOUP

Yield: 8 to 10 servings

As in many ethnic groups, some black families prepare soup from scratch, while others do not. Vegetable soup is a good way to use leftover foods, although fresh ingredients may be added for variety and taste.

1 pound stew meat, beef chuck or bottom round
1 beef soup bone (1 pound), shinbone preferred, cracked by butcher
½ pound ham hocks
3 quarts cold water
4 cups sliced potatoes
1 cup sliced onions

1½ cups sliced carrots
2 cups chopped cabbage
1 bay leaf
½ teaspoon chili powder
½ teaspoon black pepper
Salt to taste (depends on saltiness of ham)
1½ to 2 cups noodles

1. Place beef stew meat, soup bone, ham hocks, and water in a large soup kettle. Bring to a slow boil and simmer about 5 minutes. Remove any scum that has formed on surface. Cook covered for about 2 to 2½ hours or until meat is tender.
2. Add potatoes, onion, carrots, cabbage, bay leaf, chili powder, and pepper. After stirring, taste and salt if necessary. Cook for ½ hour. Add noodles and cook until tender, about 20 minutes.

VARIATIONS: Substitute other vegetables or increase the ones mentioned to suit family tastes.

GUMBO

Yield: 4 to 6 servings

From the Louisiana or Gulf region tradition, gumbo is part of the substyle of spicy dishes that some love and others consider "ulcer food." Gumbo is believed to have originated among the Bantu tribes in Africa.

3 tablespoons shortening or lard
4 tablespoons all-purpose flour
¾ cup coarsely chopped onions
½ cup coarsely chopped green pepper
2 pounds chicken wings, backs, giblets, or
  a combination of any pieces
¾ pound smoked sausage, cut in 1-inch
  pieces
2 cups water

1 pound shrimp, peeled and deveined
½ to 1 teaspoon salt
½ teaspoon black pepper
¼ teaspoon crushed red pepper flakes
¼ cup tomato paste
¼ cup green onions, cut in ½-inch pieces
1 cup okra, cut in ½-inch pieces
1 teaspoon filé (optional)
3 to 4 cups cooked rice

1. Melt shortening or lard in a large saucepan or kettle over moderate heat. Stir in flour and continue stirring until mixture turns light brown.
2. Add ¾ cup onions and green pepper and stir until well mixed. Continue to stir occasionally for about 5 minutes or until vegetables are crisp tender.
3. Add chicken and sausage and stir in water. May need to add more water if liquid appears thick. Cover pan and simmer for 35 minutes.
4. Add shrimp, salt, pepper, red pepper, tomato paste, green onions, and okra. Add more boiling water if necessary. Cover pan and simmer for 15 minutes. Add filé just before serving and do not simmer further. Serve over hot rice.

CORN BREAD

Yield: 5 to 6 servings

In contrast to the quickly assembled skillet bread or hoecake, this bread is baked in the oven and was traditionally served at relaxed or festive occasions. The hint of sugar shows a northern or commercial influence, southern corn bread is frequently unsweetened.

1 cup corn meal
1 cup all-purpose flour, spooned into cup
4 teaspoons baking powder
1 tablespoon sugar

1 teaspoon salt
2 eggs
2 tablespoons melted shortening
1¼ cups milk

1. Preheat oven to 425 degrees. Butter an 8-inch-square baking pan or a 9-inch round pan.
2. Sift corn meal, flour, baking powder, sugar, and salt together.
3. In medium-sized bowl, beat eggs well. Add shortening and milk and mix until blended. Stir in corn-meal-and-flour mixture.

4. Pour batter into prepared pan and bake for 20 minutes or until browned on top and shrinking slightly from edges of pan.

VARIATION: Recipe can be doubled and baked in a 9-by-13-inch pan for 25 to 30 minutes.

CORN-BREAD DRESSING
Yield: 8 to 10 servings

A favorite accompaniment to roast chicken or turkey, common in the South among white as well as black people. Many blacks prefer dressing cooked in a pan; the same recipe placed in the cavity of a bird is called stuffing.

1 double recipe of corn bread, baked in 9-by-13-inch pan
1 teaspoon salt
1½ teaspoons sage

1 teaspoon black pepper
1½ cups finely chopped onions
1 cup chopped celery
2 cups chicken broth

1. Crumble corn bread to yield 8 cups. (This will leave about 6 servings of bread.) Place in a large bowl.
2. Stir in salt, sage, pepper, onion, celery, and chicken broth.
3. Preheat oven to 350 degrees. Put dressing in a covered 2 ½-quart casserole with 3-inch sides. Cover and bake for 25 minutes. Remove cover and continue baking for 25 minutes or until lightly browned and crusty on the edges.

POTATO SALAD
Yield: 10 to 12 servings

A popular dish frequently taken to community or church events. Raw vegetables are commonly included in the salad.

2¾ to 3 pounds potatoes to yield 7 to 8 cups of sliced potatoes
1 cup celery, cut in ½-inch pieces
1 cup green pepper, cut in ½-inch pieces
½ cup sliced radishes
½ cup sliced green onions, including tops
1 large clove garlic, minced (more to taste)
2½ tablespoons prepared mustard

1 jar (16 ounces) sandwich spread with chopped pickles and pimentos
1 teaspoon salt
½ teaspoon black pepper
5 eggs, hard boiled
Paprika
¼ green pepper, cut in thin strips

1. Boil, peel, and slice potatoes 1 or 2 nights ahead of time. Cut potatoes the long way in half. Cut halves crosswise in ¼-inch slices. Refrigerate.
2. Place potatoes, celery, green pepper, radishes, onions, garlic, mustard, sandwich spread, salt, and pepper in large bowl. Gently stir in a folding fashion until ingredients are well mixed. Taste and adjust seasonings.
3. Peel eggs, and cut 4 eggs into chunks. Stir into potato salad. Garnish top of salad with slices of remaining egg and strips of green pepper. Sprinkle with paprika.
4. Cover and chill overnight.

VARIATION: Horseradish or Dijon-style mustard add more flavor to the salad.

CREOLE CHICKEN   Yield: 4 to 6 servings

"Creole" technically indicates origins among descendants of the early French or Spanish settlers of Louisiana, but Creole cookery has long transcended those boundaries. It is usually distinguished by a combination of spices, green peppers, and tomatoes.

1 chicken (3 pounds), cut in serving pieces
2 teaspoons salt
¾ teaspoon paprika
2 tablespoons butter
2 tablespoons vegetable oil
1½ cups green pepper, cut in strips 2 by ¼ inches
1½ cups thinly sliced onions
1 cup coarsely chopped celery
1 can (1 pound, 11 ounces) stewed tomatoes
1 can (4 ounces) tomato sauce
1 teaspoon dried thyme
½ teaspoon black pepper
1 can (3 to 4 ounces) mushrooms with juice

1. Wash chicken and pat dry. Sprinkle with 1 teaspoon salt and paprika.
2. Heat heavy deep skillet or Dutch oven over moderate heat. Add butter and oil. Brown chicken pieces well on all sides.
3. Add green pepper, onion, celery, stewed tomatoes, tomato sauce, thyme, pepper, and mushrooms with juice. Sprinkle remaining teaspoon of salt over top. Cover pan.
4. Simmer for about 25 minutes or until chicken is tender.
5. Serve chicken with sauce and vegetables over rice.

RED BEANS AND RICE
Yield: 8 to 10 servings

Another dish the popularity and endurance of which rests on its being filling, nourishing, and tasty. A spicy version of the dish is associated with Louisiana Cajun cooking, but combinations of grain and beans are common in black cooking throughout the South.

1 pound red beans or kidney beans
2 quarts water
1 pound ham hocks
2 tablespoons lard
1½ cups coarsely chopped onions

1 cup chopped green pepper
2 cloves garlic, minced
Salt and pepper
Cooked rice, about 4 to 6 cups depending
* on number of people to be served*

1. Wash beans and pick out any discolored ones. Place beans, water, and ham hocks in a large kettle. Bring to a boil and skim off any scum that collects on surface. Cover and simmer for 2 hours.
2. Remove 1½ cups beans from pot and mash them. Can use a blender or food processor. Will need to add a little pot liquid to speed the mashing. Return mashed beans to pot. Cover and continue simmering.
3. Melt lard in heavy skillet over moderate heat. Add onion, green pepper, and garlic and saute until translucent, stirring frequently. Add to bean mixture.
4. Cook about 2 hours more or until beans are very tender. Taste and adjust seasonings, adding salt and pepper if necessary.
5. Spoon over rice in bowls. Serve with corn bread.

MIXED GREENS WITH HAM HOCKS
Yield: 4 servings

A simple but nourishing meal, long a mainstay of southern black cooking. Greens may be gathered wild, home grown, or purchased at certain Twin Cities' markets.

1 pound ham hocks, smoked
2 quarts water
1 pound mustard and turnip greens

¼ teaspoon crushed red pepper flakes
⅛ teaspoon black pepper
Salt

1. In large kettle or pan, bring water and ham hocks to a boil. Cover and simmer 1 hour.
2. Sort through greens, removing pulpy stems and any bad spots. Wash

thoroughly, rinsing 3 times in fresh water. Add to ham hocks and water.

3. Stir until greens cook slightly. Cover pan and simmer for 1 hour or until greens are very tender.
4. Halfway through cooking period, taste liquid and add crushed red pepper and black pepper. Add salt if needed.
5. Serve with chile peppers.

NECK BONES AND BEANS
Yield: 8 to 10 servings

One example of a traditional black dish, as commonly eaten in Minnesota as in the South.

3½ pounds pork neck bones, fresh or smoked
1 pound Great Northern beans
2 teaspoons salt

2 teaspoons black pepper
¾ teaspoon crushed red pepper flakes
1 cup sliced onions
1½ quarts cold water

1. Wash neck bones and place in a 6- to 7-quart kettle. Wash beans well and add to kettle. Add all other ingredients. Bring to a boil and skim off any scum on surface.
2. Cover kettle and simmer. Check after 1½ hours and add more water if necessary. Test beans for tenderness and adjust seasonings. May need to cook another hour or so.
3. Carefully remove layer of fat that has accumulated on top of cooking liquid. Bean dish can be made the day before and refrigerated. Then hardened fat can be easily removed before reheating and serving.

YAM OR SWEET-POTATO PUDDING

Yield: 6 to 8 servings

Yams and sweet potatoes, both native to tropical regions, are two distinctive tubers although the names are frequently used interchangeably. Black people are generally credited with introducing these vegetables — baked plain, candied, or mashed in pies and puddings — to American cuisine.

½ cup butter
1 cup packed brown sugar
½ teaspoon ground cinnamon
½ teaspoon ground nutmeg

6 cups raw, peeled, grated sweet potatoes or yams
1 tablespoon grated lemon rind (fresh is tastiest but dried can be used)
Lemon Sauce (see below)

1. Preheat oven to 450 degrees.
2. Use cast-iron pan or other heavy 9- to 10-inch frying pan. Heat over moderate heat. Add butter, sugar, cinnamon, and nutmeg. Stir until butter is melted and mixture begins to simmer.
3. Add potatoes or yams and mix thoroughly. Place uncovered pan in oven and reduce heat to 325 degrees. Bake for 20 minutes. Remove pan from oven and stir well, mixing browned top portions with less browned under portions. Return to oven for 20 minutes.
4. Remove from oven. Reset oven temperature to 375 degrees. Sprinkle lemon rind over pudding and mix well. With back of spoon press pudding evenly into pan. Return to oven. Bake another 20 minutes or until pudding is lightly crusted.
5. Cool pudding in pan. Cut into wedges and serve with warm lemon sauce.

Lemon Sauce

Yield: 1⅓ cups

¾ cup sugar
1 tablespoon cornstarch
½ cup water

¼ cup lemon juice
1 tablespoon butter

1. Mix sugar and cornstarch in a small saucepan. Combine water and lemon juice and stir into sugar mixture until smooth. Over moderate heat, bring mixture to a boil, stirring frequently.
2. Boil about 1 minute. Remove from heat and stir in butter.

PINEAPPLE UPSIDE-DOWN CAKE   Yield: 10 to 12 pieces

A traditional dessert for festive occasions, church potluck dinners, and Christmastime. Blacks tend to bake a variety of cakes, rather than the cookies prepared by many European ethnic groups, for the Yuletide season.

1 cup packed brown sugar
½ cup butter or margarine
8 slices pineapple, drained (save the juice)
10 maraschino cherries
10 to 12 pecan halves (optional)
3 eggs, separated
1½ cups sugar

1 teaspoon salt
1 teaspoon vanilla
½ cup pineapple juice
1½ teaspoons baking powder
1½ cups plus 2 tablespoons all-purpose flour, spooned into cup

1. Put brown sugar and butter or margarine in cast-iron or other heavy 9- to 10-inch frying pan. Stir over moderate heat until melted and bubbly.
2. Arrange slices of pineapple, halved maraschino cherries, and pecans on top of sugar-butter mixture. Set aside.
3. In small mixer bowl, beat egg whites until stiff.
4. In large mixer bowl, beat egg yolks well. Add sugar gradually and mix thoroughly. Add salt, vanilla, and pineapple juice, mixing well.
5. Sift baking powder and flour together. Add slowly to batter in bowl. Mix thoroughly. Preheat oven to 350 degrees.
6. Fold in beaten egg whites. Pour batter over the arranged fruit in frying pan. Bake for 35 to 40 minutes or until firm to touch and slightly shrinking from sides of pan.
7. Remove from oven and cool for 5 minutes. Place a plate over top of frying pan and carefully turn cake and pan over so that upside-down cake rests on plate. Remove pan. Serve topped with whipped cream.

WHIPPED-CREAM POUND CAKE

Yield: 10 to 12 servings

Ingredients such as butter and whipping cream hint that this recipe was brought into black tradition by those who served as cooks in white households.

1 cup butter, at room temperature	*3 cups cake flour, spooned into cup*
3 cups sugar	*½ cup whipping cream*
6 large eggs	*1 tablespoon lemon extract*

1. Butter a 10-inch tube cake pan or bundt pan. Flour pan, leaving a light layer of flour over surface. Preheat oven to 350 degrees.
2. In large mixer bowl, beat butter until light in color, about 5 minutes. Gradually add sugar, beating well.
3. Add 1 egg and mix thoroughly. Add 1 tablespoon flour, beating in completely. Repeat these 2 steps with remaining eggs.
4. Add rest of flour. Mix well. Add whipping cream and lemon extract and mix well. Pour batter into prepared pan.
5. Bake for 1 hour. Check cake. Should be nicely browned and firm to touch, with edges slightly pulled away from pan. May need another 15 minutes baking, depending on oven temperature. If any doubt, bake a little longer.
6. Cool in pan about 10 minutes before turning out on rack. May be necessary to loosen cake from pan gently before turning it out. Cool completely before placing in airtight container or wrapping in plastic or foil. Flavors are best if cake "rests" for 1 to 2 days before serving. Sometimes served with whipped cream. Freezes well.

SWEET-POTATO PIE

Yield: 8 to 10 servings

A common denominator in most black holiday meals, including Christmas, regardless of where the family lived in the South or during subsequent moves.

1 pound sweet potatoes or 2 cups mashed sweet potatoes
4 eggs, beaten
1½ cups evaporated milk

½ cup melted and cooled butter
1 cup sugar
½ teaspoon ground nutmeg
1 unbaked 10-inch pie shell

1. Cut sweet potatoes in half and cook with skins on until tender. Cool, peel, and mash.
2. Preheat oven to 350 degrees. In mixer bowl, beat eggs. Add milk, mashed sweet potatoes, melted butter, sugar, and nutmeg. Mix well. Pour into prepared pie shell. Bake for 35 minutes.
3. Test for doneness by inserting knife into pie about 2 inches from edge. Knife should come out clean. May need to bake another 10 to 15 minutes or until pie is browned and filling set.

THE MEXICANS

GREEN CHILE SAUCE
(Salsa de Chile Verde)

Yield: 1¾ cups

The hot sauce that enhances many Mexican dishes. Typically, Mexican food is not searingly hot; instead, bowls of chile sauce are served so that people can season food to taste.

1 pound fresh tomatillos or 1¾ cups
canned tomatillos (available in Mexican
food stores and other specialty groceries)
4 jalapeño peppers, cut in pieces

⅓ cup chopped cilantro
2 cloves garlic, chopped
1 teaspoon salt

1. If using fresh tomatillos, remove husks, wash, and place in a pan. Cover with water and bring to a boil to blanch. Drain and cool.
2. Place peppers, cilantro, garlic, and salt in blender. Dice tomatillos and add.
3. Blend until smooth but do not puree.

VARIATION: For milder sauce, remove seeds and membranes from peppers.

CACTUS SALAD
(Ensalada de Nopales)

Yield: 8 to 10 servings

Cooking with cactus remains most popular among the immigrant generation, although some Mexican Americans also continue to use it in scrambled eggs, guisado, fried meat dishes, and salads.

1 cup cactus, either canned or fresh
5 cups shredded lettuce
⅓ cup thinly sliced green onions
1½ to 2 cups coarsely chopped tomatoes

Salad Dressing (see below)
1 cup crumbled farmer's cheese (Mexican,
if possible, available in specialty stores)

1. Mix cactus, lettuce, onions, and tomatoes. Stir in enough salad dressing to season well. Toss together thoroughly.
2. Crumble cheese over top of salad and serve in large bowl. If served in individual bowls, add cheese when assembling each portion.

NOTE: Some cactus is spineless; however, if you buy the variety with spines, carefully scrape or cut them away. Cut "leaves" into bite-sized pieces and cook in boiling, salted water until tender. Chill.

Salad Dressing

Yield: 1 cup

¾ cup oil
¼ cup lemon juice

1 teaspoon salt
½ teaspoon pepper

Combine ingredients and shake until salt is dissolved.

SOPA DE FIDEO

Yield: 4 servings as a main course
6 to 8 servings as a first course

"Sopa" is an ambiguous word in Mexican-American foodways. To some it means soup (also called "caldo"), to others it is a dish — such as soup — made with pasta. Fideo is similar to vermicelli.

2 cloves garlic
½ teaspoon salt
½ teaspoon ground cumin
2 tablespoons lard
1 cup fideo or vermicelli, broken into 2-inch pieces

1 cup chopped onions
¾ to 1 cup chopped tomatoes
3 cups chicken bouillon
½ recipe Chorizo (see below)

1. Using mortar and pestle, make paste of garlic, salt, and cumin. Set aside.
2. Melt lard in heavy kettle or frying pan over moderate heat. Turn heat to low and add fideo or vermicelli. Stir until golden. Burns easily if heat is too high. With slotted spoon remove pasta from pan and drain on paper towels.
3. Cook onion in remaining fat until crisp tender. Add tomatoes and garlic paste. Stir for 1 minute. Drain off any excess fat.
4. Add chicken bouillon, chorizo, and fideo. Simmer gently for 25 to 30 minutes or until pasta is tender.

VARIATIONS: A cup or more of diced chicken, beef, ham, or cheese can be added to the sopa instead of chorizo. Some cooks prefer to use less bouillon.

BEANS FROM THE POT   Yield: 4 to 5 servings
(Frijoles de la Olla)

Traditionally Mexicans ate their cooked beans "fresh from the pot," using a minimum of fat for flavoring. Refrying (making refritos) was a technique for using leftovers. Today Mexican Americans note that busy cooks may make several days' worth of beans at a time; as a result they must serve refritos after the first meal. Many people are concerned about consuming the extra lard, which gives refritos their flavor.

1 cup pinto beans
Water
½ cup chopped onions
2 cloves garlic, minced

2 tablespoons lard or bacon fat
½ teaspoon salt
Topping (see below)

1. Wash beans, clean thoroughly, and cover with water. Soak overnight. Or, bring beans to a boil over high heat, simmer 2 minutes, and let stand for 1 hour.
2. Do not drain beans. Place over high heat and bring to a boil. Add onions, garlic, and fat. Simmer for 1½ hours or until beans are tender. Stir in salt and adjust seasonings.
3. Serve in bowls with topping or make into refried beans (see recipe).

Topping   Yield: 1 cup

½ cup chopped tomatoes
2 tablespoons chopped jalapeño pepper (optional)

½ cup chopped white or green onions
¼ cup chopped cilantro

1. Mix ingredients.
2. Sour cream or grated Colby cheese can be spooned on top of each serving.

REFRIED BEANS (Frijoles Refritos)   Yield: 4 to 5 servings

Beans from the Pot
¼ cup lard or bacon fat

1. Drain beans. Melt fat in a heavy skillet over moderate heat.
2. Mash 1 cup of beans until smooth. Can use blender or food processor. Add whole and mashed beans to melted fat.

3. Stir beans while cooking to prevent sticking. Cook until fat is absorbed, about 5 minutes.
4. Serve as a side dish.

VARIATIONS: Mash all the beans. Or, add one of the following: ½ teaspoon ground cumin, ½ teaspoon chili powder, salt and pepper to taste, 1 clove crushed garlic, ¼ cup minced onion.

MEXICAN RICE (Arroz)

Yield: 4 servings as main dish
6 to 8 servings as side dish

Mexicans and Mexican Americans depend on a variety of carbohydrates to round out their meals; rice, beans, and noodles are all traditional. Mexican rice, like the bean and pasta dishes, depends on seasonings and preparation style for its ethnic flavor.

2 cloves garlic
½ teaspoon salt
1½ teaspoons ground cumin
4 tablespoons lard or vegetable oil
1 cup uncooked long-grain rice

1½ cups coarsely chopped onions
1 cup chopped green pepper
1 cup chopped tomatoes
2 cups chicken broth
Salt to taste

1. Mash garlic, salt, and cumin using a mortar and pestle. Set aside.
2. Heat 2 tablespoons lard in a heavy 10-inch frying pan or use an electric frying pan. Add rice and stir until golden brown, using moderate heat. Add onion and green pepper and stir for about 3 minutes. Add tomatoes and garlic-salt-cumin mixture. Stir for about 1 minute. May need to add remainder of lard after rice is browned.
3. Add chicken broth. Adjust seasonings.
4. Cover and simmer for about 35 minutes or until rice is tender.

VARIATIONS: 1 cup chopped celery can be substituted for green pepper or added to above vegetables. 1 box (10 ounces) of frozen peas and carrots can be substituted for the tomatoes and pepper.

TACOS

Yield: 12 tacos

Mexican Americans, while acknowledging that they eat tacos, are quick to point out that the popularity of the dish among non-Mexicans results from its visibility on restaurant and fast-food menus, not from any great significance in Mexican cuisine.

2 tablespoons lard or vegetable oil
1 pound lean ground beef
1 cup chopped onions
1 clove garlic, minced
1 teaspoon dried and crumbled oregano
¾ teaspoon salt
¼ teaspoon black pepper

½ teaspoon cumin
1 cup peeled and finely shredded or
  chopped potatoes
Jalapeño Pepper Sauce (see below)
12 flour tortillas
Oil

1. Heat fat in heavy frying pan over moderate heat. Add ground beef and break up meat into small pieces. After a few minutes of cooking, add onions and garlic. Cook until onion is tender but not browned.
2. Add oregano, salt, pepper, and cumin. Mix well. Add potatoes and jalapeño pepper sauce. Stir for 2 or 3 minutes over moderate heat. Mixture should not be soupy but on the dry side. Set aside.
3. Wrap flour tortillas in aluminum foil and place in 350 degree oven for 5 minutes or until tortillas are warmed through.
4. Pour about 1½ inches of oil in a heavy frying pan and heat to 370 to 375 degrees. Preheat oven to 250 degrees.
5. Take a warm tortilla and place about 2 tablespoons of filling in center. Fold in half. Carefully pin the 2 edges together lengthwise with a toothpick (see illustration). Fry in hot fat, turning once, until lightly browned on both sides. Drain on paper towels. Tilt slightly so excess oil drains out easily. Repeat with rest of tortillas. Keep warm in oven on baking sheets lined with paper towels.

6. Remove toothpicks. Serve with bowls of chopped lettuce, diced tomatoes, and shredded cheese. Taco can be easily spread apart to add these condiments.

VARIATION: Cooked peas or peas and carrots can be used instead of potatoes.

Jalapeño Pepper Sauce   Yield: 2 to 2½ cups

5 medium-sized jalapeño peppers
2 cloves garlic
1½ cups chopped tomatoes (peel, halve,
and squeeze juice from tomatoes)

¼ teaspoon dried and crumbled oregano
Salt and black pepper to taste

1. Wash peppers, cut in half, and remove seeds and membranes.
2. Boil pepper halves in small amount of water for 5 minutes. Drain well.
3. In blender or food processor, puree peppers, garlic, tomatoes, oregano, salt, and pepper.

CHORIZO   Yield: 2 cups or 6 patties

A spicy sausage that can also be bought in specialty stores. It accompanies eggs for breakfast and is a frequent ingredient in lunch and dinner dishes.

1½ pounds ground pork (have butcher
use ½ pound fat and 1 pound lean
meat when grinding)
¼ cup vinegar
½ cup finely minced onions

2 cloves garlic, finely minced
1½ teaspoons chili powder
1½ teaspoons ground cumin
1½ teaspoons ground oregano
1½ teaspoons salt

1. Combine all ingredients in a large bowl. Cover well with plastic wrap and refrigerate for several hours or overnight.
2. Fry in a skillet over moderate heat for 10 minutes, stirring until lightly browned. May need to add a tablespoon or more of lard or shortening if meat is too lean.
3. Can also form into patties and fry for about 5 minutes per side for use in other dishes.

GUISADO

Yield: 6 servings

A traditional, everyday dish in Mexican and Mexican-American households. The seasonings differentiate guisado from the stews made by members of other ethnic groups.

1 ½ pounds round steak, ½ inch thick
3 tablespoons flour
3 cloves garlic
2 tablespoons chopped jalapeño pepper
  (seeds removed)
2 teaspoons ground cumin
⅓ cup lard

8 whole tomatoes or 1 can (28 ounces)
  whole or stewed tomatoes
¾ teaspoon salt
¼ teaspoon pepper
1 ½ cups potatoes, peeled and cut in ½-
  inch cubes

1. Sprinkle flour on sheet of waxed paper or plastic wrap, covering an area twice the size of the steak. Lay meat on top of flour and press down so that flour adheres to bottom surface of meat.
2. Using a mortar and pestle or small jar attachment to a blender, mix garlic, pepper, and cumin into a paste. Spread paste evenly over top of round steak.
3. Cut meat into 1-inch pieces. Melt lard in heavy skillet over moderate heat. Place meat in pan floured side down and fry until well browned on underside. Turn pieces and cook for about 5 minutes on that side. This side will not brown as well as floured side.
4. In blender or food processor combine tomatoes, salt, and pepper and process until somewhat smooth. Add to meat in pan. Cover pan.
5. Simmer for 1 hour or until meat is almost tender. Depending on juiciness of tomatoes, may need to add more water, bouillon, or tomato juice.
6. Add potatoes and cook mixture until potatoes are tender, about 30 minutes. May need to add more liquid during this cooking period.

SHRIMP AND CACTUS (Camaron y Nopales)

Yield: 2 to 3 servings as main dish
4 servings as side dish

A traditional, meatless Lenten dish. Although canned and, sometimes, fresh cactus is available in specialty stores, many Mexican Americans substitute green beans (similar in size, shape, and color) for the cactus in this recipe.

1 can (6 ounces) shrimp
2 eggs, separated
⅛ teaspoon salt
1 teaspoon flour
Butter or oil for frying
2 tablespoons butter or vegetable oil
1 cup finely chopped onions

2 cloves garlic, minced
1 cup finely chopped tomatoes
1½ teaspoons ground cumin
¼ teaspoon salt
1 teaspoon flour
1 cup canned or cooked cactus or 1 cup
  canned green beans, undrained

1. Drain liquid from canned shrimp. Shred shrimp and set aside on paper towels.
2. Beat egg whites until soft peaks form. Slightly beat egg yolks. Fold yolks into whites. Sprinkle flour on top of mixture and fold it in.
3. Using a fork, gently stir in shrimp.
4. Heat butter or oil in heavy frying pan. Drop tablespoonfuls of egg-shrimp mixture in hot oil. When lightly browned, flip over and brown the other side. Remove from pan and drain on paper towels.
5. Melt 2 tablespoons butter in frying pan. Add onion, garlic, tomatoes, cumin, and salt. Stir until onion is soft. Add flour and stir well.
6. Add cactus or beans. May need to add a couple of tablespoons of water if mixture seems dry. Place shrimp patties on top of mixture. Cover and cook over low heat for 2 or 3 minutes until patties are hot.

NOTE: Canned cactus has usually been spiced with jalapeño pepper and other seasonings. If green beans or unseasoned cactus is used add 1 teaspoon vinegar, ½ teaspoon cumin (additional), and 2 teaspoons green chile sauce or ½ teaspoon chili powder to enhance flavor.

TAMALES
Yield: 24 to 26 tamales

A dish generally reserved for Christmas and special occasions because of the time and skill involved in its preparation. In some extended families one older woman prepares and distributes tamales among her kin.

28 to 30 cornhusks
2 cups Boiled Pork (see below)
6 large dried chile ancho pods
2 cups water (or enough to cover chiles when cooking)
1 tablespoon vegetable oil
2 teaspoons cumin

2 teaspoons garlic powder
1 teaspoon salt
½ cup lard
4 cups masa harina
1 teaspoon salt
1¾ cups beef broth

1. Soak cornhusks in panful of hot water for at least 2 hours.
2. Shred pieces of pork with 2 forks. Measure 2 cups and refrigerate.
3. Remove stems from chiles, cut in half, and remove seeds and dried membranes. Place in small saucepan and barely cover with water. Simmer for 5 minutes or until tender. Drain, saving liquid for later use.
4. Puree chiles and ¼ cup of cooking liquid in blender, stopping several times to scrape mixture from sides. May need to add more liquid to make a smooth, thick paste.
5. Put oil in small heavy saucepan over moderate heat. Add chile paste. Stir in cumin, garlic powder, and salt. Simmer 2 to 3 minutes. May need to add some of reserved cooking liquid to prevent mixture from becoming too dry or crumbly.
6. Place shredded pork in medium-sized bowl. Stir in chile paste. Set aside.
7. Melt lard over low heat. Remove from heat and cool to barely warm.
8. Measure masa harina and salt into large bowl. Gradually stir in lard, mixing well. Add broth slowly about ¼ cup at a time, stirring well after each addition. Dough will become noticeably fluffier as broth is added.
9. Remove cornhusks from water, shake well, and pat dry with paper towels. Put water in bottom of a steamer. Can use some kind of makeshift steamer as long as tamales are kept out of the water.
10. Spread spoonful of masa-harina dough in an ⅛-inch-thick layer over wide part of cornhusk, leaving bare the top edge of husk and the lower end where it narrows. The dough should be spread over an area about 3 by 3½ inches (see illustration). Use a spatula, knife, fingers, or whatever makes it easy to spread dough.

11. Spread about 1 tablespoon of meat filling over dough. Fold 2 long sides of husk to center, lapping one over the other. Fold pointed end of husk back and under. Top end is left open.

12. Place prepared tamales in steamer. Steam for 1½ to 2 hours. When tamale is done, dough comes away easily from sides of husks.
13. Best when eaten right after preparation. Can be refrigerated and will keep for 1 week. Tamales can also be frozen. Reheat, wrapped in foil, in a 350 degree oven.

Boiled Pork

*1 piece of pork, 2½ pounds (pork butt is
  preferred)*
Water
1 teaspoon salt

1½ cups sliced onions
3 cloves garlic, mashed
5 black peppercorns

1. Cut roast into large square chunks. Place in a large kettle and cover with water. Add salt, onions, garlic, and peppercorns and simmer about 2 hours or until meat is very tender.
2. Remove meat from stock and allow to drain.

PORK WITH GREEN CHILE SAUCE   Yield: 6 servings
(Carne de Puerco con Chile Verde)

Chile verde is a sauce that accompanies many Mexican dishes. This combination is a typical weekday dinner.

2 pounds pork, cut in ½-inch cubes (buy about a 2¼-pound butt roast, remove bone, and cube or have butcher do this)
2 tablespoons lard or vegetable oil
1 cup coarsely chopped onions
1½ cups potato, cut in ½-inch cubes
3 cloves garlic
1 teaspoon salt

¼ cup chopped cilantro
3 fresh jalapeño peppers or 1 can (8 ounces) of green chiles (remove membranes and seeds)
1 cup chopped tomatoes
1 to 1½ cups chicken broth or canned bouillon

1. Pat meat with paper towels to remove moisture. Heat lard in a 4- to 5-quart pan over high heat. Add part of meat and lower heat to medium-high. Allow to brown well on all sides, stirring as needed.
2. Remove browned meat with slotted spoon and drain on paper towels. Brown and drain rest of meat.
3. Lower heat to moderate. Add onions and potatoes. Stir and cook for about 5 minutes.
4. Using blender, make sauce of garlic, salt, cilantro, and peppers.
5. Add meat to pan with onions and potatoes. Add sauce, tomatoes, and chicken broth. Mix well. Cover pan and simmer mixture for 30 minutes. Check once during cooking period and add broth or water if needed. Sauce is meant to be thick.
6. Scoop up with warm tortillas.

NOTE: Fresh jalapeño peppers are much hotter than canned ones, which are usually labeled "mild" or "hot." Try the recipe using mild chiles and serve a dish of green chile sauce.

BUÑUELOS

Yield: 40 4½- to 5-inch rounds
or 80 3-inch rounds

Similar to a deep-fried flour tortilla, buñuelos are a traditional dessert at Christmastime.

3⅓ cups all-purpose flour, spooned into
 cup
1 teaspoon salt
1 teaspoon baking powder
¼ cup lard

1 cup milk
Vegetable oil for frying
½ cup sugar
2 teaspoons ground cinnamon

1. Sift together flour, salt, and baking powder. Work in lard with fingers or pastry blender until like coarse meal.
2. Stir in milk, adding the last ¼ cup slowly. Add only enough milk to make a dough that will hold together and can be kneaded. Turn dough out on lightly floured board and knead for about 2 minutes.
3. Divide dough in half and wrap 1 portion with plastic wrap while you work with the other. Divide dough into 20 pieces if making 5-inch rounds or 40 pieces if making the smaller ones. Shape pieces into small balls.
4. Roll each ball into a circle as thin as possible. (If dough does not roll easily, allow to stand, well covered, for 15 minutes.) Allow to lie in a single layer on plastic wrap while making other circles.
5. Heat oil, at least 2 inches deep, to 375 degrees in deep-fat fryer or in deep heavy pan. Before frying stretch each circle gently in all directions, retaining circle shape. Start pulling from center and continue toward edges. Be careful to avoid making holes.
6. Fry 1 or 2 at a time depending on size. Flip buñuelo over when underside is golden brown. When both sides are light brown, remove from fat and drain on paper towels.
7. Mix sugar and cinnamon in a paper bag. Add 3 or 4 buñuelos and shake gently to coat surface.
8. Repeat process for other half of dough.

NOTE: Can be made ahead of serving time through step 6. When cool, store in airtight container for up to 1 week. When ready to use, heat on baking sheet in preheated 250 degree oven for 5 minutes. Then proceed with step 7.

This recipe can be halved using: 1½ cups flour, ½ teaspoon salt, ½ teaspoon baking powder, 2 tablespoons lard, ⅓ to ½ cup milk — add ⅓ cup and then only enough more to make a dough that can be easily kneaded.

BREAD PUDDING (Capirotada)   Yield: 8 to 10 servings

A traditional dessert during Lent and for Easter, originally made, like most such puddings, from leftover bread. Different versions of capirotada use different fruits and omit the cheese and candy.

9 slices French bread, ½ inch thick
½ cup lard or vegetable oil
1 lump of piloncillo (available in Mexican grocery stores)
¼ cup packed dark brown sugar (increase amount to ½ cup if piloncillo not available)
1 cup sugar
2 sticks cinnamon
2 whole cloves
5 cups water

½ cup roasted skinless peanuts
½ cup raisins
1½ cups sliced bananas
1½ cups drained canned apricot halves
1 jar (1¾ ounces) red or multi-colored shots (found in the baking section and used for decorating cakes)
3 cups grated cheese, Colby, Monterey Jack, or the farmer's-style cheese found in Mexican groceries (about 1½ pounds)

1. In a heavy frying pan heat 2 tablespoons fat. Fry the bread slices, a few at a time, browning them lightly on each side and adding more fat as needed. Bread browns quickly so only ½ minute or so is needed on each side. Drain on paper towels.
2. In a heavy 3-quart saucepan combine piloncillo, sugars, cinnamon sticks, cloves, and water. Bring to a boil, stirring to dissolve sugars. Allow to boil until mixture has reduced to about 3 cups — 45 to 50 minutes. Remove cinnamon sticks and cloves.
3. Add peanuts and raisins to sugar syrup. Simmer for 2 to 3 minutes to plump raisins.
4. Butter a 2½-quart casserole, about 4 inches deep. Preheat oven to 350 degrees.
5. To assemble bread pudding, first cut bread slices into halves or fourths and arrange ⅓ of bread pieces on bottom of casserole. Slowly pour over ⅓ of the syrup, making sure to include some raisins and peanuts. Sprinkle ½ of cheese over top.
6. Arrange ½ of bananas and ½ of apricots over cheese. Sprinkle ½ of colored shots or decorating candy over fruit.
7. Arrange another ⅓ of bread pieces in casserole. Follow this with another ⅓ of syrup, peanuts, and raisins. Follow with layers of the remaining cheese, fruit, and candies.

8. Top casserole with remaining bread pieces and pour last ⅓ of syrup mixture over bread. Cover casserole with lid or tightly crimped aluminum foil. Bake 30 minutes at 350 degrees. Reduce heat to 325 degrees and bake for 25 minutes.
9. Cool for at least ½ hour, covered. Usually served warm and often topped with cream or whipped cream.

THE BRITISH

SCOTCH BROTH

Yield: 6 to 8 generous servings
8 to 10 servings as first course

Soups, such as Scotch broth, were made almost daily in the earlier days in Britain when all cooking was done in a large black kettle over an open hearth.

6 cups lamb stock (prepare as you would beef stock using lamb shanks, neck bones, rib bones, or a bone from a roast, either leg or shoulder)
3 tablespoons uncooked barley
4 tablespoons split peas, soaked overnight
½ cup diced carrots
½ cup diced turnips or rutabagas

1 small leek, trimmed and sliced (optional)
1 medium onion, diced
½ cup shredded cabbage (optional)
2 tablespoons finely chopped parsley
½ cup cooked lamb, trimmed from bones (amount can vary)
Salt and black pepper to taste

1. Combine broth, barley, and split peas in large pan. Bring to a boil, reduce heat, and simmer for ½ hour.
2. Add carrots, turnips or rutabagas, leek, onion, and cabbage and simmer for ½ hour or until barley is tender.
3. Add chopped lamb, parsley, salt, and pepper. Heat through and serve hot.

OATMEAL BREAD

Yield: 2 loaves

Oatmeal, used as a breakfast cereal, an ingredient in cookies and crackers, or in yeast bread and rolls, is a staple in British kitchens.

2 cups boiling water
1 cup regular rolled oats
½ cup water (105 to 115 degrees)
2 packages dry yeast or 2 cakes compressed yeast
½ cup melted shortening
¼ cup molasses

¼ cup honey or packed brown sugar
1½ teaspoons salt
2 eggs, well beaten
1 cup whole-wheat flour
5¾ to 6¼ cups all-purpose flour, spooned into cup

1. Bring 2 cups water to a boil and add oats. Cook for 2 minutes. Set aside to cool.
2. Dissolve yeast in ½ cup warm water. Set aside while assembling other ingredients.
3. In large bowl combine melted shortening, molasses, honey or brown sugar, and salt. Add beaten eggs, dissolved yeast, and oats.
4. Stir in 1 cup whole-wheat flour and 1 cup all-purpose flour. Mix well. Gradually add remaining all-purpose flour, stirring after each addition. Add the last cup slowly to avoid adding too much.
5. Turn dough out on lightly floured board and begin kneading. May add more flour as kneading continues. Knead until smooth, about 10 to 15 minutes.
6. Place in greased bowl, cover with plastic wrap, and allow to rise in a warm place until double in bulk, about 1 hour.
7. Punch down dough and allow to rise again, about 45 minutes.
8. Grease 2 9-by-5-inch bread pans well with vegetable shortening.
9. When dough has doubled in bulk, form into loaves, place in pans, and allow to rise and double a third time.
10. Preheat oven to 350 degrees.
11. Bake loaves for 25 to 30 minutes until brown and hollow-sounding when tapped with knuckles or handle of wooden spoon.
12. Remove from pans and cool on racks.

VARIATION: Can make 1 loaf of bread and 12 dinner rolls.

FRIED TOMATOES

Yield: 4 to 5 servings

This recipe, a favorite with war brides, is cooked quickly and adds tang and color to any luncheon or dinner plate.

4 ripe tomatoes
4 tablespoons butter

2 tablespoons vinegar
Salt and pepper to taste

1. Slice ½ inch slices of tomatoes.
2. Melt butter in frying pan over moderate heat.
3. Saute tomato slices for 2 minutes and then turn to cook other side.
4. Add vinegar to pan. Tilt pan from side to side so that vinegar is distributed about the tomatoes. Salt and pepper the slices.
5. Serve hot.

SAFFRON BREAD OR ROLLS   Yield: 24 rolls or 2 loaves

The story goes that an English pilgrim, during the reign of Edward III, stole a flower bulb from an Indian rajah. He planted it in the hills in Essex, where it flourished. The stamens provided the powder used in British cooking. "As dear as saffron" and "as yellow as saffron" are popular sayings.

1 teaspoon saffron threads	¾ cup milk (105 to 115 degrees)
⅓ cup warm water	½ teaspoon ground nutmeg
1 package dry yeast	1½ teaspoons salt
⅓ cup water (105 to 115 degrees)	½ cup golden raisins
1 teaspoon sugar	½ cup finely chopped lemon peel
2 tablespoons all-purpose flour	5 to 5¼ cups all-purpose flour, spooned
½ cup sugar	into cup
1 egg, beaten	Melted butter
½ cup softened butter	

1. Measure saffron threads, pressing firmly into teaspoon. Put in small dish and add ⅓ cup warm water. Allow to stand for several hours or overnight.
2. After saffron has steeped, measure yeast into a bowl, add warm water, sugar, and 2 tablespoons flour. Stir until mixed and allow to stand while measuring other ingredients.
3. In large bowl, combine sugar, egg, and butter. Add warm milk, nutmeg, and salt.
4. Stir saffron mixture and then, using a sieve, put liquid into mixture in large bowl. (Some cooks use threads and liquid.) Stir well.
5. Use 3 tablespoons of flour to mix with raisins and lemon peel, coating pieces well. Add raisins and lemon peel to mixture in large bowl and stir until mixed.
6. Stir in flour, 1 cup at a time, mixing well after each addition. After 4 cups, add remainder ¼ cup at a time until dough can be kneaded. Turn out on floured board and knead until smooth and satiny, about 12 to 15 minutes. May need to work in a little more flour.
7. Place in greased bowl, cover with plastic wrap, and allow to rise in a warm place until double in bulk, at least 1 hour.
8. Butter 2 8½-by-4½-inch loaf pans or 2 9-inch round cake pans, depending on whether you are making rolls or bread.
9. Punch down dough to remove air bubbles. Form dough into loaves or rolls of favorite shapes. Brush tops with melted butter, cover with plastic wrap, and put in a warm place and allow to rise until double in bulk, about 1 hour.

10. Bake in 350 degree oven for 1 hour for loaves, ½ hour for rolls. May need to cover tops with aluminum foil after 20 minutes if browning too fast.
11. Remove from pan and cool on wire rack. Freezes well. When serving at a later time, warm to improve saffron flavor.

VARIATIONS: Double the amount of sugar and raisins and add ½ teaspoon salt. Use currants or other varieties of raisins.

SCOTCH EGGS

Yield: 6 to 8 servings

These hard-boiled eggs coated with a sausage-and-breadcrumb mixture may have originated in Scotland as a breakfast food. They have served as snacking fare throughout Britain for many years, are popular in English pubs, and are relished by Britishers in Minnesota.

8 small hard-boiled eggs, peeled and dried, | *½ teaspoon dried sage*
or 6 medium-sized eggs | *¼ teaspoon black pepper*
1½ pounds bulk pork sausage | *½ teaspoon dried thyme*
¼ cup all-purpose flour | *1 egg, slightly beaten*
½ teaspoon salt | *1 cup dry breadcrumbs*

1. Divide sausage into as many pieces as you have eggs.
2. Combine flour, salt, pepper, sage, and thyme.
3. Roll each egg in seasoning mixture to coat evenly. Pat a piece of sausage around egg, so that it covers egg completely and firmly.
4. Preheat oven to 350 degrees.
5. Roll sausage-covered egg in beaten egg. Next, roll in crumb mixture, coat well, and press crumbs on firmly.
6. Bake on a lightly greased broiling pan so that fat can drip away; however, baking pan can be used. Bake for 45 minutes or until sausage coating is crispy brown all over. May be necessary to turn eggs once during baking.
7. Cut in half with a sharp knife and serve hot. Can be served cold for lunch or as an appetizer.

VARIATION: Fry in hot fat (375 degrees) until well browned, usually about 5 minutes. Drain on paper towels before serving.

BUBBLE AND SQUEAK

Yield: 4 servings

Named for the sounds the vegetables make as they cook together, this cabbage and mashed-potato dish is made throughout the British Isles.

3 tablespoons bacon drippings or
  shortening
1 cup coarsely chopped onions
2 cups finely shredded cabbage

2¼ cups mashed potatoes
Salt and black pepper
2 tablespoons bacon drippings or
  shortening

1. Heat 3 tablespoons drippings in heavy 10-inch frying pan over moderate heat. Stir in onions and cook until soft.
2. Add cabbage. Stir for 5 minutes until somewhat wilted and partially cooked.
3. Place mashed potatoes in a bowl. Stir in cabbage and onion. Season with salt and pepper to taste.
4. Add another 2 tablespoons of drippings to frying pan if there is none left from sauteing of onion and cabbage. When this is heated, add potato, onion, and cabbage mixture. Press down in frying pan into large pancake shape.
5. Cook for 5 minutes on one side or until lightly browned. Flip over and brown other side for 5 minutes. For ease in flipping over, cover pan with plate and turn pan over. Then slide bubble and squeak from plate back into pan.
6. Should be served hot.

STEAK AND KIDNEY PIE

Yield: 6 servings

Said to have its origins in Sussex, this flavorful meat dish is now made by cooks all over Britain and is still a holiday favorite in Minnesota.

1½ pounds round steak (or other stew
  meat)
4 lamb kidneys
¼ cup all-purpose flour
1 teaspoon salt

¼ teaspoon black pepper
3 tablespoons lard or shortening
¾ cup coarsely chopped onions
Pastry for deep 9-inch or 10-inch pie
1 egg yolk beaten with 2 tablespoons milk

1. Wipe round steak well with paper towels. Cut into 1-inch cubes. Remove any tubes, skin, or fat from the kidneys and cut into 1-inch cubes.
2. Combine flour, salt, and pepper in a paper bag. Add steak and kidney pieces. Shake to coat well.

3. Heat fat in large frying pan over moderate heat. Brown pieces slowly. Add onions to pan when meat is almost browned. Stir and cook mixture together for about 5 minutes.
4. Add water to pan until meat is just barely covered (no more than 3 cups). Cover and simmer until tender, about 1½ hours.
5. Remove cover. Liquid should be somewhat thickened. If still thin, mix 2 tablespoons flour in small amount of water and add to pan liquid. Stir and simmer for 2 to 3 minutes.
6. Preheat oven to 325 degrees. Grease a deep 9-inch pie pan or a regular 10-inch pie pan, including the rim.
7. Roll out pastry ¼ inch thick. Cut strips just wide enough to fit on the rim of the pie pan. Moisten this rim with cold water and then press strips all around the edge. Pour in meat mixture.

8. Moisten top of pastry on rim. Lay a circle of rolled-out pastry on top. Trim. Press layers together to seal well and crimp edges in usual manner.

9. Make several slits in crust or one hole in center so steam can escape. Brush top with egg mixture.
10. Bake for 45 to 50 minutes or until crust is nicely browned.

VARIATIONS: Add other ingredients to meat mixture: 1 tablespoon Worcestershire sauce, 1 teaspoon dried parsley, ½ teaspoon ground thyme, potatoes, or rutabagas. Use extra pastry to cut leaves, flowers, or geometric shapes to decorate crust; place on top before egg wash is used.

NOTE: Many British have a special deep dish called a basin that they use. A quiche dish makes a good substitute. Since the filling shrinks during the baking period, the crust often collapses. The British have special pie funnels or china birds that they use to prevent crust from falling during cooking. An egg cup or an inverted glass custard cup can be placed in the middle of the dish before the filling is added. Then a hole is cut in the top crust to fit over the inserted dish as it is laid in place to finish off the pie. It is still necessary to cut vents in this top crust.

CORNISH PASTY

Many of British descent still make the traditional, small pasties, but many others have modified this time-consuming process, making one large pie in a casserole or pie plate. Each serving then yields more filling and less pastry.

Pastry
3-Quart Casserole with 2-Inch Sides

4 cups all-purpose flour, spooned into cup
2 teaspoons salt

1 cup chilled lard or vegetable shortening
¾ to 1 cup cold water

9-Inch Pie Plate

2¼ cups all-purpose flour, spooned into cup
1 teaspoon salt

½ cup plus 2 tablespoons chilled lard or vegetable shortening
⅓ to ½ cup cold water

1. Measure flour and salt into medium-sized bowl. Cut lard into small pieces and drop on top of flour mixture. Using sharp knives, pastry blender, or finger tips work lard and flour until mixture resembles crumbs.
2. Stir in cold water slowly, adding only enough to hold dough together in a ball. Wrap dough in plastic and refrigerate about 15 minutes before rolling out.
3. Dough can be made 2 or 3 days in advance, wrapped well in plastic, and refrigerated. Allow to stand at room temperature for 1 hour before rolling out for pasty.

VARIATIONS: Mix all pasty ingredients together rather than layer them. Butter and salt and pepper are still added last. Substitute grated carrots for half or all of rutabagas. Replace part or half of beef with lean pork.

Filling
FILLING FOR 3-QUART CASSEROLE WITH 2-INCH SIDES

Yield: 10 to 12 servings

1½ pounds round steak, cut in ¼-inch pieces
2 cups finely diced onions
1½ cups grated rutabagas
3 cups diced potatoes

⅓ cup butter, cut in small pieces
1 teaspoon salt
½ teaspoon black pepper
Pastry (see above)

FILLING FOR 9-INCH PIE PLATE Yield: 6 to 8 servings

¾ pound round steak, cut in ¼-inch
pieces
1 cup finely diced onions
1 cup grated rutabagas
1 ½ cups diced potatoes

¼ cup butter, cut in small pieces
¾ teaspoon salt
¼ teaspoon black pepper
Pastry (see above)

1. Roll out ½ pastry for bottom crust, ⅛ to ¼ inch thick. Line dish and bring pastry up over sides leaving an inch extra all around.
2. Prepare meat and vegetables. Place them in dish in layers—first potatoes, followed by meat, onions, and rutabagas. Top with butter pieces and salt and pepper.
3. Preheat oven to 400 degrees. Roll out top crust and lay it on. Cut 2 vents. Trim and prepare edges in usual manner.
4. Bake 15 minutes at 400 degrees; reduce heat to 350 degrees and cook 45 minutes or until meat is tender and crust is nicely browned.
5. Cut in wedges if baked in a pie plate and in squares or spoon out of the casserole, depending on shape of dish.

Individual Cornish Pasty Yield: 8 medium-sized pasties

Filling for 3-quart casserole (omit salt and
pepper)
Pastry for 3-quart casserole

Salt (about ⅛ teaspoon for each pasty)
Black pepper (scant ⅛ teaspoon for each
pasty)

1. Prepare meat and vegetables as for large pasty.
2. Prepare pastry.
3. Divide pastry into 8 equal pieces. Keep covered until needed.
4. On a lightly floured board roll out each piece into a 9-inch round. Layer ⅛ of meat and each vegetable down center of round, in the same order as listed in 3-quart recipe (see illustration). Top with pieces of butter and salt and pepper.
5. Brush edge of circle lightly with water. Fold edges to center and crimp or flute together to provide a tight seal. Cut a small vent in each side of crimped edge (see illustration). Can be prepared ahead, covered well, and refrigerated until needed. Can also be frozen, well wrapped, at this point.

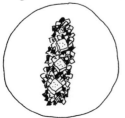 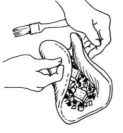 

6. Bake on baking sheet in preheated 400 degree oven for 10 minutes. Lower temperature to 350 degrees and bake for 40 to 50 minutes more or until lightly browned. Test filling with a sharp knife to be sure vegetables are tender. If frozen may need to bake additional 5 to 10 minutes.

VARIATION: 9-inch round of pastry can be laid on a large plate. Filling is then layered on ½ of circle. Moisten edges lightly with water. Fold over top half of pastry and seal edges together using a fork or crimping or fluting. Bake as above.

TOAD IN THE HOLE
Yield: 6 servings

Traditionally made with pieces of good steak or kidneys, but today, both in Minnesota and in Britain, pork-link sausages are the main ingredient.

1 pound pork-link sausages
3 eggs
½ teaspoon salt

⅛ teaspoon black pepper
1 cup milk
1 cup all-purpose flour, spooned into cup

1. Preheat oven to 400 degrees. Lightly grease a 9-inch-square pan. Place sausages in pan, pricking each one with a knife tip in several places. Bake for 5 minutes, turning once. Can be baked 10 minutes to cook out more fat.
2. Beat eggs lightly. Mix in salt, pepper, and milk. Add flour and beat until smooth.
3. Remove sausages from oven. Drain off all but 1 tablespoon of fat.
4. Pour batter over top of sausages, being sure sausages have been spread apart over bottom of pan. Return pan to oven.
5. Bake for 35 to 45 minutes or until well browned on top and puffy. Cut into squares or rectangles and serve at once.

VARIATIONS: Add 1 of the following: a few sliced mushrooms, tomato slices, 1 cup Cheddar cheese, ¼ teaspoon ground nutmeg, 1 teaspoon minced fresh herbs, 1 teaspoon prepared mustard.

SHORTBREAD

Yield: 30 to 42 cookies

Traditionally shortbread was mixed by hand, and some bakers still feel this ensures that the butter does not get too warm, thus making the shortbread oily. Busy cooks, however, may rely on a food processor to save time.

1 cup softened butter
½ cup sugar (can substitute powdered or
  superfine granulated sugar)
2 cups all-purpose flour, spooned into cup

1. In large mixer bowl, whip butter until creamy but not fluffy.
2. Slowly add sugar and mix well. Add flour, about ½ cup at a time, mixing well after each addition. Caution: mix only as much as needed as heat from mixer can warm butter too much.
3. Turn dough out onto baking sheet and press with fingers until dough is a little more than ¼ inch thick. Straighten out edges and press dough into an even rectangle or square.
4. Preheat oven to 325 degrees. With a fork prick dough in rows so that marks are about ½ inch apart, top to bottom and side to side (see illustration). Prick through dough to pan.

5. Place on shelf in middle of oven, reduce heat to 275 degrees, and bake for 30 minutes. At end of 30 minutes rotate baking sheet 180 degrees to assure even browning.
6. Check shortbread after 10 minutes. It should be golden on bottom and have a light hint of brown on top. May need up to 20 minutes more. Remove from oven.
7. While hot, use a sharp knife and cut in 1- or 1¼-inch squares or 1-by-2¼-inch finger shapes. Cool on baking sheet.
8. When cool, store in airtight container. Many cooks feel the flavor improves after several days' storage.

TRIFLE

Yield: 8 to 10 servings

This dish was originally fashioned from leftover cake, cookies, fruit, and pudding. Today it is a triumphant finale to a special meal.

1 pound cake, sponge cake, or jelly roll
   (10 to 11 ounces)
1 to 1½ cups raspberry jam
½ cup sherry (orange or other fruit juice
   can be substituted)
8 macaroons, crushed (optional)

Soft Custard (see below)
2 cups whipping cream
1 teaspoon vanilla
1 tablespoon sugar
¼ cup slivered toasted almonds

1. Cut cake into 1-by-2½-inch pieces or fingers. Spread jam on one side of each piece. Arrange pieces along bottom and sides of a trifle bowl or other 2½- to 3-quart glass bowl.
2. Saturate cake with sherry or fruit juice. Sprinkle crushed macaroons over top. Cover, refrigerate, and allow flavors to combine for several hours or overnight. If bowl size necessitates making 2 layers, divide sherry or juice in half and sprinkle an equal amount over each layer. Do the same with macaroon crumbs.
3. Pour cooled custard over top of cake, sherry, and macaroons. Cover with plastic wrap and refrigerate for 2 to 3 hours.
4. When ready to serve, whip cream, gradually adding vanilla and sugar. Spread over top of above ingredients. Garnish with almonds.

VARIATIONS: Substitute lady fingers for cake, splitting them in half lengthwise. Use strawberry jam and garnish with fresh strawberries. Add drained, thawed frozen berries, canned pears or peaches, or various fresh fruits before adding custard. Substitute ½ recipe fruit-flavored gelatin for fruit layer; allow gelatin to set before going on to step 3. Substitute 1 3-ounce package of vanilla pudding for soft custard.

Soft Custard

⅓ cup sugar
⅛ teaspoon salt
2 tablespoons cornstarch

2 cups milk
3 eggs, beaten well
1 teaspoon vanilla

1. Combine sugar, salt, and cornstarch in a medium-sized saucepan. Stir in cold milk and mix thoroughly with wire whisk.
2. Over medium heat, bring mixture to a boil and allow to boil 1 minute, stirring constantly. Remove from heat. Stir ½ of milk-sugar mixture into beaten eggs. Mix well.

3. Stir milk-egg mixture into hot mixture in pan. Cook, stirring constantly, until mixture thickens. Do not boil. Custard will thicken as it cools.
4. Remove from heat and stir in vanilla. Cool until needed for trifle. To keep skin from forming, cover with plastic wrap.

PLUM PUDDING

Yield: 14 to 16 servings

Individual servings of pudding are often decorated with a piece of holly. A more spectacular treatment is to pour a little heated brandy over the serving and ignite it at the table.

1½ cups finely ground suet
1¼ cups all-purpose flour, spooned into cup
3 eggs, slightly beaten
1 teaspoon baking soda
1½ teaspoons salt
1½ teaspoons cocoa
½ teaspoon ground ginger
½ teaspoon ground nutmeg
½ teaspoon ground cloves

1 teaspoon ground cinnamon
¾ cup buttermilk
½ cup dark molasses
⅓ cup packed brown sugar
¾ cup raisins or currants
¾ cup candied fruit (lemon or orange peel or cherries)
¾ cup chopped walnuts
Sauces (see below)

1. In large bowl, toss raisins, candied fruit, and nuts with a little flour so that they will not sink to bottom of pudding.
2. Add remaining ingredients. Mix well.
3. Grease 2 1-pound coffee cans or similar molds well. Divide the plum-pudding mix between the 2 molds. Cover with a square of any clean cloth (tied in place) or aluminum foil.
4. Place on a rack in a steamer, cover, and steam for 2 hours.
5. Serve warm with hard sauce, gorgeous sauce, or lemon sauce. Can be stored well wrapped in refrigerator for a month. Warm before serving.

VARIATION: Substitute golden raisins or sultanas for walnuts.

Fluffy Hard Sauce

½ cup butter, at room temperature
1 teaspoon vanilla or rum flavoring

2 cups powdered sugar
1 egg, separated

1. Beat egg white until it holds soft peaks.
2. Cream together butter, egg yolk, and flavoring. Add sugar and beat until fluffy.
3. Fold in egg white. Cover and allow to harden in refrigerator at least 1 hour.

Gorgeous Sauce

½ cup sugar
½ cup whipping cream
¼ cup butter

1. Boil sugar, cream, and butter together for 5 minutes over low heat. Stir frequently.
2. Serve warm.

Lemon Sauce

1 cup water
½ cup sugar
1 tablespoon butter

Juice of 1 lemon
1 egg, slightly beaten

1. Place water, sugar, and butter in small pan. Bring to a boil and boil over low heat for 5 minutes.
2. Remove pan from heat and add lemon juice. Add 2 tablespoons hot mixture to egg. Blend well. Pour into contents of pan and blend with whisk.
3. Serve warm.

THE GERMANS

WILTED LETTUCE SALAD   Yield: 4 to 6 servings

Although a common salad in traditional German-American households, it is, for some unknown reason, rarely served at ethnic festivals and food fairs.

1 quart (about 4 cups) leaf lettuce, cleaned and dried
½ cup finely sliced green onions, including tops
½ cup thinly sliced radishes

2 strips bacon
⅓ cup cream
2 teaspoons sugar
1 tablespoon vinegar
Salt and black pepper to taste

1. Tear lettuce into bite-sized pieces.
2. Combine lettuce, onions, and radishes in large bowl.
3. Cut 2 slices of bacon into ¼-inch strips. Fry over moderate heat until crisp. Drain. Pour bacon fat over lettuce, onions, and radishes, stirring well.
4. Mix cream, sugar, vinegar, and seasonings. Pour over lettuce mixture and toss gently. Dice bacon and sprinkle over top.

VARIATION: Amount of bacon can be doubled to suit family tastes.

NOTE: Serve with boiled potatoes.

SAUERKRAUT SALAD   Yield: 8 to 10 servings

One of many German-American dishes in which sauerkraut, whether homemade or commercially canned, is an ingredient. This dish is often taken to church potluck suppers.

1 can (1 pound, 11 ounces) sauerkraut,
   undrained
1 cup shredded carrots
1 cup diced onions
1 cup diced green pepper
½ cup vegetable oil

½ cup white vinegar
¾ cup sugar
1 teaspoon celery seed
¼ cup pimento (optional)
¼ teaspoon coarsely ground black pepper

1. Combine all ingredients in large bowl. Mix well.
2. Refrigerate in tightly covered container for 24 hours. Can be kept 6 to 7 days in refrigerator.

GERMAN POTATO SALAD   Yield: 6 servings

Served in homes as well as at ethnic festivals, this dish incorporates the hot vinegar-sugar-bacon dressing that is one hallmark of German cookery.

2 pounds red potatoes, boiled in jackets
6 strips thick bacon
½ cup finely chopped onions
½ cup bacon fat

⅓ cup vinegar
⅓ cup water
1 teaspoon sugar
½ teaspoon black pepper

1. Peel potatoes and slice very thin. Place in large serving bowl.
2. In heavy skillet fry bacon over moderate heat until browned and crisp. Remove from pan and drain on paper towels. Return ½ cup of accumulated fat to pan.
3. Add onions and cook over moderate heat until translucent, about 5 minutes.
4. Stir in vinegar, water, sugar, and pepper. Cook about 1 minute. Crumble bacon and add to pan. Heat through.
5. Pour hot bacon mixture over potatoes. Gently stir with a wooden spoon so that all pieces of potato are coated with dressing. Taste and adjust seasonings.
6. Serve warm or at room temperature.

SPÄTZLE

Yield: 2 cups

A tiny dumpling made in many forms — small rounds, long thin strips, short and narrow pieces. Spätzle, buttered well, is served as a side dish with sauerbraten or with any meat or chicken dish and gravy.

1 cup all-purpose flour, spooned into cup *½ cup water*
1 egg, slightly beaten *Boiling salted water or broth*
½ teaspoon salt *1 tablespoon butter*

1. In medium-sized bowl mix flour, egg, salt, and water until dough is smooth.
2. Have kettle of water boiling. Spoon dough onto a cutting board. Using large, sharp knife cut thin little strips of dough and push them into boiling water (see illustration). Or, use a spätzle maker or a cookie press

with a disc with small round holes. Or, place dough in large-holed colander and force through with a wooden spoon.
3. Boil for 5 to 8 minutes depending on size. Taste for tenderness. Remove from boiling water with slotted spoon or small strainer. Place in colander and quickly rinse with cool water. Place in saucepan, add butter, and mix.

VARIATIONS: Leftovers are fried in butter. Toasted breadcrumbs can be sprinkled over top of spätzle.

NOTE: Doubling the recipe tends to produce heavy spätzle. For best results, make only 2 cups at a time.

LIVER DUMPLINGS (Leberknödel)

Yield: 20 3-inch dumplings

German cookery is rich in recipes for dumplings, often made from potatoes or flour and eggs. These may be served in soup or as an accompaniment to any German dish with gravy or with sauerkraut.

2 slices dry bread
¼ cup warm milk
½ pound beef liver
1 cup onions, cut in 1-inch pieces
1 clove garlic
2 eggs, separated

½ teaspoon baking powder
¼ teaspoon salt
1½ to 2 cups all-purpose flour, spooned
* into cup*
Salted water or beef broth

1. In small bowl or pan, break up bread into small pieces. Pour warm milk slowly over bread, stirring so milk is absorbed. Set aside.
2. Grind together liver, onions, and garlic, using food grinder or food processor. Process until you have a smooth-textured, pastelike mixture.
3. In large bowl combine liver mixture, egg yolks, baking powder, and salt. Squeeze liquid from bread and add bread to bowl. Stir in well.
4. Beat egg whites until stiff. Heat large pan of salted water or beef broth.
5. Gradually add flour to dumpling mixture to form stiff dough. Fold in egg whites using an up-and-over motion until well mixed.
6. Try a test dumpling before forming all of them. Drop a teaspoon of dough into gently boiling water or broth. If it holds together well, then proceed forming the larger dumplings with a wet spoon so dough will drop off easily into cooking liquid. If dumpling falls apart, add 2 to 3 tablespoons more flour to stiffen dough.
7. Simmer for 20 minutes in covered pan. Remove with slotted spoon.

ONION PIE (Zwiebelkuchen)

Yield: 8 to 10 servings

Sour cream and onions hint at the Central European origins of this recipe. Some women traditionally prepared zwiebelkuchen on bread-baking day, much as Italian women made pizzas when they baked a batch of bread.

Bread for Pie Shell (see below)
1½ tablespoons shortening or vegetable oil
1½ cups finely chopped onions
2 eggs, well beaten
1 cup sour cream

1 tablespoon flour
½ teaspoon salt
¼ teaspoon black pepper
Pinch of cinnamon

1. Roll out bread dough about ¼ inch thick. Lightly grease a 10-inch deep-dish pie, tart, or quiche pan with 1½- to 2-inch sides. Place dough in pan, being sure bottom and sides are covered, pressing dough into place.
2. Melt shortening in heavy frying pan over moderate heat. Stir in onions and cook for about 5 minutes but do not brown them. Set aside to cool.
3. Beat eggs and sour cream together in medium-sized bowl. Sprinkle flour over top and beat it in. Stir in salt, pepper, and cinnamon.
4. Spread onions over dough in pie pan. Pour sour-cream mixture over the top.
5. Preheat oven to 400 degrees. Bake for 15 minutes. Reduce heat to 350 degrees and bake for another 15 minutes or until pie is nicely browned. Serve hot.

VARIATION: Can use a rich pie dough for the crust.

Bread for Pie Shell

½ package (½ tablespoon) dry yeast
¼ cup water (105 to 115 degrees)
¾ cup lukewarm water
2 tablespoons melted shortening

½ teaspoon sugar
1 teaspoon salt
2 to 2⅓ cups all-purpose flour, spooned
  into cup

1. Dissolve yeast in ¼ cup water. Stir well. Set aside.
2. In large bowl combine remaining water, shortening, sugar, and salt. Stir in yeast.
3. Stir in flour, ½ cup at a time, adding it more slowly toward the end. When dough can be kneaded, turn out on a lightly floured board, working in more flour if needed. Knead until smooth and elastic.
4. Place in greased bowl and lightly grease top of dough. Cover and let rise in a warm place until double in bulk. Punch down well and let stand 15 minutes.
5. Dough is now ready for the zwiebelkuchen.

SAUERBRATEN   Yield: 8 to 10 servings

One version of a dish that exists with many subtle variations in both
Christian- and Jewish–German traditions. Some recipes include ginger in the
marinade.

3 to 3½ pounds bottom round roast   *½ teaspoon mustard seed*
¾ cup red wine vinegar   *¼ teaspoon coriander seeds*
½ cup vinegar   *¼ teaspoon whole black peppercorns*
1 cup water   *1½ cups thinly sliced onions*
3 bay leaves   *2 tablespoons lard*
3 whole cloves   *Gingersnap Gravy (see below)*

1. Place beef roast in deep stainless-steel pan, crock, or enameled pan.
2. Combine vinegars, water, bay leaves, cloves, mustard seed, coriander, and
   peppercorns in a 2-quart saucepan. Bring to a boil and simmer for about
   3 minutes. Cool to room temperature.
3. Pour this marinade over meat. Place onions on top of roast. Cover
   container with plastic wrap or aluminum foil and refrigerate for 3 days.
4. Twice a day turn meat in marinade. May need to add ½ cup water and
   ½ cup red wine vinegar (or red wine) if marinade does not cover half of
   roast.
5. After 3 days remove meat from marinade and pat it dry with paper
   towels. Melt lard in heavy pan or flameproof casserole over medium-high
   heat. Brown meat on all sides.
6. Add marinade to browned meat. Bring to a boil. Cover pan and place in
   a 325 degree oven. After 1 hour turn meat over. Cover and return to
   oven for 1 hour or until tender.
7. Remove meat from pan to a platter. Cover lightly with aluminum foil
   and hold in a warm oven until gravy is made. Slice roast across the grain,
   arrange slices on a platter, and spoon gravy over meat. Serve remainder
   of gravy at the table.

Gingersnap Gravy

1 quart marinade   *10 gingersnaps, about 2 inches in*
½ cup water   *diameter*
3 tablespoons flour   *Salt and pepper*

1. Remove marinade from pan. Return 1 quart to pan and scrape loose any
   bits of meat and browned pieces. Reserve remainder in case gravy needs
   thinning.

2. Bring to a low boil. Mix water and flour into a smooth paste. Stir into boiling liquid.
3. Crumble gingersnaps and add to simmering gravy. Stir until dissolved and gravy has thickened. Taste and adjust seasonings.

VARIATIONS: Use rump roast or eye of round for sauerbraten. Meat can remain in the marinade for more than 3 days in the refrigerator. A more sour taste will develop.

NOTE: Sauerbraten is usually accompanied by bread or potato dumplings, spätzle, or potato pancakes and a vegetable dish such as red cabbage.

PORK HOCKS AND SAUERKRAUT   Yield: 6 to 8 servings

The primary ingredients and their manner of combination in this recipe typify German cooking for everyday meals.

6 fresh pork hocks
1 teaspoon poultry seasoning
½ cup finely chopped onions
½ teaspoon caraway seed
1 quart water

1 can or package (1 pound, 11 ounces to
  2 pounds) sauerkraut, undrained
2 tablespoons sugar
2 tablespoons vinegar, preferably white
1 teaspoon salt
1 cup peeled and grated apple

1. Wash pork hocks and pat dry. Place in 6-quart kettle or Dutch oven. Add poultry seasoning, onion, caraway seed, and water. Bring to a boil, reduce heat, and simmer covered for 2½ to 3 hours or until meat is tender.
2. Combine undrained sauerkraut, sugar, vinegar, salt, and grated apple in a bowl. Stir to mix.
3. Pour off cooking water. Add sauerkraut mixture to pork hocks. Cover kettle and simmer for at least 30 minutes. Can be cooked longer. Can be prepared the day before and refrigerated and then reheated the next day over moderate heat.

STOLLEN

Yield: 2 14-inch loaves

A traditional sweet bread for Christmas celebrations. Many families continue to bake stollen even though imported loaves are sold in specialty stores.

½ cup raisins
½ cup currants
1 cup mixed candied fruit, cut in raisin-sized pieces
½ cup candied cherries, cut in quarters
½ cup dried apricots, cut in raisin-sized pieces
½ cup rum
2 packages dry yeast
¼ cup water (105 to 115 degrees)
1 cup milk
¾ cup sugar

1 teaspoon salt
¾ cup butter, cut in pieces
6 to 7 cups all-purpose flour, spooned into cup
2 eggs, beaten
1 teaspoon almond extract
1 teaspoon grated fresh lemon peel
¼ teaspoon ground cardamom
½ teaspoon ground nutmeg
1 cup blanched and slivered almonds
½ cup melted butter

1. Combine raisins, currants, candied fruit, cherries, and apricots in large bowl. Add rum and toss fruit until well coated. Repeat several times during the next hour. At end of hour, drain and save rum and place fruit on several thicknesses of paper towels to dry. This step can be done the day before. Wrap fruit well to avoid drying out.
2. Dissolve yeast in warm water. Stir well and set aside.
3. Combine milk, sugar, salt, and butter in saucepan and heat to lukewarm, stirring to dissolve butter and sugar. Set aside.
4. Mix ½ cup flour with rum-soaked fruit. Fruit will stay mixed in dough better this way.
5. In large mixing bowl combine yeast mixture, milk mixture, eggs, almond extract, lemon peel, cardamom, nutmeg, and reserved rum. Mix well.
6. Add 2 cups flour and mix until batter is smooth. Add floured fruit pieces and almonds. Add remaining flour, 1 cup at a time, until dough can be kneaded. May not need all the flour.
7. Turn dough out on lightly floured board and knead until smooth and elastic, about 8 to 10 minutes. Use some of measured flour to keep board floured enough to prevent sticking.
8. Butter large bowl well with some of melted butter. Place dough in bowl and butter top well. Allow to rise in a warm place until almost double in bulk, about 1½ to 2 hours.
9. Punch dough down well so any large air bubbles are removed. Divide into 2 equal parts. Cover with plastic wrap and allow to rest for about 15 minutes.

10. Roll each part out to measure ½ inch thick, 9 inches wide, and 12 to 14 inches long. Brush with some of melted butter. Fold 1 side of rectangle over to center. Fold other side over, lapping about 1 inch. Press firmly to keep dough in place while it rises. Press ends together and mold into an oval shape.

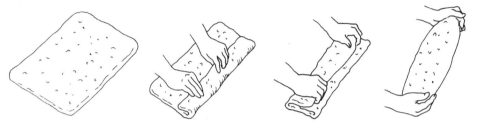

11. Butter baking sheet (at least 11 by 17 inches) with some of melted butter. Two loaves can be placed on large baking sheet. Brush tops with melted butter. Cover with plastic wrap and allow to rise in a warm place until almost double in bulk, about 1 hour.
12. Preheat oven to 375 degrees. Place loaves in center of oven and bake for 20 minutes. Reduce oven temperature to 350 degrees and bake for 20 to 25 minutes. If loaves brown too quickly, cover loosely with aluminum foil.
13. Remove from oven and cool on racks. Brush tops again with melted butter and dust with powdered sugar or spread with a powdered sugar-cream icing. Can be decorated with candied fruit and halved blanched almonds.

VARIATIONS: Use other dried or candied fruits such as citron, orange peel, or angelica.

The loaves can also be formed in the shape of a large Parker House roll. After the dough has been punched down it is rolled in the shape of a large oval and melted butter is spread over the top. Then one edge is brought over within 1 inch of the other edge and pressed gently into place (see illustration). The next steps are as in the above recipe.

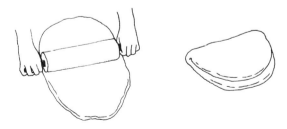

LEBKUCHEN

Yield: 48 to 60 cookies

Associated with, but not restricted to, the Christmas season. Lebkuchen ("love cookies") in Germany often carry tender messages such as "I love you" and sometimes are sold at carnivals and festivals.

1 cup honey
¾ cup packed dark brown sugar
1 egg, beaten
1 tablespoon lemon juice
1 tablespoon grated lemon rind
⅓ cup finely chopped citron
⅓ cup finely chopped walnuts
3 ¼ cups all-purpose flour, spooned into cup

½ teaspoon baking soda
½ teaspoon salt
1 teaspoon ground cinnamon
½ teaspoon ground cloves
½ teaspoon ground allspice
½ teaspoon ground nutmeg
Powdered Sugar Icing (see below)

1. In small saucepan, bring honey to a boil. Remove from heat and add brown sugar, stirring until dissolved. Pour into large mixing bowl.
2. When honey–sugar mixture is cool, add beaten egg, lemon juice, and lemon rind. Stir well.
3. Combine citron, nuts, and ¼ cup flour; mix well so that flour coats fruit and nuts. Set aside.
4. Sift together flour, soda, salt, cinnamon, cloves, allspice, and nutmeg. Stir into honey mixture. Gradually add floured citron and walnuts.
5. Cover bowl well with plastic wrap and refrigerate for at least 8 hours or overnight.
6. Grease 2 baking sheets well, or use baking parchment paper to line sheets. Preheat oven to 325 degrees. Remove ¼ of dough at a time, keeping rest refrigerated while cutting out cookies. Flour work surface and rolling pin well. Roll out dough ¼ inch thick. Cut in 2- to 2½-inch rounds or in triangles or other shapes.
7. Bake cookies for 12 to 15 minutes until set and lightly browned. Remove from baking sheet immediately to cooling racks. Repeat with rest of dough.
8. Spread with icing. When icing is set, store in airtight containers.

Powdered Sugar Icing

1½ cups powdered sugar, spooned into
  cup
3 tablespoons butter, at room temperature

2 tablespoons lemon juice
2 tablespoons milk or cream

Sift powdered sugar to remove all lumps. Combine sugar, butter, lemon juice, and milk or cream in medium-sized bowl. Using fork or hand mixer, beat until smooth.

APPLE TART (Apfelkuchen)   Yield: 12 to 16 servings

Traditionally made with fruits in season; apple was the filling for fall. Currently, canned and frozen fruits can replace fresh ones. Some cooks also substitute packaged pudding or custard mixes for the homemade variety.

2 cups all-purpose flour, spooned into cup
⅓ cup butter, at room temperature
1½ teaspoons baking powder
¼ cup sugar
½ cup milk
1 egg, slightly beaten

7 to 8 cups tart apples, peeled, cored, and
  sliced
¾ cup sugar
1 teaspoon ground cinnamon, or to taste
1 cup whipping cream
2 eggs, beaten well
2 tablespoons flour

1. Place 2 cups flour in bowl. Cut in butter as for pastry. Stir in baking powder, sugar, milk, and 1 egg in that order.
2. Grease a 9-by-12-inch pan with butter or shortening. Pat dough into pan evenly over bottom and about 1 inch up sides of pan.
3. Fill crust with prepared apples, arranging slices flat and close together. Sprinkle sugar and cinnamon over top.
4. Preheat oven to 350 degrees. In medium-sized bowl, combine cream, 2 eggs, and 2 tablespoons flour. Pour evenly over apples. Bake for 30 minutes or until apples are tender when tested with fork.
5. Serve warm. Can be topped with sweetened whipped cream.

THE SCANDINAVIANS

Norwegians

FLAT BREAD (Flatbrød)

Yield: 8 8-inch circles or
10 6-inch circles

Much like a cracker, this bread is a traditional accompaniment to fish, especially herring. It also serves as a base for sandwiches and snacks.

1 ¼ cups all-purpose flour, spooned into
   cup
¼ teaspoon salt
¼ teaspoon baking soda

1 tablespoon sugar
⅓ cup graham flour
5 tablespoons butter
½ cup milk

1. Sift flour, salt, soda, and sugar together. Stir in graham flour.
2. Using fork, pastry blender, or fingers cut butter into flour mixture. Stir in milk, mixing until well blended. Divide dough into 8 or 10 pieces. Cover with plastic wrap and allow to rest for 15 to 20 minutes.
3. Preheat oven to 350 degrees. Lightly grease 2 baking sheets.
4. Lightly flour rolling pin and board. Roll out pieces of dough as thin as possible into 6- or 8-inch circles. Use a flatbread rolling pin if possible.
5. Place rolled-out rounds on baking sheets. Prick all over with a fork. Bake 15 minutes or until lightly browned. Time varies depending on thickness of circles.
6. Remove to racks to cool. When cooled, store in airtight container. Keeps well for 1 week.

FRUIT SOUP (Søtsuppe)

Yield: 6 to 8 servings

A dessert, snack, or one course of a meal, fruit soup is a sweet eaten by Danes, Swedes, and Finns, as well as Norwegians; each nationality has preferred combinations of ingredients.

1 cup pitted dried prunes	*2 tablespoons lemon juice*
¾ cup raisins	*1 cup grape juice*
¾ cup dried apricots	*1 teaspoon vinegar*
Cold water	*½ cup sugar*
¼ cup quick-cooking tapioca, uncooked	*1 cinnamon stick*
2 cups water	

1. Combine prunes, raisins, and apricots in a 3-quart saucepan. Add water to cover, about 3 cups. Bring to boil and simmer gently for 30 minutes.
2. Bring 2 cups water to a boil in small saucepan. Stir in tapioca and simmer for 10 minutes.
3. When fruit is softened, add cooked tapioca, lemon juice, grape juice, vinegar, sugar, and cinnamon stick. Bring to a boil and then simmer for 15 minutes. Remove cinnamon stick.
4. Mixture will thicken as it cools. Add a litle more water or grape juice if mixture seems too thick.
5. Serve hot or cold. If served cold can be garnished with whipped cream.

VARIATIONS: Use currants, golden raisins, or the mixed-fruit combinations found in grocery stores. Or, substitute pineapple juice for grape juice.

LAPSKAUS

Yield: 4 to 6 servings

A hearty stew relished by Norwegian Americans; a similar dish is also popular among Danes.

1 pound bottom round beef	*1 cup chunked carrots*
¼ pound salt pork (optional)	*1 cup chunked onions*
½ pound fresh pork loin	*½ cup chunked potatoes*
1 quart water	*½ teaspoon black pepper*
1 cup chunked rutabagas	

1. Cut meats into 1-inch cubes. Put meats and water in a 5- to 6-quart kettle. Cover and bring to a boil. Remove any scum that accumulates on surface. Lower heat and simmer 1 hour or until tender.
2. Add vegetables and pepper, cover, and simmer 1 hour until vegetables are tender. Stew should have thickened. If stew has not thickened stir in a paste made of 2 tablespoons water and 2 tablespoons flour.

VARIATION: Substitute various other vegetables.

LAMB AND CABBAGE STEW (Fårikål)

Yield: 4 to 6 servings

Norwegians typically combine cooked cabbage with a variety of meats. This stew, made with an inexpensive cut of meat, is everyday fare.

2 pounds lamb shoulder
1½ cups water
1 teaspoon salt
½ teaspoon black pepper

2 tablespoons flour
2 tablespoons water
1¾- to 2-pound head of cabbage

1. Cut lamb into 1½- to 2-inch cubes. Place meat, water, salt, and pepper in a stewing kettle or large pot. Water should barely cover meat, so may need to add more depending on pan size. Bring to a boil, reduce heat, cover, and simmer for 1 hour.
2. Make a smooth paste of flour and water and stir into contents of pan. Simmer while preparing cabbage.
3. Cut cabbage in 1½- to 2-inch chunks. Add to simmering meat and cook, covered, about 45 minutes or until cabbage is tender.

VARIATION: Substitute leg of lamb for shoulder and shorten cooking period by 20 minutes.

MEAT CAKES (Kjøttkaker)

Yield: 30 to 32 patties

Enjoyed by Norwegian Americans and still typical evening fare in rural and eastern Norway, this dish is commonly served with potatoes and stewed cabbage.

1½ pounds lean ground beef
½ cup finely minced onions
1 teaspoon salt
¾ cup light cream or half and half
⅓ cup beef broth
⅓ cup pulverized breadcrumbs
½ teaspoon black pepper

¼ teaspoon ground ginger
¼ teaspoon ground nutmeg
2 tablespoons butter
2 tablespoons vegetable oil
4 cups beef broth
4 tablespoons flour
4 tablespoons cold water

1. In large bowl, combine beef, onions, salt, cream, ⅓ cup broth, crumbs, pepper, ginger, and nutmeg. Mix well.
2. Form mixture into flat cakes about 2 inches in diameter and ½ inch thick. Heat butter and oil over moderate heat in a heavy frying pan. Fry cakes about 5 minutes on each side or until lightly browned.

3. Bring beef broth to a boil in a 4- to 5-quart kettle. Slide cooked meat cakes into liquid. Cover pan and adjust heat to keep liquid simmering for ½ hour.
4. Remove cakes to serving dish and keep warm while making gravy. Mix flour and water into a smooth paste. Stir into boiling beef broth. Pour over warm meat cakes and serve.
5. Cakes freeze well in gravy.

RICE PUDDING (Risgraut)   Yield: 6 to 8 servings

One of a variety of Norwegian rice puddings that closely resemble those served by Danes and Swedes. Rice pudding is a traditional dessert at Christmastime; the person who finds the almond is guaranteed a year of good luck.

½ cup uncooked long-grain rice
1 cup water
½ teaspoon salt
2 cups milk
1 cup whipping cream
½ cup sugar

2 eggs, separated
½ teaspoon almond extract
½ teaspoon ground nutmeg
1 whole almond
2 tablespoons sugar

1. Cook rice in water and salt over low heat in a heavy 2½- to 3-quart saucepan until all water is absorbed, about 15 minutes.
2. Heat together 1 cup milk and ½ cup cream. Do not boil. Stir in ½ cup sugar and continue stirring until sugar is dissolved. Add to rice, mix well, and cover pan. Cook over low heat for at least 1 hour or until most of liquid is absorbed.
3. Beat egg yolks and mix with remaining milk and cream. Stir into rice. Cover pan and continue cooking rice mixture for 15 to 20 minutes or until most of liquid is absorbed. Mixture will be creamy. Add almond extract, nutmeg, and the almond, stirring in gently. Remove from heat.
4. Lightly butter a 8-by-12-inch pan or other baking dish of that approximate size with 1½- to 2-inch sides. Preheat oven to 350 degrees.
5. Beat egg whites and add 2 tablespoons sugar to make a meringue. Pour rice mixture into prepared dish and spread meringue over top.
6. Bake for 10 minutes or until meringue is lightly browned.
7. Cool at least 1 hour before serving. Traditionally served with rich cream or whipped cream.

FATTIGMANN

Yield: 48 to 50 cookies

"Poor man's cookies," traditional at Christmastime, but occasionally made throughout the year. Many non-Scandinavian nationalities, including Italians, Germans, and South Slavs, also make a version of this cookie.

2 egg yolks
1 whole egg
¼ teaspoon salt
3 tablespoons powdered sugar
2 tablespoons whipping cream

1 teaspoon vanilla
1¼ cups all-purpose flour, spooned into
cup
Oil or lard for deep-fat frying
Powdered sugar for dusting cookies

1. Combine egg yolks and egg in small mixer bowl and beat well for 2 to 3 minutes. Gradually add salt, sugar, cream, and vanilla. Beat well.
2. Stir in flour until stiff dough forms. Turn dough out on lightly floured board and knead a few times. If dough seems too sticky, knead in another 1 to 2 tablespoons flour.
3. Roll out dough quite thin, ⅛ inch or less. Cut into 1-inch strips. Cut strips into 2½- to 3-inch lengths. (Can make these cuts on the diagonal.)
4. Cut at least a 1-inch slash in center of each cookie. Pull one end of strip through slash and straighten it out to make a bow or twist shape (see illustration).

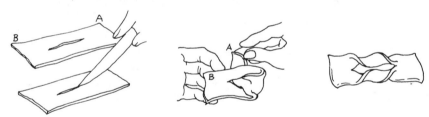

5. Preheat fat to 375 degrees. Fry a few cookies at a time, turning as they lightly brown. Browning on both sides takes less than a minute so watch carefully.
6. Using a slotted spoon, remove cookies and drain on paper towels. When cool, sift powdered sugar over them and store in airtight container. Cookies freeze well.

Danes

DANISH PUMPERNICKEL RYE BREAD (Dansk Rugbrød)

Yield: 1 large loaf or 2 small loaves

A popular base for the well-known Danish cheeses, sausages, and open-faced sandwiches.

1 package dry yeast
¼ cup water (105 to 115 degrees)
1¾ cups buttermilk
¼ cup molasses
1 tablespoon salt
¼ cup butter

3¾ cups medium rye flour, spooned into cup
1 cup whole-wheat flour, spooned into cup
1½ to 2 cups all-purpose flour, spooned into cup

1. Dissolve yeast in water. Set aside.
2. Heat buttermilk to 105 to 115 degrees over moderate heat. Add molasses, salt, and butter. Stir until butter is melted. Pour into large mixing bowl. Add dissolved yeast.
3. Add rye and whole-wheat flours 1 cup at a time, stirring well after each addition. Gradually add all-purpose flour, stirring in small amounts until dough can be turned out on lightly floured board and kneaded. May need to add more flour during kneading process.
4. Knead on floured surface for 7 to 10 minutes. Place in greased bowl and lightly grease top of dough. Allow to rise in a warm place until double in bulk, about 1½ hours. Punch dough down well.
5. Grease pans with shortening and shape dough into 1 long loaf (12¾ by 3¾ by 2½ inches) or 2 smaller loaves (8½ by 4¾ by 2½ inches). Cover lightly with plastic wrap and allow to rise until double in bulk or until dough is just a little higher than sides of pan.
6. Preheat oven to 325 degrees. Bake 1 hour. Check bread. If it sounds hollow when rapped with wooden spoon handle or knuckles, remove from oven. May need to bake additional 15 minutes.
7. Remove from pan and cool on baking rack. Cut in thin slices.

RED CABBAGE (Rød Kål)   Yield: 8 to 10 servings

A frequent accompaniment to everyday as well as holiday meals that feature beef or pork roast or chicken.

2 tablespoons butter
2½ quarts shredded red cabbage (1 medium-sized head, or about 10 cups)
1½ cups peeled, coarsely chopped apples
½ cup vinegar (pickled beet vinegar is good)

1 teaspoon salt
¼ teaspoon black pepper
¼ cup sugar
¼ cup currant jelly

1. Melt butter in heavy 4- to 6-quart kettle. Add cabbage, apples, vinegar, salt, pepper, and sugar. Stir. Cover and simmer for 1 hour.
2. Add currant jelly the last 10 minutes of cooking time. Serve hot.

VARIATIONS: Increase simmering time to 2 hours for improved flavor or make it the day before and reheat. Can bake in the oven at 325 degrees for 1½ to 2 hours. Or, add 1 cup chopped onions.

BEEF SOUP WITH MEATBALLS AND DUMPLINGS (Kødsuppe med Boller)   Yield: 6 to 8 servings

Quantities of parsley in soups distinguish the Danish variety from those of many other nationalities. The meaty portions of the roast cooked in this soup are sliced and served as a side dish or saved for later use. The broth then is heated with small meatballs and tiny dumplings.

2½ to 3 pounds chuck roast
2 pounds beef shinbone or other bones, cracked by butcher
4 quarts cold water
1½ tablespoons salt
2 cups celery, including leaves, cut in ½-inch pieces

2 cups carrots, cut in ½-inch pieces
2 medium-sized onions, cut in quarters
3 leeks, cut in ½-inch pieces (optional)
½ cup coarsely chopped parsley
Meatballs (see below)
Dumplings (see below)

1. Place roast, bones, cold water, and salt in a large soup kettle. Bring to a boil. Reduce heat and simmer for 15 minutes. Remove any scum that has accumulated on surface.
2. Add celery, carrots, onions, leeks, and parsley. Cover and simmer for 3 hours or until meat is tender. Remove meat. Strain liquid, discard

vegetables, and allow broth to stand so that fat will rise to top and can be skimmed off.
3. Heat broth to boiling and add dumplings and meatballs. Reduce heat and barely simmer until dumplings and meatballs are warmed through.
4. Serve with a few dumplings and meatballs in each bowl.

VARIATION: Add vegetables to the servings of soup. After broth is strained and defatted, bring it to a boil, add 2 to 3 cups of small pieces of carrots, onions, celery, or potatoes. Simmer until tender and then add meatballs and dumplings and allow to heat together. Do not boil.

Meatballs
Yield: 24 meatballs

½ pound finely ground lean beef
1 ½ tablespoons flour
1 egg, beaten
¼ cup milk

½ teaspoon salt
¼ teaspoon black pepper
Boiling salted water

1. Mix beef, flour, egg, milk, salt, and pepper.
2. Fill a 3-quart pan ⅔ full of water and bring to boil. Make small, teaspoon-sized meatballs. Drop into boiling water. Adjust heat so water barely simmers and cook for 5 minutes. Remove from water with slotted spoon. Set aside to add to soup broth.

Dumplings
Yield: 24 dumplings

¼ cup butter
½ cup all-purpose flour
½ cup boiling water

2 eggs
Boiling salted water

1. Over low heat, melt butter in a small saucepan. Add flour and stir.
2. Gradually add ½ cup boiling water, stirring well. Remove pan from heat.
3. Let rest for 15 minutes. Add eggs, 1 at a time, beating well after each addition. Give a final thorough beating with a wooden spoon.
4. In a large kettle bring 3 quarts of water to a boil. Adjust heat so water barely simmers. Drop teaspoonfuls of batter into water. Gently agitate pan so that dumplings will move around and turn over. Cook for about 3 minutes.
5. Cover and keep warm in cooking water until ready to add to soup. May not need all the dumplings for 6 servings of soup.

TORSK WITH MUSTARD SAUCE
(Torsk med Sennep Saus)

Yield: 4 to 6 servings

Fish occupies a major place in traditional Danish cookery, and torsk with mustard sauce is both one of the most traditional and most popular among Minnesota's Danish Americans. It is usually served with boiled white potatoes on New Year's Eve.

2 pounds frozen torsk
Cold water
1 tablespoon salt
2 bay leaves
½ cup butter
4 tablespoons flour

2 cups hot water or chicken broth
½ teaspoon salt
¼ teaspoon black pepper
2 tablespoons prepared brown mustard
(variety with seeds)

1. Place frozen torsk in a 5- to 6-quart kettle or Dutch oven. Add cold water to cover fish completely. Bring water to a boil over high heat. Add salt and bay leaves. Cover pan.
2. Remove pan from heat. Allow to stand 10 minutes. Drain fish well, patting dry with paper towels.
3. Melt butter in small pan over medium heat. Stir in flour and simmer for several minutes. Add hot water or chicken broth, a little at a time, until mixture thickens. Stir in salt, pepper, and mustard. Turn heat to low and allow to cook for about 2 minutes, stirring constantly.
4. Serve fish with sauce spooned over each portion. Pour extra sauce in gravy boat and serve at table. Traditionally a large pat of butter is added to sauce in the gravy boat.

DANISH LIVER LOAF
   (Leverpostej)

Yield: 20 to 22 ¼-inch slices

1 pound pork liver
¾ pound pork fat
1 cup finely diced onions
2 tablespoons butter
2 tablespoons all-purpose flour
1⅓ cups light cream or half and half
2 teaspoons salt

1 teaspoon black pepper
¼ teaspoon ground cloves
¼ teaspoon ground allspice
2 eggs, slightly beaten
2 teaspoons mashed Portuguese anchovies
   (optional)
4 slices bacon

1. Put liver and fat through food grinder at least 2 times; 4 to 5 times gives a more authentic texture. Or, process in food processor until meat and fat are a smooth, homogeneous mixture. Place in large bowl. Stir in onions.
2. Melt butter in small heavy saucepan over moderate heat. Stir in flour and cook for 1 minute stirring constantly. Gradually stir in cream and continue stirring until thickened. Allow thickened sauce to simmer for 2 minutes. Stir into meat mixture. Add salt, pepper, cloves, and allspice.
3. Stir in beaten eggs and anchovies. Mix well.
4. Preheat oven to 350 degrees. Put water in a 9-by-13-inch pan and place in oven to heat. Grease a 9-by-5-inch loaf pan well. Line bottom with 4 slices of bacon. Pour in meat mixture. Set pan in hot water in oven. Bake 15 minutes. Reduce oven temperature to 300 degrees and bake for 1¼ hours or until a toothpick stuck in middle of loaf comes out clean. May need to add water to pan before liver loaf is done.
5. Cool for 1 hour in loaf pan. Remove from pan and refrigerate when cold.

VARIATION: Substitute 6 slices of bacon for the pork fat.

DANISH MEATBALLS   Yield: 55 to 60 meatballs
(Frikadeller)

Distinguished from its Norwegian and Swedish cousins by its texture, seasonings, and oval shape. As cold leftovers, frikadeller are sliced thinly and arranged with garnishes on open-faced sandwiches.

1 cup dry breadcrumbs
1 cup cream
1½ pounds extra lean ground beef
½ pound lean ground pork shoulder
1¼ cups minced onions
¾ teaspoon black pepper

1½ teaspoons salt
½ teaspoon ground allspice
2 eggs, beaten
3 tablespoons butter
3 tablespoons vegetable shortening
Pan Gravy (see below)

1. Combine breadcrumbs and cream. Set aside.
2. In large bowl, mix beef, pork, onions, pepper, salt, and allspice with a large spoon or use hands.
3. Add breadcrumb-milk mixture. Mix with a wide sweeping motion using spoon or hands to work air into mixture. Add beaten eggs in same manner.
4. Melt butter and shortening in large heavy frying pan. Using a tablespoon, make an oval-shaped meatball. Before making each meatball dip spoon either in hot fat or very cold water. Flatten meatball slightly on top as it slips into pan. Fry over medium heat until light brown on both sides.
5. Do not crowd meatballs. May need to fry in 2 batches. Remove from pan, drain well, and place in casserole or serving dish while making gravy. Pour gravy over meatballs and serve.

VARIATION: Substitute 1 cup charged water (club soda) or ½ cup milk and ½ cup charged water for the cream. The charged water makes an even lighter meatball.

Pan Gravy

4 tablespoons pan drippings
2½ cups hot water

1 bouillon cube
4 tablespoons all-purpose flour

1. Remove all but 4 tablespoons of pan drippings from frying pan. Over moderate heat stir in 2 cups of water and bouillon cube. Stir and loosen all browned bits. Bring to a boil. Reduce heat and simmer.

2. Combine remaining ½ cup water and 4 tablespoons flour. Stir until smooth and slowly add to simmering mixture.
3. Cook for 3 minutes. Taste and adjust seasonings.

DANISH OPEN-FACED SANDWICH (Smørrebrød)

Yield: 1 sandwich

Usually reserved for festive occasions, these sandwiches are made to be eaten with a knife and fork. Although a great variety of appropriate toppings exists, tradition dictates the proper combinations of ingredients and garnishes.

1 thin slice pumpernickel bread
1½ to 2 teaspoons softened butter
1 to 2 slices Danish Liver Loaf (see recipe)

2 whole pickled beets
1 slice bacon, fried and cut in half
4 thin slices cucumber (optional)

1. Cut crusts from bread unless they are thin and soft. Spread softened butter to edges of bread.
2. Arrange slices of liver loaf on bread. Slices can extend over edges of bread.
3. Slice pickled beets into strips and spread equal distance apart across slices of liver loaf. Lay pieces of bacon on top of beets.
4. Place cucumber slices, slightly separated, across top of sandwich.

VARIATIONS: Slice of ham and ruffly lettuce, garnished with a slice of egg and parsley. Or, sardines and ruffly lettuce, garnished with a lemon twist and slices of stuffed green olives. Or, sliced meatballs (use frikadeller) and thinly sliced cucumbers, garnished with thinly sliced raw onion rings.

NOTE: Sandwiches are best when assembled fresh. Bread can be buttered ahead and refrigerated, well covered. To prepare an hour ahead, assemble sandwich except for cucumber. Cover with plastic wrap and refrigerate.

DANISH LAYER CAKE (Blødkage)   Yield: 12 to 15 servings

Featured at birthday parties, weddings, special anniversaries, and the annual Danish Constitution Day picnic in Minneapolis. Cooks from various regions of Denmark embellish the cake differently.

4 eggs at room temperature, separated
2 cups sugar
1 ¼ teaspoons vanilla
1 cup milk (around 105 degrees)
2 cups cake flour, spooned into cup
2 teaspoons baking powder
8 ounces dried apricots

2 tablespoons sugar
⅛ teaspoon almond extract
3 macaroons, crushed (optional)
1 jar (8 ounces) raspberry jam
Custard Cream Filling (see below)
Whipped Cream Frosting (see below)

1. Preheat oven to 350 degrees. Grease 2 9-inch round cake pans well. Dust pans with flour, making sure to discard any flour that does not cling to pan.
2. Beat egg whites until stiff. Set aside. Beat egg yolks until thick and lemony in color. Add sugar gradually. Add vanilla. Fold in egg whites until completely mixed in. Gently and slowly add warm milk.
3. Sift cake flour and baking powder together. Add to egg mixture, folding in gently with wire whisk. Can use mixer on low speed.
4. Pour batter into prepared pans. Bake for 15 to 18 minutes or until cake is lightly browned and springs back when gently pressed.
5. Remove from oven and cool on racks for 5 minutes. Remove from pans and cool further.
6. Place dried apricots in a small saucepan and just barely cover with water. Simmer until tender and drain thoroughly. Puree in blender or food processor or put through food mill or sieve. Add sugar and almond extract. Set aside.
7. Crush macaroons. Prepare filling and frosting. When cake, apricot puree, and filling are cooled, cake can be assembled.
8. Split cake layers in half, using bread knife or serrated knife to make a smooth cut. There are now 4 layers. Place first layer on a cake plate cut side up. Place strips of waxed paper under edges of cake so that plate will be protected from smears of frosting and crumbs.
9. Spread raspberry jam over layer. Place other half of layer on top, cut side down. Spread custard filling over this layer. May not need quite all of this filling (1 to 2 tablespoons for the cook).
10. Place half of next layer, cut side up, on top of custard filling. Spread pureed apricots over layer and sprinkle macaroon crumbs over top. Place last layer on top of cake, cut side down.
11. Frost stack of layers with whipped cream frosting, making sure that layers stay even and straight. After putting a thick layer of frosting all

over cake, use a pastry bag and decorative point to make some special decorations on top. Remove waxed paper from around the base.
12. Refrigerate for several hours before serving.

Custard Cream Filling

2 egg yolks, room temperature
¼ cup sugar
1½ tablespoons all-purpose flour

¾ cup half and half, heated to boiling
1 teaspoon butter
½ teaspoon vanilla

1. In medium-sized bowl, combine sugar and egg yolks, beating for 2 minutes or until mixture is pale yellow.
2. Add flour gradually. Add warm cream very slowly in a thin stream.
3. Pour mixture into heavy saucepan and set over moderate heat. Bring to a boil stirring constantly. It may lump up a bit as it begins to boil but rapid beating will smooth it out. Beat for 2 to 3 minutes until flour is cooked. Lower heat if pan is not thick enough to prevent scorching. Can use a double boiler for this step.
4. Remove from heat. Stir in butter and vanilla. Use a spatula and scrape sides of pan. Drop small pieces of butter on top of custard to prevent a skin from forming while it cools.
5. Can be made ahead and refrigerated until used.

Whipped Cream Frosting

2 cups whipping cream
¼ cup sifted powdered sugar
1 teaspoon vanilla

1 teaspoon unflavored gelatin
1 tablespoon cool water

1. Chill bowl and beaters before whipping cream.
2. Dissolve gelatin in cool water in small bowl. Place over hot water and stir to liquefy gelatin. Set aside to cool.
3. Whip cream, adding sugar gradually as cream thickens. Add vanilla. Beat in cooled gelatin. Refrigerate until time to frost cake.

VARIATIONS: Use other favorite cakes for the layers. For other fillings use packaged vanilla pudding, sometimes flavored with almond extract; chocolate sauce, pureed prunes, apricot jam, pureed strawberries, or strawberry jam. Use plain whipped cream or a buttercream frosting to cover cake. Decorate with red and green cherries, apricot halves, fresh fruit in season, or slivered almonds.

SUGARED COOKIES (Kringler) Yield: 42 to 48 cookies

"Kringle" means pretzel, and the name is often used for anything shaped in that form — coffeecake, cookies, crackers, or cakes. These cookies are part of the array of traditional Christmas sweets.

3 cups all-purpose flour, spooned into cup *½ teaspoon crushed cardamom seed*
1 teaspoon baking powder *1¼ cups butter*
¼ teaspoon salt *1 cup whipping cream*
¼ cup sugar *Sugar*

1. Combine flour, baking powder, salt, sugar, and cardamom seed in large mixer bowl. Add butter and blend with a pastry blender.
2. Stir in cream until well mixed. Refrigerate for 30 minutes.
3. Remove half of dough from refrigerator. Pinch off small pieces, about the size of a walnut. Roll each into a 10- to 12-inch rope. Form into pretzel shape (see illustration). Press each side of cookie into a plateful of sugar.

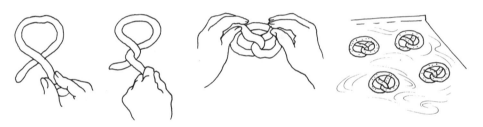

   Place cookies on greased baking sheets, about 1½ inches apart.
4. When nearly finished, remove other half of dough from refrigerator. (May need to warm at room temperature so that dough handles easily.) Repeat procedure.
5. Preheat oven to 350 degrees. Bake cookies for 15 to 18 minutes or until very lightly browned. Remove from baking sheets and cool on racks.
6. Cookies keep well in airtight containers or can be frozen.

RIS À L'ALMANDE Yield: 6 servings

A traditional Christmastime dessert, variations of which are enjoyed by other Scandinavians. The one whole almond is believed to bring good luck to the person in whose bowl it is found.

1 ¾ *cups whipping cream*
1 ½ *cups finely chopped or slivered*
    blanched almonds
4 *tablespoons sugar*
2 *teaspoons vanilla*

3 *tablespoons sherry (optional)*
Rice Porridge, cold (see below)
1 *whole almond*
Cherry Sauce (see below)

1. Whip cream to stiff stage in large bowl. Gently fold in almonds, sugar, vanilla, sherry, and cooled rice porridge.
2. Fold in 1 whole almond.
3. Cover dish and refrigerate for at least 2 hours.
4. Serve with cherry sauce or other fruit sauce.

Rice Porridge

½ *cup long-grain white rice*
1 ¾ *cups milk*

¼ *cup whipping cream*
¼ *teaspoon salt*

1. Combine rice and milk in top of double boiler. Bring water to boil in bottom of double boiler. Cover top of pan and place over hot water. Keep water at a low boil.
2. Cook for 1½ hours, stirring several times to mix rice and milk. Milk will be all absorbed at end of cooking period.
3. Cool rice for ½ hour. Stir in whipping cream and salt. Cover.

Cherry Sauce

1 *can (17 ounces) pitted Bing cherries,*
    drained (save juice)
1 ½ *cups juice (add water to make the*
    amount)

2 *tablespoons cornstarch*
1 *teaspoon lemon juice*
¼ *teaspoon almond extract*

1. Combine juice-water with cornstarch in small heavy saucepan. Stir until blended. Bring to a boil over medium heat. Stir until clear.
2. Add cherries, lemon juice, and almond extract. Set aside to cool.

VARIATIONS: Make fruit sauces using raspberries or strawberries. Some cooks use commercially canned pie filling.

Swedes

SWEDISH RYE BREAD (Limpa)   Yield: 2 loaves

Similar to a Finnish bread, this slightly sweet loaf is popular at both sacred and secular times of year.

1 package dry yeast
¼ cup water (105 to 115 degrees)
1 tablespoon packed brown sugar
2 teaspoons salt
2 tablespoons shortening or lard
⅓ cup molasses
2 cups warm water

½ teaspoon crushed cardamom seed
½ teaspoon crushed anise seed
2 cups rye (or medium rye) flour, spooned into cup
4 to 5 cups all-purpose flour, spooned into cup

1. Dissolve yeast in warm water. Add sugar and set aside.
2. Combine salt, shortening, molasses, water, cardamom seed, anise seed, and rye flour. Mix well. Stir in yeast mixture.
3. Stir in 4 cups of all-purpose flour, 1 cup at a time. Continue to add flour slowly until dough can be kneaded on a lightly floured board. Knead for about 10 minutes or until smooth and elastic. May need to work in more flour to eliminate stickiness.
4. Allow dough to rise in a well-buttered bowl, covered, until double in bulk. Punch down and allow to rise a second time.
5. Punch down well and divide dough in half. Form into 2 loaves and place in well-greased pans. Allow to rise in the pans until double in size. Preheat oven to 350 degrees.
6. Bake bread for 35 to 40 minutes or until nicely browned. Brush with melted butter. Remove from pans and cool on racks.

HASSELBACK POTATOES
(Hasselbackspotatis)

Yield: 8 servings

A festive dish, named for a favorite old restaurant in Stockholm.

8 baking potatoes of somewhat uniform
*   size*
½ cup melted butter
1 ¼ teaspoons salt
½ cup fine dry breadcrumbs

1. Peel potatoes and place in bowl of ice water.
2. Remove 1 potato at a time and slice in the following manner: place potato on a large spoon and use a sharp knife to make ⅛-inch crosswise slices (see illustration). The spoon keeps the knife from cutting all the

way through the potato. The potato will spread apart slightly when baked and browned.
3. Return scored potato to ice water and repeat process with remaining potatoes. Preheat oven to 400 degrees. Drain all scored potatoes on paper towels. Arrange them in a buttered 9-by-13-inch baking pan or dish, cut side up. Brush with half the butter and sprinkle salt over tops of potatoes.
4. Bake 40 minutes or until almost done. Remove pan from oven and brush potatoes with remaining butter and sprinkle crumbs over tops.
5. Bake 15 to 20 minutes longer until tender and nicely browned. May need to increase heat to 425 degrees to achieve browning.

VARIATION: ¼ cup Parmesan cheese can be sprinkled over potatoes during last few minutes of baking.

BROWN BEANS (Bruna Bönor)   Yield: 8 to 10 servings

Popular with the immigrant generation and still eaten frequently at present, bruna bönor is an everyday dish that also appears on holiday tables.

2 cups dried brown beans (available in specialty stores)
6 cups water
1½ teaspoons salt

½ cup white vinegar
½ cup dark corn syrup
3 tablespoons packed brown sugar

1. Pick over and rinse beans. Add water and soak beans at least 12 hours.
2. Bring beans and soaking water to a boil. Cover pan and simmer for 1½ hours.
3. Add salt, vinegar, syrup, and brown sugar. Stir to mix. Simmer for 1 hour or until beans are tender. The liquid mixture should be thick like a sauce at the end of cooking period.
4. If liquid is not thickened, turn up heat for 10 minutes or until liquid is reduced. Stir often. Serve hot.

SWEDISH MEATBALLS (Köttbullar)   Yield: about 60 small meatballs

An ethnic recipe that has been assimilated into the diet and cookbooks of mainstream America. The sauce and mode of preparation distinguish Swedish meatballs from the Norwegian and Danish varieties.

¼ cup milk
¼ cup half and half
1 egg, slightly beaten
2 slices bread, crusts removed
1 pound lean ground beef
¼ pound ground pork shoulder
2 tablespoons finely minced onions
1 teaspoon salt

½ teaspoon sugar
½ teaspoon black pepper
3 tablespoons butter
1 tablespoon vegetable oil
1 can (10¾ ounces) cream of chicken soup
½ can (10¾ ounces) tomato soup
½ soup can warm water

1. Combine milk, half and half, and egg. Add slices of bread that have been torn in chunks. Set aside.
2. Combine beef, pork, onion, salt, sugar, and pepper in large bowl. Mix lightly with hands. Add egg mixture and continue to work until mixture is light and fluffy.
3. Shape into small meatballs, about the size of walnuts.

4. Heat butter and oil in heavy frying pan over moderate heat. Brown meatballs, turning often to keep them round. Do not crowd pan. Or, melt butter and oil in a large baking pan in a 375 degree oven. Add meatballs to hot fat and brown in oven.
5. Remove meatballs from pan. Add chicken soup, tomato soup, and water to pan. Stir until well mixed and bits of browning are loosened from bottom of pan. Adjust seasonings if necessary.
6. Place meatballs in 3-quart casserole. Pour gravy over top and bake 20 minutes at 350 degrees.

JANSSON'S TEMPTATION (Janssons Frestelse)

Yield: 4 to 6 servings

Some claim that this dish originated in the vicinity of Stockholm, others, that it was first made in America and was named for Erik Jansson, a religious leader who emigrated with his followers to found the Bishop Hill community in Illinois.

5 to 5½ cups potatoes, peeled
1½ cups sliced onions
6 tablespoons butter
½ teaspoon white pepper

1 can (3½ ounces) Swedish anchovy
*   fillets, drained (reserve 1 tablespoon*
*   juice)*
¾ cup whipping cream

1. Butter 1½- to 2-quart baking dish. Preheat oven to 400 degrees.
2. Cut potatoes into ¼-inch slices and then into ¼-inch thick strips, like small french fries. Set pieces aside in dish of cold water.
3. Saute onions over moderate heat in 3 tablespoons of butter. Stir and cook for 3 to 4 minutes.
4. Drain potatoes on paper towels. Put ½ of potatoes into prepared dish. Add onions evenly over top. Arrange anchovy fillets on top of onions. Cover with remaining potatoes. Sprinkle anchovy juice and pepper evenly over dish.
5. Pour cream over mixture and dot with bits of remaining butter. Cover tightly.
6. Bake for 40 minutes. Remove cover. Reduce temperature to 375 degrees and bake 20 minutes longer or until potatoes are tender.

VARIATIONS: Swedish anchovies are only very lightly salted compared to the Portuguese variety; substitute well-rinsed Portuguese fish for a stronger, but less authentic, flavor. Or, increase cream by ¼ to ¾ cup for a much richer flavor. Can also add an extra ½ cup of onions.

SWEDISH TEA RING (Jul Krans)

Yield: 2 14-inch rings of 10 to 12 servings each

The name means "Christmas Wreath," but this festive and intricate sweet bread may be served for any special occasion.

2 packages dry yeast
¼ cup water (105 to 115 degrees)
1 cup lukewarm milk
½ cup sugar
1½ teaspoons salt
2 eggs, beaten

¼ cup lard
¼ cup butter, cut into small pieces
5½ to 6 cups all-purpose flour, spooned
  into cup
Filling (see below)

1. Dissolve yeast in water. Set aside. In large bowl combine milk, sugar, salt, eggs, lard, and butter.
2. Gradually stir in flour, 1 cup at a time. After 5 cups have been added, slowly spoon in remainder until dough is firm enough to be kneaded on lightly floured board.
3. Knead until dough is smooth and elastic, working in additional flour as needed to eliminate stickiness. Place in greased bowl. Cover and allow to rise until double in bulk, about 1 hour. Punch down and allow to rise a second time for about 45 minutes.
4. Punch dough down and divide in half. Wrap 1 portion tightly with plastic wrap. Gently knead other portion for several minutes, working out air bubbles. Divide into 3 parts.
5. On floured board roll each piece into a rope about 20 inches long. Using floured rolling pin shape rope into a rectangle about 20 inches long, 4½ to 5 inches wide, and ¼ to ½ inch thick. Spread each rectangle with ⅙ of filling.
6. Roll up each rectangle, jelly-roll fashion, beginning at the long edge. Pinch together and secure long edge and ends of rope (see illustration). Repeat with other 2 pieces of dough.

7. Braid the 3 rope pieces and shape into a ring, overlapping and securing the ends. Place on large, well-greased baking sheet. Place food can, 2¾ to 3 inches in diameter, in center of ring. Be sure to remove all glue

particles before using. This keeps the center of the ring from closing up as the tea ring rises and bakes. Cover and allow to rise until double in bulk, about 45 minutes.

8. While first ring is rising repeat steps for second ring.
9. Preheat oven to 350 degrees. Bake first ring for 35 to 40 minutes or until nicely browned. Then bake second ring. Can be frosted when cool with a powdered sugar frosting and decorated with nuts and cherries, if desired.

Filling

1 cup soft butter
1½ cups sugar
3 tablespoons ground cinnamon

Spread each rectangle with 2½ tablespoons butter, ¼ cup sugar, and 1½ teaspoons cinnamon. Then proceed with rolling up the rectangle.

KRÄM PUDDING   Yield: 6 to 8 servings

An urban adaptation of a traditional recipe, originally made from wild berries or fruits.

1 can (12 ounces) frozen concentrated   *½ cup cornstarch*
  grape juice   *1 cup cold water*
1 can (12 ounces) water   *1 tablespoon butter*
½ cup sugar   *Sugar*

1. In a saucepan, combine juice concentrate, water, and sugar. Stir occasionally until mixture boils. Remove from heat.
2. Combine cornstarch and water, mixing until cornstarch is thoroughly dissolved. Gradually stir into juice mixture.
3. Return pan to moderate heat and allow pudding to boil gently for at least 3 minutes, stirring constantly. Stir in butter. The pudding will be thick and will thicken further as it cools.
4. Pour into 1-quart dish or into individual serving dishes. To prevent a skin forming on top of pudding sprinkle lightly with sugar.
5. Cool. Serve at room temperature or chilled with cream or whipped cream.

PEPPARKAKOR   Yield: 48 to 60 cookies, depending on shape

A spicy cookie that is part of traditional Swedish and Swedish-American Christmas celebrations.

½ cup sugar
1 egg, beaten
¼ cup molasses
¼ cup shortening
¼ cup butter, at room temperature
1 ¾ cups all-purpose flour, spooned into
   cup
1 teaspoon baking soda

1 teaspoon ground ginger
½ teaspoon ground cloves
½ teaspoon ground cinnamon
½ teaspoon ground nutmeg
¼ teaspoon salt
¾ teaspoon crushed cardamom seed
½ teaspoon grated orange rind
½ teaspoon grated lemon rind

1. Combine sugar, egg, molasses, shortening, and butter.
2. Mix flour, soda, ginger, cloves, cinnamon, nutmeg, salt, cardamom, orange rind, and lemon rind. Slowly add to sugar-egg mixture to make a smooth, soft dough. Chill, covered with plastic wrap, for at least 24 hours.
3. Preheat oven to 350 degrees. Lightly grease baking sheets.
4. Remove ¼ of dough from refrigerator. On a lightly floured board (preferably a cloth-covered board) roll out dough ⅛ inch thick. Using cookie cutters, cut various shapes, such as traditional Swedish hearts, pigs, or horses.
5. Place cookies on baking sheet and bake for 6 to 8 minutes or until cookies are firm but not browned. Remove immediately from sheet and cool on racks.
6. Can be decorated with white icing.

ALMOND RUSKS (Mandelskorpor)   Yield: 60 slices

A European-style cookie, often served with coffee, into which the skorpor is traditionally dunked.

1½ cups sugar
½ cup butter
4 tablespoons vegetable oil
4 eggs
1 cup milk
1 tablespoon baking powder

1 teaspoon salt
5 cups all-purpose flour, spooned into cup
1 cup finely chopped almonds
½ teaspoon almond extract
1 teaspoon vanilla
Sugar

1. Generously butter a 9-by 13-inch baking pan. Preheat oven to 350 degrees.
2. Using mixer, cream together sugar, butter, and oil. Add eggs and beat well for 2 minutes.
3. Add milk and then the combined baking powder, salt, and flour. Add almonds, almond extract, and vanilla last, mixing only until batter is smooth.
4. Spread batter evenly in prepared pan. Bake for 1 hour.
5. Cool. Cover pan loosely with plastic wrap and set aside for 24 hours.
6. Slice into 4 even strips the length of the pan. Remove 1 strip at a time and cut into ½-inch slices. Place slices flat on baking sheet. Sprinkle each lightly with sugar.
7. Place rusks in a preheated 275 degree oven and bake 40 minutes or until crisp and lightly browned.

LUCIA BUNS (Lussekatter)

Yield: 48 single **S** buns
or 24 double **S** buns

The nickname "Lussekatter" translates "Lucia cats," reflecting a pagan belief connecting Lucia with the devil, who sometimes took the form of a cat. The shape of these buns, a stylized open cross, is thought to be powerful in warding off the devil.

1 cup milk
1 teaspoon saffron threads (or ⅛ teaspoon saffron powder)
2 cakes compressed yeast or 2 packages dry yeast
⅓ cup water (105 to 115 degrees)
⅔ cup sugar
3 large eggs, at room temperature, slightly beaten

1 teaspoon salt
½ cup melted butter, slightly cooled
1 teaspoon crushed cardamom seed (or ¾ teaspoon cardamom powder)
5½ to 6 cups all-purpose flour, spooned into cup
1 egg white
1 teaspoon water
Raisins

1. Heat milk in small saucepan to just under boiling. Remove from heat and add saffron. Set aside to cool for at least 15 minutes. Stir occasionally.
2. Add yeast to warm water. Stir to dissolve and allow to stand for a few minutes.
3. In large mixer bowl combine sugar, eggs, salt, butter, cardamom, and milk, straining it to remove saffron threads.
4. Stir in dissolved yeast and 2 cups flour. Mix well.
5. Gradually add remaining flour, stirring in ½ cup at a time, until dough can be turned out on a lightly floured board to knead. Knead about 10 to 12 minutes, adding more flour if dough is sticky.
6. Place in greased bowl and lightly grease top of dough. Cover and allow to rise in a warm place until double in bulk, about 1 hour. Punch down well. Grease 2 large baking sheets.
7. Pinch off a piece of dough large enough to roll into a strip or rope 6 to 8 inches long and about ½ inch thick. On the baking sheet form rope into an **S** with ends coiling in spirals (see illustration). If making double **S** buns, place another **S** over the first with the middle of the top **S** directly on top of the middle of the bottom **S**. Place far enough apart to allow for rising.

8. Place a raisin in center of each spiral. Brush tops of buns with egg-white wash made with egg white and water beaten together until frothy.
9. Cover buns lightly with plastic wrap and allow to rise until double in bulk, about 1 hour.
10. Bake in preheated 350 degree oven 15 to 20 minutes or until browned. Remove from baking sheet and cool on racks.

VARIATIONS: Reduce amount of saffron to give just a hint of saffron flavor. Or omit saffron and use only cardamom.

THE FINNS

PEA SOUP (Hernekeitto)   Yield: 6 servings

Originally made with whole green or yellow peas, now difficult to find, hernekeitto is a winter staple among Minnesota's Finns. The soup has become a traditional part of Laskiainen celebrations.

1 pound split peas	*1 cup chopped onions*
3½ quarts water	*1 cup diced carrots*
1 to 1½ pounds smoked pork hocks	*2 cups cubed potatoes*
4 whole peppercorns	*1 cup chopped celery*
4 whole allspice	*Salt to taste*

1. Rinse peas well and remove any darkened peas or dirt. Soak overnight. Do not drain. Use a 4- to 6-quart heavy pan to prevent scorching during cooking.
2. Add smoked pork hocks, peppercorns, and allspice to peas and water. Bring to a boil. Reduce heat, cover, and simmer 1½ hours until peas are almost tender. Stir several times.
3. Remove pork hocks. When cool enough to handle, cut off meat and return to split-pea mixture.
4. Add onions, carrots, potatoes, and celery. Cover and simmer for 1 hour or until all vegetables are tender. Stir several times to prevent scorching.
5. Taste and adjust seasonings.

VARIATION: Substitute one pound of salt pork or a ham bone with some meat on it for pork hocks. Or, add 1½ to 2 cups cubed ham.

FLAT BREAD (Rieska)

Yield: approximately 24
3-inch-square pieces

Whole-grain bread is a staple of Finnish-American foodways. In western Finland, round loaves of rieska traditionally were baked in quantity once or twice a year. They were then skewered on a pole and hung in the rafters. In Minnesota, the bread is baked frequently and eaten fresh.

1 cup water (105 to 115 degrees)
2 packages dry yeast
1 cup milk
1 egg, slightly beaten
2 teaspoons salt
1 tablespoon honey
¼ cup vegetable shortening or lard

¾ cup graham flour
½ cup cracked-wheat flour (or finely ground cracked wheat)
¼ cup rye flour (often sold as medium-rye flour)
7 to 8 cups all-purpose flour, spooned into cup

1. Dissolve yeast in warm water. Let stand 5 minutes.
2. Mix milk, egg, salt, honey, and shortening in large bowl. Shortening will remain in small pieces but will be well mixed as flour is added. Add softened yeast.
3. Stir in graham, cracked-wheat, and rye flours. Beat well.
4. Gradually add white flour, beating well after each addition. When a stiff dough forms, turn out on a lightly floured board. Cover with bowl and let rest for 15 minutes.
5. Knead until smooth and not sticky, working in additional flour if needed.
6. Lightly oil 2 9-by-13-inch pans. Divide dough in half and flatten each piece on bottom of pan. Use palm of hand to even dough over bottom.
7. Using a fork, prick firmly all over dough at 1-inch intervals.
8. Allow to rise for 30 minutes. Bake in 375 degree oven for 30 minutes or until lightly browned.
9. Remove from pans to cooling racks. May brush with butter while still hot. Usually broken into pieces when served.

BEET-HERRING SALAD (Rosolli)   Yield: 6 servings

Finnish Americans in Minnesota have adapted this recipe to suit individual tastes and occasions. Among some families rosolli is a Christmas treat; others serve it with lunch or as part of a buffet dinner.

2 cups cooked, diced potatoes
1 cup cooked, diced carrots
1½ cups cooked, diced beets
2 tablespoons minced onion
¾ cup pickled herring, cut into small pieces

1 dill pickle, chopped
1 tart apple, peeled and diced
1 egg, hard boiled
Parsley
Dressing (see below)

1. Combine first 7 ingredients. Add dressing, mix well, and cover. Refrigerate for a few hours or overnight.
2. Adjust seasonings, adding salt or pepper as needed. Decorate top of salad with slices of hard-boiled egg and sprigs of parsley.

Dressing

½ cup sour cream
1½ teaspoons lemon juice
1 teaspoon beet juice

1 teaspoon sugar
⅛ teaspoon salt
Dash of black pepper

Mix well.

VARIATIONS: Change amounts of vegetables, apple, or herring to suit tastes. Adjust proportions of seasonings in the dressing. Add garlic powder or horseradish.

RUTABAGA CASSEROLE   Yield: 6 servings
(Lanttulaatikko)

A traditional part of Christmas dinner, this dish is also served throughout the year. Lanttulaatikko is commonly made from rutabagas alone; many cooks, however, substitute some potatoes to "tone down" the flavor.

1 ½ cups mashed potatoes	*¼ teaspoon black pepper*
1 ½ cups mashed rutabagas	*2 eggs, separated*
1 tablespoon packed brown sugar	*2 tablespoons butter*
½ teaspoon salt	*¼ cup breadcrumbs*

1. Butter a 1½- to 2-quart casserole. Preheat oven to 325 degrees.
2. In large bowl, mix mashed vegetables well, using a masher.
3. Add sugar, salt, and pepper. Mix well.
4. Beat egg whites until stiff peaks form.
5. Beat egg yolks for 2 minutes. Stir yolks into rutabaga mixture. Gently fold in egg whites.
6. Spoon into prepared casserole. Dot with butter. Sprinkle breadcrumbs over the top.
7. Bake 1 hour or until lightly browned.

SALMON-POTATO CASSEROLE (Laxlada)

Yield: 6 to 8 servings

A favorite dish from the first immigrants to the present time. The salmon has always been more or less a luxury item, but in this recipe a little goes a long way.

5 cups peeled and sliced potatoes	*½ cup minced onions*
½ pound salted salmon (can substitute lox)	*¼ teaspoon white pepper*
	1 ½ cups warm milk
4 tablespoons butter	

1. Preheat oven to 350 degrees.
2. Arrange ½ of potatoes evenly in bottom of a well-buttered 2-quart casserole.
3. Sprinkle onions evenly over potatoes. Add butter, cut in pieces, salmon, and pepper.
4. Add remaining potatoes in a top layer. Pour warm milk over top. Bake for 1¼ hours or until potatoes are tender.

VARIATION: Use canned salmon and add salt to taste.

FISH STEW (Kalamojakka)

Yield: 4 to 6 servings

Mojakka — made from meat or fish — is quintessentially ethnic, a Minnesota adaptation of Finnish stews. The origin of the word is unknown, but the food is recognizably Finnish.

2 cups water
3 cups chunked potatoes
1½ pounds lake trout, whitefish, or walleye, cut in 2- to 3-inch pieces
1 cup thinly sliced onions

1 teaspoon salt
½ teaspoon black pepper
1½ cups milk
2 tablespoons flour

1. Bring water to a boil. Add potatoes, cover, and cook over low heat until potatoes are not quite done.
2. Place pieces of fish on top of potatoes. Add onions and sprinkle salt and pepper over top. Simmer for 10 minutes.
3. Mix flour into milk so that there are no lumps. Add to stew and stir gently. Cover pan and simmer for 10 minutes.
4. Spoon into bowls. Can add a pat of butter or chopped parsley to garnish.

VARIATIONS: Use evaporated milk or cream. Substitute cod for other fish.

MEAT STEW (Lihamojakka)

6 servings

1¾ pounds beef shortribs
2 tablespoons lard or vegetable oil
4½ cups boiling water
1½ teaspoons salt
3 whole allspice

3 whole black peppercorns
1 cup chunked carrots
2 cups chunked rutabagas
1 cup chunked onions
3 cups chunked potatoes

1. Heat oil in large heavy pan. Brown shortribs a few at a time.
2. Add water, salt, allspice, and peppercorns. Cover pan and simmer 1 hour or until meat is tender.
3. Add carrots, rutabagas, and onions. Cover and simmer 15 minutes.
4. Add potatoes and cook ½ hour or until all vegetables are tender. Cooking liquid remains thin; serve stew in bowls.

VARIATION: Substitute 1 pound boneless stew meat for the traditional flavor of shortribs.

OVEN PANCAKE (Pannukakku) Yield: 4 to 6 servings

A versatile dish that can be eaten warm or cold and, depending on accompaniments, can be served for breakfast, lunch, supper, brunch, or dessert.

3 eggs
1 to 2 tablespoons sugar
1 ¾ cups lukewarm milk

¼ teaspoon salt
1 cup all-purpose flour, spooned into cup
¼ cup butter

1. Preheat oven to 425 degrees. Grease 9-by-13-inch pan well with vegetable shortening.
2. Beat eggs until thick and foamy. Add sugar and beat well.
3. Add milk and salt and beat until mixed.
4. Add flour gradually and beat until batter is smooth.
5. Put butter in greased pan and place in oven to melt.
6. Gradually add melted butter to flour mixture, stirring only until mixed.
7. Pour into pan and place in center of preheated oven.
8. Bake for 25 to 30 minutes. Pancake will rise around edges of pan and in certain places in the center. Parts will be custardy and others will be crisp.
9. Cut into individual portions. Serve warm with butter, jam, fruit sauce, or whipped cream and fruit.

VARIATIONS: For a more custardy pancake, increase milk to 2 cups or add 1 more egg. For a flatter pancake, reduce the flour.

RICE PUDDING (Riisipuuro)   Yield: 6 to 8 servings

A versatile element of Finnish foodways, riisipuuro is eaten plain as a dessert or as part of a light meal. Topped with fruit sauce, it becomes a Sunday or holiday treat.

1½ cups water	*2 cups milk*
1 cup long-grain rice	*1 teaspoon sugar*
½ teaspoon salt	*Fruit Sauce (see recipe)*

1. Bring water to a boil in a 2½- to 3-quart saucepan. Slowly add rice and salt. Cook covered until water is absorbed, about 15 minutes. Watch carefully to avoid sticking. Stir if necessary.
2. Remove from heat and stir in milk and sugar. Cover pan and cook over low heat until all milk is absorbed and rice is tender, about 35 to 40 minutes. Stir several times.
3. Serve lukewarm with cinnamon, sugar, and cream or butter or with fruit sauce.

FRUIT SAUCE (Kiisseli)   Yield: 6 to 8 servings

One of the most popular and traditional treatments of berries, which are the most available of all fruits in Finland. Rhubarb kiisseli appears to be a recent adaptation.

Rhubarb

1¾ cups water	*2 tablespoons cornstarch or potato flour*
1 cup sugar	*2 tablespoons cold water*
3 cups rhubarb, cut into ½-inch pieces	*¼ teaspoon ground cinnamon (optional)*

1. Bring water and sugar to a boil, stirring well. Add rhubarb. Cover pan and simmer for about 10 minutes or until tender.
2. Mix cornstarch and water together until smooth. Remove rhubarb from heat and stir in cornstarch mixture.
3. Return to heat and simmer gently for 2 minutes, stirring several times. Add cinnamon.
4. Serve at room temperature.

Strawberry

¾ cup sugar	1 quart cleaned strawberries
4 teaspoons cornstarch	2 teaspoons lemon juice
1⅓ cups water	

1. Combine sugar and cornstarch in 3-quart saucepan. Add water. Bring to a boil and add berries.
2. Cook over low heat for 10 minutes, stirring several times.
3. Add lemon juice and cook for 5 minutes over low heat, stirring occasionally.
4. Serve at room temperature alone or over rice pudding, pancakes, or other puddings.

VARIATIONS: Substitute other berries. Sweeten to taste.

AIR PUDDING (Ilmapuuro)   Yield: 10 generous servings

A good example of how technology encourages cooks to continue making traditional foods. Most Minnesota Finns, who whip ilmapuuro in mixers, remember how their mothers beat the pudding by hand.

3 cups water	1¼ cups sugar
2 cups cranberries	½ cup farina or regular Cream of Wheat

1. Cook cranberries in water over high heat only until berries pop. Strain through a sieve.
2. Return juice to pan and add sugar. Bring to a boil, stirring to dissolve sugar.
3. Slowly add farina, stirring to prevent any lumps. Cook for 15 minutes over low heat.
4. Remove mixture from heat and pour into large mixer bowl. Beat on high speed for about 20 minutes or until light colored and fluffy. Scrape sides and bottom of bowl with a spatula several times during beating.
5. Serve cold with cream, plain or whipped.

VARIATIONS: Use 4 cups canned cranberry juice and ¾ cup sugar, eliminate step 1. Or, use 4 cups raspberry, strawberry, or apple juice, ½ cup sugar, and 1 tablespoon lemon juice to heighten flavor. Can reduce amount of sugar to taste.

PRUNE TARTS (Joulutortut)   Yield: 32 to 34 tarts

A delicacy reserved for festive occasions, especially Christmas, because it requires time and skill to prepare. Frequently, one woman will bake a quantity of tarts and distribute them as gifts to friends and married children.

Pastry

3 cups all-purpose flour, spooned into cup
1 cup ice water
1 cup soft butter

Filling

1 pound pitted dried prunes
½ cup water
½ cup sugar
2 tablespoons lemon juice

1. Mix flour and ice water together into a solid ball. May need to add another tablespoon of ice water if flour does not form a firm ball.
2. Knead for about 5 minutes. The ball will become softer as the kneading proceeds. Pat into a circle 1-inch thick. Wrap well in plastic wrap. Refrigerate for 1 hour.
3. Cut prunes into small pieces, about ¼-inch square. Place in 1½-quart pan, add water and sugar, and stir until mixed.
4. Cook uncovered over medium or medium-low heat, stirring often so mixture does not stick. Adjust heat so that mixture cooks slowly, about 10 minutes or until the consistency of a thick jam. Add 2 tablespoons lemon juice. Set aside.
5. Cut chilled dough in half. Return 1 portion to refrigerator. Roll remainder into a ⅛-inch-thick square or rectangle on a lightly floured board. May need to turn dough over and add more flour to board for easier rolling.
6. Use ½ cup of softened butter for each piece of dough. Spread ¼ cup butter over rolled-out dough, right to edges (see illustration).
7. Fold dough in thirds — right side over center and left side over top (see illustration). Spread ¼ cup butter on top of folded dough.

8. Fold this strip of dough into thirds as above. Press down on dough lightly with palm of hand. Wrap loosely in foil or plastic wrap and refrigerate for about 1 hour. Repeat process with other half of dough.

9. Repeat the rolling procedure in steps 5 through 8 at least 2 more times; 3 times will produce an even puffier pastry. Use no additional butter.

10. Preheat oven to 375 degrees. Lightly grease baking sheet.

11. Roll 1 piece of dough out on a lightly floured board to about ⅛ inch thickness. Cut into 3-inch squares. Leftover pieces of dough can be pressed together into a ball and chilled again. Reroll this dough into squares when finished with the original 2 pieces.

12. Make a slit or slash in middle of each corner of each square, from the point into the center, about ¾ inch long, leaving an uncut area for filling (see illustration).

13. Place a rounded teaspoon of filling in center of square. Lift up ½ of each corner that has been slit. Be sure to lift from the same side of each corner in order to form a star or pinwheel (see illustration).

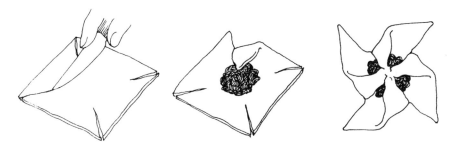

14. Pinch these 4 halves of corners together well, using a dab of water if necessary. They will come apart during baking if not well sealed.

15. Place on baking sheet and bake for 8 to 10 minutes or until lightly browned.

16. Remove from sheet right away and cool on racks.

VARIATIONS: Use dried apricots for filling, prepared the same way as the prunes. Substitute pie crust or frozen puff pastry for dough listed in recipe.

CARDAMOM BREAD (Pulla)   Yield: 2 loaves

Called "biscuit" by Finns in northern Minnesota, this sweet bread is perhaps the best-known item in Finnish–American foodways. It is eaten throughout the year and can be baked in fancy forms or served with special decoration at Christmastime.

1 package dry yeast
¼ cup water (105 to 115 degrees)
1 cup lukewarm milk
½ cup sugar
1 teaspoon salt
1 teaspoon crushed cardamom seeds (may
  prefer less if cardamom is very fresh)

2 eggs, slightly beaten
3¼ to 3¾ cups all-purpose flour,
  spooned into cup
¼ cup melted butter
Glaze (see below)

1. Dissolve yeast in warm water and set aside for 5 minutes.
2. In large bowl, combine milk, sugar, salt, cardamom, eggs, and 1 cup flour. Add dissolved yeast and stir until batter is smooth.
3. Add melted butter and stir well. Work in 2 cups of remaining flour, stirring to mix. Add flour until dough is stiff enough to knead.
4. Place dough on lightly floured board. Cover with bowl and allow to rest for 15 minutes.
5. Knead dough about 5 minutes, adding flour only if dough sticks. Return to greased bowl and let rise until double in bulk. Punch down and divide in half.
6. Divide each half into 3 parts and roll each out into a rope 16 to 20 inches long. Braid together 3 strips, working out from middle of braid, and turn ends under (see illustration).

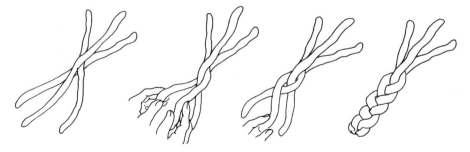

7. Let rise until double in bulk, about 30 minutes.
8. Brush with glaze. Place on baking sheet. Bake at 350 degrees for 30 minutes. Check after 20 minutes and if loaf is browning too fast, lightly cover with aluminum foil.
9. Remove from baking sheet and cool on rack.

Glaze

1 egg beaten with 1 tablespoon milk
⅓ cup chopped or sliced almonds
⅓ cup crushed lump sugar

Brush bread with egg mixture. Sprinkle almonds and sugar over the surface.

VARIATION: Brush top of loaf with melted butter before baking. After baking brush top with following mixture: 2 tablespoons hot coffee, 2 tablespoons melted butter, 2 tablespoons sugar. Follow with a generous sprinkling of coarse sugar and sliced almonds.

THE GREEKS

LENTIL SOUP (Faki)
Yield: 6 to 8 servings

Soups are an important part of the Greek diet throughout the year; during the Lenten season, when meat is generally not eaten, faki is a popular dish.

1 pound dried lentils
2 quarts chicken broth or water
1 cup chopped celery
1 cup chopped carrots
2 cloves garlic, minced
1½ cups chopped onions

1 can (4 ounces) tomato sauce
¼ to ⅓ cup olive oil
1 teaspoon dried oregano, crumbled with
  fingers
Salt and black pepper to taste
¼ cup cider or red wine vinegar

1. Wash lentils well. Drain and place in a 4- to 5-quart kettle. Add the 2 quarts of liquid and allow to soak at least 1 hour (no longer if chicken broth is used).
2. Bring to a boil, skim off any residue, and add celery, carrots, garlic, onions, tomato sauce, olive oil, and oregano. Add salt and pepper to taste. Simmer covered for 1½ hours or until lentils are tender.
3. Add vinegar the last ½ hour of cooking and adjust seasonings.
4. Soup improves in flavor if made the day before and refrigerated overnight. Can also be frozen for later use.

VARIATIONS: Add a large can of stewed tomatoes. Include other seasonings, such as mint, basil, or parsley.

CHICKEN-RICE SOUP WITH LEMON
(Soupa Avgolemono)
Yield: 6 servings

This soup is served frequently for lunch with bread and fruit or as a first course at dinnertime. Although some cooks embroider on this basic recipe, the lemon and chicken broth are constant ingredients.

8 cups chicken broth	*⅓ cup lemon juice*
½ cup uncooked long-grain rice	*Salt and black pepper to taste*
3 eggs	

1. In large heavy pan, bring broth to boil. Stir in rice and continue stirring until liquid comes to a boil again. Reduce heat, cover, and simmer until rice is just barely tender, about 30 minutes. Remove from heat.
2. Beat eggs for 2 minutes. Continue beating eggs and slowly add 1½ cups hot broth and lemon juice.
3. Stir broth-egg mixture slowly into pan of broth, using a whisk. Continue to stir for about 2 minutes. Mixture will not be thick but will be creamy in appearance with some froth on top. Add salt and pepper to taste.
4. Soup may be kept warm over low heat. Do not boil or soup will curdle.

VARIATIONS: For a thicker soup add 2 tablespoons flour or cornstarch to egg mixture while beating. Can add diced chicken, onions, carrots, or celery. Or, use orzo, noodles, or vermicelli instead of rice; starch from the pasta will make a thicker soup. Leftovers can be reheated in a double boiler or, with caution, over low heat in a heavy pan.

VILLAGE SALAD (Salata)   Yield: 6 to 8 servings

Typical of summer fare, this salad is full of garden-fresh ingredients combined with the popular feta cheese. During the winter months salads consist more of cooked and marinated vegetables.

4 to 5 ripe tomatoes	*Greek olives (number to suit taste)*
1 clove garlic, minced	*⅓ pound feta cheese, crumbled*
1 large cucumber, peeled and sliced	*Salt and black pepper to taste*
2 firm green peppers, sliced into thin rounds	*1 teaspoon dried oregano, crumbled with fingers*
3 to 4 sliced green onions, including tops	*Salad Dressing (see below)*

1. Wash and prepare all vegetables. Toss together in salad bowl with olives, feta cheese, salt, pepper, and oregano.
2. Shake dressing well, pour desired amount over ingredients, and toss well.

VARIATIONS: Add spinach, lettuce, or other greens to extend the number of servings. Or, add artichoke hearts, avocado, radishes, and zucchini as desired.

Salad Dressing

½ cup olive oil
¼ cup lemon juice
1 teaspoon salt
½ teaspoon black pepper

2 teaspoons chopped fresh parsley or 1
  teaspoon dried parsley
1 teaspoon dried, crushed basil

Mix all ingredients in a covered jar and allow flavors to blend for 6 to 8 hours. Shake well before using.

HERBED VEGETABLE CASSEROLE (Briami)
Yield: 6 to 8 servings

A classic dish designed to use whatever vegetables and herbs were ready to be picked in the garden. Cooks today freely make substitutions in this recipe.

1 medium eggplant
1 tablespoon vinegar
2 medium potatoes
2 medium zucchini
1 can (16 ounces) tomatoes, stewed or
  whole tomatoes cut in quarters (or fresh
  sliced tomatoes)
2 medium onions, chopped
1 teaspoon dried parsley

1 teaspoon dried oregano, crumbled with
  fingers
¼ teaspoon dried mint
2 cloves garlic, minced
¼ cup olive oil
Pinch of cinnamon
Salt and black pepper to taste
⅓ cup grated Parmesan cheese (optional)

1. Butter well a 3-quart casserole or a 9-by-13-inch dish or pan.
2. Cut eggplant into ½-inch squares. Soak ½ hour in bowl of lightly salted water to which 1 tablespoon vinegar has been added.
3. Cut potatoes and zucchini into ¼-inch slices or pieces. Place all vegetables in large bowl. Preheat oven to 325 degrees.
4. Drain eggplant, rinse well, pat dry with paper towels, and add to bowl. Stir in parsley, oregano, mint, garlic, olive oil, cinnamon, salt, and pepper. Spoon everything into prepared baking dish and bake uncovered for 2 hours. Grated Parmesan cheese can be added the last ½ hour.

VARIATION: To shorten cooking time by ½ hour, cover casserole tightly the first ½ hour.

ARTICHOKE PILAF (Anginares Pilafi)   Yield: 8 servings

Rice (pilafi) dishes abound in Greek menus, reflecting the influence of the Middle East. In this dish, artichokes heighten the flavors of a favorite food.

3 tablespoons olive oil
1½ cups chopped onions
2 cloves garlic, chopped or minced
1 package (10 ounces) frozen artichokes, thawed
¾ cup uncooked white converted rice
1 can (8 ounces) tomato sauce

1 can (15 ounces) chicken broth (or 1 bouillon cube and 15 ounces water)
⅓ cup water
¼ teaspoon salt (may need more depending on saltiness of chicken bouillon or broth)
½ teaspoon black pepper
2 teaspoons dried dillweed

1. Butter a 2½- to 3-quart casserole.
2. Heat olive oil in heavy skillet over moderate heat. Stir in onions and garlic. Cook until onion is golden, stirring occasionally. Preheat oven to 325 degrees.
3. In large bowl, combine artichokes, rice, tomato sauce, chicken broth, water, salt, pepper, and dillweed. Add sauteed onions and garlic. Mix well and pour into prepared casserole.
4. Bake, covered, for 20 minutes. Remove from oven and stir ingredients to mix well to ensure that rice will cook evenly. Cover casserole and return to oven for 45 minutes more or until rice is tender. Check once more during cooking time to be sure mixture is not too dry. Can add another ¼ cup water if necessary. Mix well.

VARIATIONS: To enhance flavor, brown rice in olive oil as onions and garlic are cooking. Or, try one of the following: sprinkle ½ cup Cheddar or Parmesan cheese on top of casserole the last 5 minutes of cooking; place a spoonful of yoghurt on top of each serving; substitute 10-ounce package of spinach, thawed, for artichokes; substitute mint or oregano for dillweed.

SPINACH PIE (Spanakopita)

Yield: 60 appetizers or
10 to 12 main-dish servings

Greeks serve this combination of phyllo, spinach, and feta cheese hot or cold, as an appetizer, for a main course, or as a side dish with lamb or other meat.

½ pounds fresh spinach
¼ cup olive oil
1 cup finely chopped onions
½ cup chopped fresh parsley
1 tablespoon dried dillweed
¼ teaspoon crushed mint

½ teaspoon black pepper
½ pound feta cheese, crumbled
3 eggs, slightly beaten
1 cup melted butter
12 phyllo sheets

1. Wash spinach and dry well with paper towels. Chop coarsely. Heat 1 tablespoon oil in heavy pan over moderate heat. Add spinach and stir for 2 or 3 minutes until spinach has lost some of its water. Remove from pan and drain on paper towels.
2. Heat remaining oil in pan, add onions, and saute until translucent.
3. In large bowl, combine onions, spinach, parsley, dillweed, mint, pepper, cheese, and eggs. Set aside.
4. Butter well a 9-by-13-inch baking pan. Read over "Tips for Using Phyllo." Remove 12 sheets from package and cut them to fit pan. Cover with plastic wrap. Preheat oven to 350 degrees.
5. Place 1 sheet of phyllo on bottom of pan. Brush with melted butter. Repeat with 5 more sheets. Spread spinach mixture on top.
6. Place 1 of remaining sheets of phyllo on top of spinach. Brush with butter. Repeat with remaining 5 sheets.
7. Use a large knife and cut the spanakopita into small squares for appetizers, or large squares if using for main course. Cut all the way through to bottom of pan. Sprinkle top of pie with about 2 teaspoons water.
8. Bake for 35 to 40 minutes or until golden brown.

VARIATIONS: Wash spinach well, drain, wrap in towels, and let stand unrefrigerated overnight. The next day chop spinach and proceed with step 2. Sprinkle 2 tablespoons uncooked rice over top of the first 6 sheets of buttered phyllo. This absorbs the extra moisture from the spinach and also adds another favorite ingredient to the dish. Then add the spinach mixture and proceed with rest of recipe.

Substitute 2 packages of frozen spinach for the fresh. Thaw, drain well in a sieve or colander, and pat with paper towels.

Add 4 ounces softened cream cheese to onion-spinach mixture. Add a dash of cinnamon.

Can be frozen after step 7. Add 15 minutes to baking time. Check to see that it is not browning too much — lower temperature to 325 degrees or cover lightly with aluminum foil. Brush top with 2 additional tablespoons melted butter.

TIPS FOR USING PHYLLO (sometimes called filo)

Phyllo, from the Greek word for "leaves," is a thin sheet of dough used in a great variety of recipes for appetizers, vegetable dishes, main course meats and poultry, and desserts. It is sold in 1-pound boxes in the frozen-food sections of most grocery stores. The 22 to 24 sheets in each package usually measure about 11 by 17 inches. They can be used in a pan of that size, trimmed to fit other pans, or cut in strips for making appetizers. Use a sharp knife or scissors to cut the sheets to the proper size.

1. If the thin sheets are stuck together and do not come apart easily, then you have an old box of phyllo or one that has been thawed and refrozen. It would be wise to return the box for another because you will only have problems constructing your recipe. An unopened box of frozen phyllo keeps in the freezer for about 6 months. After opening, any unused leaves can be stored in an airtight wrap for 10 days, or as the package directs. It can also be refrozen, wrapped well; however, the sheets may stick together slightly when thawed a second time.
2. The best way to defrost the package is to store it in the refrigerator for 1 to 2 days and then warm it at room temperature for at least 2 hours before using. Some microwave oven cookbooks give instructions for thawing phyllo quickly.
3. When you are ready to use the dough, open the package and unfold the sheets. Lay them on a sheet of plastic wrap on a flat surface. Cover them with a slightly damp towel as they dry out very quickly. As you use a sheet in preparing the dish, be sure to recover the others with the towel.
4. A small brush, similar to a small paint brush, can be purchased in cooking sections of stores. This is handy for brushing on melted butter, although many cooks use their fingers.

MARINATED SPICED MEATBALLS (Keftedakia Marinata)

Yield: about 60 small meatballs

Offered with wine or drinks as appetizers or as a first course. Today some cooks make the meatballs a little larger and serve them as part of a holiday meal with other meats.

1 pound lean ground beef, lamb, or pork
2 tablespoons dried parsley
½ teaspoon dried dillweed
½ teaspoon dried mint
1 teaspoon dried oregano, crumbled with fingers
¼ teaspoon ground cinnamon
½ cup finely diced onions

2 cloves garlic, minced or chopped fine
Salt and black pepper to taste
2 slices bread (crusts removed), soaked in water
Whole-wheat flour
Vegetable or olive oil
2 cups Tomato Sauce (see below)

1. In large bowl, mix meat, parsley, dillweed, mint, oregano, cinnamon, onions, garlic, salt, and pepper. Squeeze water from bread and add. Mix all ingredients lightly together.
2. Flavors will blend better if mixture is covered tightly and refrigerated for several hours or overnight.
3. Heat oil in heavy frying pan over moderate heat. Roll meat mixture into balls no larger than a walnut. Spoon some flour on waxed paper or plastic wrap and coat each meatball before placing in heated oil.
4. Fry meatballs until browned on all sides. Do not crowd pan. As meatballs brown, remove and drain on paper towels.
5. In a bowl or saucepan combine meatballs and hot tomato sauce. Cool to blend flavors.
6. Can be served cold or reheated.

Tomato Sauce

Yield: approximately 3 cups

3 tablespoons olive oil
1 cup chopped onions
2 cloves garlic, minced or chopped
2 pounds fresh tomatoes or 2 cans (28 ounces each) whole tomatoes, chopped
1 teaspoon sugar

¼ cup red wine
Salt and black pepper to taste
Cinnamon stick (optional)
2 tablespoons dried parsley or ¼ cup chopped fresh parsley
½ teaspoon dried basil

1. Heat oil in heavy pan, using moderate heat. Add onions and garlic and saute until onion is translucent.
2. Add tomatoes and juice, sugar, wine, salt, pepper, cinnamon stick, parsley, and basil. Cover and simmer for 30 minutes.
3. Taste and adjust seasonings. Simmer 15 minutes more. Remove cinnamon stick.

NOTE: Can also be spooned over fish or chicken.

BAKED FISH (Psari Plaki)   Yield: 6 to 8 servings

Fish is plentiful in almost all parts of Greece, and this recipe adapts to whatever is the day's catch.

3 pounds fish steaks or fillets (any fish in season or frozen fish)
¼ to ⅓ cup lemon juice
1 clove garlic, minced
½ cup olive oil
1½ cups chopped onions
¼ cup chopped celery
¼ cup chopped carrots
¼ cup chopped spinach

1 clove garlic, minced
1 can (16 ounces) stewed tomatoes or 4 or 5 fresh tomatoes, cut in quarters
1 can (8 ounces) tomato sauce
2 tablespoons chopped fresh dillweed or 1 teaspoon dried dillweed (optional)
Salt and black pepper to taste
¼ cup chopped fresh parsley

1. Clean, wash, and pat fish dry. Place in buttered baking dish with 3-inch sides. Pour lemon juice evenly over fish. Sprinkle 1 clove minced garlic over fish. Cover with plastic wrap and set aside for 1 hour.
2. Heat olive oil in heavy skillet over moderate heat. Add onions, celery, carrots, spinach, and remaining garlic. Stir and cook until onion is lightly browned.
3. Add tomatoes and tomato sauce. Bring to a boil over high heat, reduce heat, and simmer for 20 minutes. Add dillweed, salt, and pepper to taste.
4. May need to add a little water if sauce has become too thick. Preheat oven to 350 degrees.
5. Drain marinade from fish. Pour sauce over fish. Sprinkle parsley over top. Bake for 40 to 50 minutes or until fish is fork tender.

MOUSSAKA   Yield: 8 to 10 servings

Although the origins of this dish are in the Middle East, it is often prepared in Greek kitchens. Moussaka was designed to use whatever was fresh in the garden — for example, eggplant, potatoes, or zucchini, or potatoes combined with zucchini and tomatoes.

2½ to 3 pounds zucchini	*4 tablespoons dried parsley*
3 tablespoons olive or vegetable oil	*2 tablespoons dried basil*
Salt and black pepper	*Meat Sauce (see below)*
½ cup dried breadcrumbs	*White Sauce (see below)*

1. Butter well a 9-by-13-inch pan. Preheat oven to 350 degrees. Make meat and white sauces.
2. Wash zucchini, cut off both ends, and slice in ⅓-inch circles.
3. Heat oil in heavy 10- to 12-inch frying pan. Using moderate heat lightly brown zucchini on both sides. Drain on paper towels and season to taste with salt and pepper.
4. Sprinkle breadcrumbs over bottom of prepared pan. Layer ½ of zucchini on top. Sprinkle with ½ of parsley and ½ of basil.
5. Spread meat sauce over zucchini layer. Layer rest of zucchini over sauce. Sprinkle with remaining parsley and basil. Pour white sauce over these layers. (May refrigerate dish, well wrapped with plastic, for later baking.)
6. Bake for 40 to 50 minutes or until lightly browned and steaming. Remove from oven and allow to stand about 10 minutes before cutting into squares.

Meat Sauce

2 tablespoons butter	*2 tablespoons tomato paste*
2 tablespoons olive oil	*½ teaspoon sugar*
1½ cups chopped onions	*1 stick cinnamon*
1 pound ground lamb, veal, beef, or any combination of these meats	*½ bay leaf, crushed*
	½ teaspoon salt
2 cloves garlic, minced	*¼ teaspoon black pepper*
½ cup dry red wine	*4 tablespoons chopped fresh parsley*
1 can (28 ounces) tomatoes, chopped and drained	*½ teaspoon dried basil*
	2 egg whites, beaten until foamy

1. Heat butter and oil in heavy pan and saute onions for 5 minutes over moderate heat. Add meat and break apart into small pieces. Cook until raw color disappears.
2. Add garlic, wine, tomatoes, tomato paste, sugar, cinnamon, bay leaf, salt, pepper, parsley, and basil. Cover and simmer over low heat for 35 minutes. Taste and adjust seasonings if necessary. Cook uncovered for a few minutes if sauce is not thick. Remove cinnamon stick.
3. Fold in egg whites and set aside for later use.

White Sauce

4 tablespoons butter
4 tablespoons all-purpose flour
2 cups warm milk or chicken broth
½ cup ricotta cheese (or ¼ cup ricotta and ¼ cup Parmesan cheese)

2 egg yolks
Salt and black pepper to taste
¼ teaspoon ground nutmeg
¼ teaspoon ground cinnamon

1. Melt butter in heavy pan over moderate heat. Using a whisk, add flour and cook for 2 minutes.
2. Remove pan from heat and gradually stir in warm liquid. Return pan to heat and bring to a boil, stirring constantly. Gently simmer for 1 minute.
3. Remove from heat and add cheese, egg yolks, salt, pepper, nutmeg, and cinnamon. Taste and adjust seasonings. Should be made just before assembling moussaka.

VARIATION: Substitute eggplant for zucchini as follows: Cut off ends of 3 medium eggplants. Peel lengthwise in ½-inch strips, leaving ½-inch stripes of skin. Cut eggplant into circles, ½ inch thick. Sprinkle with salt and set aside on paper towels while preparing other ingredients. Rinse well and press very dry with paper towels. Follow recipe for sauteing zucchini.

STEW WITH ONIONS (Stifado)

Yield: 8 to 10 servings

A specific type of stew that can be made with beef, veal, lamb, rabbit, or even fish. Distinctive ingredients are little onions, vinegar, and the spices.

3 pounds lean beef from chuck or blade
4 tablespoons olive oil
1 can (6 ounces) tomato paste 1 can (4 ounces) tomato sauce
3 cloves garlic, minced
3 teaspoons crushed or ground pickling spices
2 bay leaves (optional)
¼ cup vinegar or 2 tablespoons vinegar and ¼ cup red wine

1 tablespoon packed brown sugar
2 to 3 pounds small white onions or equivalent amount of canned onions
1 can (16 ounces) tomato wedges or stewed tomatoes
Salt and black pepper to taste
1 package (10 ounces) frozen flat green beans (sometimes called Italian beans) (optional)

1. Cut beef into 1½- to 2-inch cubes and pat with paper towels so that surface is dry. Heat oil in large 4- to 5-quart kettle over moderate heat. Add meat in small amounts so that it will brown well on all sides. Well-browned meat will add to flavor of stew.
2. When all meat has been browned and removed from pan, drain off excess oil and return meat to pan. Add tomato paste, tomato sauce, garlic, pickling spices, bay leaves, vinegar, brown sugar, onions (if using raw onions), and tomatoes. Add salt and pepper to taste.
3. Cover pan tightly and simmer on top of stove or in a 300 degree oven for 2 hours or until meat is tender. If you use green beans and canned onions add them the last ½ hour of cooking. Taste and adjust seasonings when adding these vegetables.
4. Sauce around meat and onions may be a little thin. If so, reduce it by draining liquid away from meat into another saucepan and boiling it for a few minutes. Return to stew, remove bay leaves, and serve.

VARIATIONS: Add quartered potatoes, carrots, or celery during last ½ hour.

NOTE: To keep raw onions whole during cooking, peel and then cut a cross in bottom of onion.

LEMON CHICKEN (Kotolemono)   Yield: 4 to 5 servings

Lemons, a plentiful crop in Greece, are commonly used in soups, entrees, and desserts. This traditional dish combines the flavors of lemon and oregano with chicken, another popular ingredient.

3 to 4 pounds chicken pieces
¼ cup lemon juice
¼ cup melted butter or margarine
2 teaspoons dried oregano, crumbled with
  fingers

Salt and black pepper to taste
½ cup water or white wine
1 to 1½ pounds peeled and chunked
  potatoes

1. Wash chicken and pat dry. Butter well a 9-by-13-inch baking pan. Add chicken, skin side down.
2. Pour lemon juice over chicken pieces. Gradually pour butter over each piece. Sprinkle with salt and pepper. Crush oregano evenly over chicken.
3. Preheat oven to 350 degrees. Add water or wine to pan and bake chicken for 1 hour. Turn pieces once during cooking.
4. Add potatoes and baste with pan juices. Sprinkle with salt and pepper. Return to oven and bake another 30 to 40 minutes or until potatoes are tender.
5. Remove pan from oven. If potatoes are not nicely browned, turn up oven temperature to 400 degrees. Place chicken pieces on a platter and cover with foil and return potatoes to oven for a few minutes to brown. Baste with pan juices. If juices have evaporated, add a little more liquid.
6. Arrange browned potatoes around chicken and serve.

BAKLAVA

Yield: 40 to 50 diamond-shaped pieces

A good example of interethnic borrowing, this layered delicacy probably originated centuries ago in the Near East.

1 package (1 pound) phyllo pastry
2½ cups butter
3 cups coarsely chopped walnuts
½ cup sugar

1½ teaspoons ground cloves
1½ teaspoons ground cinnamon
Syrup (see below)
Whole cloves

1. See "Tips for Using Phyllo." Remove phyllo from refrigerator and allow to warm to room temperature for 1 hour before using.
2. Clarify butter by heating over moderate heat until melted. Skim off foam (can be used to season vegetables). Pour off clear butter to use for this dish (remainder can be used in soups and sauces). Amount of milky residue in melted butter varies so may have to clarify more later to brush each layer of phyllo adequately.
3. Combine walnuts, sugar, and spices in small bowl and mix well.
4. Cut phyllo sheets to fit a 9-by-13-inch pan or use a larger pan appoximately size of phyllo sheets. Butter pan well.
5. Lay sheet of phyllo on bottom of pan and brush with butter. Repeat 8 times. Put aside 8 sheets to use in step 7 for top layers. Cover with damp towel.
6. Scoop up handful of nut-spice mixture and sprinkle over top sheet in pan. Lay on 3 more sheets, buttering each. Continue this procedure until all sheets and nut-sugar mixture are used.
7. Place 8 reserved sheets of phyllo on top, brushing each with butter as was done in step 5. Preheat oven to 350 degrees.
8. With sharp knife cut baklava into diamond shapes (see illustration). Cut all the way through to bottom of pan. Pierce center of each diamond with 1 whole clove.

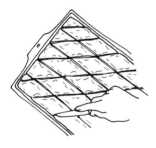

9. Sprinkle top of baklava with about 2 teaspoons water to help keep top and bottom layers from separating.

10. Bake for 1 hour, 15 minutes or until golden brown. Make syrup while baklava is baking.
11. Remove from oven. Pour syrup evenly over baklava. Allow to cool and mellow for at least 10 to 12 hours before serving. Store covered in a cool place. Do not refrigerate, or it will become soggy. Keeps for 3 to 4 days.

VARIATIONS: Substitute almonds or pecans for walnuts. Or, increase amount of nuts as desired.

Syrup

1½ cups water
⅓ cup sugar
1¼ cups honey

1 cinnamon stick
¼ cup lemon juice
Zest from 1 lemon

1. Combine all ingredients in saucepan. Bring to a boil, reduce heat, and simmer for 10 minutes.
2. Remove cinnamon stick. Set syrup aside to cool.

VARIATION: Adjust amounts of lemon juice and flavorings in syrup.

KOURABIEDES

Yield: 40 to 50 cookies

These delicacies are often called Greek wedding cakes since they are served at such celebrations. They are a favorite cookie to sell at bazaars and festivals, usually individually placed in white cupcake papers.

1 cup butter, at room temperature
⅓ cup sifted powdered sugar
1 egg yolk
1 ounce whisky or brandy
2 teaspoons fresh lemon juice

⅓ cup finely chopped walnuts, almonds,
  or pecans
2½ to 2¾ cups all-purpose flour,
  spooned into cup
½ teaspoon baking powder
Powdered sugar

1. Using a mixer, beat butter for at least 20 minutes or until very light in color and fluffy. Gradually add sugar and egg yolk.
2. Mix in whisky, lemon juice, and nuts.
3. Sift 2½ cups flour with baking powder. Gradually add flour by the spoonful to ingredients in mixer bowl. Mix well. Dough will have to be beaten by hand after part of flour has been added.
4. After adding 2½ cups of flour, break off a small ball of dough. If it holds together well, it is not necessary to add more flour. Knead for a few minutes in the bowl to mix ingredients thoroughly. Preheat oven to 350 degrees.
5. Form dough into small balls, 1¼ to 1½ inches. Flatten balls slightly or shape into a crescent about ½ inch thick or larger depending on individual tastes.
6. Place on baking sheet about 1 inch apart. On rack in center of oven, bake 15 to 20 minutes or until lightly golden. May need to turn baking sheet halfway around after 10 minutes for even baking.
7. Sift a light layer of powdered sugar on a sheet of waxed paper or plastic wrap. Remove cookies from oven and place each on sugared paper. Sift a thick layer of powdered sugar over top and allow to cool completely.
8. Store in airtight containers in a cool place. Will keep for up to 2 weeks. May also be frozen. May freeze cookies before adding powdered sugar and then dredge thawed cookies in sugar.

ST. BASIL'S BREAD (Vasilopita)   Yield: 2 round loaves

This bread, which has a coin hidden somewhere in it, is baked to celebrate St. Basil's Day on January 1.

2 packages dry yeast
2 cups milk (105 to 115 degrees)
½ cup plus 1 tablespoon sugar
7 to 7½ cups sifted all-purpose flour
¼ cup melted butter
1 teaspoon salt

5 eggs, slightly beaten
Grated rind of 1 large orange
Sesame seeds (optional)
Penny or dime wrapped in waxed paper
1 egg, slightly beaten

1. Dissolve yeast and 1 tablespoon sugar in ½ cup warm milk. Set aside.
2. Measure 7 cups of sifted flour into large bowl. Make a well in center of flour and add butter, salt, 5 eggs, orange rind, remaining sugar, warm milk, and milk-yeast mixture. Stir, gradually working flour into liquid.
3. If mixture seems sticky, add more flour. When dough forms a ball firm enough to knead, turn out on lightly floured board and knead for 15 minutes or until smooth and elastic.
4. Butter large bowl well. Place dough in bowl and grease top well. Cover and allow to rise in warm place until double in bulk, about 1½ hours.
5. Punch dough down well and divide in half. Knead each piece for about 2 minutes to eliminate any air pockets. Form into round loaves. Insert coin in bottom of 1 loaf. Butter 2 9-inch round pans well. Place loaves in pans and cover lightly. Allow to rise until double in bulk, about 1 hour.
6. Preheat oven to 400 degrees. With pastry brush spread beaten egg over loaves. Sprinkle lightly with sesame seeds.
7. Bake for 10 minutes. Reduce oven temperature to 350 degrees and bake for 30 to 40 minutes or until a deep golden color. Remove from pans and cool on racks.

THE ITALIANS

ITALIAN BREAD   Yield: 1 long or 2 short loaves

A versatile recipe, also used for pizza or pie crust. Traditionally baked outdoors in stone ovens, a practice continued in Minnesota at least until the Great Depression.

1 package dry yeast
¼ cup water (105 to 115 degrees)
2 teaspoons salt
1 teaspoon sugar

1 cup warm water
3 tablespoons melted shortening or lard
4¼ to 4¾ cups all-purpose flour,
*   spooned into cup*

1. Dissolve yeast in ¼ cup water. Stir well and allow to stand.
2. In large bowl combine salt, sugar, warm water, and melted shortening. Stir in dissolved yeast.
3. Stir in 4 cups flour, 1 cup at a time. Continue to add flour slowly until dough holds together and can be turned out on lightly floured board.
4. Knead until smooth and elastic, working in additional flour as needed to eliminate stickiness.
5. Let rise in warm place (80 to 85 degrees) until double in bulk, about 1½ hours. Punch down and allow to rise a second time, about 1 hour.
6. Shape into a long narrow loaf on greased baking sheet. Make several slashes with sharp knife in top of loaf about 3 inches long and ⅓ inch deep. Allow to rise about 50 minutes.
7. Bake at 350 degrees for 30 to 40 minutes or until nicely browned.

VARIATIONS: Form dough into 2 loaves and bake in greased bread pans. Can also brush a wash over bread before baking it, using ¼ cup cold water and 1 egg beaten well together, or can brush bread with butter when it is removed from oven.

ORANGE SALAD

Yield: 4 to 6 servings

Oranges are a popular part of Italian and Italian-American foodways. The rind flavors several desserts, and the fruit is traditionally given at Christmas. Oranges are a common dessert as well as a salad ingredient.

4 oranges, peeled and sliced ¼-inch thick
1 teaspoon black pepper

¼ cup olive oil
Lettuce

1. Place orange slices in medium-sized bowl.
2. Sprinkle with pepper and oil. Cover.
3. Refrigerate until time to serve. Arrange on a bed of lettuce.

VARIATIONS: Add salt. Can add ½ cup sliced radishes and ½ cup sliced cucumber. Or, dice oranges, radishes, and cucumber instead of slicing them.

PASTA PRIMAVERA

Yield: 4 to 6 servings

"Primavera" means "spring," and although produce in Minnesota matures much later in the season, this dish is always made with fresh vegetables.

8 ounces pasta (spaghetti or shells or
elbow macaroni)
2 cups broccoli, cut in flowerets and 1-
inch stem pieces
1 cup tomatoes, cut in bite-sized pieces
and drained
½ cup chopped parsley

2 cloves garlic, chopped
½ teaspoon salt
¼ teaspoon black pepper
½ cup plus 2 tablespoons mayonnaise, at
room temperature
1½ tablespoons red wine vinegar
Romano or Parmesan cheese (optional)

1. Cook pasta in usual manner and drain well.
2. Steam broccoli until nearly tender. Add tomato pieces and just heat through over steam. Drain.
3. Pulverize parsley and garlic in a blender or food processor.
4. In small bowl, combine parsley-garlic mixture, salt, pepper, mayonnaise, and vinegar. Stir to mix well.
5. Place pasta in serving bowl. Stir in mayonnaise mixture. Gently stir in drained vegetables. Romano or Parmesan cheese can be sprinkled on top. Chill and serve cold.

PEPERONATA

Yield: 4 servings

Some families substitute zucchini for the eggplant in this common side dish. Peperonata is served with lunch or dinner or as a snack; many enjoy dipping thick slices of bread into the liquid.

2 tablespoons butter
3 tablespoons olive oil
2 cups sliced onions
2 cups eggplant, cut in ½-by-1-inch pieces
2 cups green or red pepper (or a combination), cut in ½-by-1½-inch strips

1 ½ cups peeled, seeded, coarsely chopped fresh tomatoes
1 tablespoon red wine vinegar
¼ teaspoon salt
½ teaspoon freshly ground black pepper
¼ teaspoon garlic powder

1. Heat butter and olive oil in a 10- to 12-inch frying pan over moderate heat.
2. Add onions and saute until soft and slightly browned, about 10 minutes.
3. Add eggplant and peppers. Cover and cook 10 minutes.
4. Add tomatoes, vinegar, salt, pepper, and garlic powder. Cook for 20 minutes, using low heat so mixture steams gently. Stir once.
5. Uncover and turn heat to medium high. Cook and stir for a few minutes more until liquid in pan is reduced by half.
6. Serve hot.

VARIATION: Use coarsely chopped canned tomatoes in place of the fresh; use only ¼ cup of the liquid in the can of tomatoes. Chill and serve as an antipasto.

NOTE: Recipe can be doubled.

EASTER PIE

Yield: 12 servings

Ingredients used in the many possible variations of this recipe — fresh cheese ("basket," "hoop," or farmer's), eggs, and sprouted wheat berries in the crust — all evoke the Easter and springtime themes of new life or rebirth. This version clearly shows American influence in the choice of ingredients.

Italian Bread (see recipe)
1 pound Italian sausage, in bulk or with
    casings removed
1 pound Cheddar or Velveeta cheese, cut
    in ½-inch cubes

1 pound Monterey Jack cheese, cut in ½-
    inch cubes
8 eggs, slightly beaten

1. Prepare bread recipe. Allow to rise only once. Punch dough down. Grease a 9-by-13-inch pan well.
2. Other ingredients can be prepared while dough is rising. Over moderate heat fry Italian sausage, breaking meat into small pieces. Cook until it has lost all red color but is not crisp. Prepare cheeses. Drain meat well and mix with cheese cubes.
3. After punching down dough, divide in half. On floured surface roll out ½ into rectangle about 18 by 14 inches and ¼ inch thick. This is the bottom crust. Pat it into pan, using fingers to work the dough up and over sides. Do not trim until after filling is added.
4. Add cheese-meat filling, patting pieces into place so it is even. Pour eggs over filling.
5. On floured surface, roll out other ½ dough for top crust into a rectangle about 9 by 13 inches. Trim away any extra dough. Lay on top of filling. Trim bottom crust within 1 inch of top of pan, allowing some dough to turn over. Crimp both edges as you would a regular pastry crust.
6. Preheat oven to 375 degrees. Bake for 45 to 50 minutes or until golden brown.

VARIATIONS: Make a quick crust as follows: Use 4 cups of Bisquick and double the recipe for waffles on the package. Pour ½ of batter into a greased 9-by-13-inch pan, add sausage, cheeses, and eggs. Pour remaining batter on top. Bake at 400 degrees for 25 minutes; lower heat to 350 degrees and bake 30 minutes or until lightly browned. Or, omit top crust. Bake at 350 degrees for 45 minutes or until surface is golden and cheeses are melted and bubbling.

Substitute thinly sliced pepperoni for sausage. For more traditional taste, use mozzarella cheese instead of Monterey Jack and experiment by substituting some Romano cheese for Velveeta or Cheddar.

MEATBALL STEW (Ciambotta)   Yield: 8 servings

Hearty, everyday fare that traditionally used garden produce — canned or preserved for cooking out of season.

Meatballs (see recipe)
Pan drippings from meatball preparation
2 cups onions, cut in ¾- to 1-inch pieces
1½ cups carrots, cut in ¾- to 1-inch pieces
3 cups potatoes, cut in 1-inch cubes
1 can (28 ounces) stewed tomatoes
1 can (28 ounces) water

¼ cup red wine (Burgundy, Zinfandel, or Pinot Noir)
1 teaspoon Worcestershire sauce
Pinch of ground cinnamon
1 package (10 ounces) frozen Italian beans
Romano or Parmesan cheese

1. In 6-quart kettle combine meatballs, meatball drippings, onions, carrots, potatoes, tomatoes, water, wine, Worcestershire sauce, and cinnamon. Mix gently.
2. Cover kettle and simmer for 1 hour. Add green beans and when mixture returns to a simmer, cook 15 minutes.
3. Serve with grated Romano or Parmesan cheese.

VARIATION: As with any stew, vegetables used vary with family preferences.

MEATBALLS   Yield: 14 to 15 large or 22 to 24 small meatballs

Family custom usually dictates a preference for meatballs in tomato sauce or meat sauce over pasta. Regardless of where they are used, making meatballs that are tender is a highly valued skill.

1 pound lean ground beef
2 eggs, slightly beaten
½ cup grated Romano or Parmesan cheese
1¾ cups breadcrumbs made from fresh bread
1 teaspoon salt

½ teaspoon black pepper
1 tablespoon dried or 2 tablespoons chopped fresh parsley
1 teaspoon dried basil (optional)
2 cloves garlic, minced (optional)
3 tablespoons shortening or olive oil

1. Combine beef, eggs, cheese, breadcrumbs, salt, pepper, parsley, basil, and garlic in large bowl and mix throughly but lightly.
2. Shape into balls about 1½ inches in diameter.
3. Heat oil in large frying pan. Brown meatballs on all sides over moderate heat for about 20 minutes.
4. Use in meatball stew or add to spaghetti sauce and simmer for 30 minutes.

VARIATIONS: Adjust seasonings to suit individual taste. Or, increase the amount of cheese and decrease breadcrumbs by an equal amount.

CHICKEN CACCIATORE

Yield: 6 servings

A dish which, variations aside, transcends the north-south divide in Italian cookery. Easier to raise and maintain than cows or pigs, chickens were a mainstay in meat meals, especially in southern Italy and Sicily.

3 tablespoons butter
3 tablespoons olive oil
1 chicken (3 pounds), cut in serving pieces
Salt and black pepper

2 to 3 cloves garlic, minced
1 cup semidry wine, such as Rhine or Chenin Blanc
2 tablespoons dried, crumbled rosemary

1. Heat oil and butter in pan over moderate heat. Add chicken pieces and brown slowly on all sides. Slow browning is important. Season with salt and pepper to taste.
2. Add garlic toward end of browning time. Added too soon, garlic will become too brown and have a bitter taste.
3. Add wine to pan and sprinkle rosemary over chicken pieces, crushing it between fingers while scattering it.
4. Cover pan and allow chicken to simmer slowly for 45 minutes.
5. Remove lid and continue to simmer slowly so that liquid will reduce by half. Save enough reduced wine sauce to spoon over chicken when it is served.
6. Serve over rice.

VARIATION: Add 8 ounces of tomatoes or tomato sauce when adding wine to change flavor and yield more sauce.

HOT DAGOS
Yield: 25 to 26 patties

The name is offensive to many Italians and Italian Americans, yet this food, even in the ethnic community, goes by no other. While the ingredients and technique are common to Italian cooking, the specific dish and its title are probably of American origin.

1½ pounds lean ground beef
1 teaspoon fennel seeds
1 teaspoon garlic salt
1 teaspoon salt
½ teaspoon black pepper
¾ teaspoon cayenne pepper

2 eggs, beaten
¼ cup Parmesan or Romano cheese
1 teaspoon dried basil
1 clove garlic, chopped fine
1 quart Spaghetti Sauce (see recipe)
3 tablespoons shortening or olive oil

1. Combine beef, fennel seeds, garlic salt, salt, black and cayenne peppers, eggs, cheese, basil, and garlic. Mix lightly with hands.
2. Form into small patties, 2½ to 3 inches in diameter.
3. Heat fat over moderate heat in heavy frying pan. Fry patties until lightly browned on both sides. Do not crowd in pan; fry in several batches.
4. Drain browned patties on paper towels.
5. Pour accumulated fat from the frying pan, leaving browned bits and pieces for flavoring. Add spaghetti sauce and patties. Simmer slowly for 1 hour.
6. Serve meat and sauce with spaghetti or over slices of Italian bread.

BRACIOLIS (Beef Rolls)
Yield: 6 to 8 servings

A prime way of using steak, not a common ingredient in Italian cooking. Braciolis are generally reserved for special meals — for holidays or company.

2 whole round steaks, cut ½-inch thick
6 slices prosciutto or thinly sliced ham
* (optional)*
¼ pound mozzarella cheese, sliced thin
1 cup breadcrumbs
½ cup chopped onions
1 teaspoon salt
¼ cup chopped fresh parsley

¼ cup Romano cheese
1 egg, hard boiled and chopped
1 egg, slightly beaten
Flour
¼ cup olive oil
4 cups Spaghetti Sauce (see recipe)
String, 10 feet cut in approximately 12-
* inch pieces*

1. Wipe steaks with paper towels, trim fat, and remove bone.
2. Lay steaks on flat surface and cover each with 3 slices of prosciutto or ham and half of mozzarella cheese.
3. In medium-sized bowl, mix breadcrumbs, onions, salt, parsley, Romano cheese, hard-boiled egg, and slightly beaten egg. May need to add 1 to 2 tablespoons of water to bind together.
4. Spread ½ of stuffing lengthwise down middle of each steak, stopping about 1 inch from ends.
5. Roll up meat. Slip 5 pieces of string under each roll, evenly spaced. Tie each one, holding meat together well with fingers. May be necessary to use more string and run 1 long piece lengthwise around the roll (see illustration).

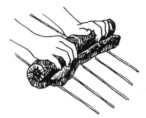

6. Heat oil in heavy pan. Dredge rolls in flour and brown on all sides over moderate heat.
7. Add spaghetti sauce and simmer for 1 hour or bake in 325 degree oven for 1 hour.
8. Remove rolls to board or platter. When cool enough to handle remove string. Cut rolls in 1- to 1½-inch slices.
9. Grease a flat casserole or 9-by-13-inch baking pan well. Spoon ½ of sauce into bottom of pan. Add slices in a single layer and spoon remaining sauce on top.
10. Cover pan and bake for 45 to 60 minutes or until fork tender.

VARIATION: Wash, trim, and cut in half lengthwise 2 stalks of celery. Place 1 strip on center of round steak before adding filling and remaining strip on top before rolling up meat. Repeat for second roll.

SPAGHETTI SAUCE

Yield: 4 to 5 cups

Tomatoes and olive oil mark this sauce as southern Italian in origin, although most contemporary Italian Americans, regardless of their Old Country roots, incorporate it into their menus. There are probably as many recipes for spaghetti sauce as there are Italian cooks.

2 tablespoons butter
2 tablespoons olive oil
1 cup finely chopped onions
1 cup finely chopped celery
¼ cup chopped fresh parsley or 2
*   tablespoons dried, crumbled parlsey*
3 cloves garlic, minced
1 can (2 pounds, 3 ounces,
*   approximately) stewed or plum tomatoes*

1 can (2 pounds, 3 ounces) water
1 can (6 ounces) tomato paste
1 teaspoon dried, crumbled rosemary
1 teaspoon dried, crumbled basil
½ teaspoon ground oregano
1 teaspoon black pepper
1½ teaspoons salt
¼ cup red wine

1. Heat butter and oil in a 10- to 12-inch frying pan over moderate heat. Add onions, celery, and parsley and saute until onions are very slightly browned. Add garlic and saute for 1 to 2 minutes.
2. In a 4- to 5-quart saucepan combine sauted vegetables, tomatoes (cut up with any hard centers removed), water, tomato paste, rosemary, basil, oregano, pepper, salt, and wine.
3. Simmer, uncovered, for about 2 hours or until sauce has thickened. Stir frequently. Taste and adjust seasonings.

VARIATION: For a spaghetti sauce with meat, cook 1½ pounds lean ground beef over moderate heat until meat has lost its pinkness. Break meat into small pieces as it cooks. Drain well to remove most fat and add to sauce in step 2.

EASTER BREAD   Yield: 2 round loaves

Family food traditions for Easter vary throughout Italy. This bread is customarily sliced, toasted, and served with butter on Easter morning in some households.

2 packages dry yeast
½ cup water (105 to 115 degrees)
½ cup all-purpose flour, spooned into cup
1 tablespoon sugar
8 eggs, at room temperature
1¼ cups sugar
½ cup melted butter
1½ to 2 teaspoons grated orange rind

½ cup orange juice
1½ to 2 teaspoons grated lemon rind
3 tablespoons lemon juice
2 teaspoons rum or rum extract
1 teaspoon salt
9 to 9½ cups all-purpose flour, spooned into cup

1. Dissolve yeast in water. Stir in ½ cup flour and 1 tablespoon sugar. Cover bowl and set aside.
2. Separate 1 egg and save white for later use. Beat yolk and remaining 7 eggs about ½ minute.
3. In large bowl combine eggs, sugar, butter, orange rind and juice, lemon rind and juice, rum, and salt. Stir in yeast mixture.
4. Gradually stir in 8 cups flour, 1 cup at a time. Add flour slowly from this point until dough can be kneaded.
5. Turn dough out on a floured board and knead until smooth and elastic, about 8 to 10 minutes, adding more flour if necessary. Dough may be a little tacky but should not stick to board or hands.
6. Cover dough in well-greased bowl and allow to rise until double in bulk, about 1 hour. Punch down and divide into 2 equal pieces.
7. Grease 2 9-inch pie pans with solid shortening or butter. Shape each piece of dough into a round and place in pan. Using sharp knife make 2 slashes about ⅓ inch deep to form a cross on top of each.
8. Whisk reserved egg white until slightly foamy. Gently brush top of loaves with egg white. Cover loaves with plastic wrap and allow to rise until double in bulk.
9. Preheat oven to 325 degrees. Bake for 1 hour to 1 hour, 15 minutes. Check loaves after 40 minutes. If they seem to be browning too quickly, cover lightly with aluminum foil.

ALMOND SLICES (Biscotti)   Yield: 30 slices

A cookie that is not associated with any particular holiday. Biscotti are traditionally served with wine or strong coffee and may be dunked into either beverage.

4 eggs, beaten
1 cup sugar
½ cup melted butter
1 tablespoon anise extract
1 tablespoon rum (optional, or can substitute whisky or 2 teaspoons vanilla)

⅛ teaspoon salt
½ cup coarsely chopped almonds
2 teaspoons baking powder
3½ cups all-purpose flour, spooned into cup
Glaze (see below)
Almonds, chopped or slivered

1. Beat eggs and sugar well. Add butter, anise extract, rum, salt, and ½ cup chopped almonds. Beat until just mixed.
2. Sift baking powder and flour. Combine with egg-sugar mixture. Dough will need to be mixed with spoon or hands as final cup of flour is added.
3. Turn dough out on a floured board. It will be sticky but can be handled with floured hands. Divide into 3 parts.
4. Grease 2 baking sheets. Preheat oven to 350 degrees. Form each piece of dough into a 7- to 8-inch roll using hands. Place roll on baking sheet and pull and pat into a strip about 3 inches wide and ½ inch thick. Strip will spread and rise during baking. Can place 2 strips on large baking sheet.
5. Bake 15 to 20 minutes or until very lightly browned.
6. Slice into ¾-inch strips as soon as removed from oven. Glaze lightly and sprinkle additional chopped or slivered almonds on top while warm.

Glaze

¾ cup sifted powdered sugar
⅛ teaspoon salt
2 tablespoons melted butter

2 to 3 teaspoons cream or milk
½ teaspoon vanilla (optional)

1. Combine sugar, salt, melted butter, and vanilla.
2. Add just enough liquid to make a spreadable icing or glaze.

RICOTTA PIE

Yield: 6 to 8 servings

The Italians invented cheesecake — a dish quite similar to this one dates back to Imperial Rome. Ricotta pie, today, is often served as a treat at Christmas or Easter.

7 eggs, separated, at room temperature
1 cup sugar
1 pound ricotta cheese (or 15-ounce carton)
1 ½ teaspoons grated orange peel

1 ½ teaspoons grated lemon peel
1 ½ teaspoons lemon juice
¼ teaspoon salt
1 teaspoon vanilla
Unbaked 9-inch pie shell

1. Beat egg whites until stiff. Set aside.
2. Beat egg yolks until lemony in color. Add sugar gradually.
3. Press ricotta through a sieve or process in food processor or blender until smooth.
4. Using low speed beat ricotta and egg-sugar mixture. Stir in orange peel, lemon peel, lemon juice, salt, and vanilla. Fold egg whites in carefully to above mixture until no streaks of ricotta mixture show. Set aside.
5. Line pie plate with pastry, making sure it overlaps rim. Flute edge so it stands high above rim, as filling will come near top. Preheat oven to 400 degrees.
6. Pour filling into prepared pie shell. Bake for 15 minutes. Reduce heat to 350 degrees and bake for 40 minutes. Check pie after ½ hour; if it seems to be browning too fast, cover loosely with aluminum foil.
7. Turn off oven and without opening door, cool pie for 2 hours. Usually served at room temperature, but may chill if preferred.

THE JEWS

SPINACH BORSCHT

Yield: 6 to 8 servings

One of a number of cold soups — including beet, sorrel, and cherry — popular among Jews of East European descent. Spinach borscht can serve either as a first course, a light lunch, or a refreshing summer drink.

6 cups water
2 packages (10 ounces each) frozen
  chopped spinach
1 teaspoon salt
½ cup minced onions

3 tablespoons lemon juice
1½ tablespoons sugar
¼ teaspoon black pepper
3 eggs

1. Bring water to a boil in a 3-quart saucepan.
2. Add spinach, salt, and onions. When water comes to a boil again, cover pan and simmer for 5 minutes. May need to break the spinach apart with a fork.
3. Remove from heat. Add lemon juice, sugar, and pepper and allow to cool for 10 minutes.
4. Force spinach mixture through a food mill or sieve or use a food processor or blender for finer puree.
5. Beat the eggs. Slowly add 1 cup of spinach mixture to beaten eggs, stirring constantly. Add spinach-egg mixture to rest of spinach.
6. Taste and adjust the salt and pepper.
7. Chill and serve with a dollop of sour cream in each bowl.

CHALLAH

Yield: 2 long loaves

The bread traditionally served at all holiday meals (except during Passover), probably because eggs and white flour were once luxury items. Challah is usually braided; for Rosh Hashanah the braids are formed into a round loaf, which signifies the cycle of life.

1 package dry yeast
1¼ cups water (105 to 115 degrees)
3 tablespoons sugar
1½ teaspoons salt
¼ cup vegetable oil
3 eggs, slightly beaten

5¾ to 6 cups all-purpose flour, spooned
*   into cup*
1 egg yolk mixed with 1 teaspoon cold
*   water*
2 tablespoons poppy seeds

1. Dissolve yeast in ½ cup warm water. Set aside.
2. In large bowl, add remaining water, sugar, salt, oil, eggs, and yeast. Mix well. Add 4 cups flour and beat until thoroughly combined.
3. Gradually add enough flour so that dough can be turned out on a lightly floured board and kneaded.
4. Knead until dough is smooth and elastic. May need to add a little more flour. Place dough in lightly oiled large bowl and cover. Allow to rise in a warm place until double in bulk, about 1½ hours.
5. Punch dough down and divide into 6 equal pieces. Take 3 pieces for 1 loaf and roll each into a rope about 20 inches long. Keep board lightly floured but work in as little flour as possible.
6. Braid ropes together loosely, tucking ends under and pinching to seal. Place on greased baking sheet. Repeat with remaining 3 pieces.
7. Cover loaves and allow to rise in a warm place until double in bulk, about 40 to 50 minutes.
8. Heat oven to 350 degrees. Brush tops of loaves with egg-water mixture. Sprinkle with poppy seeds. Bake for 30 minutes. If not lightly browned at this point, bake another 5 to 10 minutes.

TSIMMES

Yield: 4 to 6 servings

A sweet dish often served on Rosh Hashanah and Passover to accompany brisket. There are many variations of tsimmes, including one that uses carrots and pieces of brisket.

1½ pounds sweet potatoes
½ cup honey
¼ teaspoon ground cinnamon

1 cup water
1 package (12 ounces) pitted prunes
1 lemon, sliced very thin

1. Peel and cut sweet potatoes into 2-inch chunks and place in heavy 3-quart saucepan.
2. Add honey, cinnamon, and water. Bring to a boil over high heat, stirring to mix all ingredients. Turn to low and simmer until sweet potatoes are cooked but not fork tender.
3. Add prunes and lemon slices. Cover and cook over low heat until liquid is reduced and becomes thick and syrupy, at least 1 hour.

VARIATION: Bake tsimmes in a 350 degree oven for 1½ hours. If liquid has not reduced to a thick syrup, remove cover and cook 20 to 30 minutes or until juice is thick.

BLINTZES

Yield: 20 to 22 blintzes

A Jewish adaptation of the Russian blini, blintzes are a popular part of meatless meals. Fruit-filled ones may also serve as dessert.

2 eggs
1 cup milk
¼ teaspoon salt
2 tablespoons vegetable oil

¾ cup sifted all-purpose flour
¼ cup butter for frying
Filling (see below)

1. Beat eggs. Add milk, salt, vegetable oil, and flour and beat batter until smooth. Can use blender or food processor.
2. Heat a 6- to 7-inch omelet or crepe pan or a heavy frying pan over medium heat. Add a teaspoon of butter.
3. Use a ¼-cup measure and fill it almost full. Pour into heated pan, tilting and turning pan to distribute batter evenly over bottom.
4. Cook until underside is lightly browned. Blintzes are cooked only on 1 side.
5. Turn blintz out of pan onto a clean towel, with browned side up. These can be stacked and covered with a cloth until all are made.

6. Stir batter frequently while cooking so flour does not settle to bottom. If using pan without a nonstick coating, add butter from time to time.
7. With browned side up, fill each blintz with 1 heaping tablespoon of filling placed in center of circle.
8. Turn in sides and fold up blintz.

9. Heat remaining, or additional, butter in large frying pan on medium heat.
10. Place folded blintzes, seam side down, in pan and fry, turning from time to time, until browned on all sides — about 15 minutes.
11. Serve with sour cream.

VARIATION: Bake on greased baking sheet in a 375 degree oven for 15 minutes or until lightly browned.

Cheese Filling

8 ounces (1 cup) dry cottage cheese (hoop or farmer's cheese may be substituted)	*½ teaspoon salt*
	1 tablespoon sugar
1 egg yolk	*½ teaspoon vanilla (optional)*

Beat all ingredients together until very smooth. Can use sieve or food mill to break up curds in cottage cheese. Refrigerate.

VARIATION: Add 2 ounces cream cheese.

Apple Filling

4 cups apples, peeled, cored, and coarsely chopped	*¼ teaspoon ground cinnamon*
	¼ teaspoon ground nutmeg
¼ cup packed brown sugar	*2 tablespoons water*

1. Bring water to boiling in medium-sized saucepan. Add other ingredients. Stir gently until mixture is simmering. Adjust heat to maintain simmer.
2. Cover and cook for 20 minutes or until apples are tender, stirring often to avoid sticking. Set aside to cool.

KREPLACH
Yield: about 48

A dish from the era when cooks often had more time than money. Kreplach can be filled with leftover chicken or meat, and the mushroom filling can be extended with kasha (buckwheat groats).

2 cups all-purpose flour, spooned into cup
½ teaspoon salt
3 eggs, slightly beaten

2 tablespoons cold water
Meat, Chicken, or Mushroom Filling (see below)

1. Place flour and salt in medium-sized bowl. Make a well in center and add beaten eggs and 2 tablespoons water. Stir until mixed and dough holds together in a ball.
2. Turn out on lightly floured board and knead until smooth and elastic, about 10 minutes. Cover dough with a bowl and allow to rest 30 minutes.
3. Divide dough in half. Cover unused portion while working with the other. Roll dough out in a rectangle as thin as possible, at least ⅛ inch. If dough resists rolling out allow it to rest, covered well, for ½ hour.
4. Cut dough into 2-inch squares. Edge pieces that are not quite square can easily be pulled into a square shape.
5. Place a rounded teaspoon of filling on each square and fold to make a triangle or rectangle. Press edges together so they are well sealed and will not leak filling during cooking process.
6. Fill 6-quart pan or kettle ¾ full of water. Bring to boil and then drop 10 to 12 kreplach into water. Cover and reduce heat so that they do not boil vigorously and fall apart. Cook for 15 minutes.
7. Remove from pan with slotted spoon and drain well.
8. Can be used in chicken soup or baked in a 375 degree oven for 10 to 12 minutes or until lightly browned. Or fry for a few minutes in hot oil until crisp.

Meat Filling

1 pound ground beef, uncooked
2 tablespoons minced onion
1 egg, slightly beaten

1 tablespoon chopped fresh parsley
½ teaspoon salt
¼ teaspoon black pepper

Combine all ingredients.

Chicken Filling

2 tablespoons rendered chicken fat or
* shortening*
1 cup minced onions
2 ¼ cups finely minced or chopped cooked
* chicken*

1 teaspoon salt
¼ teaspoon black pepper
1 egg, slightly beaten with 2 tablespoons
* water*
1 tablespoon minced fresh parsley

1. Heat fat in a heavy 8- to 10-inch frying pan. Add onions and cook for 5 minutes, stirring occasionally.
2. In large bowl combine chicken, salt, pepper, egg, and parsley. Stir in cooked onions.

Mushroom Filling

2 tablespoons rendered chicken fat or other
* shortening*
1 cup minced onions
1 ½ pounds mushrooms, finely chopped

1 teaspoon salt
½ teaspoon black pepper
3 egg yolks, slightly beaten

1. Heat fat in a heavy 8- to 10-inch frying pan. Add onions and cook for 5 minutes, stirring occasionally. Add mushrooms and cook 10 minutes, stirring now and then. Add salt and pepper.
2. Remove from heat and set aside to cool.
3. Add egg yolks and mix well.

POTATO PANCAKES (Latkes)

Yield: 7 to 8 pancakes,
3-inch diameter

Traditional on Hanukah which requires foods fried in oil as a ritual symbol. Originally the tradition of German Jews, potato latkes have, in America, been adopted as a symbol by East European Jews, replacing, for example, the buckwheat blini fried in goose fat.

2 cups finely grated potatoes	*1 egg, slightly beaten*
¼ cup finely grated onions	*2 tablespoons all-purpose flour*
½ teaspoon salt	*2 tablespoons butter*
⅛ teaspoon black pepper	*2 tablespoons vegetable oil*
¼ teaspoon baking powder	

1. Mix potatoes and onions. Let stand for 10 minutes and drain off accumulated liquid. Press and squeeze vegetables to remove all possible liquid.
2. Add salt, pepper, baking powder, egg, and flour. Mix well.
3. Heat butter and oil in 10- to 12-inch frying pan over medium high heat. Drop batter by tablespoonful or mixing spoonful into hot fat mixture. When brown on underside, flip latke over and brown other side. Adjust heat so that cooking time is about 5 minutes.
4. Drain on paper towels. Serve with sour cream or applesauce.

CABBAGE ROLLS

Yield: 6 to 8 servings

Cabbage rolls exist in many ethnic food traditions. While this sweet-and-sour sauce hints at a German origin, slight variations of this recipe are common among Jews of East European origin.

12 large cabbage leaves (1 large head)	*½ teaspoon garlic powder*
6 cups chopped cabbage	*1 teaspoon Worcestershire sauce*
1½ cups grated potatoes	*¾ teaspoon salt*
½ onion, grated	*½ teaspoon black pepper*
1 pound lean ground beef	*Sauce (see below)*

1. Core cabbage and place in large kettle of boiling water. Adjust heat and simmer for 15 minutes or until leaves are soft and pliable. Remove from heat. Drain and cool.
2. Peel off 12 leaves. Cut out tough part of center rib of leaves. Chop remainder to yield 6 cups.

3. Grate potato on fine holes of grater. Squeeze out excess water. Grate onion and add to potatoes.
4. Mix meat, garlic powder, Worcestershire sauce, salt, and pepper. Add potatoes and onions. Divide into 12 portions.
5. Take 1 portion of meat mixture and roll into a ball. Place in center of cabbage leaf. Turn in sides of leaf and then roll up into a tight roll (see illustration). May secure with a toothpick.

6. Place chopped cabbage in bottom of 6-quart Dutch oven or heavy pan. Place rolls, seam side down, on top of chopped cabbage. Rolls can be packed tightly.
7. Pour sauce over rolls, cover pan, and bake at 350 degrees for ½ hour. Reduce heat to 300 degrees and bake for at least 2 hours — 3 hours improves flavor. Can be made ahead and reheated for later serving. Rolls freeze well.
8. May need to add ¼ to ½ cup water, broth, or tomato juice during baking period.

VARIATION: Use 1 cup cooked rice in place of potatoes.

Sauce

1 cup raisins	*½ cup vinegar*
⅓ cup packed brown sugar	*1 can (16 ounces) stewed tomatoes*
¼ teaspoon ground cinnamon	*2 bay leaves*

Mix well and pour over cabbage rolls.

VARIATION: For a less sweet sauce use: 1 can (16 ounces) stewed tomatoes, 1 can (8 ounces) tomato sauce, ½ cup water, ¼ cup vinegar, ¼ cup packed brown sugar.

QABALI   Yield: 6 to 8 servings

A Persian (Iranian) Jewish dish often served on the holiday of Sukkot that comes at harvesttime and reminds Jews of the huts that sheltered their ancestors in the wilderness after the exodus from Egypt.

½ cup yellow split peas, soaked overnight in 2 cups water	¼ teaspoon ground cinnamon
1 cup uncooked long-grain rice	½ teaspoon salt
3 cups water	½ teaspoon black pepper
2 tablespoons vegetable oil, approximately	1½ to 2 tablespoons solid shortening
1 pound beef chuck or other stew meat, cut in approximately ½-inch cubes	1 teaspoon ground cumin
1 cup chopped onions	½ cup raisins
	1½ cups grated carrots
	½ cup warm water

1. Steam rice by favorite method or bring 3 cups water to boil and stir in 1 cup rice. Reduce heat when water returns to a boil and simmer 15 minutes. Drain and rinse in cold water. Set aside.
2. Heat oil in 10-inch frying pan over medium heat; add meat and saute until lightly browned. Remove from pan and set aside in a bowl. Add chopped onions to pan. Saute for 5 minutes over medium heat. May need to add 1 to 2 tablespoons oil.
3. Using a slotted spoon, remove onions from pan and add to meat. Add cinnamon, ¼ teaspoon salt, and ¼ teaspoon pepper and mix well.
4. Heavily oil a 4- to 6-quart heavy pan with 1½ to 2 tablespoons solid shortening. Place half of rice in bottom of pan. Sprinkle ¼ teaspoon cumin over rice.
5. Add ½ of meat mixture and sprinkle with ¼ teaspoon cumin.
6. Drain split peas and layer over meat. Do the same with raisins and then carrots. Add ¼ teaspoon cumin.
7. Next layer remaining meat. Top with remaining rice. Sprinkle with last ¼ teaspoon cumin and remaining salt and pepper.
8. Measure ½ cup warm water and deglaze pan in which meat and onions were sauted, scraping loose all bits of meat and onions. Pour over meat-rice mixture.
9. Place a small clean dishcloth or 4 thicknesses of cheesecloth (folded to fit pan) over top of rice. Either one will absorb moisture and create an even, moist cooking atmosphere. Place a square of aluminum foil over top of pan and cover with lid.

10. Cook over low heat on top of stove for at least 2 hours. Check ingredients after about 1 hour to be sure there is enough liquid to keep bottom layer from sticking. If necessary add ¼ cup water. Check at end of 2 hours to see if meat is very tender and split peas are soft. Continue cooking until meat is tender. Bottom layer of rice should be crusty.
11. When serving be sure to spoon deep into pan so that each portion has all the layers of ingredients.

BRAISED BRISKET   Yield: 8 to 10 servings

A standby among Ashkenazic Jews for Sabbath and holiday dinners. This is the basic recipe; more modern variations include mustard- or tomato-based sauces.

4 pounds boneless beef brisket
2 teaspoons garlic powder
1 teaspoon black pepper
1½ teaspoons paprika

1 teaspoon salt
1 cup boiling water
3 cups thinly sliced onions

1. Mix garlic powder, pepper, paprika, and salt. Rub mixture over surface of brisket. Place in an airtight bowl or plastic bag and refrigerate overnight.
2. Heat oven to 350 degrees. Place brisket in heavy pan and add water around sides of meat. Cover brisket with sliced onions. Place pan in oven, uncovered, for 1 hour.
3. Cover pan, lower temperature to 300 degrees, and bake for another 1½ hours or until tender. May need to add ¼ cup water if pan and contents appear dry.
4. Slice brisket in thin slices across grain. Skim fat from meat juices. Serve juices as accompaniment.

VARIATIONS: Add peeled, halved potatoes the last hour of cooking. Brisket can be cooked over very low heat on top of stove.

FALAFL

Yield: 30 to 32

A common dish throughout the Middle East, including Israel. European Jews incorporate garbanzo beans into some foods, but never in this form.

*2 cups canned garbanzo beans, drained
   (dried garbanzo beans, soaked and
   cooked, may be substituted)*
*1 slice whole-wheat toast, torn into small
   pieces*
¼ cup lukewarm water
1 tablespoon all-purpose flour
½ teaspoon baking soda
3 cloves garlic, finely minced
1 egg, beaten well

2 tablespoons chopped fresh parsley
¾ teaspoon salt
¼ teaspoon black pepper
¼ teaspoon ground cumin
½ teaspoon ground turmeric
½ teaspoon ground marjoram
Oil for frying
Tahini Sauce (see below)
Relish (see below)

1. Mash garbanzo beans in large bowl or use a blender or food processor.
2. Soak bread in water, using a fork to stir bread until saturated. Allow to stand while measuring other ingredients.
3. Add remaining ingredients to beans. Add soaked bread last and mix well.
4. Add another teaspoon or more of flour if mixture appears to be runny.
5. Heat oil for deep-fat frying to 375 degrees.
6. Wet hands and form mixture into balls the size of a large walnut — about 1 inch in diameter. Fry a few at a time, until golden brown. Drain.
7. Serve hot in pockets of pita bread with tahini sauce and relish.

Tahini Sauce

*¾ cup tahini (found in most "co-ops" or
   Middle Eastern groceries)*
½ cup lemon juice
2 cloves garlic, finely minced
2 tablespoons olive oil

*2 tablespoons minced fresh parsley or
   cilantro*
½ teaspoon salt
⅛ teaspoon cayenne pepper

Combine ingredients in bowl or blender and mix well.

Relish

3 ripe tomatoes, seeded and diced
*1 medium cucumber, peeled and diced
   (seeded also if seeds are large)*

*1 medium green pepper, seeded and finely
   diced*
½ cup minced fresh parsley or cilantro
Salt and black pepper (optional)

Combine ingredients and toss thoroughly. Adjust seasonings.

HONEY CAKE

Yield: 10 to 12 servings

A dessert customarily served on Rosh Hashanah, the Jewish New Year, when families traditionally eat sweet foods to ensure that the coming year will be sweet.

1 cup honey
½ cup strong coffee
3 eggs
⅓ cup sugar
½ cup vegetable oil
3 cups all-purpose flour, spooned into cup
½ teaspoon ground cloves
½ teaspoon ground allspice
½ teaspoon ground cinnamon

¼ teaspoon salt
1 teaspoon baking soda
1½ teaspoons baking powder
Grated zest of ½ lemon
Grated zest of ½ orange
1 teaspoon vanilla
½ cup chopped almonds, mixed with 1 teaspoon flour
8 to 10 whole almonds

1. Grease and flour a 10-inch tube or bundt pan or a 9-by-5-inch loaf pan. Preheat oven to 325 degrees.
2. Mix honey and coffee and stir well. Heat mixture if coffee is not already hot so that honey will liquefy.
3. In large bowl, beat eggs until thick and lemon colored.
4. Gradually add sugar to beaten eggs. Add oil and mix well.
5. In a separate bowl, sift together flour, cloves, allspice, cinnamon, salt, baking soda, and baking powder.
6. Alternately add dry ingredients and coffee-honey mixture to egg mixture, mixing well after each addition.
7. Add lemon zest, orange zest, vanilla, and almonds to batter.
8. Pour into prepared pan. Arrange almonds on top.
9. Bake for 1 hour. Test for doneness by pressing finger lightly on top of cake. Impression should snap back immediately if cake is done. Bake another 10 minutes if necessary.
10. Cool cake in pan on a rack. Remove from pan and wrap in aluminum foil or place in airtight container. Cake should be made at least 2 days before serving as flavors improve with age. Cake freezes well.

HAMENTASCHEN I

Yield: 18 to 22 cookies

Served on the holiday of Purim, these cookies are named for the villain of the story. Different families are fiercely loyal to either the yeast or cookie-type dough; both are traditional.

1 package dry yeast or 1 cake compressed
* yeast*
¼ cup water (105 to 115 degrees)
6 tablespoons cooled scalded milk
2½ to 3 cups all-purpose flour, spooned
* into cup*
6 tablespoons sugar

¾ teaspoon salt
1 egg plus 1 egg white, slightly beaten
* together*
½ cup melted butter
Poppy-Seed Filling (see below)
1 egg yolk beaten with 1 teaspoon water

1. Soften yeast in water for 5 minutes.
2. Pour cooled milk into large mixing bowl. Add yeast and water.
3. Stir in 1 cup flour, sugar, salt, and eggs. Beat well.
4. Stir in 1½ cups flour and cooled melted butter. May need additional flour so that dough has a breadlike consistency. Turn out on lightly floured board and knead until dough is smooth and elastic, about 5 minutes.
5. Oil a large bowl, place dough in it, cover, and allow to rise until double in bulk, about 40 to 50 minutes.
6. Punch down and knead on a lightly floured board for 2 to 3 minutes.
7. Divide dough in half, carefully covering ½ with plastic wrap so that it will not dry out. Roll other ½ out to ¼ inch thickness. Cut into 3-inch circles with a cookie cutter, a glass, or a cup.
8. Place a tablespoonful of filling not quite in center of circle. Bring up 2 sides and press together. Bring up third side and seal to form a tricorn (see illustration). May have to moisten edges with water to seal well.

9. Place finished hamentaschen on oiled baking sheet and allow to rise until double in bulk in a warm place, about 40 minutes. Prepare second portion of dough while first portion rises.
10. Brush pastry with egg yolk mixture. Bake in a 375 degree oven 25 minutes or until lightly browned.

NOTE: Press scraps together, let rest ½ hour, roll out, and proceed as above.

HAMENTASCHEN II

Yield: 40 to 42 cookies

2 ½ cups all-purpose flour, spooned into
cup
2 teaspoons baking powder
⅛ teaspoon salt
½ cup butter or margarine, at room
temperature
½ cup sugar

2 large eggs
2 tablespoons milk or water or
combination of orange and lemon juice
½ teaspoon vanilla
Poppy-Seed Filling (see below)
1 egg, slightly beaten with 1 teaspoon
water

1. Sift together flour, baking powder, and salt.
2. In large bowl, cream butter or margarine and sugar. Add eggs, 1 at a time. Mix until smooth and fluffy.
3. Add milk or liquid and vanilla. Mix in flour, baking powder, and salt.
4. Chill dough in well-covered bowl for at least 4 hours or overnight.
5. Preheat oven to 375 degrees. Lightly grease 2 baking sheets.
6. Divide dough into 4 portions. Work with one portion at a time, keeping remainder well covered in refrigerator. Roll out dough on lightly floured board to ⅛ to ¼ inch thick. Cut dough into 3-inch rounds.
7. Place teaspoonful of filling on round. Bring up 2 sides and press together (see illustration for yeast dough). Bring up third side to form a tricorn. Pinch to seal well. Repeat with remaining portions of dough.
8. Brush prepared triangles well with egg mixture. Bake for 12 to 15 minutes or until lightly browned.
9. Cool on baking racks.

Poppy-Seed Filling

¾ cup ground poppy seeds
½ cup milk
¼ cup honey

⅓ cup raisins
2 teaspoons lemon juice
½ teaspoon grated lemon rind

1. Mix poppy seeds, milk, and honey and bring to a boil. Lower heat and cook, stirring constantly, for about 5 minutes or until all milk is absorbed.
2. Add raisins, lemon juice, and lemon rind. Mix well. Cool before using.

VARIATION: Use a 12-ounce can of poppy-seed filling. Substitute prune, apricot, or sweetened cheese filling.

KAMISH BREAD

Yield: 26 to 28 slices

A cookie from the East European Jewish tradition. For some families this is a Rosh Hashanah treat; others enjoy kamish bread throughout the year.

½ cup shortening
¼ cup vegetable oil
1 cup sugar
3 eggs
¼ cup orange juice
1 teaspoon orange rind
2 tablespoons lemon juice
½ teaspoon lemon rind

1 teaspoon vanilla
½ teaspoon almond extract
½ teaspoon salt
2 teaspoons baking powder
3½ to 3¾ cups all-purpose flour,
*   spooned into cup*
Filling (see below)

1. Cream shortening, oil, and sugar, using mixer.
2. Add eggs, 1 at a time, beating well after each addition.
3. Add orange juice, orange rind, lemon juice, lemon rind, vanilla, almond extract, salt, and baking powder. Mix well.
4. Add flour 1 cup at a time. Add extra flour only if dough seems too soft to roll out. It will be chilled when you roll it; the chilling will firm it somewhat.
5. Refrigerate overnight, covered tightly with plastic wrap.
6. Divide dough into 3 parts. Keep parts not being used covered in refrigerator.
7. Roll out each part on floured waxed paper or aluminum foil into rectangle about 10½ by 12½ inches.
8. Distribute filling on rectangle as outlined in Filling recipe.
9. Place greased baking sheet near work area. With filling in place, start to roll up dough with fingers. Then gently lift the waxed paper or aluminum foil underneath and dough will roll over on top of itself (see illustration). Firm up roll with hands as needed. Roll kamish bread off paper or foil onto baking sheet. Be sure edge is on underside so that roll will stay together during baking. Repeat for other 2 rectangles. The rolls spread. Unless pan is large, place rolls on separate baking sheets.

10. Bake at 350 degrees for 40 minutes or until lightly browned.
11. Cut into 1-inch wide pieces while kamish bread is still warm.

Filling (for 1 roll)

¼ *cup orange marmalade*
½ *cup raisins*
½ *cup chopped nuts*

¼ *teaspoon ground cinnamon*
1 *teaspoon sugar*
10 *maraschino cherry halves*

1. Spread marmalade over rectangle. Sprinkle with raisins, nuts, cinnamon, and sugar.
2. Arrange maraschino cherry halves in a row along 10-inch edge. Begin rolling from this edge. There will be a cherry half in each slice.

VARIATIONS: Use date, prune, or poppy-seed filling, peach, apricot, or rhubarb jam or marmalade, or add shredded coconut.

THE SOUTH SLAVS

BARLEY, BEAN, AND SAUERKRAUT SOUP

Yield: 6 servings as a main course
8 to 9 servings as a first course

Prepared with ingredients readily available to South Slav cooks in their early years in Minnesota. During depression years soups, such as this one, and homemade bread provided sustaining meals.

1 large ham hock or 2 pounds smoked
  ham pieces
3 quarts water or chicken broth
1 cup uncooked barley
1 clove garlic, minced
1 tablespoon minced parsley
1 to 1½ cups chopped celery
1 cup chopped onions

1 cup carrots, sliced in rounds
½ cup canned tomatoes or 1 whole
  tomato, chopped
1 cup cooked Roman or pinto beans
1 cup sauerkraut
2 tablespoons lard or shortening
2 tablespoons all-purpose flour
Salt and black pepper to taste

1. Cook ham hock or ham pieces in water or broth for 1½ hours or until tender. Add barley and cook 30 minutes more.
2. Add garlic, parsley, celery, onions, carrots, tomatoes, beans, and sauerkraut. Cook until all vegetables are tender, about 1 hour.
3. Place lard or shortening in small heavy frying pan over moderate heat. When heated, stir in flour and continue stirring until flour turns golden brown. (This flour–fat mixture can burn easily.) Stir into soup.
4. Simmer for 10 minutes. May need to add more water or broth. Adjust seasonings and serve.

VARIATIONS: Place slices of smoked sausage on top of soup for flavor and garnish. Or, make without ham for a meatless soup.

BROWN SAUCE (Prezganje in Slovenian, Ajmpren in Serbian and Croatian)

Yield: 2¼ cups

Used to flavor cooked vegetables, meat dishes, or soups. Lard or meat drippings add flavor; however, butter, shortening, or oil may be substituted.

6 tablespoons shortening or lard
6 tablespoons all-purpose flour
¾ cup minced onions (optional)
1 clove garlic, minced (optional)

2 cups liquid (vegetable water, chicken stock, or stock from cooking, such as sarma liquid)

1. Heat shortening in heavy frying pan over moderate heat. When melted, add flour, stirring constantly. Stir in onions and garlic.
2. Stir for several minutes until mixture turns dark golden brown. May need to adjust heat if process seems slow.
3. If using as a flavoring for soup, add to soup slowly, stirring well.
4. If using as a sauce over vegetables, slowly stir 2 cups liquid saved from cooking into flour-fat mixture. Stir until blended and thickened.
5. If using as flavoring for sarma, remove 2 cups of liquid surrounding cabbage rolls and proceed as in step 4.

MIXED VEGETABLES WITH BROWN SAUCE

Yield: 4 to 6 servings

1½ cups chunked carrots
1½ cups chunked potatoes
1½ cups chunked rutabagas
2 tablespoons all-purpose flour

2 tablespoons shortening or lard
1 cup cooking liquid
Brown Sauce (see recipe)

1. Vegetables should be cut into similar-sized pieces so that they will cook through in the same length of time. Can be diced or sliced if preferred. Put in saucepan, add water to cover, and cook until tender.
2. Prepare sauce with flour, shortening, and cooking liquid as outlined in Brown Sauce recipe.
3. Combine vegetables and sauce and serve hot.

VARIATIONS: Toss toasted bread cubes or breadcrumbs with the vegetable-sauce mixture. Use vegetable combinations, such as potatoes, carrots, and green beans, or wax beans and spinach or beet greens, or green beans and sliced potatoes.

CRACKLING BREAD   Yield: 2 loaves, 9 by 5 inches
(Spehovka in Slovenian)

In earlier days many South Slavs raised pigs for fall butchering, and quantities of fat were a by-product of this practice. Cut in small pieces and rendered until crisp, the cracklings were used to flavor many popular dishes such as this bread, casseroles, and corn-meal mush.

1 package dry yeast
½ cup water (105 to 115 degrees)
1 teaspoon sugar
1 cup milk
½ cup shortening or butter
1 teaspoon salt

1 tablespoon sugar
2 eggs, well beaten
5½ to 6 cups all-purpose flour, spooned
 into cup
Filling (see below)
Butter

1. Dissolve sugar and yeast in water and set aside in warm place until foamy, about 5 minutes.
2. Heat milk until warm enough to melt the shortening. Do not boil. Stir in shortening or butter, salt, and sugar. Set aside to cool.
3. In large bowl combine yeast mixture, cooled milk mixture, and beaten eggs. Stir in 5 cups flour. Continue to add flour until dough holds together in a ball and can be turned out on a lightly floured board. Knead dough 10 minutes or until smooth and elastic. May need to work in additional flour.
4. Lightly grease dough and place in greased bowl, cover, and allow to rise in a warm place until double in bulk. Punch down well, cover, and allow to double in bulk again.
5. Punch down dough and divide in half. Roll each half into a rectangle about 9 by 18 inches and ¼ inch thick.
6. Spread each rectangle with ½ of filling as outlined in Filling recipe. Roll up and pinch ends and edges. Place in well-greased bread pan, with pinched edge on bottom. Let rise in a warm place until double in bulk.
7. Bake in preheated 325 degree oven for 40 minutes or until evenly browned on top. Brush baked loaves lightly with butter, remove from pans, and cool on racks.

Filling

2 eggs, well beaten
2 cups cracklings or real bacon bits

2 teaspoons melted butter
⅓ cup fresh breadcrumbs

1. Spread ½ of beaten eggs over 1 rectangle of dough. Sprinkle ½ of cracklings or bacon over top.
2. Stir melted butter and breadcrumbs together in small bowl. Sprinkle ½ over top of cracklings.
3. Repeat with second piece of dough.

VARIATION: Add 1 cup chopped onions sauteed 5 minutes in 2 tablespoons butter or shortening; sprinkle ½ cup over cracklings on each piece of dough. Or, sprinkle finely chopped, fresh chives over cracklings.

POGAČA

Yield: 2 round 9-inch loaves

A flat bread made when immigrant South Slav women needed bread quickly for dinner but so good that it is still made today.

1 package dry yeast
¼ cup water (105 to 115 degrees)
3 to 4 cups all-purpose flour, spooned into
* cup*
½ teaspoon salt

2 tablespoons sugar
1¾ cups lukewarm water
¼ cup vegetable oil
Corn meal

1. Combine yeast with ¼ cup warm water, stir well to dissolve, and set aside for 5 minutes.
2. Mix together 3 cups flour, salt, sugar, 1¾ cups water, and oil. Stir in yeast mixture. Add more flour until dough can be formed into a ball and turned out on a lightly floured board for kneading.
3. Knead at least 10 minutes or until smooth and elastic. May need additional flour. Grease ball of dough, place in large greased bowl. Cover bowl and allow dough to rise in a warm place for 1 hour.
4. Grease 2 round 9-inch cake pans or 2 baking sheets with vegetable shortening. Dust with corn meal.
5. Punch dough down well to force out air and divide in 2 parts. Shape into 2 flat rounds to fit in pans or on baking sheets.
6. Prick rounds with a fork at 1-inch intervals. Lightly cover and allow to rise in a warm place for 20 minutes.
7. Bake at 375 degrees for 30 to 35 minutes.

NOTE: Good with stews, sauerkraut and bean dishes, and soups. Use any favorite bread dough to make this quick, flat bread.

CHEESE ŠTRUKLJI

Yield: 16 servings

Three favorite foods are combined in this classic Lenten dish — breadcrumbs browned in butter, cheese, and dumpling dough. Infrequently made today by younger cooks, štruklji is a treat that older women prepare for holidays.

1½ cups all-purpose flour, spooned into cup
1 tablespoon butter
¼ teaspoon salt
1 egg, at room temperature, slightly beaten
6 tablespoons lukewarm water
2 tablespoons warm melted butter

1 carton (24 ounces) cottage cheese, drained but not dry
4 egg yolks, unbeaten
1 cup sour cream
2 egg whites, beaten stiff
2 cups breadcrumbs
½ cup melted butter
Additional melted butter
Cheesecloth and String

1. Measure flour into bowl and cut in 1 tablespoon butter until mixture is like coarse corn meal. Make a well in flour-butter mixture and add salt, beaten egg, and water. Use a fork and gradually work flour into liquids until all flour is absorbed.
2. Place dough on lightly floured board and knead about 15 minutes or until dough is smooth with little bubbles under its surface. May need to add more flour but avoid adding any more than absolutely necessary. Oiling hands will help prevent sticking while kneading.
3. Pat or roll dough out to about an 8-inch circle and spread with 2 tablespoons warm melted butter. Cover with inverted bowl and let stand for at least 2 hours.
4. Make filling for štruklji shortly before dough is ready. Combine cottage cheese, egg yolks, and sour cream. Fold in beaten egg whites. Set aside.
5. In small heavy frying pan, mix together crumbs and ½ cup melted butter. Slowly brown mixture over low heat. Stir frequently to avoid burning. Set aside.
6. When ready to make cheese roll, cover a table with a cloth or sheet. (Traditionally a damask cloth was used.) Sprinkle well with flour and pat flour into cloth.
7. Place dough in center of table and brush well with melted butter. Next pull dough from all sides until very thin. Begin pulling gently, with one hand on top and one underneath. (Some cooks use a rolled fist or the top of the hand underneath.) Work from the center outward, walking around table and pulling on all sides until dough is 18 by 24 inches.
8. Spread cheese mixture along 18-inch edge of dough. Leave about 10 inches at far end of rectangle free of filling for a better seal when dough is rolled up (see illustration).
9. If edges of the rectangle are thick, cut them away with sharp knife or scissors. Start rolling up rectangle as you would a jelly roll. After

starting process by hand, the edge of cloth can be raised and dough will gently roll over on top of itself.

10. When rolled up, pinch ends and edge of roll well. Use fork to press long edge gently for a good seal.
11. Fill a large 6- to 8-quart kettle ⅔ full of water. Heat to boiling.
12. Cut piece of cheesecloth large enough to wrap around štruklji several times. Make sure it is wide enough so that ends can be tied securely. Wet cloth well and spread it out on table next to štruklji. Roll štruklji onto cheesecloth using cloth as in step 9. Roll it up loosely in cheesecloth as roll will swell as it cooks. Take string and tie 1 end of cheesecloth-wrapped roll securely. Do not cut string but continue with long end and wind it around roll, progressing to other end. Tie that end securely and trim ends of string (see illustration).

13. Adjust heat under kettle of boiling water to a gentle boil. Take wrapped roll by each end, quickly lift it, and place it in the water. Adjust heat to keep water gently boiling for ½ hour. Cover pan but leave lid ajar. Check water occasionally to be sure it is not boiling too vigorously.
14. At end of ½ hour remove roll from pan and drain on paper towels. Slide roll off paper onto plastic wrap. Cut string and gently unroll cheesecloth. It may be necessary to use the point of a knife and loosen roll from cheesecloth.
15. Cut roll into 1½-inch-wide pieces and place on a greased 9-by-13-inch pan. Sprinkle prepared crumbs over cut slices. Bake in preheated 325 degree oven for 20 minutes.
16. Serve immediately. Can be reheated but will never be as flavorful as when freshly made.

VARIATIONS: Can be made one day ahead by preparing to end of step 12. Allow to cool, wrap well, and refrigerate. Increase baking time to 30 minutes. Cook štruklji in salted water. Additional filling ingredients: ½ cup finely chopped chives or parsley or ½ cup brown sugar. For a sweeter flavor, add 2 tablespoons cinnamon and 2 tablespoons sugar to the crumb mixture.

STUFFED CABBAGE ROLLS (Sarma)

Yield: 40 to 45 medium- or
25 large-sized rolls

Often served at Serbian or Slovenian church bazaar luncheons and dinners. People come from miles away to enjoy this traditional South Slav dish that is similar to ones found in other ethnic cuisines.

1 large head of cabbage
1 pound pork sausage
3 pounds lean ground beef
1 cup long-grain rice, cooked 10 minutes, and rinsed
1 cup finely minced onions
2 to 3 cloves garlic, finely minced
2 eggs, slightly beaten
1 teaspoon black pepper

3 teaspoons salt
1 to 2 cans sauerkraut (1-pound, 11-ounce size or equivalent amount in plastic pouches)
2 cans (8 ounces) tomato sauce
2 large smoked sausages (optional)
6 tablespoons lard or shortening
6 tablespoons all-purpose flour

1. Heat large kettle of water to boiling. Remove core from whole head of cabbage and place cabbage, cut end down, in water. Can add ¼ cup vinegar to water for flavor. Cook 10 minutes or until leaves have softened enough to fold. Can be microwaved to soften.
2. Cool head in cold water. Remove leaves, 1 at a time, and trim away part of heavy vein.
3. Combine meats, rice, onions, garlic, eggs, pepper, and salt. Mix well.
4. Cover bottom of large roasting pan with 1 can of sauerkraut. If it is necessary to have 2 layers of cabbage rolls, use other can between layers.
5. Count cabbage leaves and divide meat into an equal number of portions. (Use approximately 2 tablespoons meat mixture for each cabbage leaf.)
6. Place meat over vein of cabbage leaf. Fold in 1 side; then fold in other side of leaf. Roll up remaining leaf so meat is all enclosed (see illustration). Place each roll, edge side down, on top of sauerkraut. (Can be secured with toothpick.)

7. Preheat oven to 350 degrees. Pack rolls in tightly over sauerkraut. Add 2 cans of tomato sauce and additional water to bring liquid level over top of cabbage rolls. If using sausage, cut in ½-inch pieces and layer on top. Cover tightly and bake for 1 hour.

8. Make brown roux while rolls bake. Heat heavy 8- to 10-inch frying pan over moderate heat. Melt lard or shortening and add flour, stirring until flour is golden brown. Set aside.

9. After 1 hour, take pan of cabbage rolls from oven. Using a ladle, remove approximately 3 cups of liquid from pan and stir into roux. Stir together over moderate heat until mixture thickens. Simmer for 2 to 3 minutes and then pour over cabbage rolls. Reduce heat to 300 degrees. Cover pan and return to oven for another 1½ hours.

10. Check cabbage rolls 15 minutes before end of cooking period. If sauce is watery, leave cover off for the last minutes of cooking to reduce liquid.

11. Serve rolls with some of sauerkraut and a garnish of sausage rounds. Cabbage rolls freeze well.

NOTE: Sour heads, available at some ethnic grocery stores and church bazaars, have been prepared in a brine as is sauerkraut. Leaves of sour heads make delicious cabbage rolls but, if using, then omit sauerkraut between the layers. This meat mixture is also used to stuff green peppers.

GOULASH (Golaz in Slovenian)   Yield: 6 servings

One version of a dish common in Central Europe. South Slavs traditionally served goulash with squares of cooked corn-meal mush called polenta.

2 pounds pork, cut in 1- to 1½-inch
  pieces
3 tablespoons lard or shortening
1½ cups coarsely chopped onions
3 tablespoons all-purpose flour
Water or stock (beef or chicken)

1¼ teaspoons salt
2 teaspoons paprika
½ teaspoon black pepper
⅛ teaspoon crushed red pepper flakes
1 can (10 to 11 ounces) sauerkraut
1 cup stewed tomatoes (optional)

1. Heat fat in large, heavy kettle over moderate heat. Pat meat dry with paper towels. Brown meat in heated fat. Stir occasionally to brown evenly. Add chopped onions and saute for 5 minutes.

2. Sprinkle flour over meat and stir until flour browns. Add water or stock to cover meat. Simmer for 1 hour or until meat is tender.

3. Add salt, paprika, black pepper, red pepper, sauerkraut, and tomatoes. Cover and simmer for ½ hour. Taste and adjust seasonings.

VARIATION: Increase amount of paprika and crushed red pepper for a spicier stew.

POTICA (also called Povitica)   Yield: 2 long loaves

This holiday bread is still a favorite food at special events. Some cooks take shortcuts in the preparation, such as using hot-roll mix for the dough. Most South Slavs enjoy potica served with a thin layer of butter; many Slovenians, however, relish it with a slice of ham.

1 package dry yeast
¼ cup water (105 to 115 degrees)
¼ cup butter
½ cup evaporated milk or cream
¼ cup sugar
2 eggs

3 ¼ to 3 ½ cups all-purpose flour,
  spooned into cup
½ teaspoon salt
Walnut Filling (see below)
Melted butter

1. Stir yeast into warm water. Set aside.
2. In medium-sized pan, heat butter, evaporated milk, and sugar together until milk is steaming but not boiling. Remove from heat and stir until butter is dissolved. Set aside to cool.
3. In large bowl beat eggs thoroughly with a fork. Add dissolved yeast and cooled milk mixture. Stir well.
4. Add salt and flour 1 cup at a time, stirring after each addition, until 3 cups have been added. Gradually add remaining flour until ball of dough can be turned out on a lightly floured board and kneaded. Knead dough 8 to 10 minutes or until smooth and manageable.
5. Place dough in well-buttered bowl, cover with cloth, and allow to rise in a warm location until double in bulk, about 1 hour.
6. Prepare filling while dough is rising.
7. Cover a large table with a cloth or an old sheet (a damask tablecloth was traditional). Sprinkle flour over top. Place dough on cloth without kneading or working. Pat dough down to work out any bubbles and continue patting into a rectangle. If dough seems to be sticking, lift rectangle from cloth and add more flour to the cloth.
8. Roll dough out as far as possible in all directions, making sure that rectangle is of even thickness. Make fists and place hands underneath dough, gradually stretching or pulling until it covers table top or is at least 30 by 25 inches. Stretch dough very slowly, walking around table and pulling from all sides. As center becomes thinner concentrate efforts on thick edges.
9. Generously grease a 15-by-14-inch baking sheet with vegetable shortening.
10. Spread filling over dough except for 12-inch area at the far side (see illustration). Trim away all thick edges before beginning to roll up potica.

11. Beginning at near side, roll up potica as you would a jelly roll, using fingers to start. Then lift near edge of cloth and dough will gently roll on top of itself, until potica is rolled up.

12. Use edge of small plate to cut roll into 2 pieces and to cut away extra dough at ends. Edges will seal as plate cuts through; if ends do not seal well, cover with pieces of stretched dough. Brush patched ends and entire loaf well with melted butter.
13. Cover and allow to rise about 1 hour or until loaves have doubled in bulk. Before baking prick each loaf with long-tined fork or wire cake tester in 6 places to release any air. Brush generously with melted butter.
14. Bake in preheated 325 degree oven for 40 to 50 minutes or until lightly browned. Brush with melted butter. Set on rack to cool.

Walnut Filling

½ cup butter
⅓ cup sugar
⅓ cup packed brown sugar
½ cup evaporated milk or cream
⅛ teaspoon salt

1 egg, at room temperature, slightly
   beaten
½ cup cooked dates (optional)
1 pound walnuts, finely ground

1. Melt butter and sugars together in small pan. Remove from heat and add milk slowly. Add salt and egg and stir well.
2. Stir in dates and walnuts. Set aside to cool.

NOTE: Form strips left from potica into a ball, wrap in plastic wrap for ½ hour, and then roll out into a rectangle. Cut 1-by-2- or 3-inch strips of dough. Sprinkle with sugar and cinnamon and bake in 350 degree oven until lightly browned.

Potica loaves freeze well for 2 to 3 months.

POTICA CAKE
Yield: 10 to 12 servings

A simplified version of the traditional bread, this quickly made cake has the texture of a pound cake, but the sweet walnut–cinnamon potica flavor is retained.

3 cups sifted all-purpose flour
1½ teaspoons baking powder
1½ teaspoons baking soda
¾ cup butter or margarine, at room temperature
1½ cups sugar
4 eggs, at room temperature

2 cups sour cream
1½ teaspoons vanilla
1½ cups ground walnuts
1½ cups packed brown sugar
2 tablespoons all-purpose flour
1 teaspoon ground cinnamon
Powdered sugar

1. Butter and lightly flour a 3½-quart tube or bundt pan. Preheat oven to 350 degrees.
2. Sift flour, baking powder, and baking soda together.
3. In large bowl, cream butter and sugar until well mixed. Add eggs 1 at a time, beating thoroughly after each addition.
4. To this mixture, add dry ingredients alternately with sour cream and vanilla. Beat well after each addition.
5. In small bowl combine nuts, brown sugar, 2 tablespoons flour, and cinnamon. Set aside.
6. Spread ⅓ of batter in bottom of prepared pan. Sprinkle ½ of nut mixture over batter. Add ⅓ more batter evenly to pan. Sprinkle remaining nut mixture on top. Add last of batter evenly over top.
7. Place pan in preheated oven. Bake for 1 hour or until a toothpick inserted in center of cake comes out clean. Remove from oven and allow to cool in pan for 5 minutes. Remove from pan and cool on wire rack. Dust with powdered sugar.
8. When completely cool, place in airtight container or wrap in foil or plastic wrap. Best made the day before serving.

VARIATION: Drizzle a simple icing or glaze over top instead of dusting with powdered sugar.

CHEESE DESSERT (Presnac)   Yield: 8 to 10 servings

Serbians serve this simple dessert not only for family dinners but also as one of many desserts on holidays.

¼ cup butter

4 large eggs, at room temperature

⅛ teaspoon salt

¾ cup sugar

½ cup milk

½ teaspoon vanilla

½ cup all-purpose flour, spooned into cup

8 ounces brick cheese, shredded or grated

2 pounds (4 cups) small curd cottage cheese

1. Melt butter over low heat. Use a small amount to grease a 9–by–13–inch glass baking dish. Preheat oven to 350 degrees.
2. In large bowl beat eggs well for several minutes. Add salt and sugar and beat until mixture is light and fluffy.
3. Measure vanilla into milk. Alternately add flour and milk to egg mixture.
4. Stir in brick cheese and cottage cheese until just mixed. Pour into prepared dish. Drizzle remaining butter evenly over top. Mixture will set as it bakes. Bake 50 minutes or until top of dessert is a light golden color.
5. Remove from oven and allow to stand ½ hour before serving. Usually served warm although it can be served cold.

NOTE: If you use jumbo or extra-large eggs, increase flour to ¾ cup. Can be made through point of pouring mixture into baking dish, then covered and refrigerated for later baking.

FLANCATI (also called Pohaney)   Yield: 60 to 70 cookies

The name varies from area to area in Yugoslavia, and the immigrants brought these different names with them. Slovenians seem to make and enjoy these "air nothings," as some also call them, more than other South Slavs, but all relish this delicate, fragile cookie. Many variations on the basic shape are possible.

2 cups all-purpose flour, spooned into cup
3 large egg yolks
½ cup sour cream
½ teaspoon salt
2 tablespoons powdered sugar

3 tablespoons white table wine (can
  substitute 2 tablespoons rum)
Lard or peanut oil
Powdered sugar

1. Place flour in large bowl. Make a well in center and add egg yolks, sour cream, salt, sugar, and wine or rum. Mix well, using a fork or mixer.
2. Turn dough out on well-floured board and knead until it forms a smooth ball. Dough should be soft but not sticky and some additional flour may be needed. Knead at least 15 minutes. Cover dough and allow to rest at least 1 hour or up to 3 hours.
3. Divide dough into 4 portions. Roll 1 piece at a time, keeping rest of dough well covered. Does not need to be used in a single day; can be refrigerated in airtight container for up to 3 days. Bring to room temperature before trying to roll out dough.
4. Roll dough into a rectangle about 10 by 12 inches or larger if possible. Cut into 3-inch squares or 1-by-10-inch strips. Squares are slit in 2 places and corners pulled through. Strips are wound loosely over 3 fingers and then 1 end pulled through to form a knot (see illustrations).

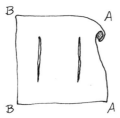 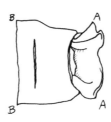 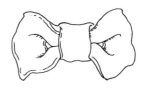

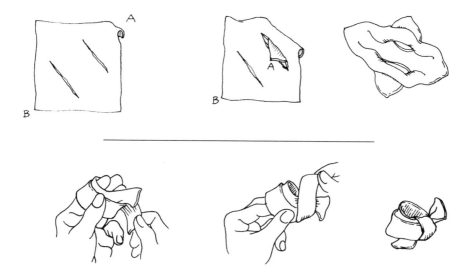

5. When several are formed, drop into hot lard or peanut oil that has been heated to 375 degrees. Fat should be hot enough to brown cookie lightly in less than 1 minute. Turn once during frying. Flancati look lighter when cooking so remove with a slotted spoon when they first show gold or light brown color.
6. Drain on paper towels. Sift powdered sugar over them or place in brown bag, add sugar, and gently tumble. Store in airtight container when cool. Keep well for 1 week.

STRUDEL   Yield: 14 to 16 pieces

Every holiday and special occasion is highlighted by strudel. Although apple and cheese are the favorite fillings, other fruits, such as blueberries, lemons, and cherries, are used today.

2 cups all-purpose flour, spooned into cup   *½ cup lukewarm water*
2 tablespoons butter   *½ cup warm melted butter*
¼ teaspoon salt   *Filling (see below)*
1 egg, at room temperature, slightly
   beaten

1. Read "Tips for Successful Strudel Making." Measure flour into large mixing bowl and cut in 2 tablespoons butter until crumbly. Make a well in center of mixture and add salt, egg, and water.
2. Slowly stir mixture, gradually drawing in the flour. Continue until well mixed. If necessary add a few more drops of water so that all dough draws together into a ball.
3. Oil hands lightly and begin kneading dough while still in bowl. Place dough on lightly floured surface and knead until smooth and elastic, at least 15 minutes and preferably 20 minutes. Dough will be sticky at first, but lose stickiness as kneading increases. Flours differ in moisture content, and it may be necessary to knead in a little more flour to make dough easy to handle. Strudel dough, however, should be soft.
4. Pat dough into a flat round and spread generously with melted butter. Cover with a warm bowl and allow to rest for at least 1 hour. To test, pull an edge of dough; if it bounces back quickly, it is not ready and must rest longer. Dough should be soft and very stretchy. (Dough can rest overnight.)
5. While dough is resting, make filling.
6. Cover kitchen table with a clean cloth or sheet. (A damask tablecloth is traditional.) The work surface should be at least 3 by 4 feet. Pat flour evenly into cloth.
7. Place dough in center of cloth and gently pat into a 12- to 14-inch circle. Spread circle generously with butter. Begin to stretch dough by placing one hand on top and one underneath and gently pulling. Walk around table stretching evenly from all sides. Some cooks place hands underneath, knuckle side up, and gently pull from all sides.
8. Continue to pull and stretch dough until it is the size of the table. Edges can hang over the sides. Sometimes it is necessary to anchor the pulled dough with a cup or plate if it has not stretched far enough to drape over the table.

9. When dough is stretched as thin as possible spread with melted butter and follow Filling recipe. Spread filling on dough within 10 inches of the far edge and 2 inches of remaining edges.

10. Cut away all thick edges.
11. To begin rolling up strudel, first fold 2 inches of dough on near edge over filling. Next, using fingers start to roll up this edge as you would a jelly roll. Then raise near edge of cloth. Dough and filling will roll gently over on itself (see illustration). May need to stop now and then to firm up roll with hands.
12. Butter baking sheet or 9-by-13-inch pan well. Place on table and with a final roll of the cloth lift or place strudel in a **U** shape on the pan. Be sure edge of dough is on the bottom.
13. Preheat oven to 425 degrees. Brush top of strudel with melted butter and place in oven. Bake for 10 minutes. Lower temperature to 350 degrees and bake for 40 minutes or until strudel is golden brown.
14. Cut into 2-inch pieces and serve warm.

Apple Filling

2 to 3 pounds apples (Jonathan,
  Cortland, or Greenings often used)
1½ cups sugar
1½ teaspoons ground cinnamon

½ cup melted butter
½ cup white breadcrumbs
1 egg, slightly beaten

1. Peel, core, and slice apples. Measure other ingredients and have ready before pulling out strudel dough.
2. Spread apples in a single layer over pulled-out dough (see illustration).
3. Combine sugar and cinnamon and sprinkle evenly over apples. Slowly pour butter over top and then sprinkle with breadcrumbs. Drizzle egg over top.
4. Roll up as outlined in step 11 of Strudel recipe.

VARIATION: Substitute ½ cup packed brown sugar for ½ cup white sugar.

Cheese Filling

4½ cups (36 ounces) small curd cottage
    cheese, drained
4 eggs, separated

½ cup sugar
½ cup melted butter
½ cup white breadcrumbs

1. Mix drained cottage cheese and egg yolks. Measure other ingredients and have ready before pulling out strudel dough.
2. Spread cottage-cheese mixture evenly over stretched dough (see illustration).
3. Sprinkle sugar over cheese, then pour melted butter over top, and sprinkle with crumbs.
4. Beat egg whites medium stiff so that soft peaks hold. Spread over top of crumbs.
5. Roll up as outlined in step 11 of Strudel recipe.

VARIATION: Brown breadcrumbs in butter, using ¾ cup butter and ½ cup breadcrumbs; stir together in a heavy skillet over moderate heat until golden brown.

TIPS FOR SUCCESSFUL STRUDEL MAKING

Strudel is relatively easy to make but every step must be followed. Read recipe through carefully before beginning. Many novices feel overwhelmed by the task of stretching strudel dough. The following are some guidelines from South Slav cooks.

1. If the dough has rested for 1 hour and still does not seem stretchy, let it rest longer. Dough that is not ready will rebound while you are trying to work with it. Many cooks are more successful with making dough the night before and leaving it well wrapped on the kitchen counter until the next morning. Then set it on a plate over warm water or place it in a slightly warm oven for ½ hour.
2. In winter it may be necessary to warm up the kitchen for good results.
3. Brands of flour contain various amounts of moisture so a measured amount of flour may take more or less liquid. Even the humidity of the day can make a difference. It is important not to add too much flour or the dough will be too stiff to pull. The dough will be sticky until it has been kneaded for a while, so use caution in adding more flour. Some flours require longer kneading times and resting periods to be ready to pull easily.

4. It is tiring to knead for 20 minutes. An alternate way is to knead for a while and then pick up the dough and slap it down hard on the work surface about 20 times. Repeat the kneading and the hard slapping of the dough for a satisfactory product.

5. It is easy to pull a section too thin and have a hole develop. The hole can be pinched together or patched with some of the thin pieces hanging over the edge of the table. Cut a piece to cover the hole generously, brush all around the hole with melted butter, and then cover it with the dough patch. Once the strudel is rolled up the patch is hidden.

6. Baked strudel can be frozen in airtight packages for up to 4 months. Some cut a strudel into 2- to 3-inch pieces and place them in the freezer on a baking sheet lightly covered with plastic wrap. When frozen, store in an airtight container or plastic bag. Individual pieces can be removed for later use. Reheat in a 350 degree oven until center is piping hot and dough is crisp. Strudel can also be frozen before baking; some claim this technique gives an improved product.

THE HMONG

CHICKEN WITH NOODLES

Yield: 6 servings

Although not a classic Hmong dish, this souplike creation combines favorite Hmong foods with coconut milk and noodles acquired from other traditions.

1 frying chicken (3 pounds), cut into serving pieces
3 quarts water
1 teaspoon salt
1 stalk lemon grass, broken into 4 pieces
3 tablespoons vegetable oil
3 cloves garlic, finely minced
1 teaspoon cayenne pepper (can be increased to 1½ teaspoons)
1 can (14 ounces) coconut milk (found at Oriental grocery stores)

42 ounces hot water (3 coconut-milk cans filled)
1½ teaspoons salt
½ teaspoon monosodium glutamate (optional)
2 cups bamboo shoots, cut into ½-by-3-inch pieces
1 package rice sticks (noodles, sometimes called "somen" in Oriental grocery stores)
2 cups chopped lettuce or romaine

1. Wash chicken pieces well. Place in a 6-quart kettle with water, salt, and lemon grass. Simmer gently for 2 hours or until meat begins to fall off bones.
2. Remove chicken from liquid. May reserve broth for some other recipe. When cool, skin and bone chicken and then shred the meat. Set aside.
3. Heat oil in a 4- to 6-quart heavy pan. Add garlic and cayenne. Saute for 2 to 3 minutes over low heat.
4. Stir in chicken and cook for 3 minutes.
5. Add coconut milk and water. Add salt, monosodium glutamate, and bamboo shoots and simmer for ½ hour.
6. While mixture is cooking, heat 3 quarts of water to boiling. Drop noodles from 4 individual packages slowly into boiling water. Simmer for 10 minutes or until tender.
7. Slowly pour off hot water and add cold water to rinse noodles in pot. Repeat until noodles are cool.
8. Using thumb and forefinger, remove bunches of noodles about 1½ inches thick from pan, squeezing and draining water from each bunch. Lay each bunch in a colander for further draining.
9. Place a serving of noodles in a soup bowl. Add hot soup and sprinkle chopped lettuce on top.

HOT PEPPER SAUCE   Yield: about 1 cup

Virtually every Hmong household makes a variation of this sauce, which accompanies most meals.

½ cup minced hot peppers (red or green,   *1 cup green onions, cut into ½-inch*
available in Oriental specialty stores or   *pieces*
supermarkets)   *½ cup fish sauce*

1. Cut peppers in half, remove seeds, and cut into small pieces. May want to use gloves to keep irritating pepper oils from hands.
2. Mash peppers and onions with a mortar and pestle or chop very finely. Mix with fish sauce.
3. Can be kept in refrigerator for up to 1 month.

VARIATIONS: Substitute 1 of the following: Use more peppers for a hotter-flavored sauce; add chopped cilantro to taste; combine peppers, onions, and fish sauce in a blender or food processor and process until smooth and liquefied; use soy sauce instead of fish sauce.

STEAMED RICE   Yield: 4 to 6 servings

Hmong cooks usually steam rice in large quantities at least twice a day since it is the mainstay of every meal. It is served in separate bowls and eaten along with other foods.

2 cups medium-grain rice
4 cups cold water

1. Wash rice to remove dirt or particles. Soak in cold water for at least 1 hour or up to 3 hours. Drain.
2. Fill bottom of rice steamer with 2 inches of water. Place soaked rice in the top part of steamer. Cover and bring water to a boil. Steam over medium heat for 20 minutes.

VARIATION: Soak rice for 5 hours. Drain and place in a large pan or bowl. Pour boiling water over rice to cover. Allow to stand for 10 minutes, covered. Drain. Fill rice steamer with 2 inches of water. Place soaked rice in top and steam for 2 to 3 minutes. Serve.

STEAMED STICKY RICE

Yield: 4 to 6 servings

Hmong make a ball of this rice in their hands and dip it into foods, pinching foods up against the rice. Food and rice are then eaten together, often dipped into pepper sauce.

2 cups sweet or sticky rice (available in
  Oriental specialty stores)
3 cups cold water

1. Soak rice in water for 3 hours. Drain.
2. Fill bottom of rice steamer with 2 inches of water. Place soaked rice in the top part of steamer. Cover and bring water to a boil. Steam over medium heat for 20 minutes.
3. Remove rice to large bowl or pan. To cool, stir with an up-and-under motion, using a large spoon. Serve either slightly warm or completely cooled.

STEAK TARTARE (Nqaij Liab)

Yield: 6 cups

Different families have different ways of preparing this dish, traditionally made with a small piece of chopped-up gall bladder added for flavor. The vegetables and spices included depend on how rare the meat is — the closer to being raw, generally, the more spices.

2 pounds filet mignon
2 cups coarsely chopped fresh mint
2 cups coarsely chopped fresh basil
1 cup green onions, cut in 2-inch pieces
  and then quartered lengthwise
¼ cup thinly sliced lemon grass
3 tablespoons finely minced small hot
  peppers
1 cup coarsely chopped cilantro

1 tablespoon fish sauce
1 teaspoon salt
3 tablespoons minced or pulverized garlic
¼ lime
2 tablespoons Rice Powder (see below)
Small green eggplants (txim lug, available
  at Oriental specialty stores)
Watercress

1. Cut meat into ¾-inch slices and broil 5 inches from unit until no longer red, turning several times. Cool.
2. Cut on the angle into small strips, 2 inches long. Then cut strips as finely as possible. Place meat in a bowl.
3. Add mint, basil, and green onions. Stir well.
4. Place lemon grass in mortar and grind into pieces as small as possible. Can use blender or food processor.

5. Add lemon grass, peppers, cilantro, fish sauce, salt, and garlic to meat mixture.
6. Squeeze juice of ¼ lime over meat. Stir well.
7. Stir in rice powder.
8. Scoop up nqaij liab with wedges of eggplant or folded pieces of watercress.

Rice Powder

Place ¼ cup uncooked sticky rice in heavy frying pan and lightly brown over low heat. Remove from heat when evenly browned. Cool. Make into a powder using blender or mortar and pestle.

NOTE: Green eggplant needed for this recipe resembles a large, unripe cherry tomato. Fish sauce is available in Oriental sections of many supermarkets as well as in Oriental specialty stores.

WATERCRESS AND BEEF
Yield: 4 to 6 servings

Watercress comes close in taste to a kind of greens the Hmong traditionally used. Cooks are pleased to find cress in the stores, but are dismayed at the price.

3 pounds beef top round
½ cup oil
2 cups vertically sliced onions
3 tablespoons minced garlic

2 quarts (8 cups) watercress, washed and drained
1 tablespoon salt

1. Cut beef into ¼-inch strips about 2 inches long. Remove all fat from beef.
2. Heat oil in heavy frying pan over moderate heat.
3. Add beef to hot oil and cook for 2 minutes stirring constantly. Add onions and garlic and stir 2 minutes.
4. Slit watercress stalks in half lengthwise. Stir into meat mixture. Add salt and stir only until watercress is slightly cooked but still crisp and bright green.
5. Serve in bowls acompanied by rice.

SPRING ROLLS

Yield: 24 to 26 rolls

Hmong in rural Laos had little or no access to the rice paper upon which this dish depends. Increased urban contact in Indochina and city life in Minnesota, however, made the product readily available; as a result, spring rolls are now a common part of holiday or special meals.

⅔ cup dried black fungus (available at Oriental specialty stores)
1 pound ground beef
1 ¼ cups finely chopped green onions, including tops
¾ cup finely grated carrots
1 tablespoon grated or finely minced ginger root

1 tablespoon finely minced garlic
1 teaspoon salt
½ teaspoon monosodium glutamate (optional)
4 eggs, slightly beaten
Vegetable oil
1 package triangular rice papers

1. Soak dried black fungus in water for 30 minutes. Cut into ⅛-inch strips and then into squares.
2. Mix ground beef, green onions, carrots, ginger, garlic, black fungus, salt, monosodium glutamate, and eggs thoroughly.
3. Heat slowly 1 inch of oil in heavy frying pan or use 350 degree setting on electric frying pan.
4. Fill shallow bowl with very hot tap water. Slowly draw a single sheet of rice paper through water, thoroughly wetting but not soaking paper. Place on working surface. Two or 3 papers can be prepared at a time.
5. Place 1 heaping tablespoon of filling about 1 inch in from rounded edge of the rice paper, shaping it into an oblong about 1 by 3 inches. Lift rounded edge of paper and lay it over filling. Fold in sides and form into a compact roll (see illustration).

6. Place on baking sheet or plastic wrap with edge down. Seam will seal by the time rolls are ready for frying.
7. Repeat until meat mixture is gone.

8. When oil is hot, slip each roll into pan with seam down. Fry about 15 minutes, turning several times, until lightly browned all over. Rolls can be fried as assembled or all can be made and fried together.
9. Drain well and serve.

VARIATION: Use larger rice papers and increase amount of filling to ¼ cup; yield will be 14 to 16 rolls.

SWEET PORK AND EGGS   Yield: 6 to 8 servings

Hmong people raised pigs and chickens in their native land and continue to depend on pork and poultry in Minnesota. The use of sugar in this dish is an unusual addition.

1¾ cups sugar
2¼ cups cold water
2 pounds pork ribs (have butcher cut the rack of ribs in half lengthwise)
1 quart water

3 cups sliced onions (cut in half vertically and then slice thinly vertically)
2 tablespoons minced or chopped garlic
12 hard-boiled eggs, shelled
1 teaspoon salt

1. Place sugar in deep, heavy pan over medium to medium-high heat. Stir with a wooden spoon until sugar dissolves and turns a medium brown in color. Takes about 10 minutes.
2. Remove carmelized sugar from heat and allow to cool a few minutes. Slowly add cold water. Mixture will spatter and steam. Return to heat and stir to dissolve any hardened sugar. Remove from heat and set aside.
3. Prepare pork by cutting each half into 1½- to 2-inch pieces.
4. Bring quart of water to boil over high heat. Add pieces of pork rib. Reduce heat so water is gently bubbling and cook, uncovered, for 1 hour. Skim off any foam. May need to add more water to maintain original amount.
5. Add onions and garlic. Stir in carmelized sugar. Add eggs and salt.
6. Cook gently until meat is tender, about ½ hour. Stir several times so eggs are evenly colored.
7. Serve in bowls accompanied by rice.

PORK AND BEAN THREAD NOODLES

Yield: 5 to 6 servings

Like rice paper, bean thread noodles entered Hmong foodways after the Hmong moved to the urban areas that were home to Lao, Thai, and other Indochinese people.

*2 pounds ground pork or 2 pounds pork
  shoulder steaks
2 tablespoons vegetable oil
¾ cup chopped cilantro
½ cup chopped green onions
1 tablespoon fish sauce
Juice of 1 lime*

*¼ teaspoon black pepper
½ teaspoon dried mint or ¼ cup chopped
  fresh mint
1 hot pepper, chopped
2 cups chicken broth
½ package bean thread noodles*

1. Saute ground pork in vegetable oil over medium heat. Use wooden spoon or spatula to break meat into small pieces. If using pork shoulder steaks, saute 5 minutes on each side. Remove from pan, cool, and dice meat finely.
2. Drain any fat from frying pan. Combine meat, cilantro, onions, fish sauce, lime juice, pepper, mint, and hot pepper.
3. Stir in chicken broth, cover pan, bring to boil, reduce heat, and simmer for 2 to 3 minutes.
4. Cook noodles according to package directions. Drain.
5. Combine noodles with meat mixture.

CHICKEN WITH VEGETABLES

Yield: 4 servings

Lemon grass, available at Korean or Vietnamese groceries, is a distinctive, traditional seasoning with chicken. Other ingredients vary according to available produce or family tastes.

*2½ to 3 pounds chicken (legs, thighs,
  and first joint of wings)
2 tablespoons vegetable oil
1 cup celery, cut in ¼-inch pieces
½ cup green pepper, cut in ½-inch
  squares
1 stalk lemon grass, cut in 3-inch pieces
½ cup thinly sliced green onions,
  including tops*

*1 cup sliced mushrooms
½ teaspoon salt
Black pepper to taste
¼ teaspoon monosodium glutamate
  (optional)
½ cup water
1 cup sliced tomatoes (optional)*

1. Wash chicken and remove skin and fat. Bone legs, thighs, and meaty end pieces of wings.
2. Cut chicken into pieces about ½ by 2 inches.
3. Heat oil in a 10-inch heavy pan or wok over medium heat. If using an electric frying pan, set at 350 degrees.
4. Add chicken and stir until pieces turn white and start to brown. Add celery, green pepper, and lemon grass and stir for 1 minute. Lower heat, cover, and cook for 2 minutes, stirring once or twice.
5. Add green onions, mushrooms, salt, pepper, and monosodium glutamate. Add ½ cup water and cover. Cook for 10 minutes or until vegetables are tender but crisp.
6. If using tomatoes, add and cook 1 minute more.
7. Remove from heat, take out lemon grass, and discard.
8. Serve with rice in separate bowls. Hot pepper or hot pepper sauce is traditionally served with this dish.

VARIATION: Substitute other ingredients, such as white onions, romaine, cabbage, or whatever is on hand, but do not increase total quantity of vegetables.

BEEF WITH VEGETABLES

Yield: 4 servings

Many Hmong brought their own chopping boards and handmade knives with them when they emigrated. Vegetables for dishes such as this one are still prepared using these traditional implements.

2 tablespoons vegetable oil
1 pound ground beef
1 cup green onions, cut in ½-inch pieces, including tops
½ cup green pepper, cut in ½-inch pieces

⅓ cup peeled and slivered ginger root
1 clove garlic, minced
¾ teaspoon salt
½ teaspoon monosodium glutamate (optional)

1. Heat oil in a 10- to 12-inch frying pan over medium heat. Add ground beef and break it up well with a fork or spatula.
2. When cooked but not browned, add onions, green pepper, ginger, and garlic. Stir for 3 minutes. Add salt and monosodium glutamate. Cover and cook for 5 minutes.
3. Serve with rice. Peppers or pepper sauce usually accompany this meal.

TOFU WITH CHICKEN

Yield: 6 servings as a main dish
8 to 10 servings as a side dish

Hmong cooks once made tofu from soybeans raised on their own land. They now either purchase ready-made tofu or prepare it in the home from a mix available in Oriental grocery stores.

½ cup vegetable oil
2 eggs, beaten
1 teaspoon salt
2 pounds tofu, sliced in 2-inch squares,
¼ inch thick
1¾ to 2 cups raw chicken breast, boned
(dark meat to supplement)

2 cups vertically sliced onions
2 tablespoons minced garlic
1 cup water or chicken broth
Salt

1. Heat ¼ cup oil in a 10- to 12-inch heavy frying pan over medium heat.
2. Combine eggs and 1 teaspoon salt. Dip pieces of tofu into mixture.
3. Carefully lay pieces of tofu in oil. Cook slowly until tofu is lightly browned, about 6 minutes per side. Do not crowd pan. Plan to cook tofu in 2 batches. Add cooking oil as needed for second batch. Drain well on paper towels.
4. Heat remaining ¼ cup oil in heavy kettle over medium heat. When hot enough to sizzle as chicken pieces are added, fry chicken 3 minutes, turning once. Stir in onions and garlic and fry for 2 minutes.
5. Add tofu pieces and water or chicken broth. Cover and simmer 10 minutes. Adjust seasoning. Serve with rice.

NOTE: If making tofu from a mix, use 2 packages (2.29 ounces each).

INDEX

RECIPE INDEX

PICTURE CREDITS

The following photographs appear through the courtesy of the institutions and individuals listed below. The names of the photographers, when known, are given in parentheses.

Pages 14, 21, 30 (Randy Croce); 22, 24 (Monroe Killy); 39; 64; 71 (Lee Brothers); 112, 117 (Gail Zucker); 184; 196; 214; 238, 241, 251 (Michael Kieger)—Minnesota Historical Society

Pages 59, 136, 148 (Joe Rossi), 201, 202, 208—St. Paul Pioneer Press and Dispatch

Page 75 (Sam Cook)—Ely Echo

Page 128 (Dave Heiller)—Askov American

Page 130 (John Rott)—Duluth News-Tribune and Herald

Pages 149, 152 (Ormond H. Loomis)—Iron Range Historical Society

Pages 157, 159—Geraldine Kangas

The following photographs were commissioned for this publication.

Pages 34, 48, 51, 90, 97, 102, 132, 135, 138, 144, 180, 186, 188, 191, 204, 210—Alan Ominsky

Pages 37, 42, 44, 45—Stan Waldhauser

Pages 56, 255—Willard B. Moore

Pages 69, 74, 82, 155, 165, 167, 168, 174, 175, 176, 219, 230—Ken Moran

Pages 86, 92, 95, 98, 110, 114, 120, 122, 125—Liza Fourré

Pages 220, 221, 228—Marjorie A. Hoover

Pages 237, 243—Patrick Kelly